Electronic
Computer
Memory
Technology

Electronic Computer Memory Technology

Edited by **WALLACE B. RILEY**
Computers Editor, *Electronics Magazine*

McGraw-Hill Book Company

New York   St. Louis   San Francisco   Düsseldorf   Johannesburg
Kuala Lumpur   London   Mexico   Montreal   New Delhi
Panama   Rio de Janeiro   Singapore   Sydney   Toronto

ELECTRONIC COMPUTER MEMORY TECHNOLOGY

07-052915-9

1234567890 HDBP 754321

Contents

Introduction

Memory performance and cost are the twin keys to computer technology. Although new electronic devices, processor organizations, and software systems have contributed to enormous advances in computer technology, they would have been worthless without the faster and cheaper memories that were developed with them.

To help electronics engineers keep up with the state of the art in each of many kinds of memories, the editors of *Electronics* presented a series of articles on the technology. These articles, together with a few others on related topics, were compiled into this convenient reference book. Each article is short, concentrates on a particular area of memory technology, and is written by an expert in that area.

Chapter 1 covers ferrite core memories—where they've been, their limitations, and ways of improving techniques of manufacturing, wiring, and operation. Core technology has become so well entrenched that the words "computer memory" have been almost synonymous with "ferrite cores." As several authors point out in their articles, the demise of cores has been predicted over and over again—but always prematurely. As fast as new technologies have arisen to challenge cores, new developments have sprung up to boost the speed and performance of cores and to lower their cost.

Cores will be with us for some time, if for no other reason than sheer momentum. Designers are accustomed to thinking in terms of cores; manufacturers have large investments in machinery for making and testing cores and stacks; and for all the producers' lamentations about the problem of threading wires through 18-mil-diameter cores, at least one manufacturer has succeeded in producing four-wire, 15-mil-core arrays.

Meanwhile, continued advances in thin films and plated wire have pushed these technologies into contention. Chapter 2 examines these technologies—emphasizing plated wires, the film configuration that seems to have the best chance of success—but without omitting the other forms. Univac pioneered plated wires in commercial computers; Honeywell Inc.'s Aerospace division pushed hard on plated wire for military applications; and in Japan, Toko Inc. uses woven plated wires in its version of Univac's 9000 series computers.

Semiconductors are coming on just as fast. Chapters 3 and 4, on MOS and other semiconductor memories, respectively, are segments that are likely to interest readers the most and at the same time become obsolescent most quickly. A leading figure in the semiconductor industry predicted that by 1973 no one would design any computer without a semiconductor memory in it somewhere—be it a scratch pad, a read-only memory, or something else. Recent events have shown that his prediction was rather conservative. The booming growth in capacity, physical size, and use of semiconductor memories from about 1967 through 1970 continues to amaze even those most qualified to write about them. Thus, if some of the figures and predictions seem rather quaint, it's because the exploding technology outraced the authors' expectations even in the few months between original publication of the articles and the preparation of this book. Even as these words are written, no fewer than three manufacturers have announced new computers within a month, each claiming to be the first with a commercially available production-line semiconductor memory; each claim has at least some degree of legitimacy.

Chapter 5 describes the various read-only memories and some of their less-obvious applications—applications that nonetheless are sure to create a boom in the use of these relatively simple arrays.

Chapter 6 describes several forms of electromechanical and acoustic memories, applications, and tradeoffs. Chapter 7 is devoted to advanced memory technologies, including electro-optic and optoelectronic forms, sonic films, cryoelectrics, and ferroelectrics. Chapter 8 describes the factors that bear on memory testing.

Chapter 9 features a discussion of several special topics, including the art of making a memory stand up under severe military applications, and the remarkable things that can be accomplished with associative memories, which are just maturing, thanks to the developments in semiconductor technology.

In Chapter 10 various systems-oriented concepts relating to memories are discussed. These include application of a core memory to a desk calculator, performance improvements in a large computer brought about through a high-speed buffer memory, and cost reductions made possible by backing away from the idea that a short cycle time is all-important.

Finally, Chapter 11 discusses some designs that are primarily of historical interest. It's interesting to note that some of these designs were current, not historical, quite recently—such is the rapid pace of technology.

I am grateful to Dan McMillan, publisher of *Electronics,* and to Kemp Anderson, Editor-in-Chief, for their permission to reprint this material. I wish also to acknowledge the assistance of Susan B. Hurlburt in laying out the articles for reproduction,

Wallace B. Riley

**Electronic
Computer
Memory
Technology**

Chapter 1

Ferrite cores

Staying ahead of the game

By Roy H. Norman

Ampex Corp., Culver City, Calif.

The trend in ferrite-core memories over the years has been toward greater speeds at lower costs per bit. These memories have from time to time been threatened by other storage techniques that promised to be cheaper and faster, but they have always managed to hold their place.

Cores are again being challenged, and the threat this time is, in some ways, more serious than ever before. It's therefore wise to take a look at what's been done and what may be done in the future.

The increases in core memories' operating speed have been due primarily to decreases in the size of the individual cores. The earliest memories used cores more than 100 mils in outside diameter—"nearly the size of Cheerios," as one expert has put it. Then came a series of reductions in standard core sizes to 80 mils, to 50 and 30 mils, and finally to the 22 and 18 mils widely used today, as shown below. It's perhaps worth noting that each new standard core could almost pass through the hole in its predecessor.

This process has been accompanied by a corresponding decrease in switching time—from the several microseconds of the old 100-mil cores to as little as 140 nanoseconds today. This, in turn, has been followed by a decrease in memory cycle time—always greater than switching time because of noise problems, current rise times, and delays in peripheral circuits.

Advances in speed have been paralleled by cuts in prices facilitated by the declining costs of semiconductors and other components. And advances in component design have permitted refinements in the design of circuits and whole systems, again reducing costs. Development of automatic wiring equipment for threading a maze of wires through thousands of cores and utilization of low-cost labor in such places as Hong Kong and Taiwan have also helped drop prices.

Economy vs. speed

For moderate storage capacities, the most economical system configuration is the coincident-current or three-dimensional organization. This arrangement, now used in the great majority of core memories, is inexpensive because it requires the minimum number of drivers and decoders. Other configurations can provide more speed than 3-D, but they're always more expensive.

Of the two basic types of 3-D memory in common use, one has four wires through each core, and the other has three. In both designs, the core's magnetic hysteresis loop must be so nearly square that the core is fully switched by currents carried in the same direction by two selection wires passing through it, but is undisturbed by either one of the currents alone. With this coincident-current scheme, the core array itself performs part of the address decoding, thus minimizing circuit costs. Instead of locating a specific core in a plane, external decoders locate two lines of cores that intersect at the address. A single set of driver circuits steers current through all cores in the data word, which are strung on a single selection wire.

A typical design stores 4,096 words of 32 bits each. It uses 32 planes each of 4,096 cores in a 64-by-64 array threaded with 128 selection wires —64 in each direction. Corresponding selection wires in all the planes are connected to each other and are driven by a single driver circuit.

In the four-wire design, two other wires are threaded through all cores in each plane, as below right, but are not interconnected between planes. The switching of any core in the plane from a 1 to a 0 generates a pulse that one of these wires carries out to the sense amplifier serving that plane. The other wire carries a current equal but opposite to one of the two half-select currents. This current can thus inhibit the action of the selection wires on a core and keep it in the 0 state.

These sense and inhibit functions are combined in a single wire in the three-wire design because the two operations need never be performed at the same time. However, this setup requires more complex circuits and is therefore somewhat more expensive than the four-wire system. This cost, though, is at least partially offset by the savings involved in threading only three wires.

With each reduction in core size have come predictions that threading four wires through every core in an array will be impractical. With 18-mil cores now coming into use, this prediction seems more realistic than ever. If the prophets are right for once, the faster, smaller cores will make the three-wire design the only practical 3-D form.

The simplest core-memory organization is the two-dimensional or linear select form, in which the cores are arranged in a single plane array with word wires and bit wires at right angles to one another, as on page 108, top. In data storage, currents on any one word wire and on the bit wires combine at the intersections to switch cores that are to store 1's or to prevent switching at cores that are to store 0's. For readout, a single, larger current on a word line—rather than the coincidence of two currents—switches all the cores on the wire. Thus currents greater than the normal full switching current can be used. The overdrive makes for very fast switching, but at a high cost because all the address decoding must be external. [For more on problems with 2-D memories, see p. 7.]

A compromise between the economy of 3-D and the speed of 2-D is found in an arrangement that has come to be known as $2\frac{1}{2}$-D [p. 5, left]. Originated in 1951, it remained dormant until rather recently, when 3-D core memories began to reach what may be their ultimate limitations.

This approach has a level of address decoding in the bit dimension. Like the 2-D memory, one wire threads the cores in a particular word, and a bit wire passes through each of these cores at right angles to the word wire. But in a typical arrangement, the same word wire threads the cores for two words, and each bit wire loops around in a U shape to thread corresponding cores in both words. Coincident currents in the word and bit lines, as in a 3-D memory, switch one or the other of these cores, the bit current's direction determining the core that switches. In the other core, the two currents oppose one another. When storing a 0, the bit current is simply not turned on. A sense wire threads all the bits common to one doubled bit line.

Since the bit current drivers control whether or not a particular core switches, the 3-D memory's inhibit drivers and windings aren't needed. Their absence reduces noise and pulse overlap, and these are the prime factors contributing to the $2\frac{1}{2}$-D organization's speed.

Bulk core memories contain perhaps 10 times as much data as computer main memories and run typically at one-third the speed. In these memories, the cost of the core array predominates over the cost of the electronics; therefore, they are usually built in the $2\frac{1}{2}$-D configuration but with only two wires. The bit and sense wires are common.

The drive circuits in a $2\frac{1}{2}$-D memory require lower voltages than do those in a 3-D memory, so that large-scale integration will be easier to apply to $2\frac{1}{2}$-D. On the other hand, if the cost of electronic circuits continues to decrease as it has in the past, the cost differential between the two arrangements should diminish.

Although no competing technology has yet displaced ferrite-core memories as the primary storage element in high-speed memories, thin magnetic

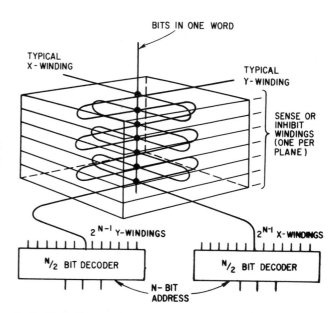

In depth. In the most common memory organization, 3-D, two sides of a stack are addressed to locate a vertical column of cores containing the stored data.

films pose a definite threat with their speed, and monolithic integrated circuits are being heralded as future challengers.

Thin films are very fast because they switch by magnetic domain rotation instead of by domain wall motion as in solid cores. A single planar thin-film element has an open flux path in most designs, which tends to make the film demagnetize itself, although this is not true in at least two proposed designs. Coupled film structures have flux paths

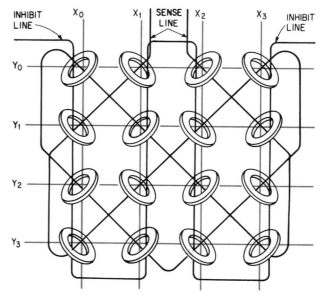

Sense and inhibit. Two additional wires in a 3-D stack sense a core's switching when reading a 1 and inhibit its switching when writing a 0.

that are closed except for two very small air gaps at the ends of the element. And plated wires usually have completely closed flux paths.

But most of these designs depend on the film's magnetic anisotropy—its higher reluctance in one direction in the plane of the film than at right angles to that direction. In the "hard" axis, the film has no magnetic threshold—its hysteresis loop isn't square—so that coincident-current organization isn't possible. The cost savings of a 3-D organization in ferrite cores are therefore not realizable in thin films. But films may be faster.

Advocates of semiconductor technology claim that prices on both bipolar and metal oxide semiconductor circuits will soon reach a point competitive with core prices. Maybe so, but monolithic arrays are still selling for about a dollar a bit, compared with a nickel a bit for million-bit ferrite-core arrays. For another thing, cores are being made today with yields of 60% or 70%, and core-stacks can be reworked if necessary, whereas monolithic arrays are unreworkable and still have yields of only a few percent.

All this suggests that IC's must undergo an order-of-magnitude improvement in this area before they can compete seriously with cores.

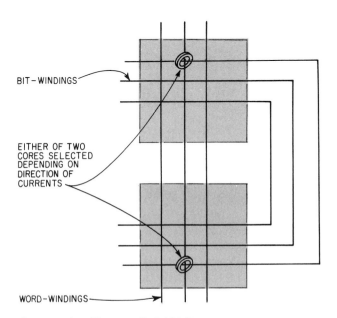

Compromise. The so-called 2½-D arrangement combines the speed of 2-D with the economy of 3-D.

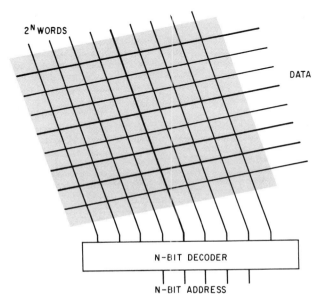

Fast plane. The simplest memory organization addresses one side of an array and brings data out at right angles to the addressing. The scheme is fast but expensive.

Challenged. This ferrite-core memory uses integrated circuits for its sense amplifiers, selection circuits, and switches. As such it is an example of "an ultimate stage of refinement" described in the following article.

Scant room for improvement

By Dana W. Moore
Computer Control Division, Honeywell, Inc., Framingham, Mass.

As in the Kansas City described in "Oklahoma!", everything's up to date in core arrays. Unfortunately, there's evidence that they, too, have "gone about as fur as they kin go."

There'll probably be a few design embellishments and some tradeoffs made in the future, but further significant improvement in the over-all cost and performance of cores is unlikely.

Cores have maintained their top position in the memory field only by fighting off the challenges of newer technologies. In the past, the threat posed by competitors offering comparable cost-performance figures and some degree of batch fabrication almost always produced core designs that were smaller, faster, more reliable, and easier to maintain than their predecessors—and less expensive, too. However, a couple of factors suggest that this will no longer hold true.

Around the edges

For one thing, most of the recent advances in core-memory technology have been made in the peripheral circuitry rather than in the arrays themselves. True, laminated frames have given way to the printed-circuit variety; the 2½-dimensional organization has been revived with its sense lines at left instead in the bow-tie configuration shown at left instead of the diagonal shown on page 4; manufacturers have capitalized on lower labor costs overseas; and high-speed core testers have been developed. But these appear to be the ultimate stages of refinement in a highly developed technology.

In fact, the peak of the core memory's cost-performance growth curve was probably reached two years ago when the 2½-D organization appeared and integrated circuits were introduced into repetitive circuitry.

The IC's were initially applied to logic circuits with standard 6-volt signal voltage swings, and to sense amplifiers. More recently, as shown on page 8, the rest of the selection circuits have been integrated and 15-volt switches have appeared that can carry as much as 400 milliamperes of current. The trend will continue as designs incorporate more complex and less expensive IC's, along with compatible packaging techniques.

The only organizational change that could bring about a core-memory renaissance with the present 18- and 20-mil standard cores would be the introduction of a linear-select arrangement with partial switching and two cores per bit—a design likely to be quite costly.

Automatic core-stringing represents one significant improvement that may yet be made on a large scale, but few manufacturers have invested in this equipment, particularly for the smaller core sizes. And with foreign labor costs on the rise, even the wide use of these machines would probably serve only to hold the line on core-memory prices rather than to reduce them.

Growing challenge

The other major factor indicating that the core-memory technology has run out of breakthroughs is the existence of well-established and strongly supported competing technologies. The top contenders —plated wire and semiconductors—have gained a firm foothold and are widening it every day. Chances are, therefore, that they, not cores, will be the subject of the largest future research and

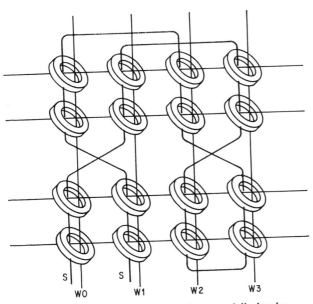

Bow-tie. This pattern of sense windings contributes to the low cost of 2½-D memories, because the wire runs parallel to the selection windings.

development efforts.

The Univac division of the Sperry Rand Corp. is heavily committed to plated-wire production, and several other manufacturers of core stacks are putting money into plated-wire studies and facilities at the expense of further core R&D. And semiconductor arrays, although now competitive only in the area of small memories, are likely to compete favorably for all sizes by 1975 or so. Semiconductors—as storage elements, peripheral circuits, or both—have a greater potential for undermining core memories than any thin-film, laminated-ferrite, or multiaperture core technology to come along so far.

Still, semiconductor circuits can help reduce the cost and improve the performance of memory systems that are designed around 2½-D arrays of 20-mil cores.

Inevitably they must cut costs. With an already integrated design, you just watch the component prices fall as volume builds and IC processing yields improve. For example, a core memory using integrated circuits, and containing nearly 300,-000 bits (16,384 18-bit words) cost $3\frac{1}{2}$ cents per bit to manufacture in volume as recently as 1968. That figure was broken down to $1\frac{1}{2}$ cents for the ferrite core stack, $1\frac{1}{2}$ for the peripheral circuits, and a half-cent for structural hardware. But circuit costs dropped by 50% in two years, and so did stack costs, so that the over-all system now costs only 2¢ a bit.

Improving the performance of core arrays is a ticklish problem, particularly when cycle times of less than 500 nanoseconds are required; that speed represents a sort of sonic barrier for ferrite cores. Attempts to break it generally take the form of a linear-select (2-D) organization and partial switching with one or two cores per bit. Both of these designs require high-amplitude pulses of short duration. With IC's, such pulses are feasible at a cost potentially low enough to overcome some other disadvantages of the designs.

Inside job

Partial switching takes advantage of the fact that a ferrite core switching from the 0 state to 1 during a write operation does so first around the inner surface of its aperture and then, rapidly but in sequence, outward in concentric rings. A high, narrow pulse of current may thus switch only the inner part of the core.

With linear selection, there are no half-selected cores to place an upper limit on the read current pulse; the lower limit is established by the need to fully reset all the cores on a selected wire from 1 to 0. Coincident-current (2½-D, 3-D) designs demand a more delicate touch; their read pulse ideally mustn't disturb any cores except those at which it coincides with another pulse, so that the upper and lower limits define a rather narrow range. With a partially switching linear-select array, not only is there no upper limit established by disturb restrictions, but the lower limit is even

IC memory. Honeywell's ICM-500 unit is characteristic of the newer developments in high-performance ferrite-core assemblies.

lower because the read current pulse doesn't have to switch as much material. On the other hand, this smaller amount of changing flux generates a smaller output signal.

Partial switching isn't practical in coincident-current designs because it creates enough delta noise to swamp the lower output signal. Delta noise—the difference in output between a half-selected 0 and a half-selected 1—can be quite large even in a fully-switched coincident-current memory. Because the outputs of half-selected cores would be more unequal if they were partially switched, the delta noise would increase to an unacceptable level. This isn't a problem with linear selection because no cores are half-selected during reading. Therefore, narrowing the width of the current pulse through a core of a given diameter makes a shorter cycle time possible, even though the cores don't completely switch.

Writing styles

There are three ways the write operation can proceed in a linear-select array, as shown at right. All of them assume that all cores in an addressed word are in the binary 0 state before the operation begins.

- In the first method, a full-select word current tends to switch all the cores in the word to 1. It is offset by a half-select digit current through those cores that should remain 0, and is aided by a half-select digit current in the reverse direction through cores to be switched to 1. This one-and-a-half select current contributes to a very high-speed write operation.

- In the second, a full-select word current, as above, switches all cores to 1 except where it is opposed by a half-select digit current.

- Finally, a half-select word current switches only those cores where it is aided by a half-select digit current; the other cores remain in the 0 state.

The first two techniques share a very serious disadvantage—they require very close tolerances on their currents. A core heavily saturated in one direction can tolerate a larger opposing current than a core that has partially switched in that direction. In either of the first two modes, the opposing digit currents, if large enough to cancel the word current, could partially reset cores already partially switched toward 0, especially if they were repeated several times. In that case, the read current would see cores that had already lost most of their flux and would produce lower than minimum acceptable 1 outputs.

But in the third writing mode, digit currents always reinforce the partially set state and oppose only the fully reset state. The digit current drivers can be of a single polarity. This mode is also inherently faster than the others because the word write current doesn't have to be overlapped as in canceling schemes.

The simplest way to implement the third mode would be to use half-select word and digit currents of nominally equal amplitudes and durations. However, the simple way is not the best way here, particularly when partial switching is involved. With impulse switching, a word current of very short duration can have an amplitude well above the core switching threshold without jeopardizing the core's remanent state, unless there's a coincident digit current.

In that case, the half-select digit current, added to the impulse word current, significantly increases the flux change from the level attainable by two equal half-select current pulses. This basic characteristic of ferrite material isn't useful in coincident-current designs because repeated impulses through unselected cores could alter the stored information.

These considerations lead to the conclusion set down earlier in this article—that only a partial-switching, linear-select design shows any promise of significantly advancing core-memory performance.

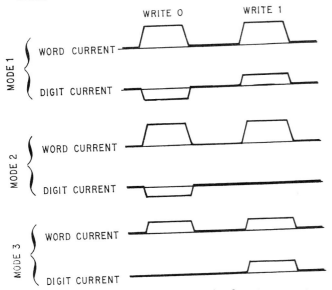

Three ways to write. Starting from the 0 state, a core switches or not depending on the digit current's direction, or on its presence or absence.

On the other hand

Unfortunately, this potential performance improvement is offset by two other factors—the noise generated by partial switching in a one-core-per-bit design, and the cost of wiring a two-core-per-bit array.

As pointed out previously, in one-core-per-bit designs, a partially switched core's output signal is smaller than the signal from a fully switched core—so much smaller that it's hard to distinguish it from a 0. Theoretically, a 0 output is characterized by absence of signal, but noise is always present because the hysteresis loop is never perfectly square. To obtain a reasonable difference between the 1 signal and the 0 noise, the core must be almost fully switched—80% or better. However, the resulting performance is only slightly better than that of a $2^1/_2$-D design with the same size cores, and the cost is much higher.

Using two cores per bit can overcome this switchng problem, but it's no answer to the cost problem. With two cores for every bit position, one is always in the 0 state and connected to the sense circuits in such a way that its noise cancels the noise from the switching core. But wiring up such an array is as complex as wiring a $2^1/_2$-D array.

Two cores per bit and two wires per core make for simple wiring, but not for particularly fast operation. Small perturbations on the digit line always persist beyond the end of a normal cycle and couple linearly into the sense circuits, so that the next discrimination must be postponed until these perturbations die away.

The use of three wires per core—with the extra one for sensing—establishes nonlinear coupling and reduces the postponement. On the minus side, though, the array is identical to a $2^1/_2$-D array in terms of wiring complexity, but twice as large for a given capacity.

A two-core-per-bit, three-wire-per-core linear select design would cost almost twice as much as a $2^1/_2$-D array. Its drive and sense circuits would also be more expensive because the selection process is less efficient, the currents are higher, and the output signals are small. Under these circumstances—and under the ever-larger threat of plated-wire and semiconductor memory technologies—a program to develop such a memory would be extensive and hard to justify.

There's still room for $2^1/_2$-D design refinements to reduce costs, improve performance, or both. These refinements take advantage of better and cheaper IC's and better packaging.

In particular, the falling prices on semi-conductors may permit the use of more circuits common to smaller memory modules; integrated sense-amplifier and preamplifier combinations, for instance, could pick up signals from shorter sense lines through smaller areas of memory. And repeated smaller X-drive matrixes would yield better drive-current wave shapes.

Another neat trick is suggested by the fact that read currents need be staggered only for read cycles. Thus, a read-regenerate cycle could partially switch the cores—in a shorter period than the clear-write—just enough to generate a reliably detectable signal. The clear-write, in turn, could turn on both word and bit currents simultaneously and complete the full switching that the clear part of a clear-write cycle requires, without staggering them. This timing, in the long run, could yield moderate reductions in cycle time. And it's feasible with integrated peripheral circuits.

Circuit improvements along this line, together with core heat sinks, represent a more sensible approach than bulldozing through a two-core-per-bit design. They should push the cycle times of 2½-D designs beyond the 500-nsec barrier at only a small increase in the cost per bit.

Past emphasis in the ferrite memory field has been on batch fabricating the arrays. Ironically, it now appears that the stress should be on discrete arrays and batch-fabricated circuits.

Bibliography

C.J. Quaitly, "A High-Speed Ferrite Storage System," Electronic Engineering, December 1959, p. 756.

W.H. Rhodes, L.A. Russell, F.E. Sakalay, and R.M. Whalen, "A 0.7-Microsecond Ferrite Core Memory," IBM Journal of Research and Development, July 1961, p. 174.

J.A. Rajchman, "Computer Memories: A Survey of the State of the Art," IRE Proc., December 1961, p. 104.

H. Amemiya, T.R. Mayhew, and R.L. Pryor, "A 10^5-Bit High-Speed Ferrite Memory System—Design and Operation," American Federation of Information Processing Societies, Conf. Proc., vol. 25, (Fall Joint Computer Conference), 1964.

G.E. Werner and R.M. Whalen, "A 375-Nanosecond Main Memory System Utilizing 7-Mil Cores," AFIPS Conf. Proc., vol. 27, part 1, (Fall Joint Computer Conference), 1965, p. 985.

T.J. Gilligan, "2½-D High-Speed Memory Systems, Past, Present and Future," IEEE Trans. on Electronic Computers, August 1966, p. 475.

D.W. Moore, "A Cost/Performance Analysis of Integrated-Circuit Core Memories," AFIPS Conf. Proc., vol. 29 (Fall Joint Computer Conference), 1966, p. 267.

W.F. Jordan Jr., "A Monolithic Decode-Drive Circuit for Magnetic Memories," Digest, International Solid State Circuits Conference, February 1968, p. 106.

R.W. Reichard and W.F. Jordan Jr., "A Compact, Economical Core Memory With All-Monolithic Electronics, AFIPS Conf. Proc., vol. 32 (Spring Joint Computer Conference). 1968, p. 253.

Four-wire performance from a three-wire memory is a valuable, attainable, but demanding goal for designers of 3-D arrays

Pairing sense and inhibit functions on one wire is a logical approach, Electronics Memories & Magnetics' *Tom Gilligan* says; but designers must be ready to come to grips with a whole new set of problems

● Three, rather than four, wires are being used in some ferrite-core memories to circumvent the problems associated with threading the smaller cores required in faster units. One approach—the so-called 2½-dimensional organization—though popular, requires lots of peripheral electronic circuits and is expensive. An alternative method employs the redundancy of one of the four wires in the standard three-dimensional array. Since the sense wire is used only during the cycle's read portion, and the inhibit wire only during the write portion, both functions can be combined on a single wire.

This approach doesn't require substantially more expensive peripheral circuitry than the standard four-wire array, and it permits smaller cores with faster switching speeds to be used. But this three-wire 3-D design poses constraints, as well as advantages, not shaped by the four-wire format. Understanding these differences and coping with them can yield a valuable design technique for small, fast, low-cost memories.

Among the factors that require attention in the design of a three-wire array are reflections in the line during a sense operation. There are also noise problems that must be compensated for differently than in a four-wire array. But once these factors are understood, a three-wire design with a given core size—that is, with a given speed—can yield a faster and a cleaner design than the corresponding four-wire design.

11

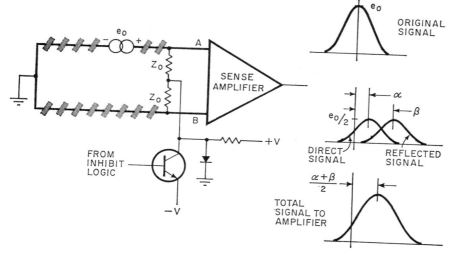

ORIGINAL SIGNAL

DIRECT SIGNAL   REFLECTED SIGNAL

TOTAL SIGNAL TO AMPLIFIER

Driver added. A current driver can be connected to a sense wire to make it double as an inhibit wire, but the circuit requires a ground return for the inhibit driver. This reflects the sense pulse and provides two overlapping inputs to the amplifier.

A sense line can be made to double as an inhibit line by adding a current driver. There are two places to connect the driver—at the end nearest the sense amplifier, or at the far end where the line doubles back on itself.

If the driver is connected at the near end, as shown above, a ground connection is required at the far end to complete the circuit. In the inhibit driver, the ground clamp on the transistor's collector serves as an equivalent ground during sensing, while permitting current pulses to be driven through the two sides of the sense-inhibit loop. But during a sense operation, the negative side of the generated pulse can't go all the way around the loop to the other side of the sense amplifier, because it is totally reflected at the far-end ground connection. This reflection changes its polarity as well as its direction, and it propagates back toward the sense amplifier, slightly behind the original positive pulse.

When a core switches at the far end of the loop near the ground connection, the direct pulse and the reflected pulse are almost simultaneous, and their sum more nearly resembles the total generated pulse than when a near-end core switches. In the latter example, one pulse arrives almost immediately at the sense amplifier, whereas the other pulse has to propagate all the way down to the ground connection and all the way back; the sum of the two pulses is considerably wider and

flatter than the original total pulse.

Only one side of the sense amplifier sees the sense signal; the other side ostensibly is at ground level. But the ground is established by the connection at the far end of the sense loop, and between the connection and the amplifier are many cores. Current pulses that switch the one core generating the signal also disturb some of these other cores, thus generating delta noise. This noise is caused by the departure of the so-called square hysteresis loop of the ferrite material from perfect squareness; its top and bottom taper off slightly, as shown below. In other words, the ferrite's remanent magnetic field strength is slightly less than its saturated strength, whereas if its hysteresis loop were perfectly square the strengths would be equal.

To overcome delta noise, the sense wire in a four-wire array is routed so that it sees half the cores tending to switch from left to right, and the other half from right to left, during a given half-cycle. This routing, shown on page 16, permits the delta noise from half the cores to cancel that from the other half. The exact routing depends on the particular core patterns; different patterns often are used for advantageous peripheral circuit packaging, but all the patterns are equally subject to delta noise.

But no routing cancels the noise perfectly, because no two cores are identical. The difference between non-

Almost square. Typical hysteresis loop of ferrite material (boundary of shaded area) is close, but not identical, to ideal square shape; departure from ideal is source of delta noise problem.

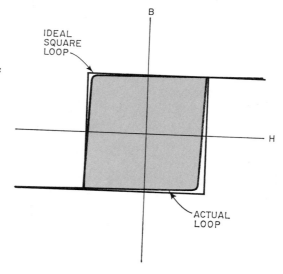

B

IDEAL SQUARE LOOP

H

ACTUAL LOOP

Four-wire fundamentals

In a four-wire array, the x and y wires perform the switching functions, while the other two are for sense and inhibit. In each plane there are as many y wires as there are columns; but the array is usually square, so that x = y. These wires are selected in pairs to address individual cores where they intersect.

Each plane also contains one sense and one inhibit wire passing through all cores in the plane. When any core in the plane changes state, it generates a pulse in the sense line that is detected by a sense amplifier. And when the inhibit line carries a current, it opposes the currents in the x and y lines to prevent the core at their intersection from switching.

In the sense wire, a switching core acts like an ungrounded generator whose output is e_o, as shown below. Because the generator is electrically floating, half of its output, $e_o/2$, travels to one input of the sense amplifier at one end of the line; the other half, with opposite polarity, $-e_o/2$, travels around the loop to the amplifier's other input. Both pulses are somewhat attenuated by line losses. At the sense amplifier the line is terminated in its characteristic impedance, so that the pulses are not reflected. Because the two branches of the line are of different lengths, the two pulses arrive at the sense

amplifier inputs at slightly different times; but because the sense amplifier's input stage is a differential circuit, it responds to the difference between the voltages of the two signals. This difference is a slight distortion of the pulse that would have been generated at the core if the core had been grounded, but it is delayed by half the propagation time of the whole line—that is, by the average of the long and short propagation times from the core. Its distortion is caused by the difference in the two propagation times.

When a core switches at the far end of the sense-wire loop, the two propagation times and the two attenuations are nearly equal. Therefore, the differential signal at the sense amplifier is larger in amplitude, and more nearly resembles the theoretical signal generated by the grounded core. This difference between near-end signals and far-end signals is quite small for a matrix of 4,096 cores, but increases rapidly for larger arrays.

These variations in pulse shape, timing, and amplitude must be taken into account in the sense amplifier design, which usually includes a strobe to guarantee clean output. This strobe must be timed to occur as nearly as possible at the peak of all the different kinds of pulses that appear at the input.

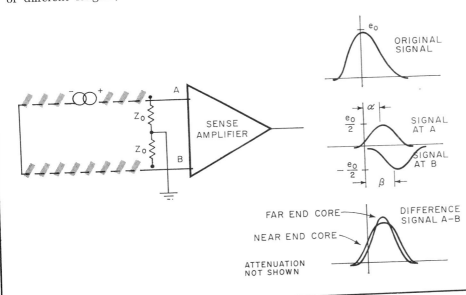

Isolated sense. When a core switches in a four-wire array, it generates two pulses of opposite polarity that travel toward the two ends of the sense loop, arriving at the amplifier at slightly different times. The position of a core along the sense wire affects shape of signal received by sense amplifier.

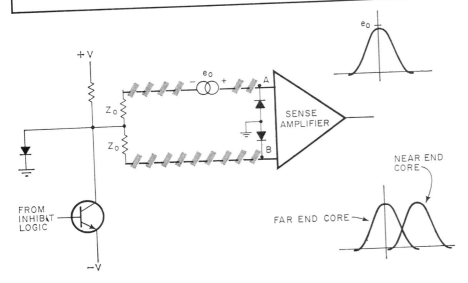

Far-end driver. With both current source and impedance-matching resistors at far end of sense-inhibit line, diodes at amplifier pass inhibit current, but present high impedance to sense signals; coupled-in ringing dies out quickly. This configuration permits sense signals to arrive at amplifier at significantly different times, depending on their position on the line.

Additive. When one core is selected at intersection of two wires, every other core on those wires generates delta noise, interfering with signal from selected core.

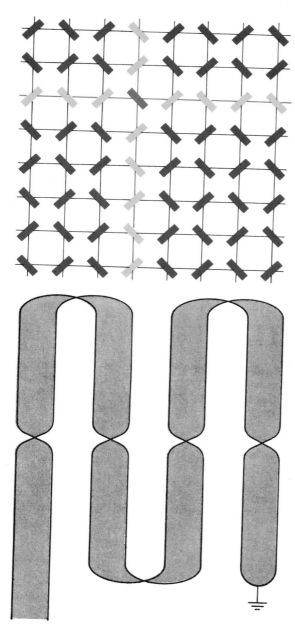

Bow-tie. This arrangement of sense-inhibit line cancels delta noise during sense operation while properly directing inhibit current to oppose the write current.

identical cores in a pair creates a residue of noise that wire routing can't overcome—hence the designation "delta"; because the x and y wires thread many cores the cumulative effect of this residue can be quite significant. For example, in a 4,096-core array, laid out as a 64-by-64 square matrix, each addressing wire threads 63 unselected cores on its way to a single selected core, as shown at left. These 126 cores—62 pairs and two unpaired cores—generate noise that tends to mask the distinction between a 1 and a 0, either of which may be stored in the selected core. The noise exists on both sides of the sense loop.

Routing a combined sense-inhibit wire is subject to an additional constraint. Just as in the four-wire array, the wire must pass through equal number of half-selected cores in opposite directions; but it must also pass through every core in the reverse direction from that of the write current. Since either the write currents or the core orientations alternate from row to row, this constraint is realized with a "bow-tie" winding, shown at left below, that interchanges adjacent rows halfway through the array.

The inhibit driver also may be connected at the far end, as shown on page 13, together with terminating resistors; the near end goes straight to the amplifier, with terminating diodes as shown. In this configuration the sense pulse's negative side is absorbed in the terminating resistor without reflection, while arriving at the amplifier's high input impedance, is approximately doubled in amplitude. The amplifier sees only the one pulse; the amount of its phase shift is determined solely by the position of the generating cores. This pulse, in addition to being detected by the amplifier, also is promptly reflected toward the far end of the line, where it also disappears into the terminating resistors.

In the configuration shown, the collector of the inhibit driver is clamped at a level just above ground; this clamp and the two diodes at the amplifier input prevent current from flowing except during an inhibit operation. But when the inhibit logic calls for a pulse, the transistor turns on; its collector drops to a level slightly above the emitter voltage, and a current pulse flows from the diodes at the amplifier to the transistor, through both sides of the loop.

This configuration is most useful in memories made from cores whose switching time is short relative to the sense line's propagation time. It's valuable because such a core generates a high, narrow pulse whose overlap with its reflection in the grounded-center configuration is likely to be small. This would cause the combined pulse to be exceptionally wide and flat, and thus to have a poor signal-to-noise ratio; in an extreme case—such as selecting the core closest to the amplifier—the two pulses conceivably wouldn't overlap at all, and the amplifier would produce a double output.

A third configuration [page 15, top] develops large voltages for fast rise times in high-speed memories. To prevent these voltages from harming the sense amplifier, this design incorporates diodes at the near end. The balun—a transformer connected between the lines, with the polarity of the windings as shown by the dots—assures that currents in the two lines are balanced. Any tendency for the current on one side to increase creates a reduced back voltage on the other side through

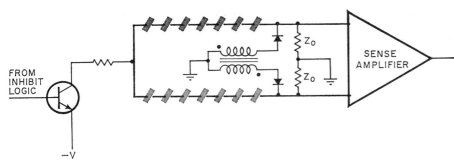

High speed. Large voltages with fast rise times can be developed with this connection; diodes prevent voltage spikes from damaging sense amplifier.

the transformer, pulling more current on that other side. Likewise, a decreased current on one side sets up an increased back voltage on the other side.

This connection also has terminating resistors at the near end; the inhibit driver draws current through the diodes and balun. During a sense operation the inhibit driver connection effectively is a short circuit between the two sides of the sense-inhibit line and an open circuit through the driver, so that the operation proceeds as in the four-wire array.

In all these sense-inhibit circuits, both the signal and the delta noise have a common-mode component—one that appears at both terminals of the sense amplifier equally—because one side of the sense loop is effectively at ground level and the entire signal appears on the other side. Another common-mode component is coupled from one of the selection wires which is parallel to the sense-inhibit line in the bow-tie configuration. And still another component is present in the inhibit current when the drivers divide the current equally between two paths; these components, although not generated during a sense operation, may continue to circulate because of ringing, and thus interfere with subsequent sensing.

In the four-wire array, the only common-mode component arising directly from the sense signal is caused by attenuation differences between the two routes from the switching core to the sense amplifier terminals. This component usually is quite small and not very troublesome. But four-wire arrays do encounter common-mode signals generated by the large capacitive coupling between the sense and inhibit lines. Furthermore, the coupled-in signals tend to ring, which interferes with subsequent sense signals. Most designs have a balun on the inhibit line; this eliminates the common-mode component of the inhibit current and breaks the path for circulating coupled-in current.

Because the sense amplifier is a differential circuit, it can, in theory, ignore common-mode inputs. But in practice, no actual circuit is as good as it should be in theory. If the common-mode component could be reduced or eliminated, the sense amplifier circuit would be more reliable.

One way to reduce the common-mode component in three-wire arrays is to use a differential driver, as shown below. In this circuit one line is driven positive while its neighbor is driven negative, forcing the common-mode component to zero.

But a less complex circuit is based on an analysis of a common-mode signal, which can be broken down into a common-mode component and a differential component. In the diagram on page 17, the two horizontal lines represent the inhibit loop, capacitively coupled to another wire represented by the vertical line, which in

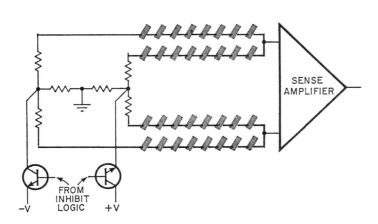

Differential driver. This circuit minimizes the common-mode component of inhibit current, which sometimes persists with a ringing effect and interferes with sense operation that follows.

Untwisted impedance

In any ferrite-core memory array, terminating resistors at one or the other end of the line match the sense line's characteristic impedance. This characteristic impedance has to be calculated differently for a three-wire array than for four wires, because the sense-inhibit line is doing double duty—whereas in most four-wire memories the sense wire has a lower characteristic impedance than the inhibit wire.

Just how reorienting the wire for a three-wire array lowers its characteristic impedance becomes clear when the factors that contribute to that impedance are considered. In a typical four-wire design, the sense wire has the configuration at upper left below. It's shown in an 8-by-8 array of cores, viewed edgewise as small black rectangles—but the pattern can be used in arrays of any size. Despite the sense wire's convolutions, it actually resembles a bifilar, or two-wire, transmission line—as the shading in the distorted version at right makes evident. In this version the arrows show an assumed current reference, which produces a net circulating current of zero wherever the transmission line crosses itself, and a nonzero circulating current in all other enclosed areas. This circulating current produces a net inductance.

If the sense wire is untwisted so that it retains its bifilar property but doesn't cross itself, it can be made to look just like the inhibit wire, shown at lower left. In this form its core inductance is the same as that of the inhibit wire because it passes through the same number of cores. Because the sense wire is almost 1½ times as long as the inhibit wire—note its diagonal configuration compared to the latter's orthogonality—its air inductance and its resistive attenuation might be expected to be more than twice that of the inhibit wire. But they're only about ten per cent higher, because the areas enclosed by the zero circulating current don't contribute to them. Therefore the sense wire's inductance and resistance are lower per unit length. These lower parameters therefore contribute to a lower characteristic impedance.

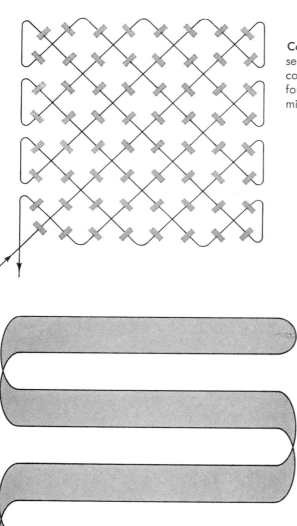

Convoluted. This sense-wire configuration in a four-wire array minimizes pickup.

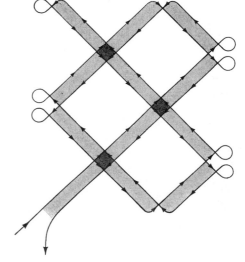

Distortion. Another view, topologically identical to the configuration at left, emphasizes the sense wire's resemblance to a transmission line.

Inhibit wire. This simple arrangement is possible because noise isn't picked up in isolated inhibit winding, and essentially is the same as the sense winding except for a somewhat higher characteristic impedance.

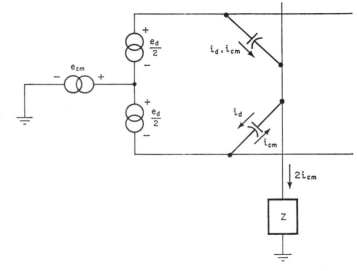

Coupling circuit. Common-mode and difference components present in any signal are represented by the three voltage sources shown here. Common-mode component can couple to external circuit, whereas differential component can't—it cancels itself.

turn is connected to ground through an impedance.

In this arrangement, the hypothetical generator e_{cm} produces a common-mode signal on both sides of the loop; the two differential generators e_d add differential signals of opposite polarity to the common-mode signal on the circuit's two sides. The diagram shows that the differential generators supply as much displacement current to the receiving line as they remove from it; thus the net current in the external circuit caused by the differential generators is zero. But the common-mode generator supplies a net current that is not zero. This current varies according to the common-mode potential and the total resistance, capacitance, and inductance in the external receiving circuit. When the common-mode input is large—as it is in a three-wire core array—the design of the external circuit can be critical.

Basically, there are two kinds of external circuits, shown in the diagrams on p. 18. These diagrams illustrate only the passive components, and they show only the connections that affect common-mode current, rather than all the array circuits.

In the grounded circuit, the drive lines are tied down at both ends. The equivalent circuit consists of a capacitance that equals the total coupling between the selection lines and the sense-inhibit lines; an inductance that is the sum of the stack inductance from nonswitching cores and the external inductance of attached circuits and parasitic effects; and a damping resistance. This resistance equals $Z_0/2N$, where N is the number of drive lines. The characteristic impedance, Z_0, typically is 150 ohms. Thus in a square array of 4,096 cores, 64 on a side, there are 128 drive lines, and the damping resistance is $150/(2 \times 128) = 0.58$ ohm.

In the open circuit, however, the drive line is open at one end with respect to coupled-in common-mode signals, and it has a high impedance at the other end. The equivalent circuit consists of the same capacitance and inductance as the grounded circuit, but the damping resistance typically is equal to $4Z_0/(2N)^{1/2}$. In the 4,096-core array, this is $4 \times 150/(2 \times 128)^{1/2} = 38$ ohms—almost two orders of magnitude greater than the damping resistance of the grounded circuit. Obviously the open circuit minimizes the need for common-mode suppression in the inhibit circuit—any spurious signals are quickly damped by the relatively high resistance.

This is one of the advantages of the inhibit-driver connection shown on page 13, which had both the driver circuit and the terminating resistors at the far end of the sense-inhibit loop, and no termination at the near end. The connection encounters only a minimum of spurious signals created by common-mode signals and ringing.

The three-wire array also affects a memory's power dissipation, inductance, and operating temperature. In a four-wire array, the inhibit wire, whose inductance is L, carries a current of I amperes, equal to the write current in one of the two selection wires, but opposite in direction. This inhibit current can be generated by a circuit at one end of the wire and grounded at the other end. The energy stored in the inductive circuit by this current is $\frac{1}{2}I^2L$.

But in the three-wire array, the sense operation requires the grounding, if any, to be at the center of the loop, not at the end. Thus the inhibit driver has to provide the I amp in each of two branches of the wire, for a total of 2I amps. The inductance in each branch is $L/2$, and the total inductance of the two branches connected in parallel is $L/4$. But the energy the driver must provide is

$$\frac{1}{2}(2I^2)\,(L/4) = \frac{1}{2}I^2L$$

This is the same as in the four-wire array. This energy

Grounded circuit. Essentials of a sense-inhibit line with coupling to drive lines in a three-wire memory. Here, drive wire is tied down at both ends.

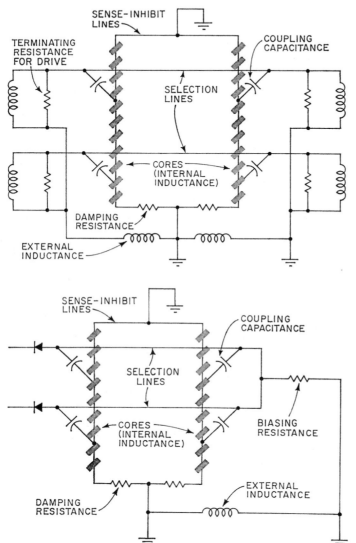

Open circuit. Permitting one end of drive line to float relative to common-mode reference and connecting the other end to a bus through a high resistance sets up an equivalent damping resistance about 100 times greater than that in the grounded circuit, largely overcoming common-mode ringing problems.

isn't dissipated as heat; it's stored in the magnetic field of the inductance, which either returns it to the source or dissipates it elsewhere in the circuitry after the current turns off.

A three-wire array is much less affected by temperature gradients than the four-wire unit because its sense-inhibit wire dissipates less power. This wire is the major resistive component seen by the inhibit driver, and the power it dissipates is I^2R. (It's not $4I^2R$, because every part of the winding carries only I amperes.) But since only three wires thread each core, the inhibit wire used with cores of a given size can be larger than in the four-wire array—perhaps by as much as three standard wire-gauge sizes. A difference of three in the wire-gauge number is about the same as a factor of two in the cross-sectional area, and therefore in the wire's resistance per unit length—and therefore in the inhibit wire's power dissipation.

Likewise, a three-wire array presents less of a problem in heat dissipation than a four-wire array, because of its sense-inhibit wire's lower resistance. Cycle time is a designer's first performance criterion, from which he obtains all other design factors. For example, from the specified cycle time he obtains the core size he must use; and with a given core size the three-wire array runs cooler. Suppose he tries to decrease the cycle time of a proven four-wire design by reducing the core size by a given factor F. Suppose further that he also reduces all other dimensions—wire sizes, wire lengths, mounting hardware, and so on—in the same proportion. He'll find that his proven four-wire design runs hot under these conditions.

What happens here is that in the scaled-down design, each piece of wire, shorter in proportion to F, has a cross-sectional area that is less in proportion to F^2. Thus its resistance proportional to its length and inversely proportional to its area, is increased in proportion to F—and so is its power dissipation. At the same time the areas of all surfaces in the design are reduced by the square of the factor. From the linear increase in power and the square decrease in surface area, it follows that the power density in watts per unit area increases in proportion to the cube of the given factor. This increase in power density increases the temperature of the stack.

The easiest way to cool it is to go to the three-wire design. ●

Smaller cores, bigger challenge

By John L. Turnbull and John J. Kureck

Ferroxcube Corp., Saugerties, N.Y.

One of the biggest problems faced by memory manufacturers is the need for smaller and smaller cores. One need creates another, and what's really needed now is a revised manufacturing and testing technology to handle the special problems presented by today's extremely small cores.

The techniques developed over the last 10 years to shape the dry powdered ferrite material into cores may be no longer usable. And quite possibly the problems encountered in testing small cores may place a more severe limit on their size than does the difficulty of wiring them by thousands into arrays.

Briefly, manufacturers are running into problems in the ferrite material itself, in the granules from which the cores are pressed, and in the density of the pressed cores, as well as in testing the finished product.

These problems, however, are not considered insurmountable. Core memories are here to stay for the foreseeable future, at least. Even though batch-fabricated elements such as thin films and semiconductor arrays are sure to give ferrite-core memories some tough competition, several companies are using cores now at speeds faster than even the fastest yet attained with the more exotic technologies. Sixteen-mil core arrays have been successfully wired, and one company is reported to be considering 12-mil cores in a two-dimensional, 100-nanosecond memory for its next generation computers.

Ferrites are ceramic materials, which are oxides of various materials. Within the crystal structure, the oxygen ions form two distinct sites, which can be occupied by smaller metal ions. The magnetic moments of the metal ions in these two sites provide the material's magnetic behavior. In the simplest case, one site contains trivalent iron ions, and the other contains a divalent ion of a transition metal—generally one of the elements in the first long horizontal row of the chemist's periodic table. The outer electron shells of these elements begin to fill before the inner shells are complete, producing a net magnetic moment.

A special case of considerable interest is lithium ferrite. Lithium, a monovalent element, can replace either divalent or trivalent ions, or both. Unique bonding in the resulting complex crystalline structure gives magnetic properties that are stable over a wide range of temperature. All ferrites in computers are mixtures of these forms.

All of the memory materials can be fabricated into cores of any size. Raw materials are prepared into ferrite powder, which is then pressed into cores. The ferrite granules are generally spherical, with the smallest being 0.4 mil in diameter, a size established by the minimum opening in currently available screens.

Granule diameter establishes the thinnest possible core wall thickness, which in turn determines the minimum core diameter attainable by pressing. This diameter should be about 5 or 6 mils, a size that is considerably smaller than the present 18- to 22-mil standard sizes or the 12-, 14-, or 16-mil sizes that have been wired experimentally. The walls of 20-mil cores are two to three mils thick.

Micrometer. This type of gauge measures the height of cores, as part of a density measurement.

But small granules have a large surface area relative to their weight, and often don't flow freely to core-pressing machines, which are fed by gravity.

A pressing matter

The nature and extent of this problem can be visualized by considering that these minuscule granules have to flow into a toroidal cylinder 1 mil thick and 15 to 20 mils deep in no more than 200 milliseconds, and keep doing it again and again at intervals of 600 msec. No sticking in the chute can be tolerated.

Once the cylindrical die of a standard core-pressing machine has been filled with powdered ferrite, a punch compresses the powder into its familiar toroidal form. The punch is ordinarily driven by a small crank on a large flywheel rotating (as the 600-msec interval makes obvious) at 100 revolutions per minute. The pressing operation creates extremely high pressures—high enough to make the ferrite granules coalesce.

The pressed core is very nearly a single homogeneous mass, although traces of the granule boundaries can sometimes be discerned under the microscope. The sintering operation that follows pressing destroys any granular structure that may remain; the oxide particles, of which the original granules were agglomerations, diffuse to form the proper crystal structure—a spinel.

Cores of all sizes are turned out by the same kinds of machines—indeed, often by the very same machines with changed punches and dies. The total force applied to the cores is thus about the same regardless of their size, so that the unit pressure is considerably larger when smaller cores are pressed. The increase in pressure is more than just a matter of applying a given force over a reduced area; the smaller cores must be pressed to a higher density than the larger ones to give them enough mechanical strength to withstand normally rough handling.

Fabricating the punch and die assemblies suitable for smaller and smaller core sizes is a difficult task. It's not impossible, thanks to modern machining techniques, but the very tiny parts now being made are likely to be somewhat fragile under the great stresses they encounter. Better die designs and materials are needed.

The smaller the cores, the shorter the tool life. The increased pressures cause more friction between the punch and the dies as they come together. And regardless of wear, the smaller tools must be maintained at closer tolerances and must therefore be replaced more often than the larger ones.

Measuring density

After the cores have been pressed, they are baked or sintered at 1,050° to 1,350°C to establish the square hysteresis loop and other magnetic and mechanical charcteristics required in memories. After baking, a sample of each batch of cores is taken for density measurements. These measurements, a necessary control on the pressing operation, cannot be made before the sintering because the smaller unsintered cores are very fragile.

It takes very sophisticated equipment to measure the density of the smaller cores. The core's volume and weight must be determined and the quotient found. Since the pressing results in quite uniform roundness and diameter, the volume measurement is reduced to measuring the core's height—not a particularly difficult job for mechanical gauges with gradations down to 20 millionths of an inch.

Weighing the core is something else again. A single core weighs about 6 micrograms and has to be measured within a tolerance of 5%. Such measurements require an ultra-microbalance accurate to within 0.1 microgram. This balance, the same kind used in biochemistry and spectroscopy, works on the principle of force applied in a magnetic field. The force deflects a coil, and current through the coil returns it to normal; the amount of current is a measure of the applied force—the weight of the object being weighed.

Obviously, measuring the heights and weights of such small cores requires close environmental control—the technician can't afford to even breathe heavily. Such control imposes restrictions on the speed and precision of measurement, and this is one of the reasons why only samples are measured.

Core tester. Cores feed from the vibrator into the vertical chute (heavy dark line at left). At the bottom of the chute, the split probe (also dark) moves through the hole in the core and makes an electrical contact on the other side. The two halves of the probe carry current pulses that switch the core and sense its output.

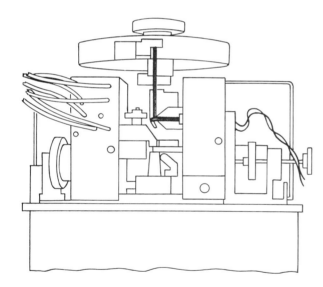

One conceivable solution to the problems involved in pressing cores and measuring their density might be to stamp the cores out of a sheet of ferrite that had been rolled out, like cookie dough, to the proper thickness. This thickness, and the weight of the stamped-out cores, would be relatively easy to control. The rolling and stamping tools might be simpler and therefore cheaper, and the tools might last longer because they would encounter less wear. This technique has been tried experimentally, and it looks promising. However, it raises some questions that in some ways might be just as troublesome as the ones involved in stamping out the cores individually. For example, the ferrite sheets, which would resemble paper tape, would be only a few mils thick and rather brittle, so they would crack easily—perhaps under their own weight.

Passing muster

Just one faulty core in a million-bit memory will cause the whole assembly to fail—a reason sufficient to justify the testing of all cores before they're assembled into a memory.

In the standard testing operation, a vibratory feeder moves the cores into a funnel-shaped chute that orients them properly and drops them into a vertical track. The track's dimensions are such that the core falls freely but maintains its orientation. The core stops moving at the bottom of the track, and a split probe is inserted through its hole to electrical contacts behind it.

A current pulse pattern is generated on one of the two halves of the probe, while the other half senses the flux changes in the core as it switches. Sense amplifiers and logic circuits determine whether the core is up to specifications. If it is, the probe is withdrawn and the core is deflected into a collector; cores that fail drop straight into another collector. This arrangement ensures that while a few "good" cores might be thrown out if the deflector mechanism failed, a bad core could never land in the good pile.

The entire operation takes place in a single machine that typically tests 16 cores per second.

Although its output rate is far higher than could be achieved with any manual process, it is plagued by problems either intrinsic to the process or related to the core sizes.

For example, a few cores are invariably broken or chipped before they get to the tester or while they're in the vibrator. These cores sometimes jam in the funnel or the vertical track so that the machine must be shut down, or they come to rest at an angle in the test fixture and break the probe as it comes through.

In addition, as thousands of cores pass through the tester, friction wears off particles of ferrite that may become embedded in the probe. These particles create noise that sometimes produces false test results, and they wear out the probe.

Reduced core size means reduced weight. Just as the fine granules of ferrite don't always drop into the press the way they should, small cores are restrained by air resistance and tend to dribble slowly down the track in the testing machine instead of dropping straight and true into position. Present testing machines run at a fixed rate and assume that a core has fallen into proper place before the probe moves in. If cores get much smaller, testers will have to be designed with positive feeding mechanisms to ensure that the core is positioned to take the probe.

With smaller cores designed to switch more quickly, the pulse generators connected to the probe will have to operate at higher frequencies than the present units, and the sense amplifiers will have to reject noise better.

Last but most definitely not least, smaller cores will require smaller testing probes, or a new testing method. Scaled-down probes may be weaker than the present models and might break sooner or wear out faster. This could be serious, because the split probes are an inherently weak design.

Ultra-microbalance. This instrument weighs single cores to an accuracy of half a microgram.

Cutting the tape

To the Editor:

We read with interest the article "Smaller Cores, Bigger Challenge" in your recent issue. Particularly deserving of comment is the statement concerning the possibility of cutting ferrite cores from a green (unfired) ferrite sheet.

Core Memories Inc., a subsidiary of the Data Products Corp., has been producing cores in this manner for about two years, first at our facility in Dublin, Ireland, and now at our Mountain View, Calif., plant. The process was developed by Walter Wiechec, head of the firm's ceramics department.

By mixing the ferrite powder with a plastic binder and rolling the mixture to a precisely con-trolled thickness, an extremely flexible sheet is formed—not at all as brittle as the article suggests. The sheets are then cut into "tapes" about 5⁄8 inch wide, and these are fed through an automatic machine that cuts a row of up to 12 cores across the tape at a rate of up to 4,000 cores per minute, 40 times the pace of a conventional press.

This technique reduces the cost of cores because it increases yield through better control of core density, lowers tooling expenses, lengthens tool life, and speeds production. And it is particularly suited to producing very small cores (under 18 mils).

William G. Rumble
Engineering department manager
Core Memories Inc.
Mountain View, Calif.

Speeding up ferrite-core memories

By Robert M. Whalen

International Business Machines Corp., Poughkeepsie, N.Y.

For nearly 20 years, the introduction of new fast computers has been confronted by the discovery of a class of problems that require even faster processors—and faster memories. However, the drive for faster ferrite-core memories has temporarily slowed, due to developments in computer architecture that make them seem to run faster than they actually do [see "Prodding memories," p. 24]. But these architectural developments themselves require fast memories that presage the even higher speeds required of future main memories.

Conceptually, the method of making today's memories faster is to make the cores smaller. Smaller cores can be made to switch faster without increasing drive current, because they have shorter magnetic path lengths which result in higher switching fields. They also have smaller cross-sectional areas, which reduces inductance, and can be placed closer together, which reduces drive line length. The result is lower transmission delay, back voltage, and power dissipation. The latter two make the storage array, as a load, easier to drive with high-density integrated circuits. The shorter line lengths even compensate for the higher resistance per unit length of the smaller wires that are required.

Signal-to-noise ratios do not deteriorate when core size is reduced, as shown on page 25, because delta noise, which is produced by half-selected cores, can be cut in proportion to signal output, and lower drive voltages and line delays reduce spurious couplings, thus generating less noise. The surface-to-volume ratio also increases as cores get smaller, increasing their efficiency in dissipating heat generated during switching.

Mechanical problems

The principal problems in smaller cores are more mechanical than electrical.[5] Making, testing, and wiring cores becomes more difficult as core size is reduced. The problems in making cores range from obtaining finer ferrite powder, to building presses with close tolerances, to controlling time and temperature in sintering. In testing, the cores must move continuously along controlled paths despite air currents and magnetized mechanism parts. And in wiring, the cores usually are vibrated into positions in a type of jig that is quite difficult to make for the smallest core sizes.

Wiring the cores—a task that up to now has been largely manual—inevitably will become completely automated. Limitations of human dexterity and, coordinately, the inability of manual threading to stay abreast of an ever-increasing bit market, will

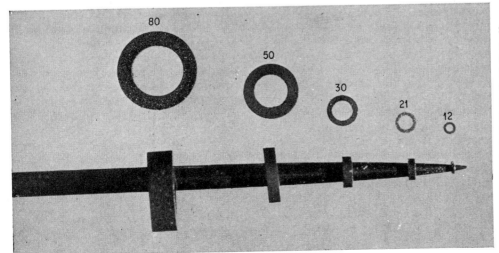

Sized for speed. Five common ferrite core sizes have been in use in computers. Each was smaller than the one before, and made it obsolete, because the new size could switch faster. Numbers show the outside diameter of the cores in mils; the lower line-up shows them mounted on the tip of a sewing needle.

Prodding memories

Ferrite-core memories with cycle times faster than 500 nanoseconds are not generally available commercially, even though designers long have been tinkering with the idea of building them,[1,3] and even though a relatively large memory with a 100-nsec cycle was demonstrated as long ago as 1966.[2]

But faster memories have not appeared for three primary reasons: the development of architectural techniques that match relatively slow memories to faster processing units; difficulties in handling and wiring the small cores that would be required, and the expense of achieving speed by switching only part of the ferrite core's toroidal volume instead of all of it.

There are two basic types of architectural techniques. The simpler of these divides the large memory into relatively small modules that can operate at the necessary speed, and are connected via a single common bus to the central processor. But even this approach is limited by transmission and switching delays, which erect a performance barrier between the processor and its large and remote memory frame.

To compensate, the architectural alternative is to add a relatively small, high-speed buffer directly in the processor to exchange data with the remote memory [see p. 241]. The processor could randomly access individual words in the internal buffer without delay while the buffer obtains new data from the external main memory in larger blocks. Although this requires more control hardware in the processor, the cost/performance tradeoffs have made it worthwhile.[4]

A high-speed buffer still requires the external main memory to transfer data at a rate commensurate with the internal buffer's cycle time, and there are techniques to accomplish this that do not impose severe requirements on the latter. For example, the accesses to separate modules can be interleaved—new cycles can be started in one or more modules before a previous cycle in a different module is complete—or long words can be transferred by accessing several modules in parallel. Thus the main memory cycle can be considerably longer than the buffer cycle.

Module capacities for these systems usually are limited to a half-million bits or less, which is desirable because, by distributing successive memory addresses, it permits an apparently very fast cycle but doesn't require individual modules to be unusually speedy. In an interleaved operational mode it reduces the statistical probability of a double access to a single module during its cycle time—this would interrupt the data flow.

But there's a tradeoff for permitting the modules to be slow: they also must be inexpensive. For this reason 3-D and 2½-D organizations are most frequently used.

---

make automation an economic must. But it will be necessary to further extend the capability of the wire insertion tools presently available, or to develop an entirely different approach to plane design—for example, a way of fabricating ferrite arrays in batches.

These mechanical problems have been solved, at least on an experimental basis, with cores that have an inside diameter of 7½ mils, an outside diameter of 12 mils, and a thickness of 2½ mils—compared with today's standard size of 20 mils o.d. A 12-mil core can switch in about 70 nsec when excited by a full-select current of 900 milliamperes. In a 3-D memory the core must switch both ways, first to read out the data and then to store it again for reuse later. This two-way switching time typically represents about 50% of the cycle of a 3-D memory in the quarter- to half-million-bit range; the other 50% permits transients to die away. These figures thus project a 280 nsec cycle. A slightly faster cycle time of about 230 nsec can be projected for a three-wire 2½-D organization, primarily because of the elimination of one of the dimensional controls.

But these projected times don't really indicate how much swifter main memories will actually become. There are too many factors that will influence future demand—for example, how much a customer is willing to pay for speed, or how quickly competing technologies develop and how rapidly they're adopted.

Buffer memories

Fast operation becomes the key requirement—if necessary, at the expense of bit capacity—when cores are used in buffer memories. Their clock cycles must match those of modern high-performance processors—usually faster than 200 nsec, and in some cases even 100 nsec. Buffer memories also must be compact enough to house the required bit capacity within or very near the processing unit. These two requirements—speed and compactness—when coupled with cost and limitations of today's memory technologies, have restricted buffer capacity to a quarter of a million bits or less.

Ferrite cores can meet the speed and compactness requirements for most buffer applications, but they lose much of the cost advantage that they enjoy in main memories. Although the necessary compactness is possible in 3-D or 2½-D organization with still smaller cores, significantly better performance is possible, with present standard core sizes through partial switching. Because it switches less flux—in effect, less of the core's toroidal volume—switch time is cut.

Switching duration could be made almost arbitrarily small, except for some practical limitations such as the 1-to-0 signal ratio; it becomes pro-

Wired up. These cores are being wired in an automatic machine. One coordinate already has been threaded and the second is being inserted through hollow needles. Use of the needles indicates that the cores are 30 mils or more in diameter; in smaller cores, a similar machine simply pushes the wires through a row of cores without the use of needles.

gressively smaller as less flux is switched. To maintain the ratio at a practical level, a second core is introduced at each bit position. The second core is used to store a reference flux; a differential flux-sensing system detects the presence of a 1 by measuring the difference between the flux stored in the data core and the flux stored in the second core.

2-D is a necessity

But the chief disadvantage of partial switching is that it requires a 2-D or word-organized system. A 3-D or 2½-D organization cannot be used because both depend on half-select current pulses that affect many cores besides the full-select core; a partially-switched core produces large spurious signals when exposed to these half-select pulses, and these can even change its flux state. In a 2-D organization a single word line is selected; it carries the full drive current, but it requires more drive and sense circuitry, which, together with the use of two cores per bit, makes an inherently more expensive system than one using full switching.

On the other hand, partially switched cores dissipate less power and use lower drive currents, which are more easily obtained with state-of-the-art semiconductor circuits. Furthermore, because even in the fastest systems only two wires thread each core, the array is easier to assemble, and therefore less expensive.

Whether 2-D ferrite core systems continue to be cost-competitive with other technologies remains to be seen, though the availability of low-cost monolithic drive and sense circuits will enhance their chances. From a performance standpoint, quarter-million-bit memories with 100 nsec cycle times can be produced with the 7-by-12 core. To attain even higher speeds, a number of design choices are available, but the most chal-

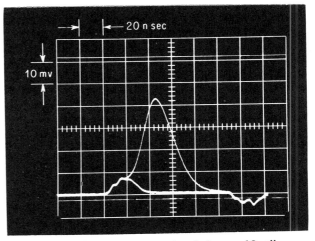

Silence, please. These 1 and 0 signals from a 12-mil core under worst-case coincident-current test conditions still show an excellent signal-to-noise ratio.

lenging and most promising in many respects is to continue to make cores smaller. This will increase core fabrication and winding problems, but will considerably ease the semiconductor and cooling requirements and permit a denser package. ∎

References

1. J.A. Rajchman, "Computer Memories—Possible Future Developments," RCA Review, June, 1962.
2. G.E. Werner and R.M. Whalen, "A 110-Nanosecond Ferrite Core Memory," IEEE Transactions on Magnetics, September 1966.
3. T.J. Gilligan, "2½-D High-Speed Memory Systems—Past, Present and Future," IEEE Transactions on Electronic Computers, August 1966, p. 475.
4. C.J. Conti, D.H. Gibson, and S.H. Pitkowsky, "Structural Aspects of the System 360 Model 85," IBM Systems Journal, Vol. 7, No. 1, 1968, p. 2.
5. John L. Turnbull and John J. Kureck, "Smaller cores, bigger challenge," this volume, p. 19.

Chapter 2
Thin films

Plated wire: a long shot that's paying off

By George A. Fedde
Univac division, Sperry Rand Corp., Blue Bell, Pa.

In the spring of 1967, plated wire was described as "Univac's bet to replace toroidal ferrite cores." Univac is still in the game, which has seen many players join in and a few drop out. The division has met its cost-performance goals and is resonably confident in predicting major improvements.

Production of plated-wire memories is expanding at about six times as fast a rate as the over-all production of random-access memories in the U.S. This is partly due to the fact that the base rate is very small, but it also indicates that significant progress has been made overcoming production problems. Current annual output of plated wire is about 2.5% of the estimated total for all types of random-access memory this year, and most of this production is going on at Univac for the division's 9000 series and 1110 computers.

By and large, plated-wire memories are being used in new products requiring higher speeds and lower costs than ferrite technology can provide. For example, the Univac 9000 series computers wouldn't operate at both the speed and cost that they do if they had ferrite-core memories. Plated wires aren't replacing ferrite-core memories, nor are they expected to replace them, in the sense of production changeovers. They're being applied in areas that core arrays haven't been able to penetrate.

But an evolutionary replacement of ferrite cores in the main memories of new computers is just starting. This period of profitable coexistence is expected to last at least through 1975, at which time plated-wire units may account for 10% to 20% of the production of random-access memories production in the U.S.

Bandwagon

Univac's decision to develop and produce plated-wire memories has been followed recently by similar decisions at other firms. Their present substantial efforts, added to Univac's, are moving plated-wire technology at an accelerating pace.

For example, Honeywell Inc. is now building plated-wire memory stacks for Government-funded programs and may soon offer them commercially. Toko Inc. of Japan and Plessey Co. Ltd. of England also offer plated-wire memories and stacks. The National Cash Register Co. has been producing plated wire with somewhat different magnetic characteristics for some time [see p. 35], and the volume could increase substantially in the wake of the company's late 1970 announcements of new equipment using the wire. However, NCR didn't use its version of plated wire in its newest large computer, whereas Univac's version was carried through into the 1110.

Other companies with plated wire products or technology include the Electronics division of the Lockheed Aircraft Corp.; the Autonetics division of the North American Rockwell Corp.; the Stromberg-Carlson Corp., a subsidiary of the General Dynamics Corp.; Nemonic Data Systems, Inc.; Memory Systems, Inc.; Goodyear Aerospace Corp.; Philips Gloeilampenfabrieken; the Nippon Telephone and Telegraph Public Corp.; Siemens A.G. and government-supported laboratories in France and Japan.

Definition

Plated wire is a specially cleaned and prepared beryllium-copper wire 2 to 5 mils in diameter that's electroplated with a layer 30 microinches thick. The alloy is about 80% nickel and 20% iron, and, like most thin films, is magnetically anisotropic—it can be more easily magnetized in one direction than in another.

A current in the wire during the plating process

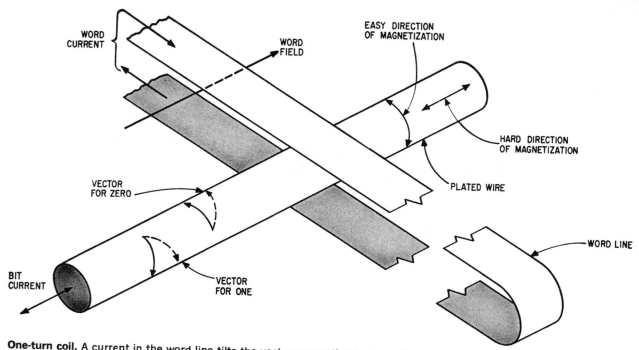

One-turn coil. A current in the word line tilts the vector magnetization from its rest position, shown in solid lines, toward the hard axis of magnetization, generating a pulse in the plated wire.

establishes the magnetic easy axis circumferentially around the wire. Thus a particular spot on the wire can be magnetized either clockwise or counter-clockwise, corresponding to the 1's and 0's of binary data. The same current applied while the wire is heated in a reducing atmosphere at the end of the plating process anneals the wire and stabilizes the film so that it retains its magnetic properties indefinitely. Without this step the wire's characteristics would deteriorate too rapidly for practical application.

The closed flux path offers significant advantages over the open path that is characteristic of single planar thin-film elements. With an open flux path, the element would tend to demagnetize itself unless it were made of a material with high coercive force —particularly if it were small. But with the closed path, the film thickness is not dictated by considerations of self-demagnetization. With no gaps in the path, the minimum bit current is obtained for a given material and path length.

Twenty bits can be stored in each inch of the wire, which is plated, annealed, and tested in a continuous process, and then cut into segments a foot or two long for incorporation into a memory system.

The size and position of the bit storage cell is set by the interaction of the magnetic drive field generated by current in the word line, as shown above, with digit write current in the wire. Each word line forms a solenoid of a few turns around all the parallel wires in a memory module, or one turn around 160 wires in Univac's 9000 series.

The plated wires are inserted in "tunnels" 30 mils apart in a layer of plastic, and the word lines are on printed-circuit boards on both sides of the plastic. An unplated dummy wire is inserted in intermediate tunnels at intervals as a noise source to cancel the common-mode noise in the plated wire, and six unconnected plated wires at each edge of the array provide the same magnetic environment for the outermost connected wires as for wires in the center.

This storage element has a number of special characteristics that are particularly interesting when compared with those of conventional ferrite cores and planar thin films. Also, the single drive line in a plated-wire storage element is its own sense-digit line. Also, plated wire has an explicit output for a 0 readout. Cores ideally would have no output, but they always generate a little noise. Planar films have explicit 0 outputs, but in most versions, the signals for 1 and 0 are smaller than those in cylindrical films; the flux path of a single planar element is open, and that of two coupled planar elements has two air gaps in it. The one disadvantage of plated wire at the present state of the art is its relatively low bit density.

Nondestructive readout

But plated wire is capable of nondestructive readout, which isn't available with the mass-produced versions of the other two types of memories. This NDRO capability reduces the amount, and therefore the cost, of the peripheral electronic circuitry required by a two-dimensional memory, and permits an organization similar in some ways to the 2½-D ferrite core layout, which attains high speed at low cost even in small module sizes. Plated-wire memories are most economical when the word drive current has the same amplitude for reading nondestructively as for writing.

[The alert reader will note an apparent contradiction between this statement and Al Bates' contention in Chapter 11, page 257, in this book that NDRO is more expensive than DRO. But both authors are correct, given their companies' approaches. Burroughs would achieve NDRO by tickling the memory with a smaller current than is used for writing. This would require either separate circuits for reading and writing, or a more complex and expensive circuit capable of delivering two levels of current. Univac, on the other hand, uses equal word currents for reading and writing; the extra wallop to wipe out old data when new data is being written comes from the bit current. This means that new data can be written in only part of a word if necessary.]

NDRO also reduces processing time in a computer by one-third, if, as is typically the case, the computer takes about four read cycles for each write cycle. With nondestructive readout, read instructions can be executed in half the time required by a ferrite-core or other DRO memory. Reading out a core clears, or destroys, the data

in it, so a rewrite is necessary after every readout. And every write instruction must be preceded by a clearing out of the old data. Thus four reads and one write require 10 operations—five read-write pairs. The same instructions require only six operations in this NDRO memory: four reads and one clear-write pair.

Few rejects

The production of plated wire at Univac has grown about 45% per year in the past three years. Although this is partly due to an increase in the number of plating machines in the production line, it also reflects improvements in yield and quality control.

The individual bit yield is now 99.61%. With 270 bits on a single length of wire, the wire yield is about $(0.9961)^{270}$ or 0.445; actually it varies between 35% and 60%.

Thus an average of one bit in every 256 is bad at the output of the plating process, where testing occurs. Most are eliminated then and there by cutting the wire as soon as a defective bit is located. A few slip through, and a few wires are found to have bad spots later on. Nevertheless,

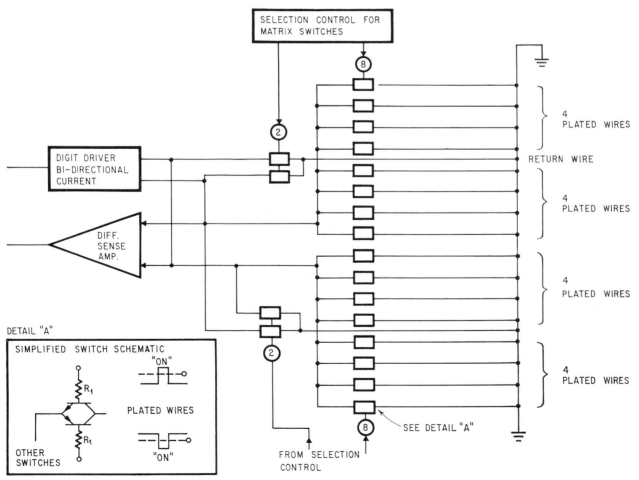

Sixteen to one. One sense amplifier or bit current driver is connected to one of 16 plated wires and to one of two dummy wires through a matrix of switches that permit high-speed operation at low cost.

FERRITE CORE

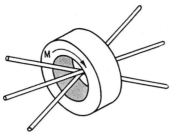

TWO SELECTION WINDINGS—
ONE SENSE WINDING

PLATED WIRE

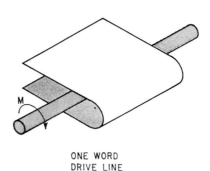

ONE WORD
DRIVE LINE

FLAT FILM

SENSE-DIGIT LINE

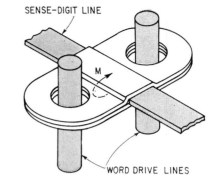

WORD DRIVE LINES

Competitors. Plated wire, like planar thin films, switches 10 to 30 times as fast as ferrite cores with perhaps 1/15 the energy per element, and occupies about 1/100 the volume. Both plated wire and planar films have bipolar output signals, but the wire's output is about 10 times as large as the film's, and 1/4 as large as the core's.

only about one in 10,000 bits is defective after the memory plane is assembled.

It's become possible in the past year to measure and control the magnetostriction coefficient, a very important parameter, on the moving wire in the plating machine.

The relative concentrations of nickel and iron in the plating bath are now being controlled continuously. This maintains the optimum levels more closely than formerly, when discrete portions of each element were added as needed.

The electronic circuits and the memory planes containing the plated wires are undergoing evolutionary changes, most of them represent attempts to improve the signal-to-noise ratio. They include a new low-gain preamplifier stage, layout changes in the sense amplifier and signal strobe circuits, and improved low-level switching circuits.

These low-level switches connect one sense amplifier or bit current driver to one of 16 sense-bit circuits, as shown on page 31, and to one of the two unplated dummy wires associated with the 16 circuits. Write current passes along both wires. If a read operation is to ensue immediately, either both the plated wire being read and the selected dummy wire must have been used in writing, or neither of them. Otherwise, one of the wires would have a decaying voltage on it that the sense amplifier would see as noncommon-mode noise.

Through any given cycle, 15 switches are off to prevent the unselected sense lines from reducing the sense signal available to the amplifier or from diverting bit current from the selected plated wire during a writing.

Three goals

Current research and development programs are giving special attention to semiconductor circuits in three particular areas.

For one thing, if the plated-wire memory is to have a 100-nanosecond cycle time, it needs a new low-level switch. The present switch produces an offset voltage when it's on; a switch made with a field-effect transistor would have no offset volt-

age, but wouldn't operate at cycle times much below a microsecond. The switch must also be capable of carrying the 40-milliampere digit drive current. The right combination of fast turn-on and turn-off times with low capacitance, resistance, and cost is being sought.

All plated-wire memories require a magneto-motive force of 750 to 1200 ma-turns. When a one-turn word coil is used, the necessary current is easily carried by discrete or hybrid-chip semiconductors. To use monolithic integrated circuits in the drive circuits, the amount of current must be reduced to about 30% to 40% of its present value. Experiments indicate that low-reluctance paths for the word-line flux may make such a reduction possible. Such paths can be established through a magnetic keeper—a layer of magnetic material on top of the word lines.

Present plated-wire memories operating at 500-nsec cycle times have a diode in series with each word line, permitting a very economical transistor switch matrix to select the word lines. These matrixes would be feasible down to about 150 nsec. An alternative scheme, which would work at both faster and slower speeds, would replace the diode with a transistor whose base and emitter are connected to switch matrixes. This method would be especially attractive with monolithic integrated circuits, and would reduce the noise coupled into the sense lines by permitting the grounding of one end of the word lines.

Not that all research and development on the plated-wire element has come to a screeching halt. A whole new optimum set of magnetic parameters will probably have to be worked out for tomorrow's high-speed systems, covering such things as film thickness, coercive force, and anisotropy field. Coercive force is the minimum magnetic-field intensity required to remove the residual magnetism from a saturated material; anisotropy field is a measure of the magnetic field that saturates an anisotropic film in its hard direction.

A thinner film would mean fewer milliampere-turns required in the word line, higher coercive force, and a smaller change of flux coupled to the sense line during readout. The output signal would be smaller, but that would be compensated for, at least in part, by the fact that a very fast memory requires a short rise time on all input and output signals, which maintains the peak amplitude and shortens the signal duration.

Some researchers are exploring the advantages of a thinner wire. For a given film thickness and bit length, a smaller diameter would reduce the flux coupled to the word drive line, without affecting the output signal's amplitude. Slimmer wires would also permit the word lines to be placed closer together, reducing the fringing of the drive field to adjacent bits and possibly leading to a higher bit density. But the thinner wire would be harder to handle than the present variety, and would tend to increase signal attenuation because of its higher resistance.

For all this, though, today's R&D efforts should produce memory systems in the not too distant future with module capacities of 100,000 to 1 million bits, cycle times of 100 nsec, and access times of 55 to 60 nsec—at a cost only slightly higher than that of present 500 to 600-nsec cycle memories. Plated wire is also attractive for very large memories of up to 100 million bits. These memories were estimated early in 1967 to cost significantly less than one cent per bit, but recent developments indicate that the estimate was quite conservative. However, until production capacity can catch up with demand, plated wires aren't likely to be used commercially in such sizes.

The next step will probably be the production of larger modules with cycle times down to about 200 nsec. The next three to five years should see the introduction of 100-nsec random-access memories with capacities up to a million bits, and sub-microsecond memories in the 100-million-bit range.

Bibliography

W.O. Freitag, J.S. Mathias, and G. DiGuilio, "The Electrodeposition of Nickel-Iron-Phosphorus Thin Films for Computer Memory Use," Electro-chemical Society Journal, January 1964, p. 35.

H.O. Leilich, "The Chain—A New Magnetic Film Memory Device," Journal of Applied Physics, March 1966, p. 1361.

J.P. McCallister and C.F. Chong, "A 500-Nanosecond Main Computer Memory Utilizing Plated-Wire Elements," American Federation of Information Processing Societies, Conf. Proc., vol. 30 (Fall Joint Computer Conference), 1966, p. 305.

G.A. Fedde, "Plated-wire memories: Univac's bet to replace toroidal ferrite cores," Electronics, May 15, 1967, p. 101.

S. Waaben, "High-Speed Plated-Wire Memory System," IEEE Trans. on Electronic Computers, June 1967, p. 335

J.R. Brown Jr., "Internal Memory Systems," Modern Data Systems, February 1968, p. 62.

C.F. Chong and G.A. Fedde, "Plated-Wire Memory, Present and Future," Proc., International Conference on Magnetics, 1968.

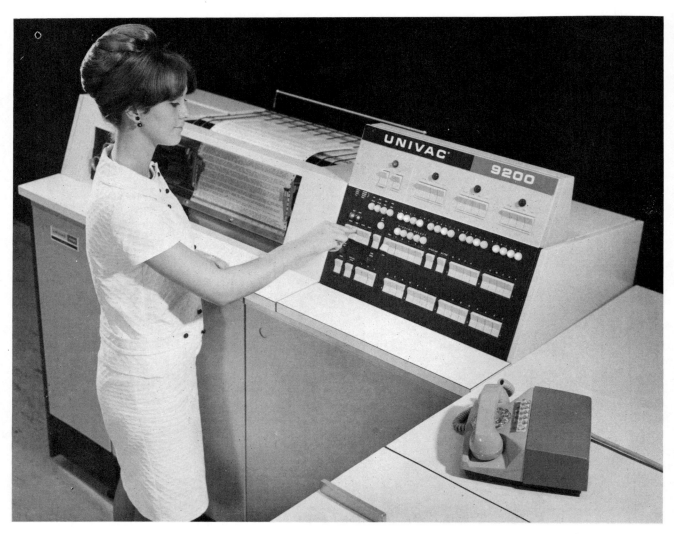

Pioneer. This computer was one of the first models commercially available to use circumferentially-magnetized plated wire in its memory (see preceding article). Axially-magnetized wires, or rods, had been in use for some time, as described in the next article.

Rods look like wires, act like cores

By Donal A. Meier

National Cash Register Co., Hawthorne, Calif.

Cylindrical, thin magnetic films plated on wire with axially oriented storage states have replaced ferrite cores as the storage medium in high-performance digital computer memories at the National Cash Register Co. Unlike those used in other forms of plated-wire and thin-film memories, these films are isotropic and are made of a material with a high coercive force.

These two film characteristics give the wires, or rods, a number of advantages. Like cores, the films retain their magnetic characteristics indefinitely without annealing even though the flux path is open. This is true whether they are repeatedly switched back and forth or made to retain a fixed magnetic state for a long period of time.

Also, the plating process can be relatively speedy —much faster than the plating of wires with a circumferential anisotropic film. Finally, problems of magnetostriction, skew and dispersion, which plague designers of planar thin-film memories and plated wires with circumferential storage states, are avoided here. [An article on skew and dispersion problems appears elsewhere in this volume, on page 45.]

Magnetic rods, which are organized in arrays like cores, have been used in many experimental and commercial memories. Of these, the most practical have been the two-dimensional organization in NCR's 315 RMC computer, the 2½-D form in the company's new Century series computers, and a structure with two rod elements per bit. This set-up, analogous to the two-core-per-bit arrangement, was used in an experimental memory that achieved 100-nanosecond cycle times.

First of its kind

Rods were introduced in the 315 RMC (for rod memory computer) machine, the first commercial computer with an all-thin-film memory. The 315, brought out in 1965, is being phased out of production, having been superseded by the recently announced Century series.

In the rods, the axially oriented magnetization reverses its direction by 180° when switching between binary 1's and 0's, as shown on p. 36. The continuous plating, an alloy of 98% iron and 2% nickel, switches when subjected to a magnetizing force greater than 16 oersteds. [The corresponding energy is about 2×10^{-10} joule; compare this with the plated-wire figure of 1×10^{-10} joule.]

The rods used in the RMC processor are made from a continuous length of beryllium-copper wire 10 mils in diameter. This wire is passed at a speed of 15 feet per minute through a series of baths that deposit the plating material on it. When the wire emerges from the last bath it is immediately and continuously tested, helically wound with a copper ribbon, and cut into pieces seven inches long.

Fine wires wound on these lengths of wire establish the bit cells, typically 10 of them per linear inch of rod. The windings are interconnected between bit cells and between rods in a two-dimensional arrangement, as shown on p. 37. Word windings are machine-wound solenoids of 10 turns over a distance of 50 to 60 mils along the wire; digit-sense windings are continuous machine-wound helixes of about 95 turns along the entire 7-inch rod. The solenoid's intersection with the helix defines a storage cell. Yield for the whole 7-inch length has been greater than 85% during the four years in which this RMC memory has been in production.

New whiskers

The newer Century series computers contain rod memories of a different design suitable to semi-automatic fabrication in large batches without the yield problems usually associated with batch fabrication.

In the Century, the memory is assembled from modules of approximately 16,000 bytes. Each module contains 32 planes of 4,608 bits in a 64-by-72 array. Each bit is stored in a separate length of rod, or "whisker," about 1/10 inch long and 6.5 mils in diameter, with its own set of windings.

Whiskers are made in essentially the same way as rods except for the on-line cutting. Following a testing step primarily aimed at monitoring the plat-

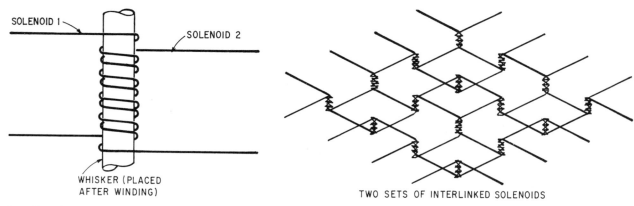

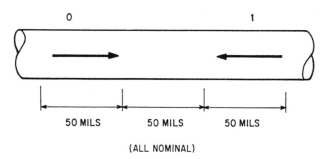

TWO SETS OF INTERLINKED SOLENOIDS

Interlinked. Two solenoid windings are interlaced in a special machine that winds them both at the same time, in a pattern for the whole plane that resembles a chain link fence. One whisker fits in each solenoid (photo, right).

Reversal. Magnetized thin film on a rod is oriented parallel to the rod's axis, in opposite directions corresponding to binary 1's and 0's.

ing process, the wire is coated with 0.2-mil layer of plastic to keep the iron from oxidizing. It is then baked and wound on a take-up spool. In a separate off-line process, the wire is tested again and cut mechanically into whiskers at a rate of 1,000 per minute.

The solenoid array in which the whiskers are mounted is made in a frame by a machine that winds interlinked 10-turn solenoids in each of two perpendicular directions as shown above. A sheet of plastic is then vacuum-formed across one side of the array to establish a "bottom." The rods are automatically dropped into place in the interlinked solenoids, using a mask and an alternating magnetic field. The mask is placed over the solenoid array, an oversupply of whiskers is poured on it, and the whole is placed in the magnetic field. The field causes the whiskers to stand upright and dance about; when the array is tilted, the whiskers march across the surface and fall into the individual solenoids through holes in the mask, as shown at right. Surplus whiskers pile up at the edge of the array, and are lifted off with the mask. Another layer of plastic is formed over the top to encapsulate the array, which is then tested as a unit. If a

On the march. An alternating magnetic field set up under the large horizontal pole piece stands the whiskers on end and marches them across the plane. One whisker drops through each tiny hole into a pair of linked solenoids beneath the plane. Surplus whiskers accumulate at the edge of the plane and are lifted off with the mask.

bad whisker happens to find its way into the array, it can be removed individually and replaced by another without endangering the array in any way.

Familiar pattern

Modules made from this standard array are laid out in a two-wire, 2½-D organization for good performance at low cost. The interconnections and operation are essentially the same as those in the two-wire, 2½-D ferrite-core array. This causes the delta noise, induced in the sense winding by half the whiskers, to cancel that induced by the other half. As a result, superimposed oscilloscope traces of all 4,608 bits in a single plane are remarkably similar to the oscilloscope trace for a single bit.

Memory cycle time in the Century series is 800 nanoseconds. In the case of the experimental 2-D, two-element-per-bit experimental organization that attained a cycle time of 100 nsec, the rods were only partially switched—that is, only part of the film under each winding was axially magnetized. The part that was magnetized was nevertheless saturated. This is possible because, just as a core switches first around the hole and then in concentric rings outward, a rod switches first at its midpoint and then in both directions toward its ends.

The two elements for each bit must be electri-cally and magnetically identical, a requirement met by arranging the elements adjacent to one another on the same rod a few hundredths of an inch apart. The wiring is basically the same as in the 315 RMC memory, except that the roles of the digit and word lines are interchanged and two digit lines are selected for each bit instead of one. The two elements store complementary bits; when writing, the noise from these bits, which doesn't decay until well into the subsequent read cycle, appears at the sense amplifier as common-mode noise, and is therefore rejected. Because the sense amplifier can recover quickly from this noise, the memory can operate at high speed.

The experimental 100-nsec rod memory contained 10 bits per linear inch of rod, even with the doubled-up windings. With further research and development, strip lines could be substituted for the digit solenoids to produce a large-capacity, high-performance rod memory.

Bibliography

D.A. Meier and M. Arbab, "A 10-Megacycle DRO Rod Memory," Proc. International Colloquium on Memory Techniques, Paris, 1965, p. 641.

Paul Higashi, "A Thin-Film Rod Memory for the NCR 315 RMC Computer," IEEE Trans. on Electronic Computers, August 1966, p. 459.

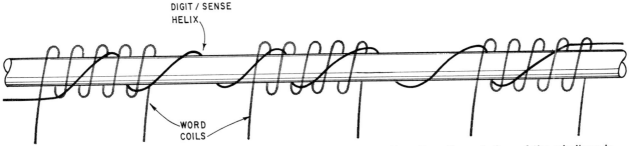

Double helix. Two windings over a section of a seven-inch rod define a bit cell on the rod. One of the windings is continuous along the full length of the rod; the other is about 1/10 inch long and connects with coils on other rods.

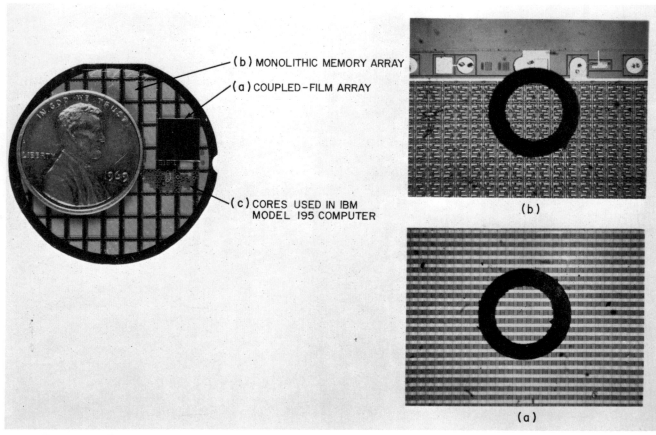

(b) MONOLITHIC MEMORY ARRAY

(a) COUPLED-FILM ARRAY

(c) CORES USED IN IBM MODEL 195 COMPUTER

(b)

(a)

Latest. The coupled-film arrays described in the following article have evolved further, as shown here. Under the penny is a wafer of silicon containing about 50 MOS memory chips; next to it is a coupled-film array and a few conventional ferrite cores. One of the 21-mil cores is shown enlarged over a part of the coupled-film array and over part of an MOS array. The core stores one bit; four MOS storage elements are visible through the hole in the core; and 38 coupled-film elements occupy the same area, at 250,000 bits per square inch.

Coupling sets thin magnetic films on closed flux path

By Hsu Chang

IBM Watson Research Center, Yorktown Heights, N.Y.

Placed face to face, pairs of thin-film memory elements, sandwiching striplines, form coupled magnetic films in which the flux lines of their magnetic fields are almost wholly contained in magnetic material. The films therefore operate with large disturb margins and produce relatively large output signals but require only small input currents. These advantages follow from the device's structure, which is at least as important as the film's intrinsic magnetic properties.

Flux closure is the key to thin-film memory performance, in terms of high speed, large capacity, and low cost. All of these parameters can be improved if the memory elements are made smaller; but only when the flux lines close in a magnetic material can miniaturization without demagnetization occur. One reason for the outstanding success of the ferrite core over the years is that its toroidal shape intrinsically offers a closed path for flux.

Miniaturized closed-flux devices such as coupled films require demanding techniques for depositing integrated multilayer structures, in which magnetic films are deposited on top of other conducting or insulating films. These techniques include controlling the properties of these films, etching the layers at various stages, maintaining the closed-flux pattern at the edges of etched lines, and adding high-permeability keepers. As a result, although the feasibility of coupled film memories has been clearly demonstrated, progress in their development has been rather slow.

At present, memory planes with storage density of 9,000 bits per square inch* have been built. This density is higher than that of any other magnetic memory, but it's still far short of that attainable by present-day fabrication technology. These planes

*See addendum, page 51.

are suitable as building blocks for million-bit memories that cycle in less than 100 nanoseconds,[1] or for much larger memories with longer cycle times. These memories operate at or near a limit imposed by thermal noise in the amplifier, indicating that further development in detection techniques should be undertaken to keep pace with coupled-film structure miniaturization.

Thin films have a number of intrinsic properties that aren't found in bulk material. Of the intrinsic properties, one of the most important in connection with memories is the film's magnetic anisotropy—the variation of its magnetic properties as a function of orientation relative to a crystalline axis.

Anisotropy in general, and uniaxial anisotropy in particular, is important because it permits thin films to be magnetized in either of two opposite directions along the easy axis; these two remanent states correspond to the binary 0's and 1's characteristic of most data storage units.

In general, if a single-crystal film is deposited in the absence of a magnetic field, it will have at least two axes of symmetry, and perhaps more. The number and angle of these axes depend on the film's atomic structure. For example, a single crystal of iron has a cubic structure, and therefore is biaxial—it has two axes at right angles to one another parallel to the film plane. When such a film has been magnetized, much energy is required to reverse or alter the magnetic state, because the anisotropy is strong.

On the other hand, in a polycrystalline film of permalloy, the individual crystals, or crystallites, are randomly oriented. If the film is deposited in a magnetic field, the field creates an artificial anisotropy, called magnetization-induced anisotropy. It's this artificial anisotropy that offers the two stable quiescent states required in a memory.

This magnetization-induced anisotropy in polycrystalline permalloy is about two orders of magnitude smaller than the material's intrinsic crystalline anisotropy. This permits the word field—perpendicular to the easy axis—to be only a few oersteds, and the bit field, parallel to the easy axis, a few tenths of an oersted, if the film's easy axis orientation is sufficiently uniform. Furthermore, a drive field parallel to the hard axis could cause the magnetization in the film to rotate sufficiently to switch the material in only a few nanoseconds, with very little energy dissipated in the material.

Another manifestation of the uniaxial anisotropy is the astroidal rotational threshold curve.[2] This is a plot of the switching threshold in the hard direction versus that in the easy direction, in four quadrants; it resembles a four-pointed star with the tips on the coordinate axes. It's an important property because in an array of thin-film elements data is stored by applying a relatively strong word field at right angles to the easy axis and a weaker bit field parallel to the easy axis; the bit field's direction is defined by the bit to be stored. If the word field is turned on alone, it twists the film's magnetization out of the easy axis. The bit field then biases the magnetization one way or the other. Toward the end of the cycle, the word field turns off before the bit field, which ensures that the magnetization returns to the easy axis in the proper direction.

Because of the astroidal threshold, the word and bit fields when applied together are substantially greater than the minimum total field required to switch the film, yet when applied separately are substantially less than the field that would disturb the film without switching it. Because the fields are usually created by currents in perpendicular conductors, each field exists alone at many points in an array of film elements. The magnitude of each separate field must be kept well within the threshold limits to avoid disturbing the film at these points. Because they add vectorially, both fields together can cause the film to switch even if their scalar sum is less than the magnitude that one field must have to switch the film alone. As a result, the four-quadrant plot resembles the four-pointed star.

Permalloy also has a smaller magnetostrictive effect than iron—that is, its magnetic properties are not as strongly affected by physical deformation. Therefore it can be packaged with less emphasis on protecting it from mechanical forces. This is another reason why permalloy is preferred as a material for thin films.

Open and closed

However, these desirable characteristics aren't sufficient to realize a workable memory in open-flux devices—that is, devices in which a substantial part of the magnetic flux lines lie outside the magnetic material itself. (All flux lines, of course, are closed; the distinction between the two kinds of devices discussed here is essentially the same as the distinction between a single bar magnet—open flux—and a pair of bar magnets with opposite poles adjacent—closed flux.) The limitations are in phenomena of arrays of film elements, as opposed to intrinsic properties of the film itself.[3, 4]

Open-flux single films in an array environment require stronger drive fields for several reasons: the films tend to demagnetize themselves; the magnetization has a tendency to spread; the switching action is retarded by an opposing magnetic field created by the motion of flux lines through nearby conductors; and the ground current tends to spread through the ground plane. These effects are more pronounced in miniaturized elements, so much so that the stronger fields far exceed the levels that the film's intrinsic magnetic properties would otherwise require. In fact the bit field must even be made almost strong enough to switch the film by itself, thus impairing the stored data's stability.

The flux lines associated with an open-flux film element close outside the element. In so doing they interact with adjacent elements. The open-flux element also sustains an internal demagnetizing field opposing its magnetization. Only if the film's coercive force is sufficiently high will it retain its magnetic state in the presence of this demagnetizing field, which is proportional to the film's thickness and also increases, but not proportionally, as the ratio of the film's width to its length increases. Thinner and narrower film elements are thus less likely to demagnetize themselves, but they also produce smaller output signals that are harder to distinguish from noise; longer film elements don't lend themselves to densely packed memories. Thus to produce an adequate output signal from a miniaturized element that doesn't demagnetize, a structure that closes the flux lines in magnetic material is a necessity.

On continuous films, which are easier to fabricate than arrays of discrete film spots, the storage elements can be defined by drive line intersections. But with permalloy's high permeability, the amount of film affected by the demagnetizing field around a particular intersection is much larger than the area immediately under the intersection.[5] This spreading problem is particularly serious in miniaturized arrays, because the spreading effect can sometimes generate a spurious output from an unaddressed bit, and if a particular bit is addressed over and over again the gradual spreading, like an oil slick on water, can actually destroy adjacent stored data. There are only two ways to prevent it—using discrete spots, or closed-flux elements.

In most thin-film designs, the word and bit currents share a common return through a ground plane. Because this return current is widely diffused instead of concentrated in a narrow conductor, it contributes little to the drive field, and its contribution is likely to be different at different points in the array. To reduce both the magnetization spread and this ground-current spread, a layer of magnetic material over the word and bit lines provides a low-reluctance path around them.

In the quiescent state, if the flux lines from a single open-flux element pass through nearby conductors such as the ground plane, they tend to hold back the element's switching action. This action occurs because the applied field from the drive lines, in altering the magnetic state of the element, moves these flux lines; their motion through a conductor generates eddy currents, which in turn create opposing magnetic fields that retard the principal switching action. This effect is called flux trapping; it can be overcome in open-flux devices only by increasing the applied field. It's not a problem in closed-flux devices because little or no flux exists outside the element itself.

Only through closed-flux devices, such as coupled films, can magnetic materials that switch quickly when driven by a small applied field be made into stable low-current devices with adequate output signals.

Memory performance

Two good ways to indicate memory cost, at least relative to other designs, are to specify the storage density on a substrate, which also affects the memory's speed and storage capacity as well as its cost, and to specify the utilization of peripheral circuits —measured, for example, by the ratio of memory elements to peripheral circuits.

Because coupled film elements permit greater miniaturization than other elements, their storage density can be made large. Also the number of elements on a substrate of reasonable size can be made large, leading to a large element/peripheral ratio. Thus the coupled film configuration offers an excellent potential for both high speed and large capacity at low cost.[6]

A magnetic film memory's cycle time is the sum of three components. The first of these, the memory elements' switching time, is almost negligible. Transmission delays in the drive and sense lines are obviously reduced by miniaturization and the consequent shortening of drive lines. And finally propagation delays in the drive circuits and sense amplifiers, particularly when these are made of high-speed integrated circuits, are very small, but these circuits for the most part can handle only

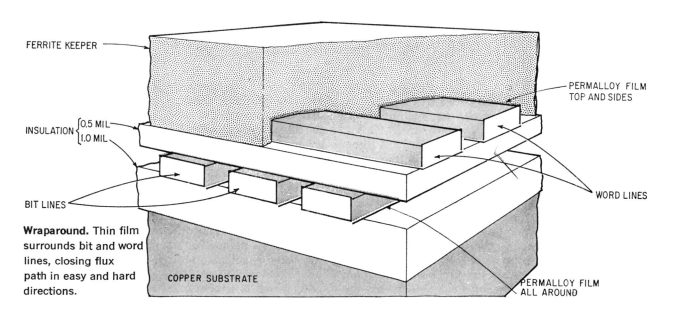

FERRITE KEEPER

PERMALLOY FILM TOP AND SIDES

INSULATION {0.5 MIL 1.0 MIL}

WORD LINES

BIT LINES

Wraparound. Thin film surrounds bit and word lines, closing flux path in easy and hard directions.

COPPER SUBSTRATE

PERMALLOY FILM ALL AROUND

Comparing memories

	Chain store[13]	Mated films[14]	Plated wires[15]	Planar films[4] (IBM)	Planar films[16] (MIT)	Coupled films[1,9]
Density, bits/in²	400	200	1,000	610	12,500	12,000
Word current, ma	800	700	900	510	500	200
Bit current, ma	400	50	20	100	190	15
Switching signal						
Amplitude, mv	10	3	10	3.8	0.13	2
Width, nsec	90	15	15	8	30	5
Flux, volt-sec x 10⁻¹²	900	45	150	30	4	10
Drive voltage	60	15	20	10	10	5
Module size						
Words	2,048	4,096	2,048	819	1,024	2,048
Bits/word	72	68	128	72	64 to 352	64 to 512
Power, watts	—	250	200	—	200	50
Cycle time, nsec	500	200	200	120	1,000	60

limited current and power. Since miniaturization, low current, and low power are all characteristics of coupled film elements, it follows that this technology is ideal for large fast memories; indeed, megabit modules with 50-nanosecond cycle times aren't unreasonable at today's state of the art.

Memories of large capacity require long drive and sense lines that can maintain adequate signal-to-noise ratios over many bits.[7] And they must be batch-fabricated. Since flux closure permits thicker films to be used, even in miniaturized devices, without danger of demagnetization, it also produces larger signals, thus improving the signal-to-noise ratio. Furthermore, if the thicknesses for both conductors and insulators are maintained, while the planar dimensions are reduced, the total impedance increases but the resistance per bit remains constant; therefore the attenuation per bit is decreased. Already 10-million-bit storage modules have been built with plated wires;[8] comparable or larger capacity is expected with coupled films, but with much lower word current requirements.

To make a film

In one coupled-film design, shown on p. 41, the storage elements consist of two layers of permalloy 1,000 angstroms thick deposited on both sides of a thin copper bit line.[9] The easy axis of the permalloy films is across the bit line, and parallel to the word lines just above. Flux closure in the easy-axis direction is through additional permalloy plated at the edges of the three-layer bit lines. The word lines are plain strips of copper with a 3,000-angstrom permalloy keeper on top and down the sides; flux closure in the hard-axis direction is through this permalloy and also through a ferrite keeper on top of the whole assembly. The bit lines are 4 mils

wide on 6 mil centers; the word lines are 6 mils wide on 14 mil centers. Both are 0.5 mil thick. The storage flux is 10⁻¹¹ volt-second, switched with a word current of 200 milliamperes and bit current of 15 ma. All the dimensions can vary over a considerable range; different working models have been built with different dimensions.

In this design, the choice of materials and dimensions is largely determined by electromagnetic requirements and materials compatibility. Between the bit lines and the copper substrate is a layer of insulation thick enough to establish a reasonably large characteristic impedance; the insulation between the bit lines and the word lines is thinner, to minimize the magnetic reluctance in the hard direction, but not so thin that capacitive loading between the two sets of conductors would be a problem. The copper conductors themselves are thick enough to have low resistance but, like the insulation, not so thick that they hinder hard-direction flux closure.

The ferrite keeper is the best way to limit current spreading in the ground plane, but it doesn't work very well at high frequencies because its permeability decreases as frequency increases. A permalloy keeper is good at all frequencies, but is effective only when the width of the word lines is much greater than the word line-bit line separation.

In addition to the general requirements for any multilayer structure—good adhesion, chemical stability, and matched thermal expansion coefficients—magnetic coupled film structures have special requirements of their own.[10, 11] For example, the electrical insulation is better if it's put down in several thin layers instead of one thick layer, because there's less probability of pinholes. It must be smooth and clean if the metallic film deposited on top of it is to have satisfactory properties. To insure this smoothness a thin layer of silicon oxide is deposited on the copper before the top permalloy layer goes down. Because the metallic layers are composites of different materials, their etching into lines requires special care.

The competition

Coupled films aren't the only structures that have closed flux paths, but they're best. Other approaches include for example, flat films with keepers, chain stores, mated films, and plated wires. But each of these other forms has disadvantages.

To speak of complete flux closure around both word and bit lines is more topological semantics than physical reality. No design provides completely closed paths in magnetic material for all the flux in both hard and easy directions. Two designs that come close are chain stores[12, 13] and mated films. Both of these use magnetic and conductive materials in intricate shapes; conductors pass through holes in magnetic material, or magnetic material is wrapped around a conductor, or both. But some of the flux has to pass through a conductor rather than exclusively through magnetic material, so the path isn't wholly closed. Also, either the flux path around one or both conductors has a nonuniform cross-section, or the film has a nonuniform thickness. The former quality increases the path's reluctance and may make some flux "leak" into the surrounding medium; the latter quality is difficult to implement, especially in small sizes. Furthermore, these three-dimensional configurations are very difficult to fabricate in batches.

Both the plated wires and the coupled films obtain complete flux closure around only one conductor. Partial closure around the other conductor is achieved with a keeper; it's partial because the insulating layer and the first conductor are in the way. This nonmagnetic gap is minimized best with flat geometry, which obviously favors coupled films and their associated striplines, rather than wires.

Nevertheless the fact that these different designs exist, as summarized in the table on page 42, demonstrates their viability. But the combined advantages of high density, low currents, low power, and short cycle time are realized only in coupled films. This clearly demonstrates that performance optimization can be achieved only through both miniaturization and flux closure.

Further development of film memory optimization through miniaturization and flux closure will be aided by advances in interconnection methods, sensing techniques, and memory organization.

Presently available interconnection techniques are the limiting factor to storage density; fabrication techniques are capable of producing integrated structures with much higher densities than anybody knows how to interconnect today.

Miniaturized memory elements always generate smaller output signals, and therefore require more sophisticated detector and amplifier designs. These are highly optimized in a planar film memory built at the MIT Lincoln Laboratory, and are approaching a physical limit imposed by thermal noise. This implies that further miniaturization, and therefore further reduction in sense signal level, is possible only with innovations in detection techniques.

Film switching dissipates so little energy that very long word lines compared to those used in ferrite core memories would be expected. However, the long word lines imply many bit/sense lines, and thus many expensive sense amplifiers. An alternative is to devise novel memory organizations, such as the 2½-D selection already proposed for plated-wire memories,[15] to reduce the number of sense amplifiers. Once the interconnection problem is overcome, even higher-density arrays will become practical, making optimum utilization through novel organization even more urgent. ∎

References

1. Q.W. Simkins, "Planar Magnetic Film Memories," Conference Proceedings, American Federation of Information Processing Societies, Vol. 31 (Fall Joint Computer Conference), 1967, p. 593.

2. J.I. Raffel, "Operating Characteristics of a Thin Film Memory," Journal of Applied Physics, 1959, p. 60S.

3. A.V. Pohm, R.J. Zingg, T.A. Smay, G.A. Watson, and R.M. Stewart Jr., "Size and Speed Capabilities of DRO Film Memories," IEEE Transactions on Communications and Electronics, 1964, p. 267.

4. E.W. Pugh, V.T. Shahan, and W.T. Siegle, "Device and Array Design for a 120-nanosecond Magnetic Film Memory," IBM Journal of Research and Development, 1967, p. 169.

5. D. Dove and T.R. Long, "Magnetization Distribution in Flat and Cylindrical Films Subject to Non-uniform Hard Direction Field," IEEE Transactions on Magnetics, 1966, p. 194.

6. H. Chang and C.P. Wang, "Characterization of Magnetic Memories—a Step toward Automated Design and Optimization," Digest, First Annual IEEE Computer Conference, 1967, p. 74.

7. H. Blatt, "Random Noise Considerations in the Design of Magnetic Film Sense Amplifiers," MIT Lincoln Laboratory, Group 23, Report 1964-6.

8. W.J. Bartik, C.F. Chong, and T. Turozyn, "A 100 Megabit Random-Access Plated Wire Memory," Proceedings, International Conference on Magnetics, 1965, paper 11.5.

9. H. Chang, "Coupled Film Memory Elements," Journal of Applied Physics, 1967, p. 1,203.

10. B.I. Bertelsen, "Multilayer Process for Magnetic Memory Devices," IEEE Transactions on Magnetics, 1967, p. 635.

11. K. Ahn and J.F. Freedman, "Magnetic Properties of Vacuum-deposited Coupled Films," IBM Journal of Research and Development, 1968, p. 100.

12. H.O. Leilich, "The Chain—a New Magnetic Film Memory Device," Journal of Applied Physics, 1966, p. 1362.

13. S.A. Abbas, H.F. Koehler, T.C. Kwei, H.O. Leilich, and R.H. Robinson, "Design Considerations for the Chain Magnetic Storage Array," IBM Journal of Research and Development, May 1967, p. 302.

14. W.M. Overn, "Status of Planar Film Memory," IEEE Transactions on Magnetics, 1968, p. 308.

15. J.P. McCallister and C.F. Chong, "A 500 nsec Computer Memory Utilizing Plated-Wire Elements," Conference Proceedings, American Federation of Information Processing Societies, Vol. 29 (Fall Joint Computer Conference), 1966, p. 305.

16. J.I. Raffel, A.H. Anderson, T.S. Crowther, T.O. Herndon, and C. Woodward, "A Progress Report on Large Capacity Magnetic Film Memory Developments," Conference Proceedings, American Federation of Information Processing Societies, Volume 32 (Spring Joint Computer Conference), 1968, p. 259.

Production line. This facility can produce over 200 million bits per year of planar thin-film elements, at Univac's Federal Systems division plant in St. Paul, Minn. Glass substrates are handled automatically, passing through the system in about an hour; the films deposited on them are closely controlled for magnetostriction, as a result of constant vapor compositions maintained electronically.

Controlling creep and skew in thin-film memories

By William M. Overn

Univac Federal Systems Division, Sperry Rand Corp., St. Paul, Minn.

It's not easy to make thin-film memory elements bistable—that is, constrained to two magnetic states corresponding to binary digits 0 and 1. To get binary operation with these elements demands careful design, precise control of the memory's external circuits and control of the film's deposition process. During deposition it's necessary to optimize anisotropy and to minimize skew. Also the film's creep threshold should be made as high as possible, and the electronic circuits designed to avoid crossing it. A mounting nearly free of strain is also important, for mechanical strain in the presence of magnetostriction increases the amount of skew.

In planar and cylindrical thin-film memories, a word field and a digit field are applied at right angles to one another in such a way that they combine at one and only one memory element. This arrangement permits a fairly large tolerance in drive currents. It permits each field to be somewhat greater than its nominal value without causing spurious switching, while permitting both fields to be somewhat less than nominal and still cause switching where they combine.

But reducing this advantage is the practice of batch-fabricating hundreds of elements on a single substrate, as discrete planar film spots or as a large continuous film on a wire. These elements have properties that differ to the extent that a current that's less than the critical value at one element may be considerably more than the critical value at another element.

A characteristic of a magnetic thin film is its anisotropy—by virtue of which each element has an easy axis of magnetization and a hard axis at right angles to it. Nominally the easy axes of all the elements are parallel, in the sense that two vectors pointing north and two vectors pointing south are all parallel to one another; the conductors carrying the word current are parallel to this easy direction of anisotropy.

When reading or writing, a current in the word line generates a magnetic field around the line. This field is thus at right angles to the easy axis of the field and to the current that generates it [see next page]. When reading data from the memory, this rotation generates a signal in the bit line; this signal is amplified and sent out as the memory's response

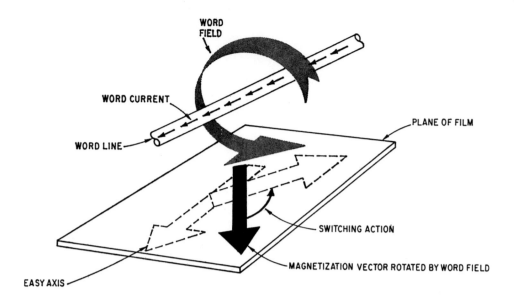

WORD FIELD

WORD CURRENT

WORD LINE

PLANE OF FILM

SWITCHING ACTION

MAGNETIZATION VECTOR ROTATED BY WORD FIELD

EASY AXIS

Rotation. A magnetic field surrounding the word line tends to rotate the magnetization vector in the thin film away from the easy axis of the film. Then the digit field (not shown) can, if desired, switch the vector to the opposite direction.

to the read command. When writing, there is current in both the word and bit lines; the word field rotates the magnetization, and the bit field tends either to rotate it back or to drive it over in the opposite direction, depending on whether the new bit being written is the same or opposite to the one stored previously.

Most planar thin films operate with destructive readout (DRO) to achieve speed. This means that the magnetization is switched quickly from the 1 to the 0 state to generate the readout signal; but the speed advantage is tempered by the need to regenerate the 1 state immediately after reading. On the other hand, most cylindrical thin films, or plated wires, use nondestructive readout (NDRO); the magnetization is rotated only slightly, giving a much smaller readout signal, but permitting a large memory to operate with a small number of electronic circuits that are shared among different parts of the memory.

Skew and dispersion

Unfortunately, the easy axes of all the elements are only nominally parallel. An individual element's easy axis may be at some small angle to the nominal direction—an angle called "skew". The extent of skew corresponds to the film's departure from ideal. In the analogy used above, if the compass directions of the four vectors were a degree or two away from due north and due south, they could be described as nominally parallel, yet slightly skewed.

Skew has two principal effects in thin film memories; it increases the amount of digit current required to write, and it reduces a parameter called the reversible limit.

The required digit current must be increased because skew creates a component of the word field along the easy axis, as shown on page 48 –a component that should be zero, but isn't. When the digit field then tries to switch the magnetization of

the element, it's opposed by the nonzero skew component; thus considerable digit current is needed to first overcome this opposition, and then switch the magnetization.

The reversible limit is the angle to which a word field may repeatedly drive the magnetization during successive nondestructive read operations, without causing the stored bit to deteriorate. Skew reduces the reversible limit because some elements are closer to the limit than others in the absence of a word field; this situation limits the amplitude of the word current—but only in NDRO mode.

Another factor related to skew is "dispersion." Although skew is defined in terms of the actual position of an element's easy axis relative to its nominal position, skew can actually vary from point to point within a single element. Dispersion is an indication of how much it varies in an element, and by extension how much it varies across a continuous sheet containing many elements. A measure of dispersion is the angle of skew in either direction not exceeded in some standard percentage—usually 90%—of the area of film. Like skew, dispersion tends to increase the digit current and limit the amplitude of the word current—again, only in NDRO mode.

Both skew and dispersion are effects of the film's polycrystalline nature and the failure of all the crystals to line up perfectly with the magnetic field in which the film is deposited.

However, the real villain in thin-film arrays is neither skew nor dispersion but rather magnetostriction. Recent improvements in the economics of thin-film memories are, in fact, due to new ways of controlling magnetostriction. Skew and dispersion, although serious, are well under control; ways were worked out years ago to produce large thin-film arrays with suitably small values of skew and dispersion. But magnetostriction causes the skew to increase greatly when a small mechanical strain appears in the element. Strain is almost impossible

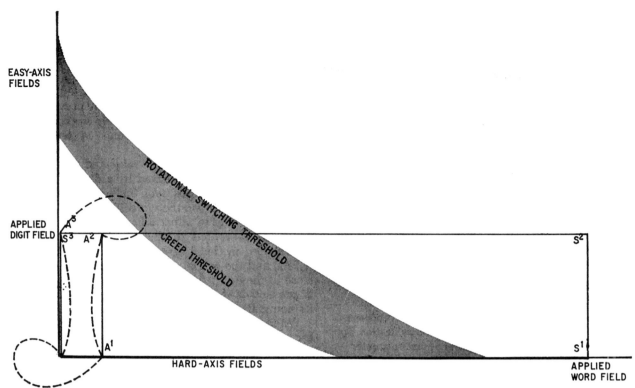

EASY-AXIS
FIELDS

ROTATIONAL SWITCHING THRESHOLD

CREEP THRESHOLD

APPLIED
DIGIT FIELD

A³
S³ A²

S²

A¹

S¹

HARD-AXIS FIELDS

APPLIED
WORD FIELD

Indirect path. Transients induced in inactive digit lines can cause brief excursions of the magnetic field (dashed lines) into the creep region of an unaddressed memory element. If repeated often enough, such excursions can destroy the information stored in such an element.

to avoid completely; even if a mounting could be devised that would completely free an array of strain, the slightest external force or tremor would introduce new strains. Thus magnetostriction is the single factor that kept film elements in the laboratory before suitable controls were developed.

When a bit is written in a thin-film memory element that consists of a spot with well-defined edges, the edges of the spot don't switch along with the center unless the same bit is rewritten many times. But, when the element is part of a large continuous film and is defined only by the intersection of the word and digit fields, repeated writing of the same bit in that element can eventually cause the magnetization to creep, or to spread into an adjacent location and to disturb the bit stored there.

But when many such cycles do occur, followed by a single cycle of the opposite type—many 0's followed by a single 1, or many 1's followed by a 0—a subsequent read may produce an undesirably small output signal. This is called an adverse-history condition.

Creep also can occur in and near elements when one of the driving fields is present in normal switching magnitude and a residual field is present on the other axis. This residual field may be the fringe of a switching field for an adjacent element, or it may simply be the effect of skew. In either case it causes domain nucleation, which arises from flaws in the film and on the film's substrate.

In a perfect film deposited on an absolutely

smooth substrate, the presence of fields that are too small to affect the film's magnetization would never have any effect, no matter how often they were repeated. But near a flaw in the film or a bump in the substrate, irregularities in the film's crystal structure react to small fields more readily, and their magnetic state is likely to change. The effect is analogous to the way water vapor condenses on ions created by the passage of nuclear particles in a cloud chamber.

This change is the beginning of a magnetic domain, which is itself a larger "flaw" in the film. Other small domains are found at bit boundaries—the remnants of previously recorded information on continuous cylindrical films, and irregularities at the edges of discrete film spots. Additional small fields impinging on these domains induce them to grow and propagate across the film, thus causing the memory element to creep. Thus the creep threshold is lower than the switching threshold.

Since these stray domains arise at bit boundaries as well as at actual flaws, it's useless to strive for a perfect film or an ultrasmooth substrate. On the contrary, these flaws can block the growth of a domain as well as initiate it; so that the beryllium-copper wire and the initial copper layer under the magnetic plating of a plated wire are made with a controlled roughness rather than with maximum smoothness.

Difficulties caused by both creep and adverse histories, shown above, can be avoided by proper design of the word and digit lines and the elec-

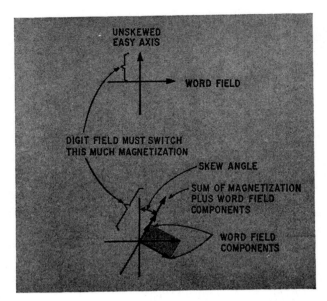

More oomph. When the thin film's easy axis has skew, the word field has a component along it, which opposes the digit field's tendency to switch the magnetization. To meet this opposition, the digit current must be greater than in the absence of skew.

tronic circuits that drive them.

In general, either a sufficiently large word field alone or a sufficiently large digit field alone can switch the magnetic state of an element. If both fields are present, their sum can switch it if the sum is represented by a point in the diagram above and to the right of the rotational switching threshold curve.

But if the sum of the two fields is just below the rotational threshold, the element's magnetization won't switch unless the driving pulses are repeated many times; the more times they are repeated, the further below the threshold they can be and still cause switching. The curve below the creep region is the theoretical limit if the pulses are repeated infinitely many times.

If the sum of the two fields is below the creep region, it has no effect on the element. The trick is to make sure that a field that should be below the creep region stays below it, even in the presence of small electrical transients.

In the absence of skew, the word field would be plotted directly along the horizontal axis as shown, and the digit field along the vertical axis. But skew causes one or the other of these fields to effectively appear at a slight angle to its axis, and thus to bring the sum point closer to the threshold of the creep region. Thus, with skew, transients become more dangerous.

Suppose that a particular element is being addressed in a thin-film array and a very large word field, as shown, is required to obtain high speed in the DRO mode. Here, the sum of the word and digit fields is represented by the point S_2; if the word field is turned on before the digit fields, and the two are turned off in the same order, the element will be exposed to the four fields S_1, S_2, S_3, and the origin, in that order.

Neighbors cause problem

These conditions tend to create a creep problem in the element adjacent to the one addressed. Proper design of the memory system prevents the problem from appearing; for if creep appears even in a single element the entire memory system might as well have failed.

The adjacent element is subjected to the full digit field, which is generated by a digit current in a conductor that passes over the adjacent element. Furthermore, because the word field is so large, its fringes are likely to affect adjacent elements. Thus the fields presented to the adjacent element are represented in the diagram by the four points A_1, A_2, A_3, and the origin. The point A_2 is dangerously close to the creep threshold—particularly so if skew is present or if the creep threshold is lower than its nominal value.

When the word driver turns off, the word field for the addressed element decays from S_2 to S_3. But as the current in the word line decays, in a poorly designed memory it would generate a voltage in the adjacent word line, because the two are parallel over a considerable length and inductively coupled. Although the adjacent word line isn't operating, it probably isn't a completely open circuit either; it has some high-impedance connections somewhere, and it is capacitively coupled here and there too. Therefore a current spike would accompany the induced voltage in the passive line, in the forward direction. This spike would create a transient field that is added to the fringes of the decaying field from the word line next door; the net result would be a field that as it decays from A_2 to A_3, does so not along the solid line, but along a stray path such as that shown dotted—which crosses the creep threshold.

The mechanism described in this example is the principal mode of failure that involves creep. It could be controlled by turning off the word current slowly, so that its long fall time wouldn't generate the spike in the adjacent conductor. But this slows down the memory. Other controls can be applied that don't impose a speed penalty. Some kind of control is essential, because attempting to control the element behavior is impractical in the presence of uncontrolled transients.

Some of the recent developments that overcome creep include better film materials, better manufacturing techniques, better mechanical design, and magnetic keepers over the word lines.

Closed flux paths, as in plated wire memories and the mated-film design [*Electronics*, April 1, 1968, p. 31] effectively raise the creep threshold and reduce the digit current, which obviously makes creep less of a problem. ∎

Bibliography

W.M. Overn, "Status of Planar Film Memories," IEEE Transactions on Magnetics, Sept. 1968, p. 308.

Packing data tightly in thin-film memories

By Judea Pearl

Electronic Memories and Magnetics Corp., Hawthorne, Calif.

High packing density in planar and cylindrical thin-film memories—the latter more popularly known as plated-wire memories—is limited more by creep than by almost any other characteristic. How creep can be overcome, therefore, is of paramount importance to designers of these systems, particularly with regard to plated wire, a growing technology.

The nature and causes of creep were discussed at length in the preceding article [see page 45]. When memory elements are packed tightly together in a flat film or along a wire, obviously, the field that switches an individual element must be relatively strong at the element, but must taper off very rapidly to avoid affecting neighboring elements—in other words, it must be strongly localized. It's easy

to make small conductors capable of carrying enough current to produce the necessary field at the element, but preventing this field from dispersing is not so easy. This dispersion arises from two facts. The first is that the nature of the fabrication process requires that at least one of the conductors be slightly separated from the film. The second is that the nonuniform magnetization in the film itself has an effect on the field around the conductor —an effect similar to that of like poles on two ordinary bar magnets, whose fields tend to push one another apart.

This effect is shown more precisely in the diagram and graph at left below. The diagram shows a cylindrical film between two narrow word straps,

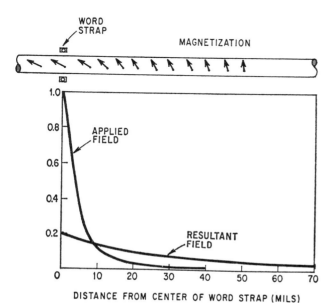

Dispersion. Magnetic film on wire reduces the magnetic field under the word strap but increases it by a large factor on each side of the strap.

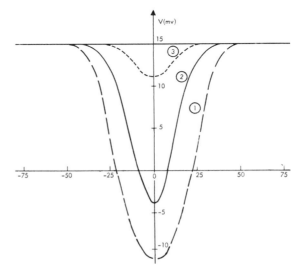

Profiles. These curves show voltage decreasing from the no-disturb case (1) when adjacent cells are 35 mils (2) and 25 mils (3) apart.

and the film's effect on the magnetic field created by the current in the straps. Without considering the film, the magnetic field distribution is easy to calculate from the current distribution in the straps; it's shown by the black curve in the graph. But magnetic monopoles on the film's surface create a demagnetizing field that opposes the field directly under the straps and aids it on either side, thus causing it to spread. The resultant field distribution is in color in the graph. Clearly the dispersion at points well removed from the strap is several times larger with the film than without it.

Mathematical expressions have been derived[1, 2] relating this dispersion to the film's thickness, its magnetization at saturation, and its degree of anisotropy (difference in magnetic properties in the hard and easy directions). For planar and cylindrical fields, the dispersion lengths are respectively:

$$\lambda_{pf} \approx \frac{t}{2} \frac{M_s}{H_k}$$

$$\lambda_{cf} \approx \left(rt \frac{M_s}{H_k} \right)^{1/2}$$

In these expressions, t is thickness, M_s is magnetization, H_k is anisotropy field, and r is the radius of the wire.

Clearly, to localize the field as much as possible, and thus to reduce interference with adjacent cells, the film should be as thin as possible, with a low magnetic saturation level and a high anisotropy. Unfortunately, these characteristics also produce lower outputs and require higher drive currents. In this respect plated wire is superior to planar films in that its dispersion can be reduced by using smaller wire without reducing output signal amplitude.

Furthermore, since wire employs a closed magnetic flux path along the easy axis, it has no demagnetizing field in that direction, and therefore no inherent minimum spacing between adjacent wires. Planar film, on the other hand, requires a minimum bit length along the easy axis to guard against self-demagnetization, especially during readout. This is one reason why planar films with several memory words on a single word line have never been successful.

Shaping the field

In a memory cell with suitably localized fields, the area interrogated during a read operation should be as large a proportion of the area switched when writing as possible. This condition is best achieved with a magnetic field whose cross-section is as nearly rectangular as possible. (A perfectly rectangular field, of course, would have no dispersion at all—an unrealizable ideal.) There are two ways to approximate such a distribution: with multiple-turn word straps and with magnetic keepers.

When the distributions of a double word strap are combined, and when the two straps are properly spaced, the resultant field distribution is nearly rectangular.

The second method requires a keeper, a piece of magnetic material that completes the magnetic circuit and prevents demagnetization. In a plated-wire memory without a keeper, the demagnetizing field opposes and disperses the applied field. But when a keeper made of a high-permeability material is placed over the word lines, both the applied field and the demagnetizing field tend to enter and exit the keeper at a 90° angle to its surface—much as if identical word lines and plated wire were behind the keeper surface, at the position of a mirror image. These image currents and image magnetic charges reduce the demagnetizing field and tend to localize the resultant field. Similar considerations apply to planar films.

However, keepers do have some disadvantages. Even though a high demagnetizing field requires higher drive currents and puts a lower ceiling on packing density, it tends to wash out nonuniformities in film properties and dimensions. For example, in the presence of a large demagnetizing field, the variations in drive line width affect the resultant field only slightly, whereas with a keeper and consequently with a small demagnetizing field, the resultant field is inversely proportional to the drive line width.

Although analytical and numerical methods of calculating magnetic field distributions can often help the memory designer understand how the field spreads and therefore how his cell size for a given overall configuration is limited, they are based on ideal films that have never existed even in the laboratory, much less on the production line. Therefore, such methods should be complemented with experimental measurements before attempting to make a final design.

A simple technique for measuring the most important parameters of a cell on a plated wire relies on the film's nondestructive readout property. To use this method, a technician records a data pattern on the wire, and then measures it by moving it between the word straps as if it were a piece of magnetic tape passing under a read head.

The parameters measured are the cell lengths—taken after writing once with minimum current, and again after writing many times with maximum current—the length of the interrogated area during a read, and the minimum spacing between cells.

First, the wire is magnetized in one direction over a considerable length with maximum word and bit currents. (The word current is in the strap around the wire; the bit current is in the wire itself.) Then these currents are turned off; the wire is positioned with its midpoint under the strap, and then the currents in the opposite direction are turned on. This remagnetizes the wire in the opposite direction; half the entire length is remagnetized in this way. The result is a sharp transition of magnetization from one direction to the other at a short distance X_h from the center of the wire. Now the word current alone is turned on to read what is on the wire, and the sense voltage on the wire itself is plotted as the wire moves under the strap. This voltage has a transition similar to that of the magnetization on the wire, but less sharp because of the field dispersion. The spread of this transition is measured by the slope of the voltage profile. And this profile crosses the zero axis at a point coinciding exactly with the magnetization transition. This yields a simple measurement of X_h, which is half the maximum cell length. The voltage profile indicates the system's response to a unit step function of magnetization. From this response, the magnetization distribution can be reconstructed from any arbitrary voltage profile.

Measuring the minimum cell spacing initially requires that a minimum-current 1 be written in the middle of a row of maximum-current 0's, and that the voltage profile be measured using the moving-wire technique [see curves at bottom right, page 49]. Then new maximum-current 0's are written on both sides of the 1, at gradually decreasing distances, until the 1's profile begins to shrink. The curves show the amount of shrinkage at two cell spacings. ∎

References

1. D.B. Dove and T.R. Lang, "Magnetization Duatribution in Flat and Cylindrical Films Subject to Nonuniform Hard Direction Fields," IEEE Transactions on Magnetics, 1966, p. 194.

2. Judea Pearl, "Field Distribution of Plated-wire Memory Elements and its Effect on Memory Characteristics," International Conference on Magnetics, 1968.

Recent advances in thin films

Since my article, "Coupling sets thin magnetic films on closed flux path," (page 39) was originally published, there have been several advances in both thin films and plated wires.

For coupled films, the storage density has been increased to 250,000 bits per square inch, as compared to the 9,000 b/in² cited in the original article. The word current is 60 milliamperes and the bit current is 30 ma; output signal is 150 microvolts and readout is nondestructive. Details are given in a paper, "0.25 × 10⁶ Bits/In² NDRO Coupled-film Memory Elements" by Chang, Mazzeo, and Romankiw, in the IEEE Transactions on Magnetics, December, 1970, p. 774.

For plated wires, higher storage density is now available because 2-mil-thick wires have replaced the original 5-mil wires. Densities of up to 40,000 b/in² have been reported. But the highest storage density with adequate signal amplitude and low drive current is still obtained with coupled films.

—Hsu Chang
IBM Research Center
Yorktown Heights, N.Y.

Post-and-film memory delivers NDRO capability, low noise, high speed, but avoids problem of creep

Fixing one or two continuous films on a grooved ferrite wafer forms a batch-producible memory with paths for flux closure; *Robert F. Vieth* and *Charles P. Womack* of Litton Systems discuss the process in detail

● A hybrid technology has been devised that combines anisotropic thin-film and ferrite-core memory technologies. It grants a designer the advantages that thin films have over ferrite cores, such as batch fabrication, high speed, wide temperature range, capability for nondestructive readout, and low noise; but at the same time it overcomes thin films' disadvantages, such as close tolerances on drive currents and tendency to creep.

The memory produced by this technology, called the post-and-film memory, comprises either one or two continuous films atop a ferrite wafer that has two sets of closely-spaced grooves cut into it at right angles, thus creating an array of square posts that provide a path for flux closure, thereby preventing creep. Word wires are in the grooves parallel to the film's easy axis of magnetization; digit wires are in the orthogonal grooves. The one-film memory, shown below, reads data destructively, so that data read out must be regenerated for later use; the two-film version, on the opposite page, permits non-destructive readout (NDRO).

This design offers high reliability and wide operating tolerances, as well as manufacturing costs as low as 2¢ per bit. These memories also dissipate very little power, so that their drive and sense circuits can be built with monolithic integrated circuits. Their speed—250 nanoseconds in the current model—is limited more by their associated circuits and connecting transmission lines than by an intrinsic characteristic of the memory elements.

Each ferrite wafer is one inch square and contains 64 grooves in each direction. The film stores one bit above each pair of groove intersections in the basic design; this density can be doubled by using one intersection per bit—straight digit lines instead of the U-shaped ones shown below—but the electronics costs more. Shortly, the designers expect a further increase in density; they plan to decrease the groove spacing and to use 2¼-inch square film substrates to achieve a 50,000-bit capacity per substrate.

Simple thin-film technology has significant advantages that are retained in the post-and-film approach:

▶ The array can be batch-fabricated. Other batch-fabricated memory forms have turned out either to have severe problems in development, or to be difficult or impossible to manufacture in quantity, or to pose operating or packaging problems due to magnetostriction.

▶ Like simple thin films, the post-and-film structure is potentially capable of 100-nanosecond cycle times.

▶ It is potentially capable of producing large output signals, which are possible for two reasons: first, the film's permeability is much higher than that of ferrite; and second, the volume of each film element is less than that of a core. Thus, the total magnetization is about the same order of magnitude.

▶ It can operate satisfactorily over a wide tempera-

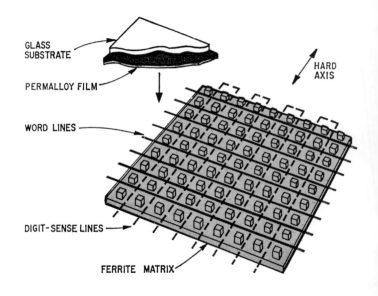

GLASS SUBSTRATE

PERMALLOY FILM

WORD LINES

DIGIT-SENSE LINES

FERRITE MATRIX

HARD AXIS

Open book. Current model of post-and-film memory has memory elements mounted on one side of base plate, electronics on opposite side; two plates, hinged together, close up for compactness, or open for maintenance.

ture range, because the film is made of materials that have high Curie temperatures and which therefore retain their magnetic properties.

▶ It is capable of nondestructive readout, without maintaining tight tolerances on the drive current, as long as the film's magnetic hard axis remains unsaturated.

▶ The signal is inherently less noisy than that from a ferrite-core memory.

This noiseless operation is a critical factor in a memory's speed. In the presence of noise, the output signal has to be much larger or of a significantly different character from the noise in order to be distinguished from it, which tends to lengthen the cycle; and the noise generated during a given memory cycle must be allowed to die away before a new cycle can begin, otherwise the new output signal will be contaminated not only by its own noise but also by noise left over from a preceding cycle.

There are three reasons, or three and a half, for this nearly noiseless operation in thin films: first, a core, being much bulkier than a film element, necessarily has part of its magnetic material considerably more distant than other parts from the wire carrying the drive current. The more distant parts are subjected to weaker fields than the nearer parts, so that the core switches more or less gradually. This gradual switching generates noise.

Second, when the magnetization vector in a core switches, it does so all the way from a positive maximum to a negative maximum relative to a particular reference, whereas a film switches from the positive maximum to zero as the vector rotates through a right angle.

Third, core arrays are usually wired with the cores at an angle to the wires, so that only a fraction of the applied field acts to switch the cores. The remaining component is parallel to the core's axis and therefore has no effect on switching.

The half-reason is related to this angular wiring; it's the fact that the sense wire is usually parallel to the drive wire, permitting a high degree of coupling from one to the other. In thin films the conductors are necessarily orthogonal to the storage elements and to each other, for maximum coupling to the elements and minimum coupling to each other.

These advantages in simple thin films are accompanied by a number of disadvantages, which have been overcome in the post-and-film technique:

▶ Unlike simple thin films, the post-and-film's NDRO capability resides in its structure—the two films set against the ferrite wafer—rather than in the control of its drive currents. Therefore, the tolerances on these currents can be much looser in post-and-film than in simple thin films. The latter require such tight tolerances that, in fact, they are rarely designed for NDRO.

▶ In the post-and-film technology the flux paths from the film, which stores the data, close in the ferrite posts,

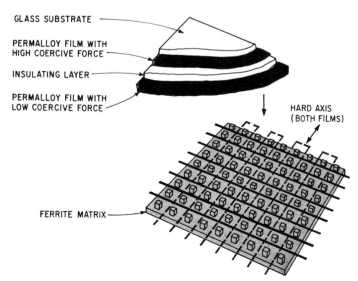

GLASS SUBSTRATE

PERMALLOY FILM WITH HIGH COERCIVE FORCE

INSULATING LAYER

PERMALLOY FILM WITH LOW COERCIVE FORCE

HARD AXIS (BOTH FILMS)

FERRITE MATRIX

Two versions. In the one-film version of the post-and-film memory (far left), data is stored in film, read and written with the aid of wires laid in the grooves between the posts. In the two-film model, flux from hard film restores data in soft film after reading, thus permitting nondestructive readout.

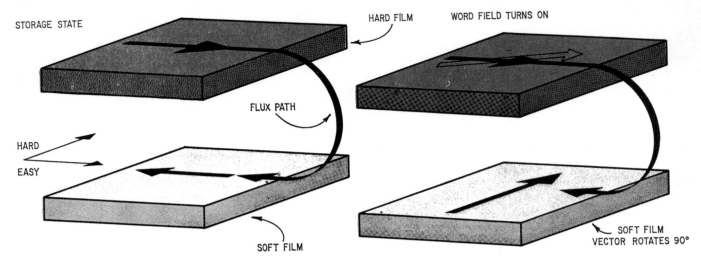

as shown below. This control of the flux also enhances the output signal. In simple planar thin films, the flux paths close in air, so that the magnetic patterns representing stored data are subject to creep, a phenomenon caused by repeated reading and writing at one location, which tends to affect the data stored in nearby locations.

Various artifices have been employed to avoid this difficulty. One strategy uses a coupled-film design, in which two film spots on separate substrates are placed face to face to provide a flux path entirely within magnetic material except for a small air gap separating the two films; this gap is established by the drive lines passing between the films. Another approach would be to use a keeper, which is a slab of ferrite or other magnetic material placed over an array of film spots or a continuous film. It specifically provides a closed flux path. In a way, the post-and-film memory is an extension of the keeper concept. Almost all planar thin film designs utilize one of these or a similar strategy.

▶ The films in the post-and-film structure are plated in an electron-beam evaporation process, in which only three parameters must be controlled: the substrate temperature, the melt composition from which the evaporation takes place, and the thickness of the evaporated film. Many ordinary thin films are electroplated. This process is difficult to control because it involves many variables: the temperatures of the various solutions, the plating

current, the substrate's surface roughness, the magnetic field in which the plating takes place, and many others. There is no one-to-one correspondence between variations in any of these parameters and variations in some specific quality of the plated film.

Development of the post-and-film memory was initiated at Litton as an in-house research project, and is being continued for the Naval Air Development Center under contract N62269-69-CO239.

The single-film version of the post-and-film memory operates in much the same way as simple thin films. When a saturating field is applied at right angles to the single film's anisotropic easy axis, the magnetization vector rotates to align itself with the field. Removing this word field permits the vector to rotate back to the easy axis. It may rotate back in either direction; a small digit field parallel to the easy axis "tips" it back toward the proper direction before the word field turns off.

A current in a word wire parallel to the easy axis generates the word field; a digit wire at right angles to the word first carries a readout pulse generated by the magnetization vector's rotation, and then carries a current to generate the digit field. This is the method used to write new data in thin film and regenerate old data following a destructive readout.

All simple thin-film memories operate this way. Without the small restoring field following readout, the vec-

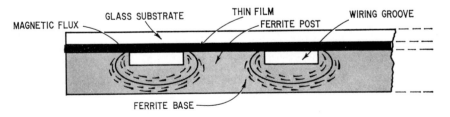

Closed path. Flux lines from magnetic storage elements close in ferrite posts, for high reliability at low cost.

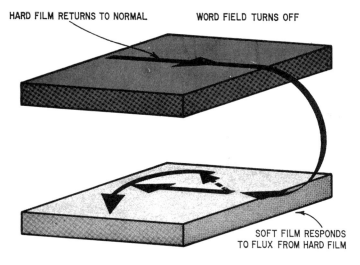

HARD FILM RETURNS TO NORMAL   WORD FIELD TURNS OFF

SOFT FILM RESPONDS
TO FLUX FROM HARD FILM

Turn vs. twitch. Flux lines of data stored in two magnetic thin films close within the films (left). But a word field large enough to saturate the soft film in its hard direction (center) has hardly any effect on the hard film. As a result, the hard film restores the magnetization in the soft film (right) for nondestructive readout.

tor would drop back to the easy axis in either of two directions, at random, and the stored data would have been destroyed; in this case, readout would be destructive. For NDRO, the vector would have to rotate far enough to generate an adequate output signal, but not so far that its dropping back to its original orientation can't be guaranteed; this requires impractically precise word currents.

The principal advantage of the post-and-film memory over simple thin films is its flux closure in ferrite rather than in air.

In the double-film version, one of the films is "hard" —that is, it has a much higher coercive force than the other, so that it requires a much stronger external field to significantly affect its magnetization. A small read pulse in the word wire rotates the magnetization in the "soft" film to read out the data, while having only a very small effect on the magnetization of the hard film. When the read pulse turns off, the magnetization in the hard film drags that of the soft film back to its previous orientation, without the need for an external digit field, as shown above. To write new data in the double-film memory, a much stronger word current rotates both the hard and soft magnetizations.

This description ignores the effect of the ferrite posts on the flux paths. Because they provide low-reluctance paths for the flux, the posts bend the magnetization away

from true alignment with the easy axis, as shown below, but the memory operates essentially as described.

Currents for the post-and-film memory are only 40 and 250 milliamperes in the digit and word lines respectively—as against 125 and 800 ma for plated wire or 300 and 800 ma for ferrite cores. A memory of 8,192 words of 16 bits each dissipates only 22 watts, compared to 70 for cores.

Three different batch fabrication techniques are applied in manufacturing the post-and-film memory. These are the film evaporation process, the ferrite base preparation, and the wiring of the array.

The film evaporation apparatus, shown on page 56, is basically similar to that used in the semiconductor industry and elsewhere; it contains an electron gun that shoots a beam of electrons down onto a water-cooled copper block serving as the anode. But sitting on the block in the path of the beam is a container holding a small quantity of permalloy, which melts at about 1,500°C under the electron beam's bombardment. Because the apparatus is evacuated, a significant vapor pressure quickly builds up, and metallic permalloy precipitates on the relatively cool substrates, which are mounted around the block but out of the beam's path.

The substrates to be coated with film are mounted in holders that have two pole faces and two field coils. These apply a magnetic field across the substrate while

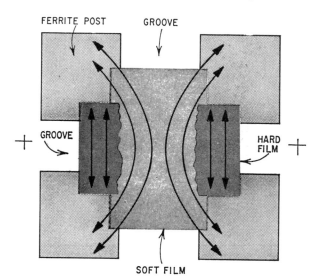

FERRITE POST   GROOVE

GROOVE

HARD FILM

SOFT FILM

Curved axis. Ferrite posts, having much lower reluctance than air, distort the magnetic vector in the soft film, but without destroying its basic anisotropic character.

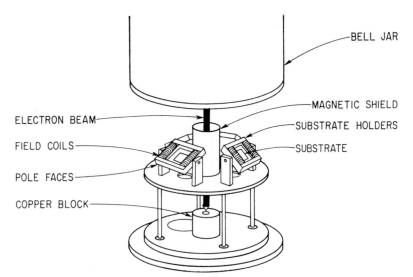

BELL JAR

ELECTRON BEAM

MAGNETIC SHIELD

SUBSTRATE HOLDERS

FIELD COILS

SUBSTRATE

POLE FACES

COPPER BLOCK

Evaporator. Electron beam (shaded) melts piece of permalloy on hearth; permalloy evaporates in vacuum, and vapor precipitates on relatively cool substrates.

the film is being deposited, to establish the direction of the film's easy axis. They are maintained at a temperature of about 400°C.

In the process currently in use at Litton Systems, four large substrates are coated in a single operation; each is 2¼ by 2¼ inches, thus containing enough surface to hold four of the inch-square ferrite wafers. Thus enough thin film is prepared with each evacuation of the evaporator, assuming 100% yield, to make 16 post-and-film memory arrays of over 2,000 bits each. The substrates are cut apart later to the smaller size.

Only two tests are required on the film. The films are not etched, nor do they age or deteriorate in any way as a result of mechanical or thermal stresses. As a result, their yield is indeed very nearly the 100% assumed in the preceding paragraph.

The ferrite bases are stamped out from powder in the same way as other ferrite components, and the grooves are cut in them using the same standard techniques as for dicing semiconductor wafers. There are two ways to do this: one method relies on a small circular saw with diamond teeth, and the other uses an oscillating wire and a slurry of abrasive material. Both techniques use several of these cutters ganged together, so that a whole ferrite wafer is grooved in only two operations, one for each orthogonal set of grooves.

The wires that thread the posts are preformed and drop

quickly in place. Although details of the preforming process are proprietary, in general, the conductor pattern is etched from a piece of copper-clad epoxy board, new layers of copper and insulation are then built up, and the epoxy is removed. This leaves a preformed structure that resembles a small piece of fine screen, and that fits over the ferrite wafer.

After the wires are in place, the ferrite wafers are attached to printed-circuit boards to which the wires are connected. Then the films, on glass substrates, are placed on the wafers, film side down; alignment isn't critical because the films are continuous. However, the film's easy axes must be closely aligned with the direction of the word wires; to achieve this the substrates are slightly rotated by hand until the output of a sampling of bits is a maximum. Because some of the thin-film elements may have easy axes with a certain angle of skew relative to the nominal easy axis, the substrates' final position may appear to be rather carelessly out of line with the wafers.

Finally, the substrates are thermally laminated to the ferrite wafers and the assemblies given a final test.

Repairs can be made at each of these stages, if necessary. For example, individual preformed wires can be cut out and replaced if faults are detected before the films are put in place. Even after the laminating step, the ferrite wafer with the film in place can be removed and replaced, if necessary.●

Simple electroplating process allows high-density waffle-iron memory to be built easily, inexpensively

A thick-film layer atop a grooved ferrite block produces a memory whose performance approaches that for plated wires, say *Peter Langlois, Nye Howells,* and *Alan Cooper* of Standard Telecommunications Laboratories

● Another batch-fabricated memory superficially similar to the post-and-film memory [page 52] is the waffle-iron memory. Although it uses square wafers of ferrite, grooved to make an array of posts, it uses a one-layer film about 10,000 angstroms thick—perhaps two orders of magnitude thicker than Litton's film—that is magnetically isotropic.

In the waffle-iron memory, shown below, each wafer has 5-mil grooves spaced 15 mils apart. The word and digit lines define a storage element at every pair of groove intersections—two intersections per bit. The storage density is thus very high; but even so, improved mechanical techniques, such as for grooving the ferrite wafers, could double the density.

One set of grooves contains the digit lines, which are U-shaped—they go "out" and "back" in adjacent grooves. The other set, at right angles to the first, contains the word lines, which are straight. Simultaneous word and digit currents magnetize the film over their two intersections diagonally from left to right, as shown on page 59, for either direction of digit current. In general, the digit current magnitude is smaller than that of the word current, so it doesn't destroy data in cells where no word current is present.

A reverse current in the word line, in the absence of a digit current, destroys this diagonal pattern and switches the flux to directly adjacent ferrite blocks, from right to left. This switching generates readout pulses in the digit line; the readout is destructive. Nondestructive readout techniques are being developed, but are still experimental.

Design characteristics of a typical waffle-iron memory appear in the table on page 59, compared with a typical plated-wire design. The waffle-iron is easier to build, and therefore costs less, and its performance competes with the plated wire.

Fabrication of the waffle-iron memory occurs in three main steps; the ferrite preparation, the film and substrate, and the mating of the two parts.

Plates of ferrite are lapped flat to within 6,000 angstroms, or approximately one wavelength of visible light. Then they are grooved with a multiple blade cutter, polished to make a good mating surface, and cut into ¼-inch squares.

The storage film is electroplated on a metal substrate an inch square. Because the film is thick and isotropic, the plating process doesn't require the stringent physical controls used in most thin-film memories, the electroplating yield is very high.

These substrates have 16 times the area of the ferrite wafers. This is done to permit the wafers to be interchanged more readily; one-inch square wafers could be made just as easily as the ¼-inch square ones, and at about the same cost.

Continued on page 59

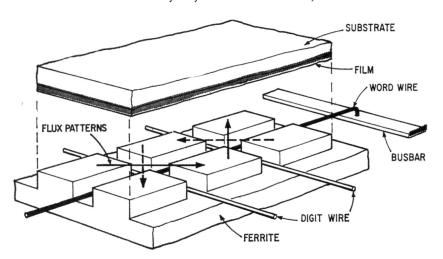

Groovy. Ferrite wafer has 5-mil grooves spaced 15 mils apart, to hold word and digit wires. Thick magnetic film on substrate laid over the grooves stores data, is switched by currents in the wires.

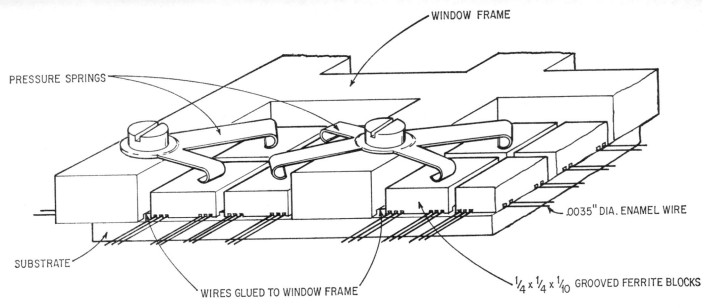

WINDOW FRAME

PRESSURE SPRINGS

.0035" DIA. ENAMEL WIRE

SUBSTRATE

WIRES GLUED TO WINDOW FRAME

$\frac{1}{4} \times \frac{1}{4} \times \frac{1}{10}$ GROOVED FERRITE BLOCKS

X-shaped clamp. Eight of the ferrite wafers are held in place in a frame containing word and digit wires by X-shaped spring clamps that permit individual wafers to be removed for maintenance and repair.

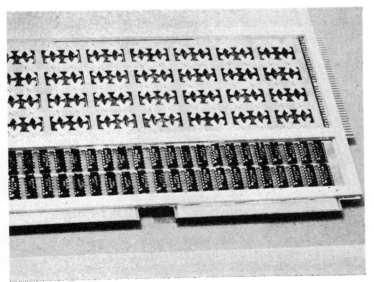

Working models. At far left is waffle-iron array storing 512 words of 64 bits each, showing spring clamps, and IC diode packages, 12 per chip. With hole-storage diodes, only one per word is needed, not two. Small photo shows reverse side of same array; diamond-shaped plates (one removed) hold film substrates. Below left is closeup of different array showing wires and ferrite wafers.

Different recipes for waffles

Besides the versions at Standard Telecommunication Laboratories and at Litton Industries, waffle-iron-shaped memories are also being worked on at a number of other places.

In Japan, at the government-owned Electrotechnical Laboratory, researchers are working on a version of the waffle-iron that uses plated-wire as the sense-digit line instead of plain wire [Electronics, Dec. 22, 1969, p. 167]. They do not use the overlaid thin film on top of the ferrite plate. And lukewarm efforts are said to have been made at a number of private laboratories, including those of Tohoku Metal Industries Ltd.

Performance comparison

	Waffle Iron	Plated Wire
Bits per sq. inch	2,000	200-300
Switching time	25 nsec	15-25 nsec
Word current, read	+500 ma	+500 ma
Word current, write	—180 ma	+500 ma
Digit current	±80 ma	±50 ma
Output	±20-25 mv	±8-10 mv
Capacitive coupling	0.05 pf	0.3-0.5 pf

Continued from page 57

Word and digit wires are stretched over a 1-by-½-inch aperture in a frame, and bonded to the frame's sides. Into this window eight of the ¼-inch ferrite squares are placed, so that the wires fit into the grooves. They are held in place by a simple spring clamp, as shown at left. The film on its substrate is secured on the underside of this assembly, against the ferrite and covering the grooves.

If necessary, for repairs or inspection, either the film or the ferrite can be easily removed. A single ¼-inch square can be removed and replaced without disturbing its neighbors; the wires are kept in place by the other squares and the frame.

Skeleton models of memories as large as half a million bits—4,096 words of 128 bits—have been built; they achieved cycle times of less than 250 nanoseconds. A smaller memory of 256 by 128 bits has been completely assembled and is in satisfactory operation, and one of 1,024 by 64 bits is being tested. ●

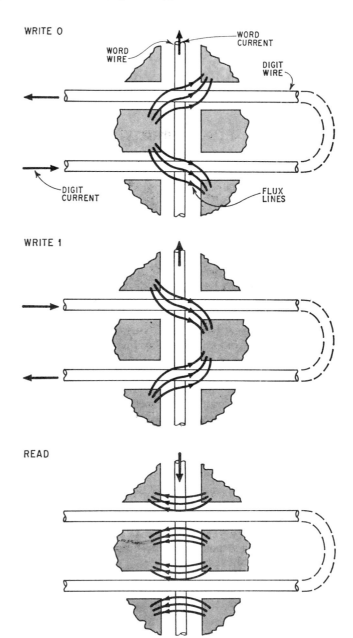

Catercorner. Flux paths in the thick film lie diagonally over the intersections of two grooves; two intersections store one bit.

At Thomson-CSF in France, two versions have been developed. One of these resembles Litton's two-layer post-and-film memory; the company is shooting for a 72,000-bit production prototype sometime this winter, with a 100-nanosecond cycle time.

The other is a read-only memory in which squares are etched out of the film wherever a binary 0 is stored; the memory can hold microprograms, mathematical tables, a cathode-ray tube character generator, and so on. A 16,000-bit prototype has been built, with an access time of 55 nsec.

At Iowa State University, in Ames, Iowa, researchers under the direction of A.V. Pohm are working on a similar idea using, instead of the waffle-iron

plate, a fabricated keeper formed by pouring a slurry over an array of wires and letting it dry. The wires are either plated wires—cylindrical thin films—or the drive and sense wires for a planar thin film. The slurry is made of powdered magnetic material of low permeability dispersed in an organic solvent, which dries by evaporation.

At AC Electronics, a division of the General Motors Corp., some work was done a few years back on what its designers called a waffle-iron memory, but it was different from the waffle-iron memories which used film structures. It was a read-only memory comprising a grooved ferrite plate, drive and sense lines in the grooves, and iron slugs on a printed-circuit card

to complete the flux paths across the intersections of the grooves. The slugs lay in either of two diagonal directions, thus coupling from the drive line to the sense line in either of two polarities, corresponding to 1's and 0's.

Bell Telephone Laboratories did most of the original work on waffle-iron memories in the United States. But it got the idea from a Philips Gloeilampenfabrieken patent on a method for batch-fabricating core arrays. Philips used a flat ferrite slab across the top of the ferrite waffle-iron to complete the flux paths around wires in the waffle-iron grooves. Bell Labs discontinued its waffle-iron work to begin plated-wire investigations—which it has now also discontinued.

Chapter 3

MOS memories

MOS arrays come on strong

With their low power dissipation, the circuits can be densely packed
on a chip; they promise to find a place in main storages and in read-only
and associative memories, too, yielding to bipolars only when speed is essential

By William F. Jordan
Computer Control Division, Honeywell Inc., Framingham, Mass.

The Establishment has been taking its lumps lately in every field—including computer memories. Like the authority of political leaders, university presidents, and movie censors, the reign of ferrite cores is being challenged from several directions. And perhaps the most serious challenger is a ceramic plane containing a hybrid assembly of p-channel metal oxide semiconductor chips and bipolar sense and drive chips.

Much of the work in this area, and with all-bipolar arrays as well, has so far been limited to scratchpad memories. But commercial systems holding tens of thousands of bits are already in production—for the IBM 360/85 computer, for example, which has a bipolar semiconductor buffer memory between its main storage and processor.

And the trend may lead to the evolution of computer architectures employing several random-access, read-write memories with more specialized functions—an evolution possible only through the use of semiconductor memories. Because all memories are composed of many identical elements, and because they function in an essentially orderly and repetitious manner, they stand to benefit more from microelectronic packaging developments than would any other part of the computer.

MOS technology is also applicable to the fast-growing area of read-only memories. And the heretofore slow development of content-addressable memories may be speeded by the large-scale integration of MOS circuits.

As main memories, p-channel MOS circuits are attractive for their ease of fabrication, low power dissipation, relatively high yield, and high density.

These circuits can be processed in 25 steps, compared to about 150 for bipolar circuits and 50 for complementary MOS circuits, which use both p- and n-channel devices. And because the MOS transistor is controlled by an insulated gate, it dissipates practically no power through its gate electrode, and none at all when it's not switching.

Up tight

As for density, MOS circuits—unlike bipolars—can be closely packed on a chip without danger of interaction or overheating because of their low power dissipation and because they don't need the isolation regions required by the bipolar circuits. All the action in MOS technology occurs between, rather than around, two deposited areas—source and drain—so there's no need for a wall of oppositely doped material to isolate collector leads from spurious signals produced by adjacent transistors. In bipolar circuits, this wall takes up space with its own volume and that of the biasing leads.

Read-only memory applications

Function tables
Character conversion
Logarithmic tables
Trigonometric tables
Memory location tables
Transducer calibration

Emulation
Of software for competing computers
Of software for older computers

Microprograming
To minimize single-purpose control logic
To permit specialized instructions
To streamline changes as designs evolve
To reduce costs of initializing and fault diagnosis

Input/Output
To adapt different devices to a standard computer interface

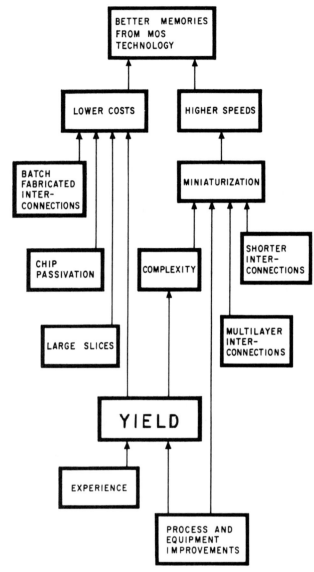

Common factor. Yield is a major influence on both the cost and speed of MOS memories.

supplies whose current outputs vary as temperature varies over the design range.

Coming attractions

There'll be several developments in the near future that will make MOS circuits more attractive in many memory applications, developments chiefly involving cost and speed, as shown at the left.

■ Lower costs, for instance, will accrue from the automating of face-bonded interconnections, from the development of new techniques for chip passivation—putting down the hermetic layer on top of the chip—and from the use of larger slices of substrate. The traditional 1-inch and 1¼-inch slices have already been replaced by 2-inch slices at many plants.

■ Higher speeds will be possible with miniaturized circuits and devices. The interconnections will be shorter and multilayered, and thus will have less capacitance—the factor limiting speed. Process and equipment improvements should lead to greater degree of miniaturization.

■ Yield, that old bugaboo of solid state devices, directly influences both cost and—through greater complexity of integration—the degree of miniaturization. Improvement in this area depend again on process and equipment improvements, plus just plain experience.

Isolated storage

The concept of the read-only memory goes back many years—farther than the electronic computer itself. With the advent of integrated bipolar and MOS arrays, the concept has matured.

Any read-only memory has two basic functions: bit storage and bit isolation. The storage in bipolar arrays is provided by array interconnection in one of the final process steps. In MOS arrays, an oxide pattern is generally used to establish the data. A thin oxide layer over the channel area of an MOS transistor separates the channel from the gate electrode; if the layer is thick, the gate won't work. Thus, stored 1's and 0's in the read-only memory are established by thin and thick regions in the oxide. Oxide thicknesses, in turn, are determined by the mask used at the appropriate process step.

However, another storage scheme involving gate connections has been proposed. In this process, certain connections are made by very narrow metal patterns, which melt when heavy currents are passed through them. Under program control, such currents can be made to establish the pattern of stored data.

This process is likely to be rather expensive, though, because the fuse-links must have both close tolerances and direct access for fusing through external connections. And this means that decoders and sense amplifiers cannot be integrated with the storage array.

Isolation in this context means that bits must be individually addressable, with no false outputs caused by "sneak paths" from other bit positions. It does not refer to the kind of isolation mentioned

And the relatively high cost of bipolar chip "real estate"—silicon surface area—is aggravated by the fact that the accumulative yield isn't as high with these circuits as with MOS.

Present p-channel MOS memories also have several advantages over magnetic memories, as summarized in the table, page 65. For one thing, they are capable of much higher speeds. For another, their peripheral circuitry can be much simpler because they don't need such closely controlled drive currents and because their sense signals are more easily discriminated and are accompanied by less noise. And although semiconductors in general are highly sensitive to temperature variations, MOS memory circuits can be designed to operate under worst-case conditions at the extremes of a suitable temperature range. Magnetic memories, on the other hand, require currents of a specific magnitude at any temperature and therefore need power

Memory characteristics

	Ferrite cores	Plated wire	PMOS
Cell spacing	25 x 25 mils	50 x 50 mils	2 x 4 mils
Sense signal	50 mv	15 mv	100 mv
Word current	400 ma	600 ma	100 ma*
Word voltage	25 v	25 v	20 v
Cycle time**	600 nsec	450 nsec	300 nsec
Access time	320 nsec	250 nsec	300 nsec

* For capacitance charging
** 250,000 bit system

earlier—the separation of transistors on a single substrate by a wall of material between them. Bit isolation is often achieved with diode arrays, because a diode conducts current in only one direction and therefore cannot be part of a sneak path. But in bipolar technology, transistors aren't significantly more expensive than diodes, and employing them for sneak-path isolation makes their gain available to increase speed.

The need for read-only memories is clearly growing, as indicated in the table on page 63. For the peripheral function tables, p-channel MOS is fast enough and its low cost makes it attractive. For computer microprograms, cycle time must be a small fraction of the computer's main-memory cycle time, so bipolar arrays, with their higher speeds, get the nod.

By content

The concept of content-addressable storage also goes back several years—12, to be exact—but this type of memory isn't yet in wide use. A content-addressable, or associative, memory, is one from which data is fetched in terms of its content rather than its location.

Alone among memory forms, the associative requires both storage and logic in its arrays—storage to "remember" the data and logic to compare stored data with input keys that identify it. Because of this, it was assumed for a long time that these memories would have to be cryogenic; no other technology seemed feasible. To be sure, a few investigations were carried out with magnetics and even with transistor circuits. But the projected 1972 cost with either of these technologies was somewhere between $1 and $10 per bit—expensive even for small memories.

But large-scale integration should make a content-addressable memory feasible at a cost as small as 1 to 20 cents a bit by 1972. Furthermore, because of its requirement for fault-tolerant structures, LSI provides the need as well as the means for such a memory. A defect in one word of a large mono-lithic array wouldn't be cause for rejecting the entire array if it could store data associatively; it would simply reduce the capacity by one word.

Even so, a cryogenic memory may turn out to be the best form of large-scale content-addressable file storage because it's relatively nonvolatile. Unless they're backed up by batteries, semiconductor memories lose their data almost instantly when primary power fails. A power failure in a cryogenic memory, shutting down its refrigerator, would also destroy the data—but the array would take at least several minutes to warm up to the danger point. The high fixed cost of refrigeration would be prohibitive for smaller memories, however.

Quite possibly one of the first commercially successful LSI products will be a medium-size content-addressable memory for use as an auxiliary input-data processor for a conventional computer. At least one MOS content-addressable memory containing 128 words of 48 bits each has already been built, and bipolar memories now locate programs in large commercial computers' segmented main memories.

Hierarchy

A small content-addressable push-down memory, installed between a computer and its main storage, would make the main memory appear very fast. In such a memory, every word written is entered at the top, and the word that has been unused the longest is at the bottom, disappearing permanently when the memory "overflows." Since most cycles fetch words that have already been used at least once, such a push-down memory would serve as a "window" into the main memory through which the computer can see the words it's most likely to need—namely, those that have been recently used.

Rather than a straight shift of old words down as new words came in at the top, efficiency demands an external address counter to keep track of the words in the memory, together with a content-addressable capability for fetching data. To be of greatest value to a system, the memory would have to operate at high speed, and therefore should be built of bipolar circuits.

In addition, bipolar scratchpad memories and p-channel MOS serial memories should become quite common. And their progeny will appear in strange new computer architectures and exotic packaging. But one thing is absolutely clear—the enormous investment in LSI will stimulate higher-speed and lower-cost memory technologies.

Bibliography

A.E. Slade and H.O. McMahon, "A Cryotron Catalog Memory System," National Joint Computer Committee, Conf. Proc., Vol. 10 (Eastern Joint Computer Conference), 1956, p. 115.
Alan Corneretto, "Associative Memories, a Many-Pronged Design Effort," Electronic Design, Feb. 1, 1963, p. 40.

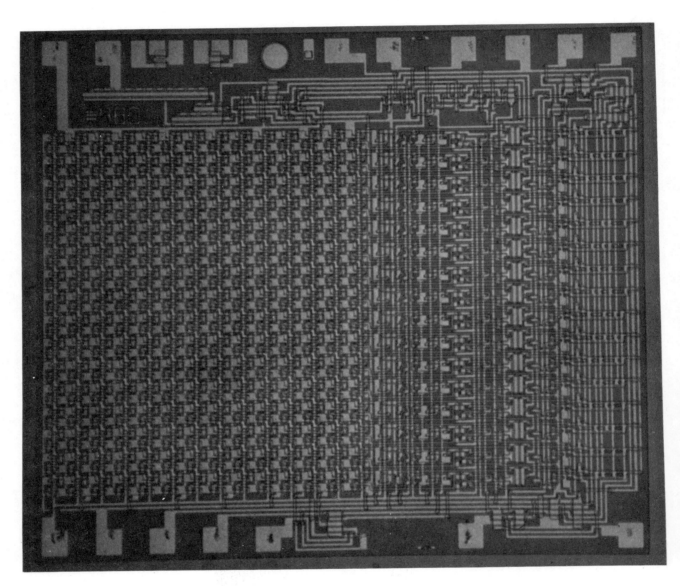

Random-access array. This Philco-Ford microcircuit is a MOS 16-by-16 random-access serial memory. The chip is 100 by 120 mils. This circuit illustrates improvement obtainable by use of new circuit forms to increase functional density.

MOS random-access arrays

By Burton R. Tunzi

American Micro-systems, Inc., Santa Clara, Calif.

Large-scale integration through MOS technology promises to enhance the performance and cut the cost of random-access memories. Larger and larger chips are being designed every day, and they are leading to larger memories assembled from many chips on a common substrate, driven in parallel or separately as required by the memory's capacity.

The circuits on these chips can be either static or dynamic. The dynamic type requires refreshing from time to time, but its elements can be densely packed and it therefore lends itself to memories of large capacity. Both kinds of circuits can include decoding transistors on the same chip; the address decoding can be partial or complete, but the more complete decoding often involves a speed penalty. With or without the decoding, both circuits can be made compatible at input and output with diode-transistor and transistor-transistor logic circuits.

A typical single chip contains 256 individually addressable bits, which may be considered 256 words of 1 bit each. A memory with a longer word, say of 16 bits, could be assembled from 16 of these 256-by-1 chips driven in parallel. Or a memory with a larger number of one-bit words, say 4,096, could be made from 16 chips driven separately.

Organized either way, 16 chips can be packaged in about 1.5 cubic inches, and will dissipate about 2.4 watts supplied from sources of +5 and −12 volts when operating.

Two modes

Data is stored in MOS memories in either a conventional cross-coupled pair of d-c NOR gates or in the form of a charge on a capacitor in a dynamic circuit. The charge is maintained by periodic refreshing. Such dynamic circuits dissipate very little power and can be packed densely on a small chip.

Either kind of circuit may be produced by American Micro-systems' proprietary low-threshold-voltage process, which yields transistors with turn-on thresholds of only −2 volts. Conventional processes produce transistors with thresholds of 5 to 10 volts.

In the d-c storage element [top of page 68], transistors Q_1 and Q_2 are the cross-coupled elements of the flip-flop and have relatively low impedances. Transistors Q_3 and Q_4 have higher impedances and serve as load resistors. As their gates are permanently connected to the − 12-volt supply, they are always on. The circuit's output is the drain of Q_2 coupled through decoding transistors Q_5 and Q_6 to a sense amplifier. This point is also the circuit's input; data to be written comes in through the decode transistors and forces the flip-flop into the desired state.

This cell, with addressing lines, takes up about 40 square mils of silicon and dissipates less than 1 milliwatt of power.

The dynamic storage circuit [lower diagram, p. 68] is essentially a one-bit continuously recirculating shift register. The recirculation requires strobe pulses, but they can have a relatively low frequency—a few kilohertz—and need be only a couple of hundred nanoseconds wide, for a duty cycle of less than 0.1%. These same pulses initiate the read-write action in the dynamic cell. Power dissipation is roughly proportional to the strobing frequency, and can be as small as 100 nanowatts per bit at slow strobing rates.

With no d-c current paths in the circuit, all the transistors can have the same impedance. This impedance can be relatively high, and the area occupied by each transistor small. Furthermore, the same line can be used for both reading and writing, saving still more area.

Data is stored in this cell as a charge on capacitor C_1, which is actually only the parasitic capacitance on the line to which it is shown connected in the diagram. Transistor Q_3 is biased on if the charge on C_1 is negative.

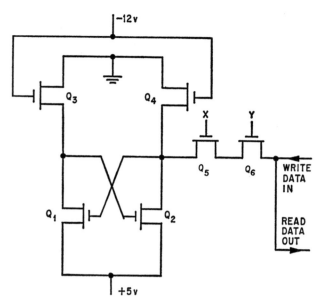

Static. The cross-coupled transistors retain a stored bit indefinitely without refreshing.

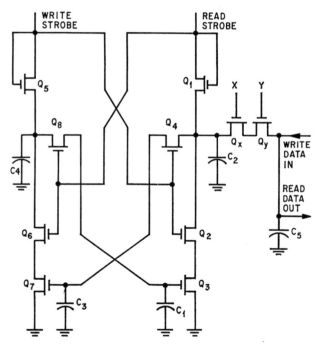

Dynamic. Parasitic capacitance store data but require refreshing; the entire circuit can be quite small, however.

The drain of Q_1 is normally maintained at $+5$ volts, but a read strobe pulse appearing from time to time momentarily drops it to -12 volts, thus turning on Q_1 briefly. During this short interval, capacitor C_2, which is also simply a parasitic capacitance, charges to the -12-volt level.

Some time before the next read strobe occurs, a write strobe turns on Q_2. (In the absence of other activity, the read and write strobes occur alternately about 500 microseconds apart.) Because C_1

has Q_3 biased on, C_2 discharges through Q_2 and Q_3 to ground. After the write strobe, therefore, C_1 and C_2 are oppositely charged.

Besides discharging C_2, the write strobe discharges C_3 through Q_4—biasing Q_7 off—and puts a negative charge on C_4. The following read strobe turns on Q_6 and Q_8; with Q_7 off, nothing happens in Q_6, but the negative charge on C_4 is transferred through Q_8 to restore the level on C_1, which may have leaked off somewhat since the last read strobe.

The two halves of the circuit are obviously identical, and their operation is exactly reversed if C_1 is initially discharged. The capacitances are small, as are the resistances of the transistors biased on, so that the charging and discharging can occur very quickly.

Between the read and write strobes, C_2 is always charged to -12 volts and therefore contains no useful information. But between the write and read strobes, the charge on C_2 represents the data stored in the circuit. At this time, therefore, the address decoding transistors, Q_x and Q_y, can be turned on, transferring most of the charge on C_2 to C_5. The latter is the parasitic capacitance on lines external to the circuit and is as much as two orders of magnitude larger than C_1 and C_2. The voltage on C_5 is therefore much smaller than the one on C_2, but it is still well above the threshold of an ordinary sense amplifier.

If transistors Q_x and Q_y are turned on at the time of the write strobe, C_2 and C_3, instead of discharging, acquire whatever voltage level is impressed on the output line and on C_5 by a write driver. The following read strobe transfers the newly written information to C_1—discharging it if C_3 is charged, charging it if C_3 is at ground.

These dynamic circuits are examples of two-phase clocked circuits, but other versions require more or fewer phases. Where, for example, four-phase clocking is employed, the phase pulses often relate to different stages and overlap in various ways to improve circuit operation. These multiple phases, however, place an additional burden on the systems designer, who has to provide properly timed phase pulses over a wide area.

Two-phase dynamic storage elements have been laid out on silicon slabs as small as 16 mils square —less than half the area required by the d-c cell. With such a small area, a 256-bit array can be fabricated on a chip only 100 mils square; and a 512-bit random-access array and 2,048-bit associative memory are not far off.

Although the diagramed d-c and dynamic circuits include both x and y addressing transistors, only one such transistor is actually needed for each cell in the array. The other can serve a whole row of cells, as shown opposite. Using two transistors on every cell not only needlessly increases the area of the whole array, but means that all the cells must produce an output on a single common line, presenting a large capacitive load.

In the 16-by-16 cell array, any one cell can be addressed by driving one of the x and one of the y lines. This partial decoding method requires a minimum of silicon area and achieves the maximum possible speed. However, it also requires 32 address input leads, and the external decoder that selects two of these 32 leads as an address must have a supply voltage greater than 5 volts because the gate of an MOS transistor must be at least 5 volts more negative than the source and drain if the device is to turn on. But the drain voltage in the decoder equals the gate voltage in the array because the two are electrically common; if the array operates from a 5-volt supply, therefore, a

higher voltage is needed in the decoder.

Full decoding on the chip permits selection of the x and y lines from a single binary input address—eight lines in the case of the 256-bit array. This setup can be driven with TTL-compatible input signals, but the extra circuits dissipate more power, add about 100 nsec to the access time, and take up space on the chip. The most straightforward decoder would use 32 four-input NOR gates and eight inverters to generate the address-line complements. A more sophisticated decoding matrix would use fewer gates but add delay. ■ ▓

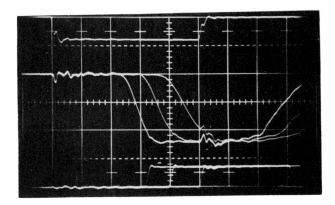

Slower when hot. Traces are, top to bottom, input, memory output, and load output, repeated at −55°, +25°, and +125°C. This unusual slowing, characteristic of MOS, follows because circuit is an RC network with positive temperature coefficient of resistance.

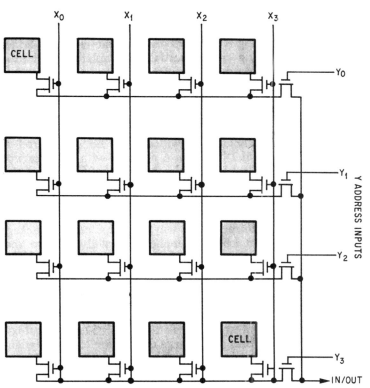

Common address. Single transistor to access full row increases array density and decreases output capacitance.

Getting more speed from MOS

By Oliver S. Saffir

American Astrionics Inc., Palo Alto, Calif.

So far as speed goes, MOS and bipolar memories often appear to be in two different leagues. Actually, however, they are by no means as poorly matched as they are sometimes taken to be; in fact, metal oxide semiconductor technology is capable not only of superior packing densities and lower power dissipation but also of an unexpected turn of speed.

For example, it's generally believed that the speed of MOS circuits is limited to a few megahertz, corresponding to access times of several hundred nanoseconds. But MOS memories built by American Astrionics Inc. for use as buffers with high-speed digital conversion and processing equipment can operate at up to 50 Mhz. This figure, though well below the 120 Mhz achieved by emitter-coupled-logic circuits, is comparable to the speed level of the more expensive transistor-transistor-logic circuits and ahead of the 15-to-25-Mhz rates of the cheapest ones.

The factor that limits speed in the simplest MOS designs is the transistor's resistance and capacitance, which form an RC network with an intrinsic time constant.

Speeds can be boosted by clock pulses from low-impedance sources, which charge portions of the circuit to levels that are permitted to decay through the RC network. One-, two-, and four-phase techniques have all been tried. But the highest speeds attained so far have resulted from the use of small output-signal swings in conjunction with amplifiers that restore the level required at the next stage, along with multiplexers that permit several medium-speed circuits to operate in parallel.

MOS memories are actually only long shift registers, or arrays of flip-flops; these, in turn, are combinations of simple logic blocks. A discussion of high-speed memories therefore begins with logic.

Examination of a typical MOS logic stage suggests ways to make it go faster. For example, the oldest and simplest form is the resistance-ratio logic stage shown at right, so-called because its binary 0 level is proportional to the ratio of the two resistances of its transistors. It's very slow, being constrained by its built-in resistance and by the unavoidable gate capacitance of the following stage.

In the resistance-ratio circuit shown, transistor Q_1, called the pull-up device, is always turned on because its gate is connected to its drain—though a separate voltage supply is sometimes used instead of the feedback connection. The transistor therefore acts like a resistor, the value of which depends on its size; the longer and narrower the transistor, the higher its resistance.

When the input signal is a binary 0 (at ground), Q_2 is turned off, and the output is a binary 1. When the input becomes negative, Q_2 turns on and the output becomes 0. The 1 level at the output is approximately the same as the supply voltage because the load draws essentially no current and there is no voltage drop across the resistance of Q_1. But the 0 level is generally not at ground because Q_1 and Q_2 become a voltage divider when both are turned on. More precisely, the 0 level is

$$V\{1/[(R_1/R_2) + 1]\}$$

where R_1 and R_2 are the resistances of Q_1 and Q_2, respectively. R_2 is usually much smaller than R_1

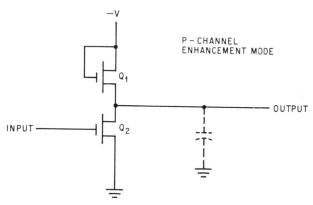

Resistance ratio. The speed of the logic stage in this simplest MOS design is limited by its size and input capacitance.

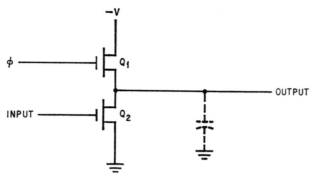

Clocked stage. The clock pulse permits some speed improvement, but the ceiling is still under 2 Mhz.

because the 0 level must be kept below the threshold that turns on the next stage; the 0 level is therefore approximately $V(R_2/R_1)$.

The output of the logic stage always sees a node capacitance—the sum of the next stage's gate capacitance, the capacitance of the line connecting the two stages, and a few other parasitic odds and ends. This node capacitance charges slowly through Q_1 when the circuit is switching from 0 to 1, and discharges quickly through Q_2 when the switch is from 1 to 0.

This difference in speed arises from the difference in the two resistances. But if the designer tries to reduce both resistances to increase speed, he must make both transistors larger, thereby increasing the capacitance at the gate and at the junction between source and substrate. He therefore soon encounters the law of diminishing returns.

In most applications, Q_2 has a resistance of about 1,000 ohms when it is on, and Q_1 of 7,000 to 10,000 ohms. Charging and discharging the node capacitance through these resistances limits the circuit's speed to about 1 or 2 Mhz.

Two early attempts to increase the speed of resistance-ratio logic involved the use of clock pulses instead of the gate-to-drain connection. In the simpler form, shown at left, a clock pulse turns on Q_1 at regular intervals—say, once a microsecond with about a 10% duty cycle. While Q_1 is on, the output takes on a value opposite to that of the input, just as in unclocked resistance-ratio logic. Between pulses, the output tends to retain its last state, although some decay through various leakage paths may occur. This decay is of little consequence, though, since the following stage is also clocked and therefore uses the output only before the decay can begin.

The other scheme, the precharge node method, uses a two-phase clock to turn on two identical pull-up transistors alternately, as at left below. The first clock pulse connects the output directly to the supply voltage, regardless of the input state. The output thus becomes a 1, and the node capacitance charges to the level of the supply. The second pulse turns on a parallel connection and admits the input signal through Q_4 to Q_3. If the input is 1, therefore, Q_3 turns on and the output becomes 0 as the node capacitance discharges.

This technique takes advantage of the fast transition from 1 to 0 occurring with the second clock pulse—just the time the following stage looks at the signal. The transition from 0 to 1 occurs only at the time of the first clock pulse, when no one is looking. However, the technique still doesn't produce speeds above 2 Mhz because it still leaves the circuit shackled by the restrictions of line and gate capacitance.

Four-phase or polyphase techniques are employed in some circuits to increase internal speeds without boosting power consumption or enlarging transistor size. In some circuits, all four clock phases are externally generated; in others, only one phase is external, the rest being generated within the circuit. The latter arrangement works best with low-voltage MOS circuits.

Four-phase clocking can be used with many circuit configurations and with a variety of time relationships between the phases. But with all these variations, the usual approach uses MOS transistors

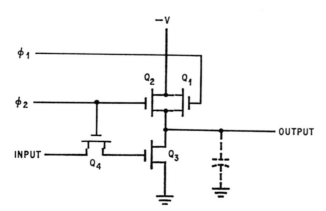

Precharge. Two alternating clock pulses set up the stage before its logic state is acquired, for further speed improvement.

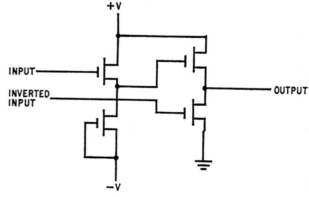

Push-pull. Driving the signal both up and down using the signal and complement overcomes the high capacitance of a load outside the chip.

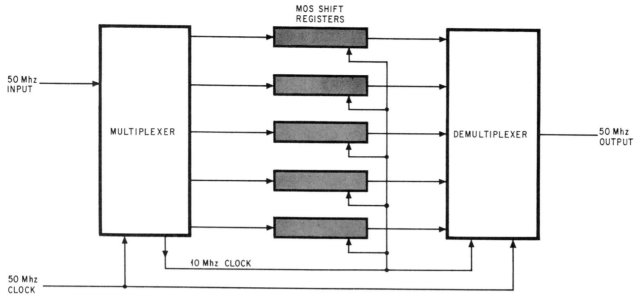

Parallel. Dividing a high-speed signal into several parts—each handled by a separate, relatively slow shift register —makes the memory appear to have high speed.

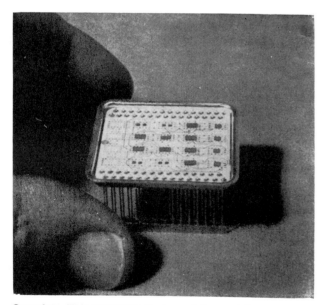

Complete. This hybrid memory contains registers, a multiplexer, and a demultiplexer on a single substrate.

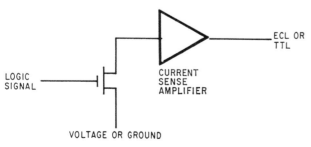

Booster. Low-level signals are intrinsically fast; an amplifier gives them the oomph to drive an external stage.

as switches to charge and discharge capacitors rather than as resistors.

In these switching designs, the input logic signals appear during the first phase and turn the gates of an isolated MOS switching network on or off. Due to the residual charge on the gate, these switches retain their states when the logic signals are disconnected.

In the second phase, another isolated switch is turned on. It stays on until the third phase arrives, at which time it discharges through the logic network established in the first phase if that network was turned on, or stays on if that network was off.

Finally, during the fourth phase, the logic network is disconnected again and the switch that was turned on during the second phase produces its new state as the circuit's output.

The transistors in a four-phase circuit can be small and thus have a high resistance. Because they charge open-circuited capacitors, the voltage drop across them is relatively unimportant. Likewise the capacitors are very small and charge quickly, so that the circuit's speed is high. Finally, the circuit dissipates very little power because the energy loss when charge passes from one capacitor to another is proportional to the capacitor and to the square of the voltage difference, but is independent of the resistance. The only power dissipation stems from leakage in the capacitors and diodes, an almost negligible factor.

Push and pull

Capacitance is most severe in circuits whose loads are external to the chip. The approach most frequently applied to these high-speed output circuits employs a push-pull stage made of two transistors of the same size, as shown at bottom right

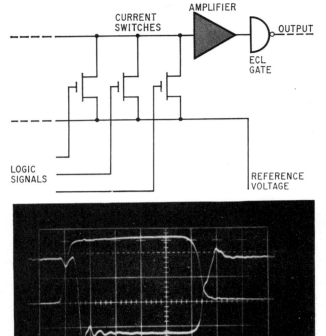

CURRENT SWITCHES

AMPLIFIER

OUTPUT

ECL GATE

LOGIC SIGNALS

REFERENCE VOLTAGE

→| |← 10 nsec

Fast. Several low-level stages driving a single amplifier put out logic signals at high speed. Rise and fall times are only a few nanoseconds, and the propagation time is less than 10 nsec.

on page 72, and therefore with the same resistance when on. This stage is faster than the simple resistance-ratio stage and it switches both ways in the same time. Both polarities of the input signal are required, but this is easily obtained with an inverter. Combining this technique with the precharge node or four-phase method yields speeds of up to 10 Mhz, or access times of 100 nsec.

And the circuits can be made to appear to operate at even higher speeds—by multiplexing several parallel circuits, for instance. A four-phase shift register with push-pull output circuits will operate as a serial dynamic storage unit at the 10-Mhz level. But five such registers can be connected in parallel, as shown at top of page 73, to the outputs of a multiplexer made from TTL or ECL circuits; their outputs are connected in turn to the inputs of a similar demultiplexer, which produces a bit stream identical to the input but delayed the length of a single shift register. Such a hybrid package containing registers, multiplexer, and demultiplexer on a single substrate is shown in the photograph on page 73.

Fast random-access memories require fast access time. Multiplexing tricks don't apply here; they speed up the access rate, but not the access time. The only answer is to make the basic MOS circuit operate faster.

The biggest roadblock in this area has been the idea that output signal swings have to be comparable to input logic levels. When this concept is set aside, significant improvements in speed are possible.

Using the MOS transistor as a high-speed switch reflects this change in concept. The output stage now used by American Astrionics [bottom, p. 73], is an amplifier that senses currents of about a half-milliampere through a current switch. The voltage swing at the input to this switch is only about a half-volt—even less than the customary ECL swing.

To demonstrate a quantitative result, the oscillogram in the photo at left shows what can be obtained from the circuit just above it. The total propagation delay of the circuit is well under 10 nsec, and the rise and fall times are only a few nanoseconds. This represents a significant improvement over the hundreds of nanoseconds required when the MOS device drives a voltage load instead of the amplifier. It also permits the fabrication of a 32-bit chip with access time of less than 150 nsec, including external address decoding and sensing time.

Additional speed can be attained by putting the address decoding right on the chip with the memory array. This reduces the number of wires and packages, and thus the amount of noise and parasitics that hold back the circuits. ■

COS/MOS:
the best of both worlds

By Gerald B. Herzog

RCA, Princeton, N.J.

Flip-flops built with complementary symmetry metal oxide semiconductor circuits (COS/MOS) dissipate negligible power and are stable in the presence of noise and heavy loads. These characteristics make the flip-flops excellent elements for arrays that can be used as memories with capacities of up to several hundred bits per chip.

Furthermore, the trend to MOS memories is toward more use of complementary symmetry as techniques are perfected and as additional manufacturers begin supplying COS/MOS devices.

The low dissipation and the high stability result because the circuit has both n-channel and p-channel transistors in series. Only one of these transistors can be conducting at a time, except during a switching operation; and the non-linearity of the series combination is greater than that of either transistor working by itself.

Only the difficulty of fabricating complementary MOS devices on a common substrate has slowed the development of these circuits so far. All the many variables involved in the dual process have to be just right at the same time; otherwise the process won't work. But recent breakthroughs in ways to make oxide and metal layers that are free of impurities have overcome the problem.

Digital circuitry requires devices whose characteristics have a particular kind of non-linearity, in which a small increase in the input over part of its range causes a much larger decrease in the output. When two such devices are cross-connected to drive each other, they form a bistable circuit. A small increase in the input of one of the devices causes a large decrease in its output and thus in the input of the other; the second device's output then saturates, strongly reinforcing the original small increase in the input.

The MOS transistor, though nonlinear in this way, is by no means ideal. Its transfer characteristic is much more nearly linear than that of a bipolar transistor—so much so that a MOS transistor is widely used in radio tuners as a mixer and r-f amplifier.

When used with a high-impedance linear load, the voltage transfer characteristic of the MOS transistor is marginally acceptable for a digital switching element. The transfer characteristics of the two cross-connected low-threshold transistors, when plotted with the appropriate relationship to one another, as shown below, indicate the stable operating points of the flip-flop. With a 10-volt supply these are approximately 1 volt and slightly

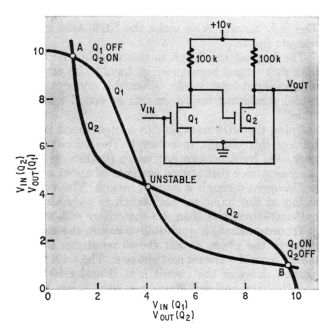

MOS characteristic. Although MOS transistors can be connected in a bistable configuration, their linearity makes the circuit only marginally reliable.

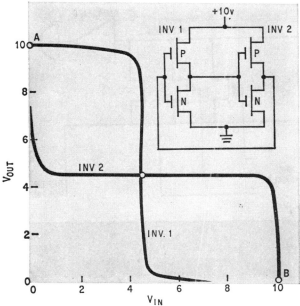

COS/MOS characteristic. Connecting opposite types of MOS transistors in series multiplies their nonlinearities, thus reducing noise sensitivity and power dissipation.

less than 10 volts. The shape of the two loops indicates the d-c stability of the circuit. The diagram is drawn for n-channel devices; that for p-channel transistors would be similar.

Noise transients, excessive loading during the readout of the flip-flop, or transients on the power supply voltage could cause the characteristics to move or change enough so that the stable intercept points would be lost and the circuit would lose its stored data.

Wide margin

When two COS/MOS inverters are connected as a flip-flop, as at lower right on page 75, the characteristics of the two types of devices are effectively multiplied together, and the transfer characteristic of the two in series becomes extremely nonlinear. The cross-connection provides large noise margins, and well-defined output levels of 0 and 10 volts, for a 10-volt supply.

Since each leg of the flip-flop always contains one conducting and one nonconducting transistor, there is always a relatively low impedance path from the output terminal to either the power supply or ground, depending upon the state of the inverter. The low impedance minimizes the capacitive noise pickup. And whatever noise signal is received, has only a slight effect because the circuit has a large noise margin.

Furthermore, through this same low-impedance path, more current can be drawn from the circuit than from a flip-flop made from a single kind of transistor without disrupting the state of the flip-flop. This larger output current—available, for example, to a sense amplifier—makes sensing faster. At the same time, the nonconductive transistor lowers the COS/MOS flip-flop's standby power dissipation, because it blocks the current flow from power supply to ground.

Because MOS transistor circuits that use only one type of transistor usually operate with higher voltages, the wider voltage level translation costs time, especially if the address signals come from bipolar transistor logic. But the highly nonlinear characteristic of the COS/MOS inverters permits devices with low threshold voltages to be used; its source voltage can be well below 10 volts. With these lower voltages, compatibility with bipolar transistor logic levels can be obtained, leading to higher memory cycle speeds or lower costs for the peripheral circuitry or both.

In applications requiring more complex arrays, address decoding on the chip containing the storage elements reduces the number of leads from the package. Complementary MOS transistors in a decoder tree can also achieve higher addressing speeds than can the single-channel type, again because complementary transistor pairs are more nonlinear and have lower impedances, and thus can generate larger currents to charge circuit capacitance.

In the decoder tree shown on page 78, all the transistors are n-channel except the output

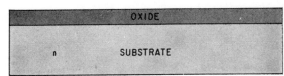

INITIAL CHIP WITH OXIDE LAYER ON TOP

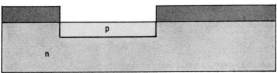

OPEN OXIDE LAYER, DIFFUSE p WELL

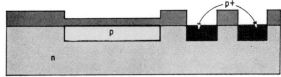

GROW NEW OXIDE LAYER, OPEN TWO NEW HOLES, DIFFUSE p+ SOURCE AND DRAIN

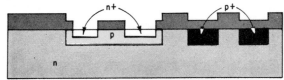

GROW OXIDE OVER p+, OPEN TWO HOLES OVER WELL, DIFFUSE n+ SOURCE AND DRAIN

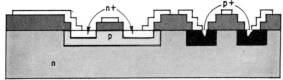

OPEN CONTACTS TO p+ SOURCE AND DRAIN, METALIZE

Ticklish problem

Complementary symmetry isn't easy to achieve in integrated circuits. Although either n- or p-channel transistors have been used in MOS IC's for several years, both types have been combined in a single chip only recently—processing techniques had to be greatly refined first. The editors of *Electronics* checked around to see how different companies approach the task. At RCA, ultra-precise control of diffusion makes the complementary MOS chip possible. Other firms take different approaches: Westinghouse has used elaborate and critical mechanical operations to form the complementary channels; General Telephone and Electronics Laboratories uses a substrate of extremely high resistivity.

RCA uses the substrate for the p channel and diffuses a p-type well for the n channel. The sequence of operation is shown above. First the oxide layer is opened and the p well diffused into the n substrate. A new oxide is grown, and two new holes are opened for p+ diffusion; these regions become the source and drain of the p-channel transistor. After the oxide is regrown over the p+ regions, two new holes are opened over the well and n+ regions are diffused through them; these become the source and drain of the n-channel transistor.

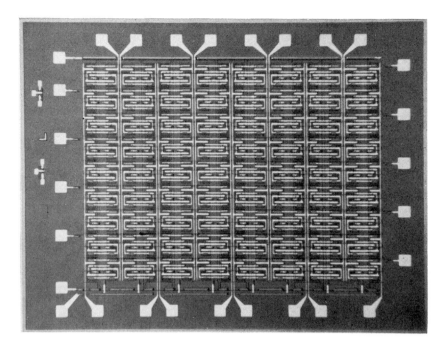

72-bit memory. This array, now in production, is the prototype of one, four times the size, that will be used in a high-speed scratchpad application.

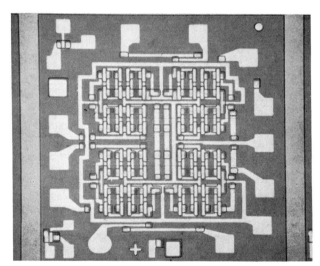

Commercial. This 16-bit array, RCA's type CD4005, is part of a 4,096-bit scratchpad with 100-nsec cycle time.

stage. The p-channel output transistors are normally kept on, except when the strobe signal goes positive; this turns them off and turns on the single n-channel master gate. When the output transistors turn off, all but one of the output lines are left floating at their positive level, while the line specified by the input address lines are grounded through the tree and the master gate.

Although circuit designers have long recognized advantages of the circuit, only recently has the process technology become commercially practical for fabricating both n- and p-channel devices on the same substrate. While the principal processing steps look easy [see "Ticklish problem," p. 76], they require exceptionally clean oxides and metal layers. Impurities, which tend to contaminate the

semiconductor material, are more deleterious in n-channel devices, which is why semiconductor engineers have swung toward p-channel devices in the past several years. With the new techniques, n-channel is coming back into favor; its carriers are more mobile, so that the devices switch faster.

Since COS/MOS uses both n- and p-type devices, the new techniques are as important here as in single-channel designs. They've made possible the memory array shown above, with 72 bits of memory and 432 MOS transistors; it's being experimentally fabricated now with modest yields—still under 10%—of perfect arrays, that is, arrays where all 72 bits are operational. This particular array is being produced for the U. S. Air Force* as part of an effort to fabricate a 4,068-bit high-speed scratchpad memory. Arrays of 288 bits with partial address decoding will be used in this memory.

More representative of what can be done in the factory is the 16-bit memory array [photo at left], which RCA is selling commercially. It operates at 10 volts and dissipates 100 nanowatts in standby; its set time is 50 nanoseconds and its read time is 15 nsec. It is the basic storage element of a scratchpad memory containing 512 bytes (4,096 bits) that has an access time of 50 nsec and a full cycle time of 100 nsec. The bipolar decoding limits these speeds, which include internal translation from and to emitter-coupled logic.

What's to come

Work on silicon-on-sapphire substrate material at RCA Laboratories promises to make available the higher speed of complementary symmetry in larger semiconductor memories. As the size of any memory is increased, the limit of its operating speed decreases because of parasitic loading ef-

* Air Force contract No. AF33(615)3491

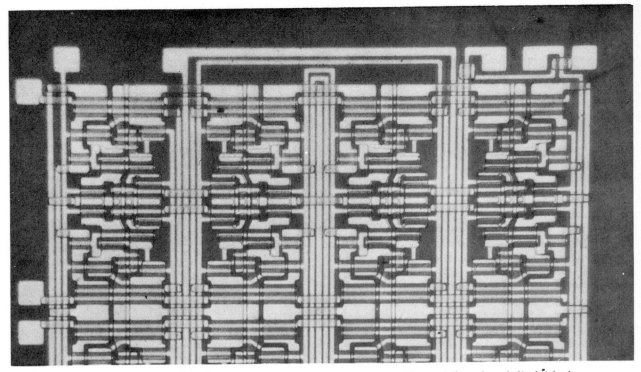

SOS. Another 16-bit array made of a thin film of silicon deposited on sapphire and then doped. Its intrinsic capacitance is very small, thus it is ultimately capable of very high speed.

fects. In COS/MOS devices fabricated in silicon on sapphire, rather than in bulk silicon, the line capacitance is closer to the free-space capacitance of a wire than to the parallel-plate capacitance of a wire over the insulator covering the relatively conductive substrate; thus the capacitance is much lower and these parasitic effects are minimized.

Fabrication of COS/MOS devices in silicon-on-sapphire films, although a more difficult materials processing problem at the present time, promises eventually to be a much simpler process. Processing complementary MOS devices in bulk silicon requires the silicon material to be converted from n-type to p-type or vice-versa for the fabrication of the opposite polarity devices; but an undoped film of silicon on a sapphire substrate can be converted either to n or to p [see following article]. Thus both kinds of devices can be fabricated in the same substrate material, both with low threshold voltages. These advantages can be achieved by novel processing techniques that require only one diffusion furnace, instead of the half-dozen or more furnaces in the bulk-silicon process.

The cost of MOS storage elements is unlikely to drop as low as that of magnetic cores operating at about one-microsecond cycle time. But a market is highly likely to develop in the few hundred nanoseconds region. At these speeds semiconductor memory elements can compete on a cost basis with magnetic memories, because high-speed drivers and sense amplifiers for magnetic memories cost more than those for semiconductor memories. Cur-

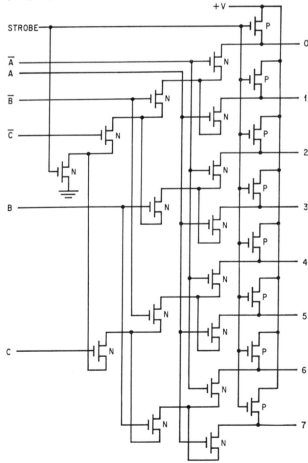

Decoder. Complementary pair at output can generate larger currents to charge circuit capacitance, thus can operate faster than single-channel circuit.

rently, small magnetic scratchpad memories cost approximately $1.00 per bit; whereas the total system cost for a small semiconductor scratchpad memory that operates at two or three times the speed of a magnetic memory is about the same.

There seems to be every indication that complementary devices can be fabricated with as good a yield as single-channel devices. The improved performance of a COS/MOS memory offsets its slightly higher processing cost—which might well be masked by the usual engineering and overhead costs. Consequently, the advantages of COS/MOS memory arrays make them the logical choice for modules with which to build future high-speed memories of moderate to large size. ∎

Bibliography

J.R. Burns, J.J. Gibson, A. Harel, K.C. Hu, R.A. Powlus, "Integrated Memory Using Complementary Field Effect Transistors," Digest of technical papers, International Solid State Circuits Conference, February 1966.

G.B. Herzog, "Large Arrays of Semiconductor Devices for Computer Memories," Third Annual Integrated Circuits Seminar, Stevens Institute of Technology.

F.P. Heiman, "Thin-Film Silicon-on-Sapphire Deep Depletion MOS Transistors," IEEE Trans. on Electron Devices, December 1966.

A. Medwin, "Fabrication of Complementary MOS Circuits," RCA reprint PE-375.

J.F. Allison, F.P. Heiman, J.R. Burns, "Silicon-on-Sapphire Complementary MOS Memory Cells," IEEE Journal of Solid-State Circuits, December 1967.

R.W. Ahrons, P.D. Gardner, "Interaction of Technology and Performance of Complementary Symmetry MOS Integrated Circuits," Digest of technical papers, International Solid State Circuits Conference, February 1969.

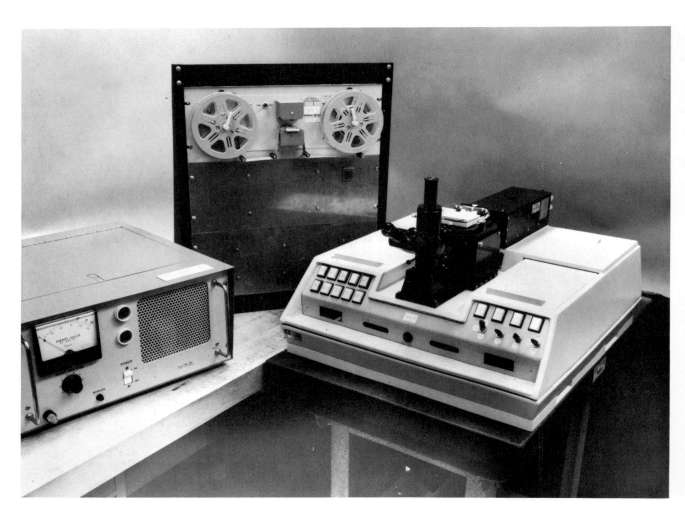

Micromachine. With this laser tool, North American Rockwell Microelectronics Co. (Narmec) encodes a silicon-on-sapphire diode array quickly. A computer translates the data to be stored in the array into taped instructions from which the laser encodes the array automatically. Narmec was formerly known as Autonetics.

SOS brings new life to read-only units

By J.A. Luisi

North American Rockwell Microelectronics Corp., Anaheim, Calif.

Silicon on sapphire is a semiconductor technology particularly well-suited to diode arrays used as read-only memories. The simple structure and processing make the arrays easy to build; the low capacitance of the SOS diode's junction makes the arrays fast, and the silicon film's large sheet resistance permits resistors to be included in the array without taking up too much room. Furthermore, the arrays are highly radiation resistant.

A recently developed automatic laser micro-machining technique [*Electronics*, Dec. 23, 1968, p. 37], for custom bit-pattern encoding makes SOS technology practical by permitting fast, low-cost production of memories. This is especially helpful in speeding implementation of engineering changes. These read-only memories achieve lower cost, higher speed, larger output signals, decreased size

and weight, reduced dissipated power, and better radiation hardness, both in themselves and in the equipment they're used in.

In the marketplace, the SOS read-only memory is expected to do well in the fields of process-control computers, test equipment, and input-output equipment. In process control applications, special high-speed sub-routines, data tables, and microprograms can all be implemented with read-only memories. In test equipment, the read-only memory can store instructions, generate test waveforms and bit sequences, and hold the model outputs for comparison with the response of the system under test. In a remote computer terminal with a cathode-ray tube display, the memory can be used for a character generator.

The fabrication of an SOS integrated circuit be-

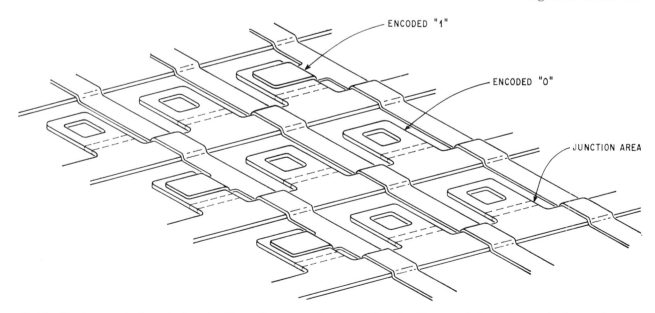

Matrix. The lower set of conductors is silicon, the upper aluminum. Tabs in silicon contain diodes; contact is made through similar tabs on the aluminum layer.

Resistant to radiation

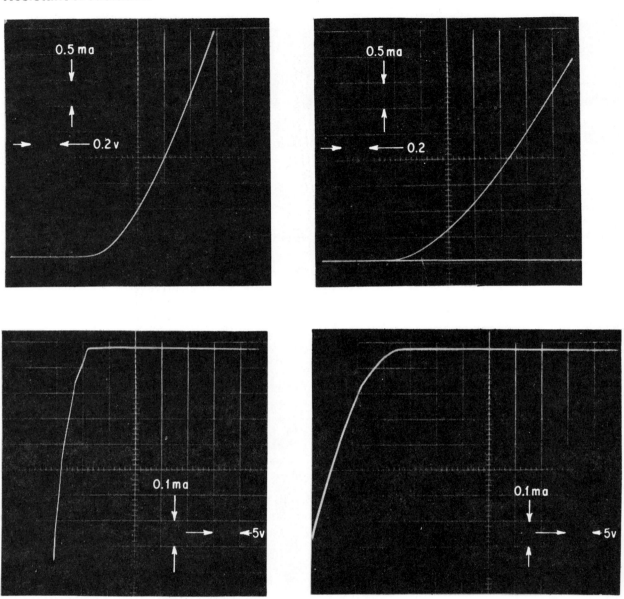

Hardy. Heavy doses of radiation have hardly any effect on SOS diodes. Upper traces show diode's forward characteristic before (left) and after exposure to neutrons; the lower traces are the reverse characteristic.

gins with the growth of a thin single-crystal layer of silicon on a polished substrate of sapphire (aluminum oxide). Because silicon and aluminum oxide are different substances, the thin film must be grown heteroepitaxially. Autonetics was the first to do this successfully in 1963; RCA is apparently the only other organization to have investigated it extensively. Much of this work has been proprietary. The fabrication difficulty is probably the main reason that research and development in SOS has been limited.

After the silicon film is grown on the sapphire, it's selectively doped, using conventional oxidation, photolithographic, and diffusion processes, to form semiconductor junctions. The two diffusions—one

with n dopant and one with p—need not be precisely controlled, because the dopants are driven at high concentration, through selectively exposed areas of the silicon, all the way to the silicon-sapphire interface. After these junctions have been formed, the unwanted parts of the silicon film are etched away to produce electrically isolated islands of silicon supported by the insulating sapphire substrate. A layer of oxide, grown over the remaining islands, seals them and reduces the probability of short-circuits at the crossovers. The final steps in the procedure open contact holes in the oxide, deposit an aluminum film, and etch the metalization pattern.

In an early SOS diode array, shown on p. 81, the diodes are connected by a matrix consisting of two

Production version. Autonetics' ROM-2206 stores 1,024 bits on a chip 220 mils square.

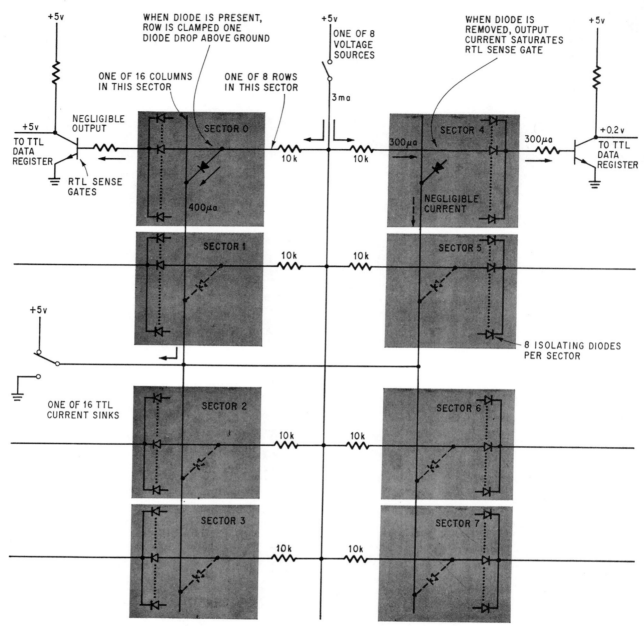

Eight in parallel. A single access selects one diode in each of eight 128-diode sectors, producing a read-out signal in 50 nanoseconds.

orthogonal sets of conductors [*Electronics*, Feb. 20, 1967, p. 171]. One set is formed from heavily doped silicon, the other from the vapor-deposited aluminum. An oxide layer insulates the two conductors at the crossovers in the matrix. Diodes are built into silicon tabs, extending from the silicon conductors. These diodes can be made with either the anodes or the cathodes electrically common, depending on the selected doping. Because this array is produced with just five photomasking steps, the yield is excellent.

An SOS junction is formed along a diffusion front that advances down to the silicon-sapphire interface and laterally under the oxide. The resulting junction is sometimes called vertical because its plane is perpendicular to the substrate plane, rather than parallel to it as in other technologies. One of the dimensions of the junction area, then, is the thickness of the film—typically 1 micron, or 10^{-4} centimeter. If the tab is 2 mils wide, the area of the junction is 50 square microns, and the corresponding junction capacitance is only about 10 femtofarads (0.01 picofarad).

As a result, even large diode arrays have only a small capacitance, which is quickly charged and discharged while the array operates. For comparison, the junction capacitance of conventional diodes is on the order of 100 times greater. Thus an SOS read-only memory can achieve higher speed at any given capacity or greater memory at any given speed than arrays of other kinds of diodes.

Reducing the number of access leads on a read-only memory reduces the number of external connections, simplifying the memory's incorporation into a system and improving the latter's reliability. In SOS technology, integrating resistor-diode circuits to produce selection and sensing functions reduces the number of leads; besides that, it's quite easy.

It's easy because the thin film, besides having a small junction area, also has a large sheet resistance—the quotient of the resistivity divided by the thickness of the film. Material of 0.5 ohm-cm produces 5 kilohms per square—more than 10 times the sheet resistance of a base diffusion in monolithic silicon.

The area on a chip occupied by resistors is a kind of "overhead" because it isn't available for memory diodes. With SOS, overhead is low, because large SOS resistances can be formed in a small area by etching; the large sheet resistance and ease of isolation permit a complex resistor-diode network to be integrated in a small area.

The crystalline quality of the silicon film material is poorer than that available in bulk silicon, and this limits the yield of certain devices, such as MOS FET IC's. But it doesn't cause significant problems in diode arrays. Variations in diode reverse-breakdown voltage or in leakage current, or difficulties in controlling the value of the sheet resistance, are not troublesome because the operation of a read-only memory does not depend on the uniformity or precision of these parameters. In fact, the crystal imperfections in SOS work to advantage when the memory must operate during or after heavy neutron bombardment.

For example, the oscilloscope traces on page 82 show the characteristics of an SOS diode before and after exposure over a period of time to 5×10^{15} neutrons per square centimeter. This radiation level, produced by a 15-minute exposure in the core of a nuclear reactor, produces severe perma-

nent damage to bipolar IC's. The small diode-junction area and the dielectric isolation of SOS also limit the transient photocurrents generated by radiation. Heavy gamma radiation also has much less effect on an SOS diode. Therefore the SOS part of a read-only memory module will not be the limiting component for survival in an environment in which severe radiation is present.

Six arrays

The first SOS diode array was fabricated at Autonetics in 1965. Since then, five other versions have been designed. The largest was a giant 96×70 array on a half-inch square wafer. This array had so many leads—166—that it was hard to package. A modified version of it was fabricated in 1967 with integrated silicon resistors included to permit on-wafer decoding. The number of leads dropped to 31.

A still later version has been dignified with a name, ROM-2206. This chip has 1,024 bit storage locations and integrated silicon resistors. In contrast with earlier whole-wafer designs, 9 to 12 of these smaller chips are obtained from each sapphire wafer. The Autonetics pilot line has produced more than 1,000 ROM-2206 circuits for evaluating. The results have been encouraging in every respect; Autonetics no longer considers the device a laboratory model. Customers' interest has been established, and production in large quantities will begin as soon as customers' requirements have been established.

The ROM-2206 chip, shown on page 83, is 220 by 220 mils; the conductor matrix has a center-to-center spacing of 4.5 mils. This chip connects to bipolar transistor logic circuits in a memory module of 32 chips; the module's specifications are tabulated below.

The chip contains eight 8-by-16 sectors, labeled 0 through 7 in the diagram on page 84. A single access selects eight bit locations, in parallel, one in each of the eight sectors.

When a diode is present at the selected row and column in a sector, the diode clamps the row to the column, the applied voltage drops across the 10-kilohm resistor, and virtually no current goes to the sense gate. Approximately 400 microamperes passes to the current sink, limited by the resistor and the memory diode drop of about 0.7 volt in its path.

When a diode is not present at the selected row and column, the sense gate gets all the current in the row—only about 300 μamp in this case because the path includes the isolating diode and the sense gate base-to-emitter drop. The access time, defined as the delay from the 2-volt level on a read command to the 2-volt level on the TTL data register output, is 50 nanoseconds with a 100-nanosecond read cycle time.

Custom encoding

Encoding memory chips cheaply and with pre-

Read-only SOS memory module	
Capacity	1,024 words
Word length	32 bits
Access time	300 nsec
Cycle time	500 nsec
Power dissipation	3 watts*
Volume	20 cu. in.
Radiation resistance	
Neutrons	3×10^{14} n/cm^2
Transient gamma	10^8 rads/sec
* Including peripheral circuits	

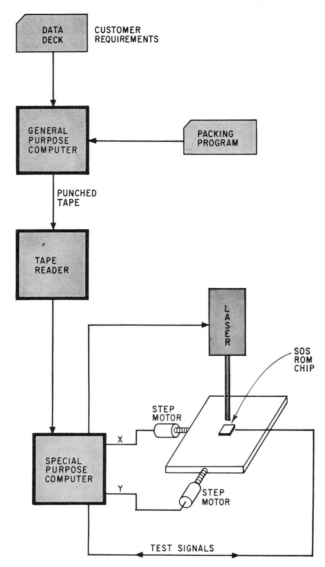

Zap machine. A laser machine tool encodes data in diode array by burning out unwanted connections.

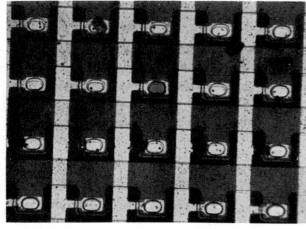

Encoder array. The laser has burned out all the diode connections in one horizontal row, where the light-colored connection is missing.

cision for fast changes is essential to the acceptance of read-only memories by project engineers, who otherwise would be likely to oppose the idea because it supposedly limits reprograming flexibility. This is a particularly sensitive point during a hardware development program. Changes in programs and in internal data stores are frequent, and the thought of repeated delays for memory substitution is intolerable. Therefore the encoding and testing process must be automated so that a read-only memory can be changed in less time than the programer can identify the change.

The recently developed laser micromachine tool, under punched-tape control, as shown at the left, meets all the necessary specifications. A deck of punched cards contains the data to be stored, which can be organized as 1,024 words of one bit, 512 words of two bits, 256 words of four bits, or 128 words of eight bits. A general-purpose computer reads the cards and produces, in 30 seconds, a punched paper tape. This tape contains a list of simple instructions for custom encoding on ROM chips. These instructions are read sequentially into a special-purpose computer, which controls the motion of a precision x-y table, commands the laser to fire when a diode is to be disconnected, and immediately checks that bit location to confirm that the connection has been broken.

A small experimental neodymium-glass, water-cooled laser makes five zaps per second; commercial lasers are available that could encode 10 times as fast. The energy per zap is 10^{-3} joule, focused onto a spot about 1 mil in diameter; the pulse lasts about 30 μsec. No redeposition of aluminum debris has been observed, either by electrical tests or by careful inspection of microphotographs at 200$\times$ magnification. Presumably the violent local heating changes the vaporized metal into nonconducting oxides or nitrides.

Of course, read-only memories can also be coded by chemical etching, whenever one needs a large number of identically encoded arrays—for example, trigonometric tables. If more than about 100 identical chips are required, chemical encoding would be cheaper than laser encoding.

What's coming

The developmental success of the ROM-2206 chip is expected to lead to volume production and stocking of blank SOS memories. The masks and the process will be refined first, test programs will be expanded to characterize the devices more completely, and a large number of chips will be used in a wide variety of applications.

The designers are now considering increasing the bit storage capacity by quadrupling the chip bit-density to 4,096 bits in approximately the same chip size. The device structures on ROM-2206 are crude by contemporary standards of photo-lithography and reflect the caution born of a need for success. There is no substitute for achieving the greatest bit density within the limitations of process yield when competing in a cost-sensitive market. The immediate goal is to crack the penny-per-bit sales price barrier for one-of-a-kind, custom-encoded arrays made in small quantities.

At the moment, packaging of the chips is less than satisfactory. The 40-lead flatpack in which ROM-2206 is mounted is all right for testing. However, more extreme miniaturization could be achieved by assembling uncased complex chips into functional aggregates if techniques for assembly of the machines can be developed.

In this respect, SOS has some interesting possibilities. For example, the data in an SOS memory can be established by shooting the laser through the 10-mil-thick sapphire substrate. Thus, the sapphire becomes a window in a face-down approach that might even permit laser bonding. The transparent sapphire permits registering two face-to-face metalization patterns, which can be locally heated. Experimental work in this direction is just starting; special attention is being given to the problem of chip substitution.

Work is also in progress to add active devices to the arrays. Complementary MOS circuits are being designed and fabricated to provide decoding, current-drive, and sense-gate electronics on the chip. A yield penalty is expected, and radiation effects are forcing the consideration of unconventional gate insulation, but the potential gain in speed with further reductions in size and power justifies these experimental efforts. ∎

SOS to bow in
as 5,120-diode ROM

Silicon on sapphire (SOS) appears ready to live up to its promise of high-speed circuits. Last year, James Luisi of the then Autonetics Products division of North American Rockwell Corp. said the division had redirected its SOS efforts toward a high-speed array of 5,120 diodes [*Electronics*, June 8, 1970, p. 88]. Now the unit is in customers' hands, in "developmental production quantities," Luisi says [*Electronics*, Jan. 18, p. 26].

Luisi is a member of the technical staff at North American Rockwell Microelectronics Co. (NRMEC), which inherited the development from Autonetics. NRMEC's data sheet describes the unit as a 40-by-128-diode read-only memory, but Luisi says it can be used in logic applications, too. "Its charm and power is that it's so simple to build that it offers the potential for high-volume production," Luisi asserts, "and it gives the circuit design engineer a good alternative to conventional memory and logic circuits."

The unit "operates conveniently" at 20 megahertz, Luisi says, compared to about 3 or 4 MHz for the fastest MOS read-only memory components on the market. Its speed allows typical cycle times of 50 nanoseconds with 30 ns minimum, and access times as fast as 20 ns. Luisi points out that one semiconductor manufacturer has introduced a Schottky-clamped bipolar ROM with speed comparable to that of the NRMEC SOS device but only one-fifth the storage capability. "So we have a product that's as dense as MOS parts and as fast as bipolars."

He believes it's the first truly commercially available SOS part anywhere but emphasizes that it's still in the prototype stage. NRMEC estimates an array could be custom encoded for less than $100 for a single part, but Luisi is anxious to find out if there's enough interest in the unit to justify volume production. "We'd have to be able to slug it out right now at a cent a bit if we committed to production," he says, but adds that the price probably will drop to a tenth of a cent within a year or two. Another company pursuing SOS technology, RCA, which showed a 50-bit SOS shift register at last March's IEEE show, hasn't a product yet.

The former Autonetics SOS work resulted in more complex circuits than the present one at NRMEC. "We've changed our circuit philosophy toward simplification," Luisi explains. The prototype unit is organized as 128 rows of diodes connected through a series resistor to a common power supply. With 40 columns of these rows, any word length from 1 to 32 bits at a time can be retrieved.

The arrays are now stored as blanks with aluminum links connecting all the diodes. For small quantities, the customer's program will be encoded by removing the aluminum links or selected diodes with a laser micromachining tool [*Electronics*, Dec. 23, 1968, p. 37], creating the desired patterns of 1 and 0. For larger production runs, NRMEC will create a custom metalization mask to encode the customer's data pattern.

The array can be customized in three ways, Luisi says. Custom row decoding will allow row selection via a code applied to the row leads. Then another set of rows may be selected and committed to the output function. This usually leaves 3,328 bits for custom data storage.

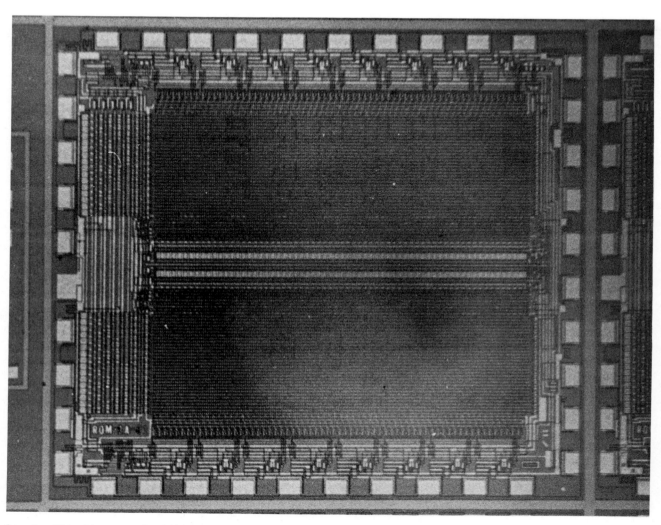

Complex. This chip, measuring 140 by 155 mils, contains Four-Phase Systems' 8,192-bit read-only memory, used in the company's System IV/70 computer. Its access time is 1 microsecond; when this is compared with the earlier prediction on page 91, it shows how quickly events outrace forecasts in the semiconductor business.

Cutting systems costs with MOS

By Lee Boysel

Fairchild Semiconductor, Mountain View, Calif.*

The great strides made in the past year in developing metal oxide semiconductor memories—both read-write and read-only forms—reflect the technology's potential for cutting costs.

Read-only memories are taking on many applications, including control as well as pure storage functions; and automated mask-making simplifies the task of reworking a read-only memory.

Read-write memories are built of pure MOS or bipolar assemblies, or in hybrid arrays containing both types of circuit, and are available in a wide range of capacities and speeds.

Large dynamic MOS read-only memories are now available in sizes from 1,000 to 5,000 bits and at projected volume prices of a half-cent a bit. These low costs should give these arrays jobs as microprogram sequencers, hard-wired memory subroutines, tables of data, and alphanumeric character generators. They may also create interest in the relatively unexplored area of random control logic.

This form of logic includes distributed controls and common bidirectional data buses. The latter route data from any register in a group to any other, with appropriate input and output gating to control their paths rather than separate connections between every pair of registers.

Distributed controls represent a new departure from control techniques in conventional digital systems—a departure that is becoming feasible only with large-scale integrated circuits. The collection of logic gates in the system that control timing and data routing would be controlled in turn by signals that are additional inputs to the chips, where they're decoded internally. The technique requires a number of redundant gates, duplicated on different chips, but it sharply reduces the number of interconnections; in LSI, interconnections cost money, but gates don't.

Both of these techniques reduce the number of pins per package and give gate-to-pin ratios as high as 10 or 15 to 1—thus simplifying the problem of partitioning the system into modules.

Decentralized control

Read-only memories are ideal means for implementing random control logic, particularly in an LSI system. For example, a read-only memory acting as a sequencer can drive a bank of eight parallel memories, each containing 256 words of 64 bits each. The bank's output is thus a long word of 512 bits, each of which is an input to one or more standard logic blocks in a data-flow path.

Such decentralized control memories typically contain about 10 bits for each gate they replace, representing at least 90% of the total control logic and 40% to 50% of the system's components. The

*Now with Four-Phase Systems, Inc., Cupertino, Calif.

Read-write memories

Type	Bits	Access Time (μsec)	Full Cycle Time (μsec)	Power Per Bit (mw)	Power Per Chip (mw)	Pads	Chip Size (mils)	Probable Volume Price Per Bit (Cents)	
								1970	1971-72
Static p-channel	32	1	1	2	64	14	65x65	20-30	10-15
Static p-channel	64	2	2	2.5	160	16	90x90	15-25	7-12
Static p-channel	128	3	3	3	470	17	125x125	—	10-15
*MOS/bipolar drive & sense	64	0.2-0.3	0.2-0.3	1	32	24	70x70	8-10	3-5
*MOS/bipolar drive & sense	128	0.2-0.4	0.2-0.4	1	64	32	90x90	8-10	3-5
*MOS/bipolar drive & sense	256	0.2-0.5	0.2-0.5	1	128	40	120x120	8-10	3-5
*MOS/bipolar drive & sense	512	0.3-0.6	0.3-0.6	1	256	56	170x170	8-10	3-5
4φ dynamic	256	1	2	0.2	50	20	95x95	4-5	3-4
4φ dynamic	512	1	2	0.15	80	22	125x125	5-7	2-3
4φ dynamic	1,024	1.5	3	0.1	100	24	150x150	—	2.5-3.5

*Hybrid subassembly

remaining control logic is combined in an array of conventional logic gates—the same kind as those used in the data flow path.

This approach to random control has three benefits. First, at a half-cent per bit for the memory and 10 bits per gate replaced, the cost is 5 cents per effective control gate, compared to 10 to 20 cents per bipolar logic gate.

Second, in a system designed around a read-only memory, a 2,000-bit memory can replace a 200-gate LSI array with many fewer interconnections, greatly reducing hardware and assembly costs.

And third, meeting customer demands involves merely specifying the contents of a read-only memory—an easy job with small risk of error, simple documentation and testing, and no rework. Turnaround on an order for such a circuit can be as little as six weeks, compared to several months for a complete custom circuit.

Read-only memories as random control devices have their disadvantages, too, of course. The biggest of these is the fact that errors can't be corrected by the addition of wire jumpers, or the clipping of something out; a whole new mask has to be made. Consequently, the wise course is to simulate the system's operation on a computer before the mask is made, or to first build the memory out of discrete diodes and to then convert to an MOS read-only memory after debugging. Even with this precaution, occasional reworking is inevitable.

To minimize the reworking, most MOS manufacturers either have a fully automated mask-generating system or are planning to install one. When such a system is available, the customer supplies the data that the memory is to contain on punched cards or on a Fortran coding form that the manufacturer converts to punched cards. These cards are then fed into a computer that cuts the working

mask on a plotting table and draws a copy on Mylar. This copy is numbered for documentation and checking purposes because it's very difficult to verify a pattern on a working mask directly. The computer also prints the data in tabular form, prints coding errors if the input is in Fortran, and generates paper tapes for automatic LSI testers.

These computer-controlled systems generate masks rather quickly at very low cost. They keep initial memory development costs as low as $500 on small-quantity orders and permit the customer to receive his complete shipment only a few weeks after placing his order. They also very nearly eliminate masking errors and circuit reworks.

Since read-only memory wafers are essentially identical, they can be mass-produced and stockpiled in readiness for the gate mask and tester code pattern that adapt them to a customer's requirements. Using this approach, the manufacturing lines can produce a single high-volume item with standard packages, test fixtures, and other accessories at very low costs.

Static and dynamic

MOS read-only memories come in static and dynamic forms. Static memories read out and hold indefinitely the word addressed by the input without clocks or strobe pulses; their projected costs during the next few years, with the high-volume techniques described above, are about 1 cent per bit. Dynamic memories have outputs that must be continuously restored at some minimum clock rate, and it's their costs that are expected to drop to about a half-cent per bit.

In a static memory, the address decoder and the memory matrix itself must be made of NAND/NOR gates with large fan-ins and resistances. The matrix as a whole looks like a large capacitance when

Read-only memories

Type	Bits	Access Time (μsec)	Power Per Bit (μw)	Chip Size (mils)	Pads	Words x Bits	Probable Volume Price Per Bit (Cents)	
							1970	1971-72
Static	256	2-3	250	75x75	16	64x4	5-7	2.5-3.5
Static	1,024	3-4	120	90x90	20	128x8	1.5-2.3	0.8-1.3
Static	2,048	8-10	80	125x125	22	256x8	—	1-1.5
4φ dynamic	2,048	0.7-1	50	90x90	24	Variable	0.5-1	0.3-0.5
4φ dynamic	4,096	1	20	125x125	24	512x8	1-2	0.3-0.5

viewed from the input. Charging the capacitor through the resistance takes time, so that access is gained to a static memory in 3 to 4 microseconds. These arrays also dissipate something like 150 microwatts of power per bit.

At the present state of the art, a 1,024-bit static memory can be fabricated at lowest cost on a chip 90 mils square cut from a 2-inch wafer. A memory with twice the number of bits on a somewhat larger chip is feasible, but its greater parasitic time constant would slow its access time to about 10 μsec. Furthermore, a 90-mil-square chip gives the maximum yields per bit under present production-line conditions. A memory twice as large could be built on a chip 120 to 130 mils square, but this size isn't expected to be economical until the early 1970's.

Dynamic read-only memories typically provide twice the bit density, five to 10 times the speed, and a quarter the power consumption of static memories. The 90-mil chip can hold 2,048 bits; again, a larger chip with more bits is feasible, but it will cost slightly more per bit. In applications where pin count, size, and power dissipation are critical, however, the extra cost is justified.

Storing and fetching

Read-write MOS memories come in three major forms: complete assemblies of p-channel MOS devices, p-channel storage cells addressed by bipolar decoders and containing bipolar sense amplifiers, and complementary systems using both p-channel and n-channel devices. And they come in three performance levels: high-speed scratchpad memories of a few bits with access times of a few nanoseconds; medium-speed, medium-capacity memories; and rather slow bulk-storage units.

The applications of high-speed scratchpads, the oldest form of semiconductor memory, generally justify costs of a dollar a bit. Bipolar integrated circuits dominate this area at present, though, and probably will continue to do so.

Medium-performance memories are most practical at today's state of the MOS art. In the range of 32 to 256 bytes (256 to 2,048 bits), bipolar circuits are prohibitively expensive and magnetic memories are inefficient. Typical MOS costs of 25 to 50 cents a bit are therefore justifiable.

Fairchild Semiconductor recently announced a static p-channel read-write memory with 64 bits on a chip 90 mils square. Each bit is accessible in 2 μsec and dissipates 2 milliwatts. This unit is priced at 25 cents a bit in large quantities.

The third level—bulk storage—is the most attractive for solid state technology in terms of potential profit, but it's also the most difficult to attain because of the entrenched position of ferrite cores and other competitive technologies. The most common approach in this class is an array of MOS flip-flops driven by bipolar decoders and sensed with bipolar sense amplifiers. However, the bipolar circuits dissipate considerable power, and the MOS chips require a large number of leads because they must be on separate chips within a hybrid package.

One solution to these problems lies in the use of a quasi-static four-phase circuit with dynamic decoding on the chip. This circuit requires a four-phase clock and continuously circulates data bit for bit within itself. To the outside world, though, the memory as a whole looks like a d-c circuit—hence the designation quasi-static. The cell itself occupies only about a third the area of a static flip-flop, but the chip area is about two-thirds that of a static memory with an equivalent number of bits because of the space taken up by the decoding circuits. This size reduction, together with the eliminated bipolar circuits, halves the cost—but at another price.

That price is in performance. A dynamic read-write memory is limited to a 1-megahertz clock rate, corresponding to a 1-μsec access time; its full cycle time is just twice its access time because the data has to be regenerated after being read out. Nevertheless, just such a memory, holding 256 bits, dissipating 0.2 milliwatts per bit, and containing all decoding read-write controls and two bidirectional input-output buses, is now available. Its price for delivery this year is about 7 to 10 cents per bit, but this is expected to drop to about 4 or 5 cents in 1970. The MOS-bipolar system's cost is two or three times as much.

These figures, along with those quoted for speed, may seem conservative when compared with some recent optimistic forecasts. However, they will appear on data sheets in the foreseeable future and are therefore quite realistic. ■ ▮

Main memory. The 1,024-bit MOS chip described in the following article is the building block of this one-card memory, which contains 1,024 words of 24 bits each with an access time of 1 microsecond, and all peripheral circuits.

Random-access MOS memory packs more bits to the chip

Lee Boysel, Wallace Chan and *Jack Faith* of Four-Phase Systems eliminated the separate feedback for each bit in the design of a 1,024-bit memory; within three years, the cost per bit could be as low as a fraction of a cent

● To manufacturers of semiconductor memories, the name of the game is putting more and more memory capacity on a single silicon chip. Ground rules usually call for more components for more capacity. But now, what may be the most compact memory array yet produced in quantity—a 1,024-bit random-access memory that fits, with decoding circuitry, on a 150-mil-square chip—achieves its greater capacity without a substantial increase in circuitry. The trick is elimination of separate feedback stages for each bit.

The metal oxide semiconductor memory is based on a modified dynamic memory cell whose stored information must be periodically refreshed. Generally, this is accomplished, as in a dynamic shift register, with a separate charge-refreshing feedback stage for each bit. But in Four-Phase Systems' new design, separate feedback stages are eliminated because a single feedback stage is shared among many bits. The result: a very dense array that occupies 20% less chip area than even a conventional 1,024-bit dynamic shift register, and with four times the random access capacity of monolithic semiconductor arrays now on the market.

The 4,500 active components on the memory chip, which will be available in a low-cost computer system, are organized into 1,024 1-bit words in a 32-by-32 word array. Access time is 1 microsecond (full cycle time is 2 microseconds) and the chip dissipates about 200 milli-watts. Within three years, the cost per bit will approach a few tenths of a cent, about an order-of-magnitude improvement over the cost of large-scale random access core memories available now. Thus far, large-scale integration of MOS arrays has been too costly for anything but limited scratch-pad applications.[1]

One of the common MOS arrays uses a familiar reset-set, or RS, flip-flop in its memory cell, as shown below. This basic cell has not changed in the five years since it was developed,[2] though new decoding schemes have been developed for moving data.[3,4]

The resistor-like symbol in this and subsequent schematics represents an MOS transistor which functions as a gated impedance. Its impedance is relatively high—100 kilohms, against 20 kilohms in the usual four-phase MOS transistor—and it is switched on and off by its gate connection. The high impedance is obtained by laying out the transistor on the silicon chip with a very long, but quite narrow, channel. The long channel takes up much more space on the chip than those of transistors used simply for logic functions.

In the RS flip-flop, data is stored statically in a cross coupled pair of NOR gates using transistors with both high and low impedance. With MOS technology, the low impedance transistors occupy a large area because conductance is proportional to the area—and hence the width—of the conducting channel between the

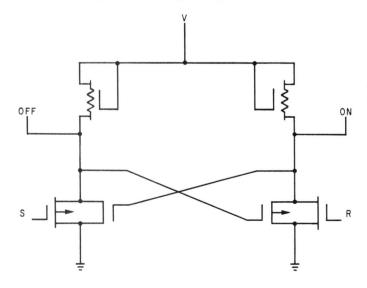

Old standby. Conventional reset-set MOS flip-flop which stores data statically takes up too much area and dissipates too much power, limiting the number of units that can be put on a single chip. The resistor-like symbol represents an MOS transistor which functions as a gated impedance.

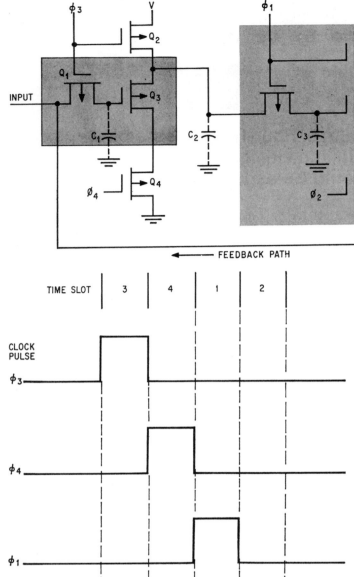

TIME SLOT	3	4	1	2

CLOCK
PULSE

ϕ_3

ϕ_4

ϕ_1

ϕ_2

FEEDBACK PATH

$C_2, C_4 \gg C_1, C_3$

Dynamic standard. Feeding back one bit of a dynamic MOS shift-register cell yields a dynamic memory cell. Data held on capacitor C_1 (and redundant data on C_3) is refreshed by charge from the large output capacitors C_2 and C_4. The four clock pulses occur during a single memory cycle. Two gray shadings distinguish the basic storage unit (left) from the feedback circuit (right) that refreshes the charge on the data-holding capacitor, C_1.

source and drain. This type of cell also dissipates a lot of power and requires high-voltage and high-current line drivers to get data in and out in a typical coincident-current memory scheme. These factors, combined with the requirement for external decoding, drive, and sense circuits, appear to limit at 256 the number of bits on a chip, and the cost from going much below 2 to 3 cents per bit.

To break this price barrier, Four-Phase Systems' new design approach is based on the dynamic storage scheme found in a conventional MOS shift-register cell, shown at the left with the four-phase clocking waveform needed for operation. In a dynamic cell data, stored in the form of a charge on a parasitic capacitor, must be periodically refreshed because it tends to leak off. But the big advantage is offered by relatively high transistor impedances so the area occupied by each transistor is small.

(In this and in the figures to follow, capacitors drawn with dashed lines are parasitic. Capacitors drawn with solid lines, although also technically parasitic, have been purposely augmented to increase their value by enlarging the p+ region of the silicon in their vicinity.)

The operation of this shift register cell, which actually consists of two inverter stages, starts with the precharging during the first phase of the four-phase clock cycle of capacitors C_1 and C_2. These capacitors are discharged later in the cycle, but the discharge is con-

Reading and writing. A row-address decoder selects the row in the memory that's to be read out. This read-row signal also triggers a delayed write row circuit that rewrites the readout data, restoring the voltage level of the signal on the storage capacitor.

Sharing the stage. The redundant stage of the dynamic shift register memory element is shared among more than one data-holding capacitor in Four-Phase Systems' design. The feedback stages refresh the charge levels on capacitor C_0, C_1, C_2, and C_3, each storing one information bit within a memory cell containing three active elements. Five gray shadings identify storage and feedback circuits as in the dynamic cell shown on page 94.

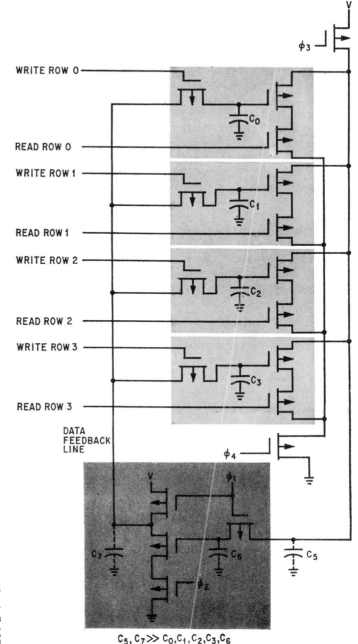

$C_5, C_7 \gg C_0, C_1, C_2, C_3, C_6$

ditional—whether they are discharged depends upon the data stored in the memory cell.

The precharging occurs during the first clock pulse, ϕ_3. Transistor Q_1 is turned on and capacitor C_1 is charged to the input signal voltage level—either a logic 1 or a 0. Simultaneously, Q_2 is turned on and C_2, the output signal-holding capacitor of the first inverter stage, is charged to the supply voltage level, V.

Conditional discharging occurs next. When clock pulse ϕ_3 goes to 0, pulse ϕ_4 comes up, turning on Q_4. If the charge on C_1 is at the high, logic-1 level, Q_3 turns on and C_2 discharges to ground through Q_3 and Q_4. But if the input and the charge on C_1 had been a logic 0, capacitor C_2 would not have discharged; a charge equivalent to a logic 1 would have remained.

Passing the signal on C_2 through the other half of the cell reinverts it, restoring the original signal level at the cell's output. And tying the output back to the input, as shown by the solid feedback line in the schematic shown on page 94, converts this one-bit shift register into a binary memory element—a dynamic flip-flop that stores one bit of information.

However, there's a basic information redundancy in this flip-flop cell—the basic information bit held on C_1 is also held on C_3, although in complement form. C_3 and the second half of the flip-flop bit keep restoring or refreshing the charge on C_1, which otherwise would

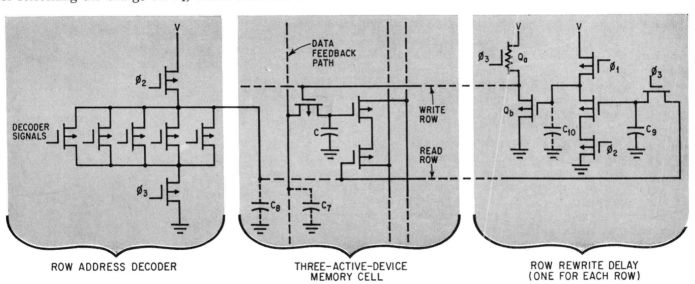

ROW ADDRESS DECODER

THREE–ACTIVE–DEVICE MEMORY CELL

ROW REWRITE DELAY (ONE FOR EACH ROW)

leak off within a few milliseconds. For shift registers and other dynamic circuits on the market today, the maximum charge-holding time is about 100 μsec. This means the minimum clock frequency for restoring data must be 10 kilohertz.

To reduce this information redundancy, Four-Phase Systems shared a common feedback, or charge-restoring, stage among many shift-register bits as shown at the right of page 95. Each memory cell contains three active devices and one data-holding capacitor. In this cell, the second, or redundant, stage of the conventional shift-register flip-flop has been replaced by the single feedback stage shown at the bottom of the schematic. This stage refreshes each of the four data-holding capacitors, C_0, C_1, C_2, and C_3 in sequence under control of the read row gates, which have been added to the basic dynamic cell. Only four memory cells are shown for illustrative purposes. However, in the actual memory, a single feedback stage refreshes a column of 32 cells.

A memory sequence begins when the fourth clock pulse, ϕ_4, comes up. Read row 0 also is high at the same time, so that the signal on C_0 conditionally discharges C_5 previously charged to the supply voltage during ϕ_3.

The charge on C_5 is transferred to C_6 during ϕ_1 and then is inverted and placed on the data feedback-return line capacitor, C_7, during the ϕ_2 pulse. The write row 0 line rises, and during the ϕ_3 pulse the charge on C_7 is transferred to C_0, restoring its original level.

The process repeats itself during the next sequence of four clock pulses. But the read row 1 line is activated during ϕ_4, and C_5 is conditionally discharged by the data-storing capacitor, C_1. This sequence, restoring the last bit interrogated and reading out the next sequential bit, is repeated continually. Thus, four bits of information can be stored with only 18 transistors—three for each cell, five in the feedback stage, and one to charge C_5 at ϕ_3—rather than the 32 required if each bit were stored in a single shift-register cell.

The actual circuit mechanism that generates signals on the read row and write row lines is shown at the bottom of page 95. Each of the 32 rows is addressed through a standard decoder network consisting, at each row line, of five transistors in parallel. Each transistor is connected to one address bit or its complement.

When the ϕ_2 pulse is present, the output of the parasitic capacitance, C_8, at the output of the decoder network[5] is precharged to the supply voltage. This precharge is retained on the read row line until ϕ_3, when the five-bit address supplied to the decoder discharges C_8 on 31 of the 32 lines through one or more of the five parallel transistors connected between each read row and ground. On the remaining row, the address keeps all five transistors off. Capacitor C_8 on this row retains its charge, and the corresponding read row stays high. During the next clock pulse, ϕ_4, the charge enables the capacitors in each of the memory storage cells to discharge conditionally.

Also during ϕ_3, the state of the one read row that's high is transferred to C_9 in the restore-delay circuit, which stores it long enough to bring up the one corresponding write row line 1 μsec later during the next cycle. The read row actually is inverted twice, by precharging C_{10} at ϕ_1 and then conditionally discharging it at ϕ_2. At the next ϕ_3 pulse, if C_{10} were discharged,

Write the first time. To change the contents of the memory, new data is placed on the data feedback path through this feedback circuit, which replaces the feedback stage shown at the right of page 95.

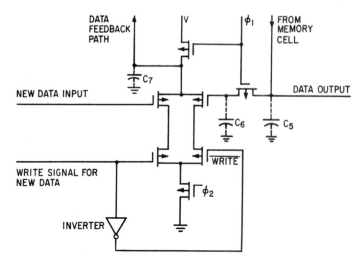

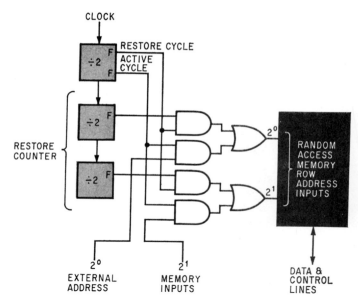

Reading and restoring. Charges on the data-holding capacitors are restored periodically by switching the memory's row inputs to a binary refresh counter. Restore cycles are alternated with command cycles which come to the random-access memory from the computer.

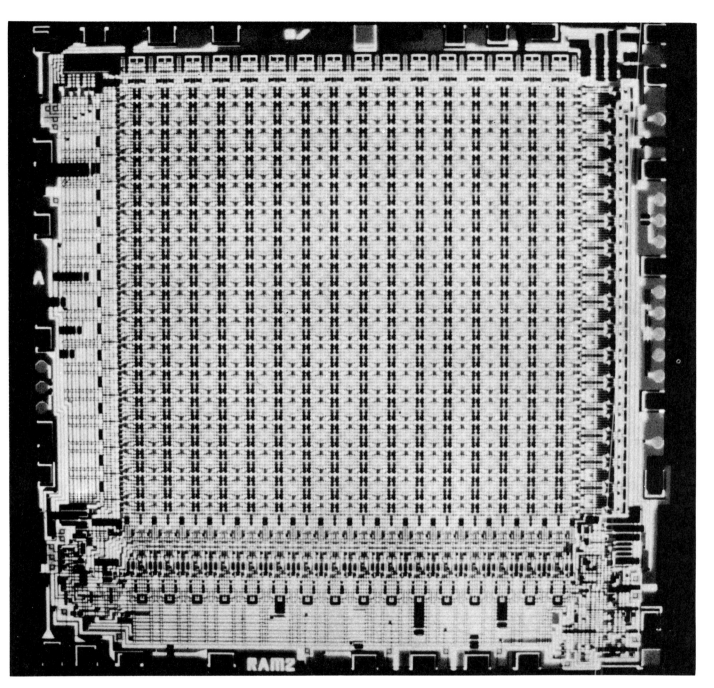

Full chip. Some 4,500 devices squeezed into a 150-by-150-mil-square silicon chip form a complete 1,024, 1-bit-word, four-phase random-access memory. Included on the chip are full binary decoding, chip selection gates, and read-write circuits. 3,072 8-bit-bytes of memory fit on a single 8-by-11-inch printed circuit card (see page 92) that includes clock generation and driver circuitry and memory-buffer registers. At a 1-megahertz clock rate, the card dissipates only about 7 watts of power, low enough so that the memory can be driven by a battery in the event of a power failure. Entire computer for which the memory is designed will dissipate only 10 to 15 watts.

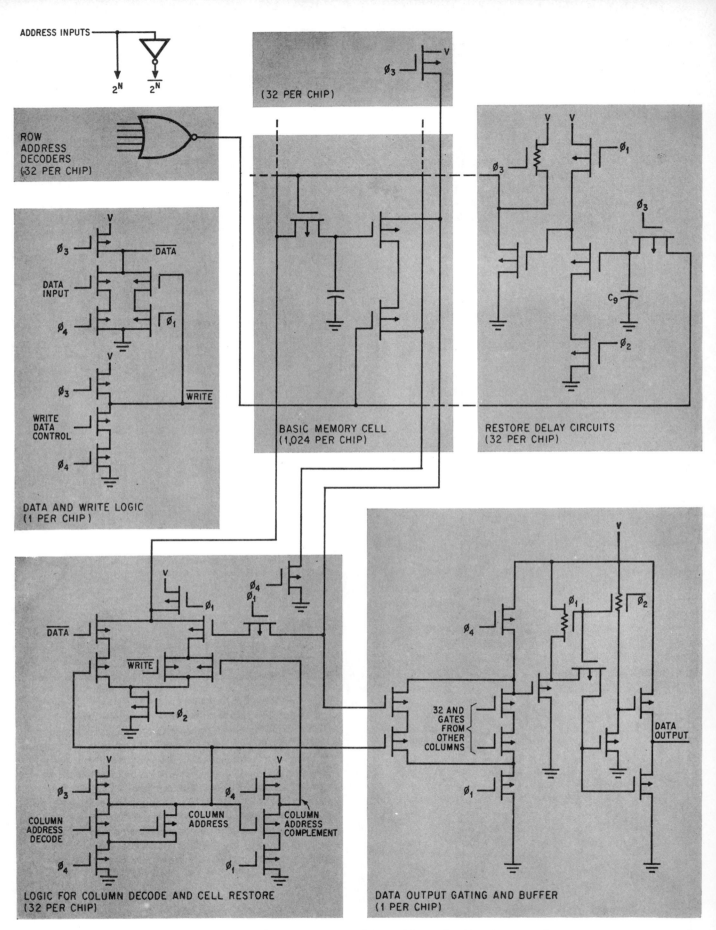

One-chip design. The memory contains all of the circuits required for a 32-row by 32-column random-access memory on a single silicon chip—including one write data input logic stage, one output buffer, and 64 row- and column-selection gates.

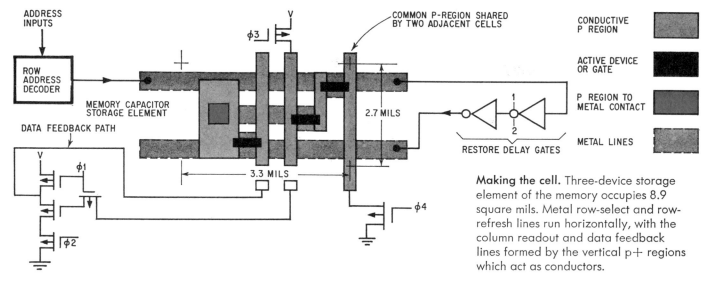

ADDRESS INPUTS

ROW ADDRESS DECODER

V
φ3

COMMON P-REGION SHARED BY TWO ADJACENT CELLS

MEMORY CAPACITOR STORAGE ELEMENT

DATA FEEDBACK PATH

V
φ1
φ2

3.3 MILS

2.7 MILS

φ4

RESTORE DELAY GATES

CONDUCTIVE P REGION

ACTIVE DEVICE OR GATE

P REGION TO METAL CONTACT

METAL LINES

Making the cell. Three-device storage element of the memory occupies 8.9 square mils. Metal row-select and row-refresh lines run horizontally, with the column readout and data feedback lines formed by the vertical p+ regions which act as conductors.

the write row line would rise to restore the charge in the memory cell. If C_{10} were not discharged the write row line would stay down. The line's level is controlled by the 30:1 ratio of impedances Q_a to Q_b, which form a voltage divider.

This voltage-divider or ratio circuitry depends on the ratio of two MOS impedances; it's an old form of MOS logic. It takes up more room than four-phase logic because the different impedances are obtained by varying the chip area occupied by the individual transistors. However, the ratio circuitry is needed to control the write row lines in spite of the extra space it occupies. This is because the write row lines cannot be controlled by precharging, as are the read row lines, during the four-phase clock times. The memory system would need either extra clock phases, or additional logic to insure that precharging the write rows would not interfere with other aspects of the memory's operation. The ratio logic approach actually is the simplest way to control the write row line. And there are so few of the circuits on the chip—32 out of thousands—that the extra space required is negligible.

New data may be written into the memory merely by putting it on the feedback path using the circuit shown at the top of page 96. With this circuit, the memory could perform all of the functions of a true random access memory. The integrity of the stored data

levels must be assured by interrogating and then refreshing each row at least once every 100 μsec.

To make certain the data will be restored within the allotted 100 μsec each active random-access cycle consisting of the four clock pulses ϕ_1 thru ϕ_4 is followed by a row-restore cycle. Over a long period, data is available from the memory only half the time. It's similar to the situation in a destructive readout core memory, where full cycle time is twice as long as access time—the dead time is needed to rewrite the data that was held in the core location.

In the Four-Phase MOS memory, this dead time—during which the next four clock pulses occur—is used to refresh the data somewhere in the memory. Successive rows are refreshed in successive restore cycles. And these are alternated with random-access cycles.

The addresses of the rows to be refreshed are generated by alternately switching the memory's row inputs between a binary restore counter and the actual address input coming from the computer, as shown on page 112.

The entire memory contains 32 vertical columns, with 32 memory cells in each column. Every column is self-contained and automatically restores its own bits. An entire horizontal row of 32 cells is refreshed during every refresh cycle. This also applies to multiple-chip configurations where chip-select lines are used. Write data input logic and the output buffer appear only once on the chip. There are 32 row address decoder gates, 32 column decoders and 32 restore-delay circuits. Since only rows are refreshed, one five-stage binary counter connected to the row address is all that is needed to cycle through the rows, irrespective of the number of words in the memory.

The memory cell is laid out with the metal row lines running left to right and the p regions, which act like another conductor strip, running up and down, as shown above. Cell size is about 9 square mils, compared to 20 to 30 square mils for a shift register bit. ●

References

1. Lee Boysel, "Cutting system cost with MOS," Electronics, Jan. 20, 1969, p. 105
2. Jack Schmidt, "Integrated MOS Transistor Random Access Memory," Solid State Design, January 1965, p. 21.
3. Jack Schmidt, T. Asai, and J. H. Freidrich, "Hybrid LSI Memory," IEEE Computer. Convention, Los Angeles, June 1968.
4. Lee Boysel and Joe Murphy, "100-Nanosecond Memory: 4φ Techniques Used in High Speed Logic," EDN, June 1968.
5. Lee Boysel, "Memory on a chip: A step toward LSI," Electronics, Feb. 6, 1967, p. 92.

Chapter 4
Other semiconductor

Semiconductor arrays get bigger and denser

By Ury Priel

Signetics Corp., Sunnyvale, Calif.

Memory circuits are being offered as standard products by almost all semiconductor manufacturers. These products now cover a wide range of speed, both read-write and read-only functions, serial and random-access operations, and such special designs as content-addressable organizations. Furthermore, the capacity per chip is steadily rising as both chip size and element density increase.

Custom-designed storages are still much in demand, but they no longer dominate the market for semiconductor memories. The shift to volume production of standard memories stems from the built-in affinity of semiconductor technology for batch fabrication, which, in turn, is well suited to turning out arrays of identical cells that are characteristic of all memories.

Metal oxide semiconductor and bipolar circuits will soon be fabricated on chips measuring 150 mils a side or more—against the now standard sizes of under 100 mils square. MOS circuits are decreasing in price and increasing in density almost daily, while bipolars are benefitting from better yields and better circuit design.

As noted in the article in this volume beginning on pg. 63, bipolar circuits' major advantage over MOS in memory applications is speed. Because their elements cannot be as closely packed as those of MOS circuits, bipolars will continue to be used in small arrays requiring high speed. Although the large-memory field today is monopolized by MOS, recent significant developments in the bipolar memory technology indicates a close battle.

Computer designers have come to rely heavily on read-only memories as sequence controllers, code converters, character generators, look-up tables, and even program storages in some cases. A read-only memory cell is an inherently simple device for which MOS technology is ideally suited—provided the cycle time isn't less than 100 nanoseconds. Built-in capacitance precludes the operation of individual devices at higher speeds.

American Micro-systems Inc. and the General Instrument Corp. have both developed a read-only memory with 2,048 bits on a chip measuring 84 by 106 mils. The memory dissipates 130 milli-watts when operating at 2 megahertz (500-nanosecond cycle), and its outputs and inputs can be connected directly to transistor-transistor, diode-transistor, or MOS logic circuits.

Philco-Ford Corp., Texas Instruments, and the Fairchild Semiconductor division have each brought out a 1,024-bit read-only memory, and other manufacturers are expected to join the club.

For higher speeds, bipolar circuits must be used, but only with increases in size, cost and power dissipation. Radiation, Inc., offers a 100-bit read-only memory in the form of a 10-by-10 diode matrix, and Motorola Inc. is working on a 128-bit memory. The Signetics Corp. is developing a 256-bit read-only memory that works with DTL or TTL and can be programed either at the factory or by the user.

Signetics is using a fusing link approach; the customer defines the data stored in the memory by melting away certain metal interconnections, or links, corresponding to stored 0's. In this new organization, access to each link can be gained with fewer external connections than earlier fusing link designs required.

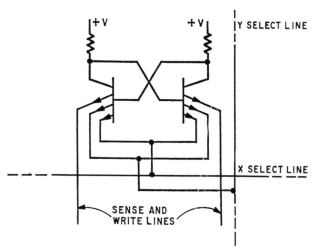

Standard. Originally a custom design, this bipolar circuit is now being used routinely by several manufacturers.

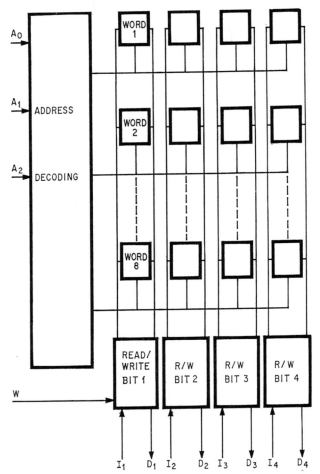

Scratchpad. This 32-bit memory is one application of the circuit shown schematically on page 103.

TI is working on a 512-bit bipolar read-only memory having a 30-nsec delay from the word driver input to the external detector output; the interconnections are made with a computer-controlled discretionary-wiring technique, and, in general, no two chips are wired alike. The aim here is to utilize all the good cells on a large chip and none of the bad ones. This approach, which is unique to TI, can be applied to any kind of large chip, but it offers a special advantage in read-only memories. Cells defective because they're open-circuited can often be included in the wiring as 0's, while short-circuited cells can be included as 1's. The approach thus has the potential to improve yields.

Long shift registers can be used as serial memories in much the same way as acoustic delay lines or even magnetic drums are used. [An article comparing the virtues of shift registers and delay lines as serial memories appears on page 163 in this volume. To get a sufficiently long delay time, the shift register must contain dozens or hundreds of bits, and only MOS technology provides the necessary packing density on a chip of reasonable size. Bipolar shift registers are being manufactured, but their bit capacities are low and their applications

lie in processing and control rather than in the memory field.

Of the MOS shift registers now being marketed for memory applications, American Micro-systems is offering three different units. One has three 66-bit registers on a single chip—with the three externally connected to one another if desired—another has two 40-bit registers, and the third has a pair of multiplexed 213-bit registers.

Philco-Ford has a 256-bit dynamic shift register from which the stored data disappears if the shifting action stops. And the National Semiconductor Corp. offers a dual 100-bit dynamic shift register and dual 32-bit and 64-bit static registers.

But none of these wholly MOS memories work to advantage with high-speed logic circuits. To offset the technology's speed limitations while realizing its savings in space and cost, MOS must be combined with bipolar, either by putting both types of circuit on one large substrate or by mounting the two circuits on separate chips in a hybrid package. This approach is being investigated by Amperex, the Solid State Scientific Corp., and Signetics, and Siliconix has already marketed a monolithic MOS-bipolar analog switch, which proves the feasibility of this approach.

Random happenings

Semiconductor technology—both MOS and bipolar—holds out as much promise in the field of random-acccess memories as in the read-only types. Up to now, most of the emphasis in this area has been on scratchpad memories—small, fast units that act as buffers between a processor and a large random-access memory.

MOS scratchpads now on the market include a 32-bit memory from American Micro-systems, another of 32 bits from General Instruments, and a 64-bit unit with a 300-nsec access time from Philco-Ford. Motorola and TI are each developing 256-bit MOS random-access memories.

Bipolar scratchpads have generally been developed as custom circuits and later marketed as standard products. One example is a 16-bit memory using a coincident selection scheme and TTL circuits, shown on p.103. This unit is now available from the Transitron Corp., Sylvania, and Fairchild. And Motorola has successfully combined the TTL saturated cell with nonsaturating current-mode sense and write circuits in a 16-bit memory that's said to cycle in as little as 50 nsec and to dissipate only 250 milliwatts.

Fairchild has developed a 64-bit scratchpad element that has 16 four-bit words. The words are accessible in about 30 nsec, but the chip requires external decoding. Signetics has an eight-bit memory with address decoding on the same chip, and it is developing a similar 32-bit unit that will be integrated on a 100-by-100-mil chip, shown above. The individual cells are essentially the same as those on page 103, except there are three address lines instead of two. The three-bit address picks out one of eight four-bit words, and is decoded through the multiple-emitter structure at the cell; the box labeled "decoder" in the diagram is actually only a bank of inverters. The 32-bit memory's access time is about 20 nsec.

These developments point to the eventual development of larger bipolar memories that will rival MOS memories in terms of density and cost, but exceed them in terms of speed. These improvements will result both from circuit innovations and from adaptation to the "terrain" of an IC.

Today's largest MOS circuits are shift registers holding a couple of thousands bits on a chip 100 mils square; the largest bipolar circuits are on chips of a similar size but are limited to about 100 bits—bits, however, that are randomly accessible. Thus, MOS density is now about 20 times that of bipolar circuits, but carries a penalty in the form of serial versus random access.

By the end of 1970, it should be economical to put a thousand or more bits on chips 150 or 200 mils square, and gain access to these bits in as little as 20 nanoseconds through bipolar circuits.

One of the major merits of integrated circuits is the easy implementation of combinations of memory and logic—in content-addressable, or associative, memories, for example. In an associative organization, the memory is presented with a bit pattern, or key, that may or may not be as long as the words in the memory. The entire array is searched in parallel, and those words whose bits match those in the key are taken out.

These memories can be used for list processing, information retrieval, language translation, and air traffic control. They will also offer a hardware solution to complex software problems when their costs are reduced.

Signetics is developing the TTL associative memory shown at right. It contains four two-bit words on a 100-by-100-mil chip, and it can get at any of these words in 20 nsec. It dissipates 420 milliwatts.

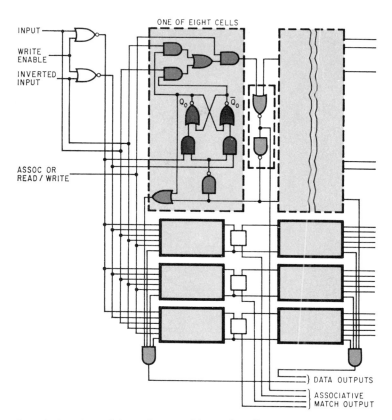

Associative. Any of these four two-bit words, all on a chip 100 mils square, is content-accessible in 25 nsec.

Future developments will result in more complex but lower-cost semiconductor devices. These developments include improvements in the isolation between circuits on a chip, the use of complementary transistors on a single substrate in both bipolar and MOS technologies, increases in yield, and greater reliance on computers in design. ■ ■

Update

Very many things have changed in the semiconductor memory industry since my original survey article was published. Many of the products mentioned have become obsolete or have been replaced by others.

For example, Electronic Arrays, Inc. now has a 4,096-bit dynamic read-only memory and recently announced a 5,120-bit static unit. Hughes Aircraft Corp. is developing ion-implanted arrays that are more quickly accessed than older forms. And bipolar technology is making significant inroads in the read-only memory market; ROMs will be available with at least 2,048 and possibly 4,096 bits on a single chip. Already they have access times of 50 nanoseconds and dissipate only 0.3 milliwatts per bit—characteristics that are certain to improve even more as time goes by.

National Semiconductor and Intel today have the largest variety of long MOS shift registers; American Micro-Systems, Texas Instruments, and Mostek also have versions. Shift registers as long as 1,000 bits have been developed by Intel and by Signetics. Other suppliers of shift registers include General Instrument Corp., Amelco, Electronic Arrays, Philco-Ford and Intersil Corp.

Static MOS random-access memories are available or under development by Intel, Motorola, Fairchild, and National Semiconductor. Dynamic memories are more cumbersome to use, but are packed more densely; Intel, Advanced Memory Systems, Mostek, and Intersil, among others, make 1,024-bit versions.

—Ury Priel
National Semiconductor Corp.

Semiconductor memories at a glance: What's here now, what's on the way

Claims and counterclaims are put in perspective to help you choose the best kind of semiconductor memory for your specific application

By Stephen Wm. Fields

Electronics staff

Proliferation is the word for semiconductor memories. Every integrated circuit manufacturer, it seems, wants to get into the act; lured by the prospect of a vast computer-age market, they announce new memory IC's almost daily. To complicate the situation, as the large companies like Texas Instruments, Motorola, and Fairchild have been developing memory product lines, many of their engineers and marketing people have seen their chance to grab a piece of the action. They've struck out on their own, establishing small companies to produce semiconductor memories exclusively.

So today there are no less than 18 companies making or planning to make some form of semiconductor memory. This active and competitive situation has led to an unending stream of claims and counterclaims of the biggest or fastest or most inexpensive memory.

The equipment or system designer who will use these products is understandably in a state of confusion. Should he go with metal oxide semiconductor bipolar technology, multichip or completely monolithic? When will these devices be available in quantity? What will access time and cost per bit be at the time the system is ready for production?

In spite of the confusion, it's possible to put things in order and draw some conclusions. Most semiconductor memory houses will agree on these points:
▶ An acceptable semiconductor re-

placement for the large mainframe computer core memory hasn't yet arrived, and won't until 1971 at the earliest. Although devices that could be used in mainframes do exist, they are not available in volume and at a price where they would become a serious contender for the mass memory market.
▶ Nevertheless, semiconductor memories are already replacing cores in smaller computers—those with 10,000-bit capacity or less—and in peripheral equipment.
▶ Bipolar circuits will be used when access time of 100 nanoseconds or less is needed. MOS circuits will be used for access time of 300 nsec or more. The best device for the middle range is anyone's guess.

Summing up the view of most manufacturers, Jerry Moffitt, manager of semiconductor memory programs at Texas Instruments, doesn't look for much large equipment to be introduced this year or next with semiconductor memories; there will be only "a few" systems in 1971 with semiconductor random-access mainframe memories. He doesn't expect any big influx until 1974 or 1975 "because the bulk of the market is at 1 to 2 microseconds. This is the speed at which cores go best—they're not pushing the state of the art. We have to offer something besides technology for people to change."

On the other hand, the overall feeling in the industry is that semi-

What's new

This article, describing the state of the semiconductor memory art, originally appeared in Electronics' Probing the News section. Most of the predictions it contains came to pass during the preparation of this volume; but some of them didn't. Motorola, for example, discontinued the 8,192-bit module described briefly here; on the other hand, SEMI began shipping its memory systems in July, not August, 1970. SEMI has decided to concentrate on bipolar circuits for now; its 256-bit MOS storage chip, mentioned on page 109, is "on the back burner," according to Don Winstead. Dave Conrad of Computer Microtechnology mentions his company's new 8,192-bit unit that is exactly like the 4,096-bit one mentioned in the story except that it is built with 512-bit chips instead of 256-bit chips. Advanced Memory Systems Inc. brought out its 4,096-bit memory card on schedule, but its 256-bit chip is still "in the works," says Jerry Larkin. But his fast bipolar registers, quoted at $1.50 to $2.00 per bit in the story, are down to 50¢ now and will be 20¢ by 1973.

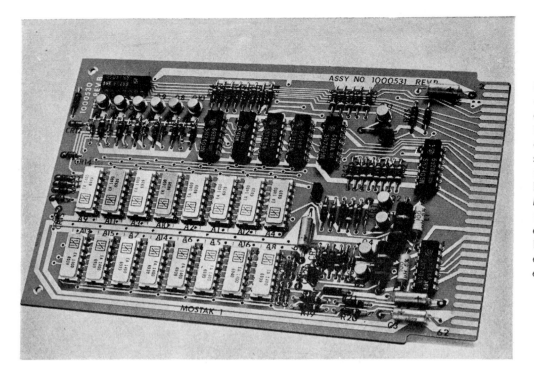

Subsystem. A popular approach to the semiconductor memory market is to manufacture a complete memory subsystem on a card, suitable for use as a scratchpad or buffer memory. The Mostak I random-access read-write memory, for example, manufactured by Electronic Arrays Inc., employs 16 MOS chips, each with 128 bit capacity.

conductor memories should soon, if they haven't already, start replacing cores in smaller systems, those that require 10,000 bits or less. Gordon Hoffman, who has responsibility for Mostek's applications and device characterization, is looking for semiconductor random-access memories in computer peripheral equipment in the next year. Hoffman includes terminals, data sets, and information retrieval systems requiring a small amount of memory—say 1,000 bits—in this category. The latter is a region where cores can't compete, Hoffman says, because a 1,000-bit core memory might cost $500 to $600, but a semiconductor RAM costs less. For example, the Intel Corp. is selling its model 1101 fully decoded 256-bit RAM with an access time of one μsec for $40 in unit quantities. Thus, a 1,024-bit semiconductor RAM can be bought today for $160, and in quantity the price drops to $94.

Semiconductor RAM's won't start making a dent as a core replacement in the minicomputer market until 1973, Hoffman predicts. However, the dissociation of bulk storage and mainframes of computers could hasten the onset of semiconductor RAM's. Although Hoffman hasn't yet seen any machines being designed this way, he expects the mainframes and bulk-storage units to be "spread around the machine,"

and this could trigger a faster introduction of semiconductor RAM's —first in the mainframes and then in the bulk-storage section.

Source of confusion. Much of the confusion that memory users face is due to the fact that, in general, semiconductor memories are available in three speed categories: high speed (10 to 60 nsec), medium speed (100 to 400 nsec) and slow speed (500 nsec to 2 μsec). And, because all of the semiconductor memory manufacturers don't agree on what is fast and what is slow, there is a gray area surrounding each category. Further complicating the problem is the packaging terminology. Memories can be bought as individually packaged chips or memory elements, as multichip modules, or as complete systems or cards.

There are three companies—at the present time—who are sticking to memory systems only. These are the Cogar Corp., Advanced Memory Systems Inc., and Semiconductor Electronic Memories Inc., (SEMI). For its first memory product, Advanced Memory Systems has staked out a narrow sector of the memory market: very high-speed memory cards.

AMS's ECL memory cards are probably the fastest units available, with an access time of 15 nsec. The cards contain two types of devices—a 16-bit bipolar ECL memory

element and a storage-support chip that contains the buffers and card and chip selection circuits. Four types of cards are available—a 32-word-by-eight-bit and a 32-word-by-nine-bit memory, each of which is either transistor-transistor logic or ECL compatible. According to Jerry Larkin, vice president of marketing at AMS, the market for these high-speed memories is not as a replacement for mainframe cores, but rather for replacement of scratchpad, small buffers, and discrete registers.

Complete and competitive. Presently, high-speed bipolar registers, says Larkin, cost about $1.50 to $2.00 per bit, not including the support circuits. AMS's units are complete and are competitive at about $2.00 per bit in quantities of 100, he says. Also included on the card are termination resistors and bypass capacitors. By the end of March, AMS expects to have a 4,096-bit memory card on the market. This will also be a high-speed ECL memory, but will use 64-bit chips instead of the 16-bit chips. Also in the works is a 256-bit chip for even larger systems.

Cogar is also sticking to memory systems, but, unlike AMS, is using multichip modules rather than cards to make up the system. Cogar's basic memory line will include a system for each of the three types of memory markets—

slow, medium, and high speed. The high-speed line will employ bipolar chips—to interface with ECL circuitry—and have an access time of 40 nsec. Each card will contain about 9,000 bits. William Taren, Cogar's marketing manager, says that sample cards will be available in April and expects to be able to deliver in quantity by July.

The medium-speed line also uses bipolar chips and interfaces with diode-transistor logic or TTL circuits, and up to 18,000 bits are available on a card. Access time is 125 nsec, and these too will be available in quantity by July. The slow speed, or "cost/performance" line as Taren prefers to call it, employs MOS chips, has an access time of 250 nsec, and interfaces with DTL or TTL circuits. With this system, up to 144,000 bits can be put on one card. Volume production for the MOS system won't begin until November. The price, including decoding circuits, but not the power supply, is 30 cents per bit for the high speed, 12 cents per bit for the medium speed, and 5 cents per bit for the cost-performance line.

Use two active modules

SEMI's approach is to use two active modules: a storage module with two bipolar 64-word by two-bit memory chips and a support module of one bipolar chip that contains the decoder, sense amplifiers, memory-address register, and eight current drivers. All memory systems, which SEMI will begin shipping in August, consist of different arrangements of these two types of modules on a printed circuit card. The systems will range in size from 1,000 to 9,000 bits and will have an access time of 200 nsec. Prices will range from about 20 cents per bit for a 128-bit-by-eight-word system to 10 cents per bit for a 1,024-by-nine unit.

SEMI's storage element is now bipolar; but a 256-bit MOS storage chip is in the works. According to Don Winstead, marketing vice-president, "The prime reason for going to MOS is to double the bit capacity and keep the chip size the same—so we can cut our costs." But, he stresses that bipolar is a known technology, and SEMI, being in a start-up situation, doesn't want to take many risks, so the

initial thrust will be in bipolar.

SEMI, like Cogar, is using a flip-chip bonding technique to attach the chips to a substrate, making up a module. The technique, called liquid-phase joining, is based on IBM's solid-logic technology. And, again like Cogar's, the assembly process is entirely automated.

Beam-lead bonding. Companies that make memory modules include Motorola and Computer Microtechnology Inc.; both employ beam-lead bonding as opposed to the system makers who use flip-chips. Motorola's memory is an 8,192-bit module employing 256-bit MOS storage arrays, ECL bipolar driver chips, and a laminated beam-lead interconnect scheme. The module consists of six packages; four contain eight each of the 256-bit memory chips, plus one bipolar array-selection circuit. One of the other packages contains the bipolar sense amplifier and the digit driver arrays, and the sixth package holds two chips that make up the bipolar decoding circuit. Access time is about 125 nsec.

The unit will be available about mid-year in evaluation quantities. Volume production is slated for late 1970 or early 1971. Roger Helmick, manager of digital IC planning at Motorola, projects a price of about 15 cents per bit in 1971, which, he believes, will make it competitive with cores in buffers and scratchpads. Further down the road, Helmick expects the price to drop close to 5 cents per bit in 1972 and close to 2 cents in 1974, prices that should compete with those of mainframe core memories.

Computer Microtechnology's module is a 4,096-bit unit on a ceramic substrate that is about 1.5 inches square and has an access time of 150 nsec. It incorporates 22 chips—four bipolar 1-out-of-8 decoders, three bipolar dual-sense amplifiers, and 16 MOS storage arrays of 256 bits with partial decoding. Sample quantities are available now, and the price is about 50 cents per bit. But, Dave Conrad, vice president of marketing at CMI, says that the price should drop to about 1.5 cents per bit by mid 1972. Conrad doesn't see high volume for his memory in mainframes until 1972 or 1973, although a market exists now in computer peripherals and instruments.

Motorola has introduced three memory elements to date. One is in the ECL family (MC1036, 1037), with a 17-nsec access time; the other is a TTL unit (MC4004, 4005) with an access time of 35 nsec. Both of these bipolar components are coincident-select 16-bit read-write devices. The third product is a 64-bit (16 by 4) MOS unit designated the MC1170, which includes all decoding and read/write circuitry on the chip. Motorola is also working on a 64-bit TTL memory component, estimated to be a few months away from production.

Helmick maintains that any or all of these smaller components are applicable to minicomputers and computer peripheral equipment, and could challenge cores in small systems because the price is in the 15-cent to 25-cent per bit range for buffers and scratchpads, essentially the same as core memory cost for similarly sized systems. In addition, Helmick points out, semiconductor memory speed is five times faster than cores and their readout is nondestructive vs. a destructive readout from cores.

Without decoding. To date, TI has introduced a 256-bit MOS RAM without decoding on the chip but with two-dimensional address—a product that has been on the market more than a year. Its sole TTL memory component is a 16-bit-by-one-word unit that has been available for about a year. There's also one memory component in the firm's ECL 2500 family—a four-word-by-two-bit device. For these one-chip-per-package components, semiconductor-memory manager Moffitt says TI can deliver possibly a couple of orders of 10,000 to 100,000 units per month. But, it will be 1971 before TI has a significant capacity in multichip packages. These will range in size from 4,000 to 8,000 bits.

For the future, Moffitt sees integration of bipolar and MOS components as the way to go rather than pursue these as individual technologies. TI's moves in this direction are not unlike Motorola's in that the firm is using MOS storage elements, bipolar drivers, and beam-lead interconnects. TI forms beam leads using an approach that is slightly altered from that of Bell Labs, but more conventional than the beam-lead laminate used in Motorola's 8,192-bit memory module.

Mostek has preliminary data sheets on seven products after being in business just about eight months. One of these is the MK4001P, a 256-bit-by-one-word MOS RAM without decoding, much like the TI chip. Mostek was scheduled to deliver its first parts in January or early February, and by the end of the year, Hoffman predicts the firm will be able to ship 100,000 parts per month. This is an aggregate figure for all lines.

Fairchild Semiconductor's announced devices include a 16-bit TTL RAM, a 64-bit TTL RAM, a 64-bit MOS device, and a 128-bit memory module that is made up of eight 16-bit chips bonded face down to a 1-inch-square ceramic substrate, and has an access time of 25 nsec. According to Fran Krch, marketing manager for standard MOS and memory products, other devices to be shortly introduced are a 256-bit MOS unit and the other is a 256-bit bipolar RAM that Fairchild has been supplying to Burroughs for Illiac 4. Called the 4100, it is organized as 256 by one and has an access time of 70 nsec. Pricing for the 4100, according to Krch, will be in the "10 cent-a-bit area in 1970; but, this should drop to below 5 cents as soon as volume production—around 100,000 units—allows."

Exotic isn't final word

Krch says that large, exotic chips are not necessarily the answer. The winner in the memory market will be "the guy who is building the big one at a high price, but who also has a smaller device that he can sell in volume to compete with cores—the most economical chip is one level down from the top." In the bipolar area, the top might be a 1,024-bit unit, and for MOS, it might be 2,048, Krch says, but it is still too early to tell.

Intel is another company that is playing it close. Its present products are a 64-bit bipolar RAM with an access time of 60 nsec, and a 256-bit MOS RAM with an access time of one nsec. Both units are priced at $40 in unit quantities. Intel will soon introduce a 256-bit bipolar unit that will have an access time of about 70 nsec and will be half the price per bit of the 64-bit unit. Also down the road

is a 1,024-bit MOS memory that will come in two versions; 1,024 by one with an access time of 150 nsec, and 512 by two with a 300 nsec time.

Against multichip. Robert Graham, Intel's marketing vice president, is predicting a cost of 1 cent per bit for the 1,024-bit MOS RAM by 1971. Graham doesn't favor the multichip approach. There is no cost advantage; he says it would be cheaper, for example, to put the 1,024-bit unit in a plastic package—"and this is not far away," he adds.

Raytheon, on the other hand, is counting on beam-lead multichips to produce large arrays. Presently, Raytheon has two bipolar random-access memory chips—a 16-bit and a 64-bit chip. Raytheon's scheme is to beam-lead 16 memory chips to a ceramic substrate. Thus, a 1,024-bit array can be fabricated now, and when the company's next device—a 256-bit bipolar unit with an access time of 25 nsec—becomes available in July, a 4,096-bit array will be tops. Marketing manager Marshall Cox points out that beam-lead chips offer several advantages in building memory arrays. First, because the chips are etched apart instead of being scribed, die yield is higher and so the cost per chip is lower. Secondly, beam-leading lends itself to automatic assembly of arrays, and this also will help reduce costs. And the costs, Cox says, will be on the order of 8 cents per bit in 1971, 4 cents in 1972, and 1.5 cents in 1973, in large quantity.

Cost not sole factor

But, Cox is quick to point out that cost won't be the sole factor. "Computer architecture is changing," Cox says, "and the memory is being dispersed throughout the main frame so that instead of finding 50,000 bits in one place, you'll find 4,000 here and 4,000 there—memory elements will be replacing some logic circuits. With this change, it won't matter if memory costs 2 cents, or 5 cents, or 10 cents per bit because it will still be cheaper than logic."

Among the companies that manufacture MOS memories, Electronic Arrays is taking two approaches: MOS elements and MOS cards. EA now has 128-bit and 64-bit memories on the market, and a 256-bit unit with an access time of 300

nsec will be introduced soon. A memory card that will employ 16 units of 128-bits—organized as 512 words by four bits—with an access time of 800 nsec will also be introduced soon. The memory elements provide flexibility to the memory system designer while the cards offer a package—complete with clock and interface circuits—for the small (under 10,000 bits) memory.

Signetics, American Micro-Systems Inc., and Intersil are also in the MOS random-access memory field. Signetics has a 256-bit, 700-nsec memory that it is supplying to National Cash Register. AMI has a 512-bit unit with an access time of 150 nsec, and a forthcoming 128-bit device that can be electrically altered to form a 128-by-one, or 64-by-two, or 32-by-four memory. Intersil's memory is a 256-bit unit with a 350-nsec access time.

RCA currently has two semiconductor memories on the market. One is a 16-bit complementary MOS device with an access time of 15 nsec and features a quiescent power dissipation of 100 nanowatts. Regular 16-bit p-channel MOS devices dissipate about 50 microwatts. The other is a 16-bit bipolar ECL circuit which has an access time of 6.5 nsec. Both devices have been in production for about a year. According to Frank Rohr, market planner for digital IC's, RCA intends to concentrate on what it calls performance-type-memories—either low power dissipation or high speed. Next on RCA's list is a 64-bit complementary MOS memory with an access time of 50 nsec and 150 nanowatts of power dissipation for August introduction.

It appears that the newcomers to the memory business have a more advanced product line than the "old guard" IC houses. Companies like Cogar, AMS, Mostek, SEMI, Intel, AMI, and EA, have concentrated their efforts in the memory area. Still, the largest contracts to supply semiconductor random-access memories for computer mainframes are the Fairchild-Burroughs and NCR-Signetics deals—although NCR is reportedly evaluating other firms and is also developing its own 256-bit RAM in an effort to qualify more suppliers. A question remains, however; who does the market belong to? The answer: there's enough for everyone.

Semiconductor memory systems: How much do they really cost?

Those who seek to avoid high costs of complete systems by starting with packaged chips may wind up paying much more than anticipated once the necessary components, assembly, and testing are factored in

By William Taren, *Cogar Corp., Wappingers Falls, N.Y.*

☐ The seductive sound of low cost per bit is a strong selling point among manufacturers of both core and semiconductor memories. Many buyers seek to avoid the seemingly greater expense of complete memories by assembling their own systems from packaged chips. They have found, however, that the real cost of a memory system—including support components, assembly, testing, and engineering—often turns out much higher than their initial expectations. In fact, the lower the quoted price, the higher the proportionate increase incurred in the ultimate cost.

The tendency to underestimate actual cost took root and still flourishes in core memories. Quoted prices for core memories often exclude necessities such as power supplies, controls for shutting down power in the proper sequence, registers, decoding, and self-testing equipment. Sometimes only cost per bit for a naked core plane is quoted; the purchaser is stuck with the task of assembling the planes into stacks, interconnecting them, and adding the support circuitry.

The very low price quoted by some semiconductor memory manufacturers often covers little more than the equivalent of a core plane. Although the user, in return, gains maximum flexibility for his particular application, he may overlook how much the added hardware and engineering is going to cost him.

In general, the hardware requirements for any semiconductor memory includes, in addition to the storage array itself, such things as support circuit packages, printed-circuit cards, decoupling capacitors, terminators, and connectors. And using these components implies that the purchaser has or will need to have assembly and memory test capabilities.

As a basis for examining the cost of these components and operations, look at today's readily available semiconductor memories. These ordinarily come in dual in-line packages with one chip per package; each chip carries from 64 to 256 bipolar circuits or 256 to 1,024 metal oxide semiconductor circuits. Both circuit types sell for about $25 per package. This corresponds to about 40 cents per bit for bipolar circuits with cycle times of 50 to 100 nanoseconds, and 10 cents per bit for MOS cycling at about 1 microsecond.

It's not unreasonable to expect this $25 figure to drop 50% within 1 to 2 years and the MOS cycle time to decrease to about 25% of those quoted. During this time, technological improvements together with lowering prices should make 256-bit bipolar chips and 1,024-bit MOS chips considerably more attractive and widely used than they are today. Such popularity would also bring the price down. By 1972 the price per bit could be down to 10 cents for bipolar and perhaps 2 cents for MOS, presupposing an optimum price/performance ratio for both types.

However, even these projections, once arrived at, still exclude the additional hardware and engineering required to adapt the memories to particular applications. The additional cost depends on the price quoted for the individual package. And although the absolute cost added decreases as the basic cost decreases, it doesn't fall off as quickly, so that the percentage of added cost rises sharply for the lower costs per bit. For example, an unmounted chip in a dual in-line package, at 10 cents per bit costs 2.8 cents, or 28%, more to incorporate in a complete memory. At 5 cents per bit, the necessary extras add 2 cents, or 40%. And where the quote is 1 cent per bit, added outlay cost is 1.4 cents per bit, or 140%.

The first and most obvious additional expense is support circuitry for the memory. This includes selection and decoding, to pick out one of a number of DIPs on a single printed-circuit card; latches, for address and data input and output; and timing pulse generators. Furthermore, if the memory circuit's output is at a logic level unacceptable to such standard logic circuit forms as diode transistor, transistor transistor, or emitter coupled, more support circuitry is necessary to convert from the memory level to the logic level or vice versa.

After the memory circuits and the support circuits have been purchased, the DIPs are still up in the air, so to speak: they need a printed-circuit card to hold them. The size and number of pc cards required depends on the kind of memory being built. A small buffer, for example, containing 256 words of 16 bits each would need 64 memory packages of 64 bits each, along with another 12 to 24 packages containing support circuitry. This number of packages might be possibly mounted on one card; however, if two cards

111

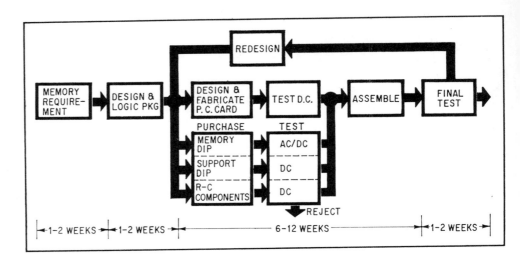

| MEMORY REQUIRE-MENT | DESIGN & LOGIC PKG | DESIGN & FABRICATE P. C. CARD | TEST D.C. | ASSEMBLE | FINAL TEST |

REDESIGN

PURCHASE / TEST
MEMORY DIP — AC/DC
SUPPORT DIP — DC
R-C COMPONENTS — DC
REJECT

|← 1-2 WEEKS →|← 1-2 WEEKS →|←——— 6-12 WEEKS ———→|← 1-2 WEEKS →|

are needed, a few more packages would be required to compensate for longer signal paths. In a few cases one DIP occupies no more than a square inch; 1½ to 2 in.² is more typical, leaving space for interconnections and for connectors, test points, and stiffeners. Today the larger pc cards have an effective area of 60 to 120 in.² Thus a single card can't hold the 256-by-16 buffer mentioned; two cards are necessary, together with extra support circuits.

A typical main memory for a minicomputer contains 4,000 words of 16 bits each, and can be packaged in 256 DIPs, each containing 256 bits in MOS circuitry. To these should be added 24 packages of support circuits, all of which should require about six pc cards. A larger memory is likely to have an even larger proportion of support packages.

Packages in a memory can be fitted more closely together on the pc card than the above figures suggest, if one spends more time and money designing the voltage and signal distribution system, or if the memory system's performance objectives are adjusted to permit the dense packing. Another factor that controls packing density is the available laminating and etching facilities for making the cards.

For example, a double-sided pc card with gold-plated card tab connections and no internal interconnection planes costs around 20 cents per square inch. Adding multiple internal planes increases the cost radically, as does the use of conductive line widths and spacings as little as 0.010 in.; the cost may reach $2 per in.², but performance of the system, interconnection problems or noise may justify the expenditure. In any case, it's much less expensive to solve these problems at an early stage in the design than to grapple with them after a system has been installed.

Not all the components of a memory assembly are high-technology devices or expensive frills. Take decoupling capacitors and terminating resistors, for example. The capacitors cost maybe 25 cents to a dollar, and the resistors are at the nickel and dime level. These necessary components add perhaps $2.50 to $7 to the cost per card.

This takes care of all the components required for assembling a semiconductor memory on a production-line basis. And at this point another cost factor raises its head—inventory. To support normal manufacturing procedures, at least a six week's supply of all components should be kept on hand. Inventory includes not only the cost of the stocked pieces themselves, but also the interest on the investment the stock repre-

Double-sided. This pc card's wiring is much denser than that on the multilayer card at right.

Multilayer. Simpler connections and higher performance are obtainable at the cost of extra internal planes.

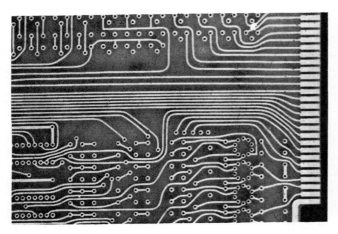

Summary of a memory's true cost

A. Cost of testing DIPS
1. First tester
   a. Capital depreciation $50,000
      based on purchase price of $150,000, five year life, no salvage value, and sum-of-digits depreciation
   b. Cost of operation in man-years

Operator	1.0
Supervision	0.2
Load, unload	0.5
Programing	0.5
Documentation	0.5
Returns to vendor	0.2
Maintenance and calibration	0.5
Inventory and miscellany	0.4

Total man-years	3.8

   3.8 man-years @ $26,000 = $100,000

   Rate includes wages, support costs, fringe benefits, etc.

2. Additional testers
   Each tester tests 500 DIPS per hour maximum
   Shifts are 8 hours, shift efficiency 0.6, less than 1.0 because of operator breaks, maintenance, and other pauses. If the production rate is higher, more than one tester is necessary. Additional testers have the same capital depreciation but only half the operating cost, because of functions shared with the first tester.

3. Total cost of testing
   a. Number of DIPS
      = (500 DIPS/h) × (8 h/shift) × (0.6 shift efficiency) × (5 shift/wk) × (50 wk/yr) = 600,000 DIPS/yr per tester
   b. Cost per DIP, first 600,000 = 25 cents

   c. Cost per DIP over 600,000 = 17 cents

   Total cost:
   $$D_y[(1 + R_d)(1 + R_s) - 600,000] \times 0.17 + 150,000$$

B. Cost of raw cards
   $$= (B_y/B_d)(1 + R_d)(1 + R_s)(A_d)(C_c)$$
   $$= (D_y)(1 + R_d)(1 + R_s)(A_d)(C_c)$$
C. Cost of support DIPS
   $$= (D_y)(R_d)(C_s)(1 + R_s)$$
D. Cost of termination and decoupling
   $$= (C_t/D_c)(D_y)(1 + R_d)(1 + R_s)$$
   $$= (C_t/D_c)(D_{yg})$$
E. Cost of storage DIPS $= (D_y)(1 + R_s)(C_{sd})$
F. Cost of assembly $= (D_{yg})(C_a)$
G. Cost of card test $= (D_{yg})(C_{ct}/D_c)$
H. Cost of inventory $= (I)(T/52)(D_{yg}) \times [(A_d)(C_c) + (C_t/D_c) + (C_s) + (C_{sd})/(1 + R_d)]$
J. Cost of DIPS rejected at incoming inspection
   1. Number of faulty DIPS $= (R_i)(D_{yg})$
   2. Number of faulty DIPS rejected $= (E_i)(R_i)(D_{yg})$
   3. Cost of rejected DIPS
      $$= (E_i)(R_i)(D_y)(1 + R_s)(C_s R_d + C_{sd})$$
K. Cost of card repair, as a result of faulty DIPS that pass incoming inspection
   1. Number of faulty DIPS installed in cards
      $$= (1 - E_i)(R_i)(D_{yg})$$
   2. Number of cards repaired at card test level
      $$= (E_t)(1 - E_i)(R_i)(D_{yg})$$
   3. Number of cards repaired at system test level
      $$= (1 - E_t)(1 - E_i)(R_i)(D_{yg})$$
   4. Cost of repair, card and system test levels
      $$= [(C_{ra})(E_t) + (C_{rs})(1 - E_t)][(1 - E_i)(R_i)(D_{yg})]$$
L. Cost of quality and reliability test samples
   $$= (C_s R_d + C_{sd})(R_q)(D_y)(1 + R_s)$$

Definitions

Symbol	Definition	Example
A_d	Card area per DIP	1.5 in.²
B_d	Bits per DIP	256
B_y	Bits per year	100 million
C_a	Assembly cost per DIP	$ 0.10
C_c	Cost per in.² of card	$ 0.50
C_{ct}	Testing cost per card	$ 5
C_{ra}	Cost per repair at card level	$ 20
C_{rs}	Cost per repair at system level	$200
C_s	Cost per DIP, support circuit	$ 2
C_{sd}	Cost per DIP, storage circuit	
C_t	Cost per card, termination and decoupling	$ 4

Symbol	Definition	Example
D_c	DIPS per card	40
D_y	DIPS per year net $= B_y/B_d$	
D_{yg}	DIPS per year gross $= D_y(1 + R_d)(1 + R_s)$	
E_i	Efficiency, incoming inspection	70%
E_t	Efficiency, card test	80%
I	Interest on investment	8%
R_d	Ratio, support to storage DIPS	1:3
R_i	Rejection rate, incoming inspection	2%
R_q	Sample rate, reliability check	1%
R_s	Proportion of spares at DIP level	1:10
T	Inventory and assembly time	12 weeks

Expensive but invaluable. Although testing equipment like this is almost frighteningly expensive, its use on purchased components is essential. Its rejection rate may be as high as one component in 10.

sents. This interest period begins when the stock appears on the shelf and continues through the assembly process. An inventory time of six weeks and an assembly and testing time of six weeks make the total investment period 12 weeks; if the stock to produce 100 million bits costs $6 million, the interest over a 12-week period at 8% is over $100,000.

All components are presumably tested by the supplier before shipment. Nevertheless, the user must test them again. Past data on medium-scale integrated logic circuits indicates that rejection rates at incoming inspection are likely to be between 1% and 10%—much too high to be neglected.

A purchaser may be tempted to minimize these rejection rate percentages when he looks at the $50,000 to $250,000 price for functional memory component testers. Furthermore, the tester's cost of operation per year can equal the required initial capital investment. However, these dollar outlays can be justified if the testing facilities have a high throughput: 250 to 300 DIPs per hour, on a single work shift for the year, add

up to more than 500,000 DIPs or 100 million bits.

Unfortunately, even at these production rates and dollar outlays, no component tester is perfect. Normally 60% to 90% effective, the testers invariably let a few bad, marginal, or intermittently failing components slip through to inventory. In the case of the 500,000 DIPs per year mentioned previously, with a 2% incoming defect level, between 1,000 and 4,000 faulty units each year can make it to the shelves.

In addition to incoming inspection, all purchased components should be subjected to a quality-control or reliability test—a destructive procedure. Although the proportion of parts used for this purpose can be decreased after an extended period of purchasing from well-qualified vendors, the tests will still consume anywhere from 0.1% to 2% of incoming parts.

Assembling these components to the cards, with the attendant soldering, marking, and inspection operations is the next cost item. With automatic insertion and wave-soldering equipment, the amortized cost for assembly averages 5 cents per component; but if cards of many types are produced in low volume, the cost can easily reach 20 cents per component.

To a great degree the total cost involved in these operations is inversely related to the investment in card assembly equipment. For example, if a 256-bit MOS DIP costs $25 and if 40 of these are used per card, then the card costs $1,000—not counting the card itself or any other components mounted on it. If the least expensive assembly process spoils 1% of the cards produced, this effectively adds $10 to the card cost, or 25 cents for each DIP. But if spending an extra nickel per component on assembly equipment —such as automatic insertion machines—eliminates the spoilage of cards, the investment is worth while. In fact, the investment proves valuable if the cost increment is less than the 25 cents per component that the cost of spoilage—provided, of course, that the costlier equipment does reduce spoilage measurably.

After soldering, the assembled card must also be tested—to screen faulty assemblies, not to repair them. Screening is usually a semiautomatic operation; the cards are plugged by hand into a test fixture, and a computer-controlled test sequence compares the cards with a set of performance specifications, including a full range of power supply and timing variations. These tests, depending on their degree of complexity can cost as little as $1.50 per card or as much as $10— but, like the component tests, they still are not perfect. In any event, the identified bad cards must be repaired—another cost item.

Unquestionably, the most expensive place to find a failure is at the system level—when the flaw that got past the component test and the card test finally shows up. The cost includes the down time for the system as well as the cost for labor and equipment to locate and repair the failed component. The time involved ranges from an hour to a full day, and the costs, if a large system is down, runs into thousands of dollars.

Although far from complete, this analysis of the true cost of a semiconductor memory provides a relative guide. The costs are summarized on page 113. □

Shelf cost. The sooner tested assemblies can be shipped after completion, the less their total cost.

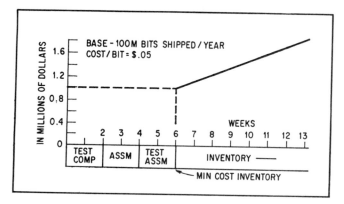

Cost summary For shipping 100 million bits per year

All figures in thousands of dollars

Item	In 256-bit chips*			In 64-bit chips**
	10¢/bit	5¢/bit	1¢/bit	10¢/bit
A. Testing DIPs	160.0	160.0	160.0	436.9
B. Raw cards	429.6	429.6	429.6	1,716.0
C. Support DIPs	283.6	283.6	283.6	1,166.0
D. Termination/decoupling	57.4	57.4	57.4	228.8
E. Storage DIPs	11,000.0	5,500.0	1,100.0	11,000.0
F. Assembly	57.3	57.3	57.3	228.8
G. Card Test	71.6	71.6	71.6	286.0
H. Inventory	213.2	114.7	33.7	339.1
J. Rejected DIPs	158.0	81.0	19.4	218.3
K. Card repair	196.0	196.0	196.0	769.4
L. Quality, reliability	165.4	57.9	13.9	123.2
Totals	12,792.1	7,009.1	2,422.5	16,512.5
Total cost/bit	$.128	$.07	$.024	$.165

*In dual-in-line packages, 4K by 16 bit system
**In dual-in-line packages, 256 by 16 bit system

Chapter 5

Read-only memories

There's a read-only memory that's sure to fill your needs

ROM's are handy design tools, say Memory Technology's *John Marino* and *Jonathan Sirota*; take your pick, you're bound to find what you want

● Inside most modern central processors, data handling systems, computer peripherals, and special-purpose digital machines is, most likely, at least one read-only memory. Systems designers now acknowledge it to be a very useful building block and design tool: complex functions can be implemented in a single unit rather than in a distributed fashion. Dramatically high-lighting this trend is the control sequence generation now used in central processors. What, in the past, took a great deal of distributed hard-wired logic is now done by a read-only memory with a microprogram.

Today, it's also quite common to find read-only memories applied as code converters, character generators for displays, trigonometric function generators, and process controllers.

In some computer peripherals, for example, where conversion between fixed codes is important, read-only storage units are the best choice. Specifically, a read-only memory can be a character generator converting six-bit code into a pattern in an array of dots; or it can mediate between two computers, or between a computer and a data terminal, that communicate with each other in different languages. And some read-only memories are used for storing large fixed portions of often-used programs, assemblers, and compilers.

Special-purpose computers can be implemented very easily with read-only memories. Depending on the task,

the system can range from a general-purpose computer with a special-purpose read-only-memory controller, to a read-only memory and some simple digital devices for a relatively low-level computational tasks.

Some kinds of read-only memories are also being employed as logic subassemblies. Logic functions can be implemented with read-only memories in two ways. In the more important of these ways, if two or more address lines are addressed simultaneously, the OR function of the data in the two locations appears at the output. The AND function is similarly obtained from the complement of the data, using de Morgan's theorem: $\overline{A \cdot B} = \overline{A} + \overline{B}$. This operation corresponds to an instruction built into many general-purpose computers to permit manipulation of individual bits.

In the other read-only-memory implementation of logic, the memory contains the truth tables for a number of different binary functions of a given set of binary variables. Each combination of these variables corresponds to a particular address; the bits in the word at that address represent the values of the various functions for the given combination [see following article].

The type of read-only memory that's best in any particular application depends upon the specifications for that application. However, general statements can be made concerning the various criteria, and are summarized in the table on page 121.

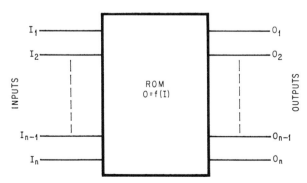

Relation. Read-only memory's only function is to maintain a fixed relationship between its inputs and outputs at all times during normal operation.

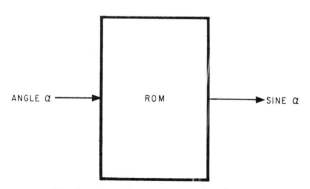

Trig function. A good example of a read-only memory application is as a function generator whose inputs are angles and whose outputs are functions of those angles.

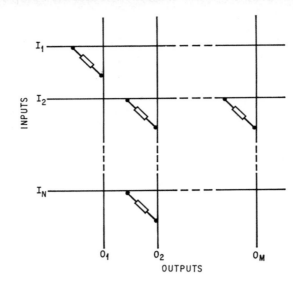

Matrix. Read only memory's basic structure is an array of intersections, with a coupling element either present or absent at each to define the stored data.

The read-only memory, despite its rather grandiose name, is only a device that maintains a functional relationship between a set of inputs and a set of outputs, as at left on page 117. This relationship is usually committed to a physical structure that cannot be altered while the system is running; but in a few cases an electrically alterable design has been used. In any case, during normal operation, the relationship cannot be changed by electrical means.

Usually, the read-only memory is considered to have an address for each combination of input variables; information permanently or semipermanently stored at that address establishes the relationship between the memory's inputs and outputs.

The trigonometric function generator is a good example of how a read-only memory stores the functional relationship between inputs and outputs. The input data is simply the angle, expressed in a suitable digital code, and the output data is the sine or other trigonometric function of that angle, also suitably encoded. All of the other applications for read-only memories are just more or less complex examples of this functional relationship.

Basically, the read-only memory is an N-by-M matrix of intersections between a set of input and output data lines, as shown above. Ordinarily, only one of the N inputs can be active at any given time; but, when

an array is used as a logic assembly, two or more inputs can be active. A signal on an input line energizes one or more output lines, as determined by the stored data. The presence or absence of a coupling element at each of the intersections of the matrix determines the data content of the read-only memory; the kind of coupling element determines the type of memory. Practically any active or passive electrical component can serve as a coupling element; in fact, the element need not be electrical—the presence or absence of holes on cards or tape is a familiar form of nonelectrical read-only memory.

The most commonly used active elements are diodes and bipolar and metal-oxide-semiconductor transistors; common passive elements in use are resistors, capacitors, and various kinds of transformers, as well as the punched holes previously mentioned. Each of these types of read-only memory is subject to a number of tradeoffs with respect to cost, flexibility, speed, fabrication, external circuits, reliability, ruggedness, capacity, and commercial availability.

Of the commonly used active elements that can provide a connection at each of the intersections of the matrix, the simplest is the diode, as shown below. Two types of diode array memories are in use—those using discrete diodes and those using monolithic diode arrays. In their simplest form, both types use a diode at each intersection in the matrix that corresponds to a

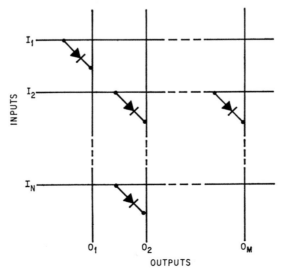

Diodes. Simplest active element that can store data in a read-only memory is the diode; the array can be of discrete diodes or a monolithic structure.

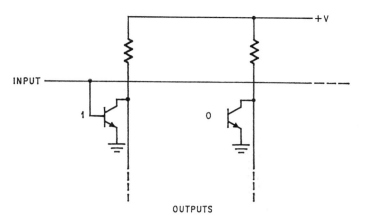

Bipolar array. A read-only memory can have bipolar transistors as its storage elements if the presence or absence of a base connection corresponds to 1's and 0's.

binary 1, and leave the other intersections unconnected. But a slight sophistication makes use of de Morgan's theorem: if the number of 1's stored in the array is greater than half the number of intersections, the array contains a diode for each 0, and the inputs and the outputs are inverted. This is particularly valuable for arrays of discrete diodes, because it uses the least number of diodes and, therefore, the least insertion labor.

These discrete arrays are simple and flexible, and are easily built without special equipment, using inexpensive components. But the relative cost per bit for the system, including the peripheral circuits, is fairly high, ranging between 10 cents and 25 cents per bit, largely because of the labor involved in assembling an array. The arrays' flexibility is due to the fact that the stored information can be changed by manual inserting or removing a discrete diode in the array. Their speed is relatively good, ranging from 250 nanoseconds to 1 microsecond.

The external circuits used with a diode memory are very simple. Because the diode matrix is a d-c network, the outputs are the same shape as the inputs; thus, if the inputs are d-c, the outputs are also d-c, so that no output register is required to hold the information.

Discrete diode arrays are very reliable and can be made rugged. In addition, their economical capacity can range from about 100 to 10,000 bits; however, outside

this range, the added cost becomes unreasonable. But there are no discrete diode array systems commercially available as separate products. On the other hand, of course, discrete diodes are available, and most electronically oriented companies can build their own arrays.

While the monolithic diode array read-only memory enjoys all the operational advantages of discrete arrays, it is economical only when many memories are required with the same contents. Generating the masks for specific diode arrays is too expensive for a short production run; even automatic equipment that removes particular diodes from a fully populated matrix is too expensive, although it eliminates the mask problem. But by sacrificing flexibility and simplicity, monolithic diode arrays offer significant advantages in speed and physical size, and in cost for large quantities. These advantages are such that small monolithic diode arrays are easily obtainable commercially.

Like diode arrays, monolithic bipolar transistor arrays can be very reliable and rugged and have been introduced by a few large semiconductor manufacturers. However, bipolar fabrication is complex and requires expensive production equipment. Basically, the arrays are fully populated matrixes in which a connection is made from an input line to the base of a transistor wherever a 1 is to be stored; transistors corresponding to stored 0's are left unconnected, as shown above.

While the array's bit capacity ranges from a few to about a thousand, large capacities rapidly become prohibitively expensive. This is true whether the large capacities are placed on single chips or acquired with hybrid assemblies; in the latter case, the interconnection costs increase with capacity at about the same rate as chip costs.

But the speed of these arrays is potentially the highest of any read-only memory type—under 100 nsec. This is considerably faster than the speed of diode arrays, because the transistors don't present the capacitive load to the input that diodes do. On this account, many companies are about to enter the field.

Recently, a great deal of interest in MOS techniques has arisen, because of their application to shift registers as well as to read-only memories. MOS read-only memories, like bipolar memories, comprise fully-populated matrixes with the gate connected to an input for a 1 and left disconnected for a 0, as shown at the left. These

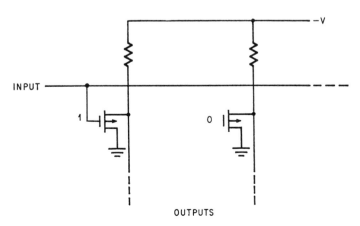

MOS FETs. As with bipolar transistors, at top of page, an array of MOS transistors can store data by a gate connection.

arrays include one or two levels of decoding, and store 1,000 to 2,000 bits, each accessible in about a microsecond. In small or moderate quantities, the devices sell for prices competitive with other types, and projected price in quantity is quite low, particularly for larger capacities.

But of those companies that have demonstrated their production capabilities for these devices, few, if any, have demonstrated long-term large-volume capability. Hence, yield and cost is still somewhat doubtful.

Furthermore, like diode arrays and bipolar transistor arrays, the facilities required to produce MOS arrays are extremely complex and costly. Also, the peripheral circuits required to read data from the MOS memory are moderately complex; this is because p-channel MOS, the most common type, uses negative levels and negative pulses, whereas most systems that would use memories are designed with integrated circuitry using positive voltages. Thus, these systems require an interface conversion to enter and leave the memory. This conversion problem is lessened somewhat with complementary MOS circuits, which have both n- and p-channel transistors on the same chip, or with low-threshold MOS circuits; quite a bit of work is being done in both these areas. But none of these units have been in use for a long enough time to provide more than the scantiest data on reliability.

The ruggedness of MOS read-only memories is also somewhat in question; they are susceptible to destruction by excessive voltages on their inputs or by the charge and discharge of static electricity. Again, circuits have been developed to alleviate this problem, but little data on their effectiveness is available at the present time.

As opposed to the active elements, the most widely used passive elements are punched tape or cards. Although these systems have been in use for a long time and are familiar to everyone, not many people think of them as a form of read-only memory. Although they are inexpensive, they are also very slow and limited to sequential access.

Resistor arrays, used as read-only memories in some applications, have excellent qualities of reliability and ruggedness. Their cost is usually very low; but the cost of their peripheral electronics is high, because the arrays' operational characteristics are poor—for example, their high power dissipation and low signal-to-noise ratio. The latter is a result of the many sneak paths that exist in the array.

As with diode arrays, the flexibility of resistive arrays is high when they are made with discrete resistors. Monolithic resistor arrays are available which, while they will eventually cost less, sacrifice this flexibility. Resistive read-only memories are capable of high speeds —in the 150 to 500 nsec region—again faster than diodes because of the lower capacitance, but not quite up to the performance of bipolar transistors.

A typical capacitive read-only memory is made from a matrix of plates on either side of a dielectric. These plates are interconnected with a set of parallel conductors on one side of the dielectric, and with another parallel set at right angles to the first on the other side of the dielectric. They are made either by deposition or etching. A high capacitance defines a 1 and a low capacity a 0; the low capacitance is obtained either by removing a plate on one side or by removing the dielectric between plates. Capacitive read-only memories are in moderately large usage in the data processing industry. However, because their users manufacture them exclusively in-house, cost data is not available; but the memories are probably competitive.

This loyalty continues despite the moderately poor flexibility of capacitive arrays caused by the manufacturing techniques used. However, systems that can be plugged in like a printed-circuit board have been designed around capacitive subarrays. Speeds of capacitive read-only memories range from 250 nsec to 1 μsec. These memories, in general, seem to be very reliable and rugged, and can hold up to tens of thousands of bits.

Perhaps the oldest of the read-only memory technologies is that of inductive read-only memories, which have been used in many applications for approximately 25 years. They have usually taken one of two forms. The oldest and simplest of these is a matrix of input and output wires with a discrete toroidal transformer at each intersection where a logic 1 is desired, as shown below. The toroid inductively couples the input to the output. The discrete toroidal array works well, but is costly because the array is handmade.

The other form of inductive read-only memory is the braid transformer array, in which the input wires —one per word—are encoded with data by weaving

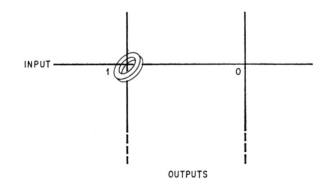

Old-timer. A toroidal transformer at each intersection corresponding to a 1 is perhaps the oldest form of read-only memory, but the array is handmade and thus expensive.

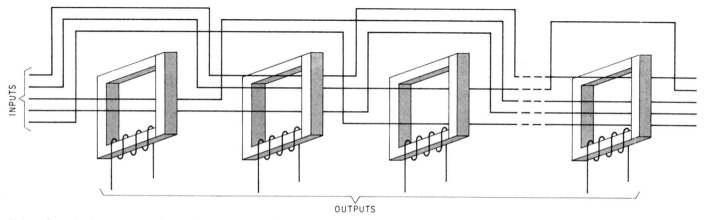

Up-to-date. In this more modern inductive read-only memory, word wires pass either through or around successive ferrite cores. A current pulse in a word wire generates a voltage pulse in the sense wire of those cores that it passes through. U-shaped cores have ferrite caps that complete the flux path.

them either through or around discrete transformer cores, as shown above. There is one core for each bit in the word. Only where the wires pass through the cores, are they inductively coupled to the outputs. The cores are U-shaped, so that the wires can be preformed in advance and dropped into place; the preformed bundle of wires resembles a ladder-shaped braid, hence the name. Ferrite caps laid over the U's complete the flux path in the core.

The braid approach has largely replaced the discrete transformer array because of its excellent flexibility, low cost, and capability for high speed—cycle times can be as short as 150 nsec. The braid transformer is being produced presently by automatic machinery, making its cost low. The cost of a braid transformer system varies from 2 cents to 9 cents per bit, including all of the peripheral circuits, depending on the system's capacity. This type of system is very flexible because replacement braids, or arrays of wires, can be made and plugged onto the cores. These braids can be made by a complex machine that automatically interprets the contents of the truth table and weaves the wires accordingly; minor corrections can be implemented very simply and inexpensively by hand.

Another form of transformer array, called the rope memory, contains one core for each word and one wire for each bit in the word. The rope memory is thus the reverse of the word-per-wire, core-per-bit braid memory. A pulse of current in the core winding of a rope memory makes the core switch from saturation in one direction to saturation in the other, and this change generates pulses in those wires of the rope that pass through the core.

The rope memory has recently, although obscurely, been in the public eye. It stores the program in the Apollo computer [*Electronics,* Jan. 9, 1967, p. 109], which has been largely responsible for the successful navigation and pinpoint landings on the moon. But, in spite of this illustrious role, it has largely fallen into disfavor because it must be handmade—the weaving process for braids can't be applied to ropes. Furthermore, it requires a large drive current and produces very small output signals.

By contrast, the word lines in the braid read-only memory require only small currents, and the pulse transformers can provide large output signals. As a result, the peripheral circuits used for read out can be extremely simple. In addition, the output signals are usually large enough to drive standard integrated circuit logic gates directly; the signal-to-noise ratio of the output signals is about 5 or 6 to 1. The simple electronics also make the braid memory very reliable and rugged. Moreover, the capacity of the braid transformer matrix can range from a few thousand bits to many millions of bits. ●

Specification	Matrix
Lowest cost:	Braid transformer
Greatest flexibility:	Braid transformer
Fastest:	Bipolar transistor
Easiest to fabricate:	Discrete diode
Easiest to read:	Diode or braid transformer
Best reliability and ruggedness:	Braid transformer, diode or transistor
Best commercial reliability of components or elements:	Diode or resistor
Best commercial availability of system:	Braid transformer

Standard read-only memories simplify complex logic design

Large-scale integration of semiconductors has made standard memories practical for use in implementing combinational and sequential logic; *Floyd Kvamme* of National Semiconductor explains how this is achieved

● Complex logic functions in control and arithmetic applications can now be implemented economically with semiconductor read-only memories, thanks to recent technological advances that make them mass producible with large capacities and good yields. These applications are in addition to their classic chores of microprograming, table lookup, and data conversion. As implementations of logic functions, they replace arrays or assemblies of gates and flip-flops at lower cost and provide more efficient use of silicon real estate, without sacrificing the direct interface with the logic circuits in the data path. Furthermore, they're simpler to design than gate arrays, and can be manufactured and tested in the same way as read-only memories for conventional uses.

Of course, they have always been capable of acting as combinational and sequential logic networks, but past proposals often depended on core ropes, arrays of resistors, or the like. These complex structures, as logic networks, were economically and technically incompatible with the structure of then-conventional digital systems.

In general, digital systems comprise a series of registers that store data temporarily during the process, combinational logic that operates on the data as it passes from register to register, and control logic that determines both when data transfer occurs and what happens to the data during the transfer. When these systems were built with vacuum tubes or transistors, or even with individual integrated-circuit gates, they had to be carefully designed to execute the desired functions, and only the desired functions, with a minimum number of components. The cost of these components, their physical arrangement in a machine, and other gross considerations imposed severe constraints on system organization—constraints that precluded the use of bulky and expensive read-only memory structures like core ropes.

Today, large-scale integration of both logic and memory circuits has removed this preclusion. With the metal-oxide-silicon process, read-only memories with capacities of up to 2,048 bits per chip are in mass production, and 4,096-bit units will be available soon. In these units the cost of individual components is almost negligible, and packaging constraints are more likely to involve interconnections a fraction of an inch long rather than to involve 50-foot cables under the floor.

Thus, economic incentive to reorganize systems now exists, because these memories provide the functional equivalent of 100 to 200 logic gates. And read-only memories are among the least expensive forms of LSI because they comprise arrays of identical cells instead of collections of miscellaneous gates randomly connected.

Nor do the technical barriers remain. MOS read-only memories can be an integral part of a logic system because they are electrically and physically compatible with logic ICs and have self-contained decoding and

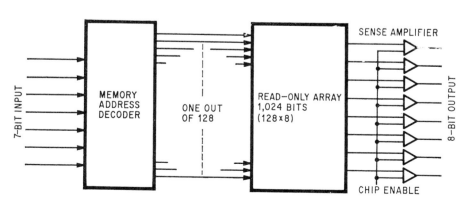

Logic or data. The seven-bit input can be regarded either as an address for one of the 128 eight-bit words, or as a combination of seven logic variables controlling eight independent functions.

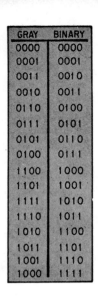

GRAY	BINARY
0000	0000
0001	0001
0011	0010
0010	0011
0110	0100
0111	0101
0101	0110
0100	0111
1100	1000
1101	1001
1111	1010
1110	1011
1010	1100
1011	1101
1001	1110
1000	1111

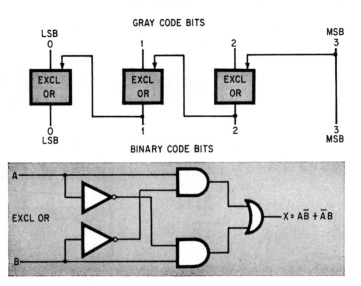

Conversion. A read-only memory containing 16 four-bit words can convert from the Gray code to binary code just as well as the logic network of three exclusive-OR circuits; the read-only memory contains merely the truth table for the conversion (left). This is a simple example, because both conversions require only a single chip—in fact, a chip with four exclusive-OR's is available, which would have a spare circuit left over in this application.

sense circuitry. Before MOS and LSI arrays became common-place, read-only memories were generally treated as subsystems because they required special control, sense and power-supply circuitry, and were assembled and packaged differently from logic circuits.

Although it is not a new idea, very little of a practical nature has been written about read-only memory logic. Therefore, the system designer will find little to guide him in this field. One pitfall to avoid is trying to force read-only memories into the established molds for relay and gate logic, by using, for instance, logic equations intended to minimize the number of gates or wiring crossovers. These do not apply to MOS read-only memories.

In conventional logic design, redundancies cost money, and it's well worth the time and effort to eliminate them from the design. But the advantage offered by memory logic lies in the fact that redundancies add little to the cost; the designer is spared the effort and expense of trying to produce a read-only memory without redundancy. Traditional logic design techniques that delete storage elements within each memory must be dropped in favor of a method that reduces the number of read-only memory packages in a function. The cost of these individual packages, and therefore the cost of the system as a whole, is kept low by using standard production memories with standard capacities and custom internal wiring patterns, even though such a route would traditionally entail ex-

pensive or inefficient designs using arrays of gates.

System development usually can be divided into six steps: describing the system, designing the architecture, generating the truth tables, generating the logic equations and diagrams, building the hardware, and checking out the system. In this sequence of steps, the input for programing a read-only memory would be a truth table, which brings the memory's manufacturer into the picture after the third step. But at the outset of development, the system designer should decide where he can use the memories, and he should be definite about this before committing himself to a particular architecture—that is, before taking the second step. Otherwise, he will find himself asking the manufacturer for rush changes, at great expense.

In general, a truth table lists various combinations of a set of input variables, with one or more output functions for each combination; as such, it governs the locations of 1 and 0 bits stored in the read-only memory. Most memories contain standard groups of decode and sense circuits flanking a standard array of MOS field-effect transistors. Data is loaded into this array by etching away part of the gate oxide of MOS FETs corresponding to 1 bits, so that when they are selected, they begin to conduct and thereby produce a 1 output. The other MOS FETs in the array can't conduct even if selected—the unetched gate oxide at each transistor is thick enough to prevent the potential due to the gate voltage from opening a conducting channel in the transistor, thus producing a 0 output.

Using a read-only memory for logic requires only a different point of view, not a change in the hardware. Many classic read-only memory applications—for example, converting a word in one code to a word in a different code—are really combinational logic functions. A network that implements one of these functions generates a specific output for each specific combination of input variables, regardless of the network's past history. Viewed functionally, the memory's input is an address and its output is a bit or a word corresponding to the address; but the concepts in this memory-oriented terminology can be replaced one-for-one by combinational logic terminology.

This one-for-one replacement is apparent in the 1,024-bit memory shown on page 123; produces an eight-bit output word when one of 128 seven-bit addresses is re-

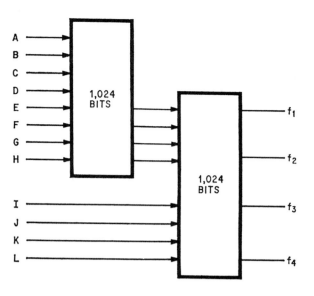

A
B
C
D
E
F
G
H

1,024
BITS

1,024
BITS

f₁

f₂

I
J
K
L

f₃

f₄

Cascade. Complex logic functions can be executed simply when small memories are cascaded. At the left, only 2,048 bits define four independent functions of 12 variables each, a task that would require eight times as many bits in a single read-only memory, or in parallel read-only memories wired to act as a single array. On page 126, 3,072 bits. take the place of 32,768 in a similar layout.

ceived. The seven bits in the address can be called seven variables and the eight bits in the output word can represent eight independent functions of these variables.

A programer specifying data to be stored in a read-only memory thinks in terms of storing certain words in certain addresses. But a logic designer working with the same memory can think in terms of the output functions and ignore the fact that words are stored. These two viewpoints correspond to looking at the memory either horizontally or vertically [see tables, pages 127 and 128]:

▶ In the horizontal view (table 1) a word at the input produces a word at the output, and all bits in the input word are related to those in the output word. However, no output word is related to any other in the memory. Here, the read-only memory performs its classic function.

▶ In the vertical view (table 2), the output bits for a given input may be totally unrelated to one another. Instead, bits in corresponding positions for all the input combinations represent values of an output variable as a Boolean function of the inputs. Seen in this way, the memory is a bit-for-bit implementation of a truth table.

A third approach, partly horizontal and partly vertical, divides each input word into subwords (table 3). This viewpoint is more flexible than the other two aspects.

With programing variations, the horizontal view in table 1 could represent the conversion of a communications code such as the American Standard Code for Informa-

tion Interchange (ASCII) to a machine language such as the standard Hollerith punched-card code. Or, it could stand for the generation of an error-correcting code from binary-coded decimal numbers or represent a micro-program. For instance, the read-only memory can interpret keyboard instructions to a business machine or control how an "intelligent" computer terminal manipulates data when addressed by instructions from the central processor. In each example, the data in one form addresses the stored words representing the data in the converted form.

The vertical representation in table 2, a classic truth table, is generally useful in logic synthesis. A logic designer, beginning with a combinational function to be implemented or with an equation, makes a truth table that describes the function. Every combination of the input variables should be entered. The logic sum of those entries containing a 1 in the output column is the standard sum, which fully defines the function but is generally full of redundancies. Each term in the standard sum is called a minterm.

In conventional logic design the standard sum is the starting point for the logic designer's most exacting task —determining the least redundant sum. Its result, the minimum sum, is a sum of products; each product is implemented by an AND gate, and their sum by an OR gate. An exactly parallel procedure resulting in a product

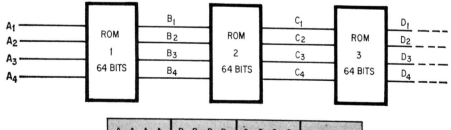

A_1 A_2 A_3 A_4	B_1 B_2 B_3 B_4	C_1 C_2 C_3 C_4	••••
0 0 0 0	0 0 0 1	0 0 1 0	
0 0 0 1	0 0 1 0	0 0 1 1	
0 0 1 0	0 0 1 1	0 1 0 0	
0 0 1 1	0 1 0 0	0 1 0 1	
0 1 0 0	0 1 0 1	0 1 1 0	
⋮	⋮	⋮	

Brute force. A type of sequential operation is possible simply by stringing read-only memories together; the output of each is the input to the next, whose output is the next in the sequence. For a particular input A, all the outputs would remain fixed, and pseudo-sequential operation would require looking at the ouput of successive read-only memories.

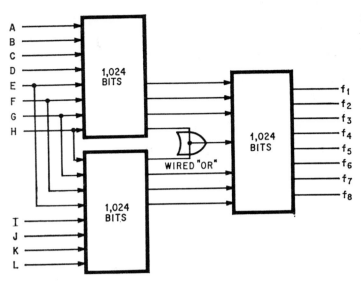

of sums is also sometimes used.

But all this hard work is avoided when the minterms are programed directly into a read-only memory. This can be done directly from the truth table, for each of several functions at once, bypassing the minimization process.

The vertical view in table 2 shows seven input variables, A through G, describing 128 different combinations of seven events, and eight possible output functions, shown as f_1 through f_8, for each event combination. To realize a function of the seven variables the designer would simply place a 1 in the column corresponding to that function wherever the function was to contain a given minterm.

Each function thus contains a set of minterms that is different from the sets contained by the other functions and independent of them.

By using a truth table that is efficiently implemented in the read-only memory, the logic designer avoids not only the task of minimization but also minimization errors that might creep into a gate array. For example, a designer can save gates by reducing the expression

$$Z = \overline{A}\,\overline{B}\,\overline{C} + \overline{A}BC + A\overline{B}\,\overline{C} + A\overline{B}C$$

to

$$Z = \overline{B}\,\overline{C} + A\overline{B} + \overline{A}BC$$

In a read-only memory this expression, in its unreduced

form, can be implemented with eight bits—eight because the expression involves three binary variables, and $2^3 = 8$. Minimization produces no savings, because the minimized expression still involves three variables. On the other hand, even the minimized expression requires dissimilar gates—two ANDs and an OR.

Logically, if the number of minterms for a given function of n variables is greater than 2^{n-1}, it is easier to program the complement of the function and invert the read-only memory's output rather than program the function itself in the memory.

It is unlikely that very many terms would occur in an equation in practical applications. Because control functions vary widely, there is no agreement in the literature on a typical number of minterms in a control function. But functions like those in table 3 would probably take about 12 gates to implement, and eight such functions would therefore require about 100 gates. In other words, one 1,024-bit read-only memory is generally the equivalent of 100 gates; thus 10 bits in a read-only memory can generally replace a gate in combinational logic. However, this is a conservative estimate; it's easy to find examples in which three or four bits equal a gate.

One such example, which incidentally is also a simple example of the equivalency of conversion and logic, shown on page 124, is in changing a four-bit Gray code representation—one in which successive values differ in no more than one bit—into its binary equivalent. These representations are often used where a continuously varying quantity, particularly a mechanical one, is converted to digital form. When the conversion is implemented in conventional logic, it requires three exclusive-OR gates, or a total of 15 simple gates. But a read-only memory containing 16 four-bit words—64 bits in all—could be programed to generate the corresponding binary output for any Gray-code input. In this case, 64 bits in the read-only memory replace 15 gates in the logic implementation, so that each gate is equivalent to approximately four bits.

Nearer to a logic designer's interest, perhaps, is an example such as the trigonometric lookup table (table 4). Read-only memories so programed are made as standard components for signal processors and fast-Fourier-transform applications. In this table, an input word is a seven-bit binary fraction that represents an angle that is a multiple of 0.703125, which is 1/128 of 90°; the cor-

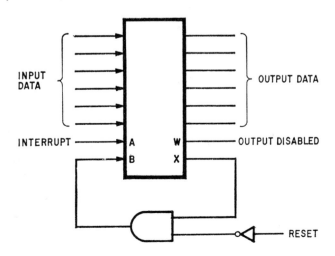

Truly sequential. A feedback loop from at least one output to the input is necessary for true sequential operation, which requires knowledge of the inputs' past history as well as their current state.

Table 1	
INPUT WORD	OUTPUT WORD
$A_1\ A_2\ A_3\ A_4\ A_5\ A_6\ A_7$	$X_1\ X_2\ X_3\ X_4\ X_5\ X_6\ X_7\ X_8$
0 0 0 0 0 0 0	1 1 1 1 1 1 1 1
0 0 0 0 0 0 1	0 1 0 0 1 0 0 1
0 0 0 0 0 1 0	0 1 0 1 1 1 0 0
0 0 0 0 0 1 1	0 0 0 1 0 0 0 0
0 0 0 0 1 0 0	1 0 1 1 0 0 1 1
0 0 0 0 1 0 1	1 0 1 1 0 ·1 0 0
0 0 0 0 1 1 0	0 0 0 0 1 1 0 1
0 0 0 0 1 1 1	1 0 0 0 0 0 1 0
0 0 0 1 0 0 0	0 1 1 0 1 0 0 0
0 0 0 1 0 0 1	0 0 0 1 0 0 1 0
⋮	⋮

Table 2	
INPUT VARIABLES	OUTPUT FUNCTIONS
A B C D E F G	$f_1\ f_2\ f_3\ f_4\ f_5\ f_6\ f_7\ f_8$
0 0 0 0 0 0 0	1 1 0 1 0 0 0 1
0 0 0 0 0 0 1	1 1 0 0 1 0 0 1
0 0 0 0 0 1 0	1 1 0 1 1 1 0 0
0 0 0 0 0 1 1	1 0 0 1 0 0 0 0
0 0 0 0 1 0 0	1 0 1 1 0 0 1 1
0 0 0 0 1 0 1	1 0 1 1 0 1 0 0
0 0 0 0 1 1 0	1 0 0 0 1 1 0 1
0 0 0 0 1 1 1	1 0 0 0 0 0 1 0
0 0 0 1 0 0 0	1 1 1 0 1 0 0 0
0 0 0 1 0 0 1	1 0 0 1 0 0 1 0
⋮	⋮

responding output word is the binary representation of the sine of that angle.

In general, the number of inputs to a memory is the logarithm, base 2, of the number of words. Thus, doubling the number of words increases the number of address bits by one. When applied to read-only memories that replace logic networks, this rule seems to require a doubling of memory bits with every additional variable. Not so—several methods are available to significantly reduce the number of read-only memories needed to perform large combinational functions. One of the best methods is cascading them, as shown at the top of page 125, a technique that becomes more efficient as the number of variables increases.

A simple example is an AND function of four variables, ABCD. This function can be performed by 16 bits of one read-only memory, 15 of which are 0, or by 4 bits in each of three memories for a total of 12 bits. A 4-bit segment in one first-stage memory would form the AND function of A and B; the second memory would similarly form C and D. The A·B and C·D outputs of these read-only memories would then be the inputs to a third 4-bit read-only memory, producing a second-stage output representing A·B·C·D.

It's impractical actually to use read-only memories for four-input ANDs, but this example shows the technique. The progression in the number of bits as the number of variables increases, shown in table 5, is much slower than the exponential growth of a single read-only memory. Note that the first of two read-only memory levels for a 7-input AND contains three read-only memories—two 4-bit and one 8-bit.

The cascades accomplish, with 2,048 and 3,072 bits, functions that would require 16,384 and 32,768 bits, respectively, with a single read-only memory or with parallel memories. They also illustrate two other points: the flexibility of read-only memories following the $\log_2$ capacity rule, and the efficiency of a few medium-sized memories relative to one giant—and expensive—special memory. In the three-memory cascades, two of the interim outputs are combined in an OR gate, which effectively "doubles" the second memory's capacity by reducing the second-stage inputs from eight to seven. Truth tables permitting such combinations are easy to prepare when the first-stage read-only memories have input subwords in common. Either a hardware logic gate may be used or, as shown on page 125, the memory outputs can simply be mixed together. Another technique uses a logic gate at an input to "double" memory capacity; what is actually doubled is the system's logical flexibility.

The cascade technique's versatility is due to the fact that any large group of functions usually contains many common variables or minterms. This appears in table 3, for example, in which the most significant bits of eight

TABLE 4	1024-BIT SINE LOOKUP TABLE	
ADDRESS	DEGREES	BINARY OUTPUT
0 0 0 0 0 0 0	0	0 0 0 0 0 0 0 0
0 0 0 0 0 0 1	0.7	0 0 0 0 0 0 1 1
0 0 0 0 0 1 0	1.4	0 0 0 0 0 1 1 0
0 0 0 0 0 1 1	2.1	0 0 0 0 1 0 0 1
⋮	⋮	⋮

Table 3

CHARACTER ADDRESS				LINE ADDRESS			OUTPUT CHARACTER							
A_1	A_2	A_3	A_4	B_1	B_2	B_3	f_1	f_2	f_3	f_4	f_5	f_6	f_7	f_8
0	0	0	0	0	0	0	1	0	0	0	0	0	0	1
0	0	0	0	0	0	1	1	1	0	0	0	0	0	1
0	0	0	0	0	1	0	1	0	1	0	0	0	0	1
0	0	0	0	0	1	1	1	0	0	1	0	0	0	1
0	0	0	0	1	0	0	1	0	0	0	1	0	0	1
0	0	0	0	1	0	1	1	0	0	0	0	1	0	1
0	0	0	0	1	1	0	1	0	0	0	0	0	1	1
0	0	0	0	1	1	1	1	0	0	0	0	0	0	1
0	0	0	1	0	0	0	1	1	1	1	1	1	1	1
0	0	0	1	0	0	1	1	0	0	0	0	0	0	0

a row, line or column related to that character. The 1 bits in the first eight rows of the output matrix outline the letter N; these bits could display the character on a cathode-ray tube by gating the crt beam with output line-by-line or column-by-column.

Assume, however, that N represented a large group of functions containing the corresponding minterms in the first eight sets of input variables. If the letter **M** represented a different large group of functions, the f_1, f_2, f_3, f_4, and f_8 columns would be identical to those for the N-group. In this case a majority of the minterms that could be represented by the input variables are, in fact, common. These read-only memory minimization techniques do not recreate the design and debugging problems of gate-logic minimization. The validity of a truth table doesn't have to be checked out in prototype hardware, because it is easily verified with a computer. Programs are available to print out truth tables from logic expressions or vice versa, mechanizing an otherwise tedious manual process.

Also, standard read-only memories will generate all eight output functions for a given input combination in about 1 microsecond. As a result, delays found in large combinational nets are avoided, and therefore need not be compensated with high-speed logic, which brings in its own problems of noise, races and clock skew.

Read-only memories can also be programed to perform a sequence of logic events, or a mix of combinational and sequential events. Feedback makes the sequential operation possible.

Any series of read-only memories can simulate sequential logic in a straightforward manner. For example, the memories shown at the bottom of page 125 are merely programed to shift the binary value of each set of outputs up by one from stage to stage. The collection of read-only memories simulates a counter. Shift registers and other sequential functions could be implemented in this fashion, but the design would be inefficient because it would require many read-only memories.

But only one would be needed to make a counter if the output from the first read-only memory were returned directly to its input. A binary 0000 input would generate an output of 0001, changing the input to 0001 and the output to 0010, and so forth. To keep the read-only memory from rippling through all its states, at least one additional input is required for a clock pulse.

The memory is programed to generate an output for each clock pulse that matches the other 4 bits of the input. This match can be made to occur at the rise of the clock pulse, at its fall, or at both.

This highly efficient counting technique employing the clocking and feedback techniques was introduced a few years ago,[2] considerably ahead of its time. It was implemented with a small read-only memory—64 by 4—limiting the counter modulus to eight. Modern read-only memories make this counting technique much more powerful. Any arbitrary number of stages can now be implemented with memories of up to 2,048 bits, since additional inputs and outputs are available for carry, borrow, and special feedback functions.

Any design of a counter, or for that matter design of any sequential logic function, must answer several important questions. Where does the sequence start? Where does it stop? If it gets into a wrong or disallowed state because of noise or other perturbation, how can this condi-

input words are alike. Likewise, in the two-memory 12-input cascade, the shared terms combine with the unshared terms to drive the second memory. The principle of the three-memory arrangement is similar. It is most useful when a group of input variables, such as EFGH, are common to several output functions. But cascaded read-only memories, like cascaded logic gates, have a longer propagation delay than does a single rank.

Many variations of these basic cascades are possible, and they can be used in combination with read-only memories of different sizes. Determining the best way to rearrange the original truth tables is an ideal task for a computer, since a great many variables must be compared and shifted around to match common terms in a convenient order. These techniques stem from the table 3 approach, which the National Semiconductor Corp. uses to organize large conversion read-only memories and character generators for displays.

For example, National uses the three-memory cascade to translate from the 12-line Hollerith code to the 8-line ASCII. Read-only memories like table 3 serve as alphanumeric fonts, and read-only memory kits are available to generate 5-by-7 matrixes of 1 and 0 patterns, for example, from ASCII 6-line inputs for various types of displays and printouts.

In this approach, the 4-bit input subword would address a character, and the 3-bit subword would address

TABLE 5 NO. OF INPUTS TO AND FUNCTION	BITS REQUIRED IN SINGLE ROM	BITS REQUIRED IN 2 CASCADED ROMs
4	16	12
5	32	16
6	64	20
7	128	24

tion be detected and how can the device be forced out of the wrong state loop?

With read-only memories these questions are answered more simply than with conventional logic design. In fact, starting the counter is easy—just force the address to its initial value and bring up the clock signal. This design avoids the additional reset input or its equivalent, required in conventional sequential circuits. And the counter stops whenever the clock signal stops or the events being counted stop happening; the only precaution is to make sure the counter counts every event, yet doesn't count a single event more than once. In designs that have many bits changing at nominally the same time, another problem is avoiding false sequences when the changes involve slight differential delays—as in fact they invariably do.

One way of solving these problems is to count in Gray code, which easily converts to straight binary, as was illustrated earlier. Gray-code counting is easy to accomplish with read-only memories, as are many of the arithmetic techniques developed in synthesizing relay-type logic and in avoiding race conditions that occur in asynchronous counter-type logic systems.

A simple design using a read-only memory is a counter that can count either up or down. Such a counter, shown below, can be built with a 1,024-bit memory, so that it has 16 stable states; it can be connected to similar units to

increase the number of states and the count range. Its two most significant input bits are the up/down controls. The two most significant outputs are the carry/borrow lines, which can be connected to the count-up and count-down lines of another read-only memory counter to expand the range. Stable states are reached as they are addressed, and the counter is drawn by feedback into the next stable state.

This design is basically the elementary sequential logic circuit proposed in 1967 for implementation with read-only memories—with two major improvements. First, it has additional capability for generating additional outputs, such as carry and borrow. Second, it takes advantage of a technology—MOS—that permits far more complex functions than this to be built monolithically, whereas the original design used up a whole bipolar memory for a simple counting operation. Bipolar technology's lower component density and more complex construction have yielded to MOS in this respect.

It is not necessary to feed back all output lines to form new inputs. Some outputs may represent combinational functions and some may be fed back for sequential functions. In addition, the feedback loops might themselves act as outputs to control subsequent circuits.

At first glance, these random-logic techniques seem to require asynchronous operation, which is difficult to control. But in read-only memories that have controls for

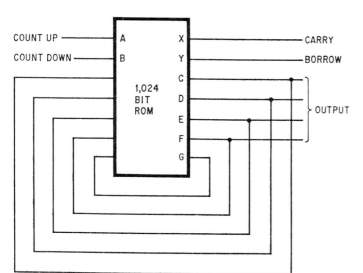

Up-down counter. This simple sequential circuit, essentially similar to one first proposed in 1967, offers two improvements: it generates additional outputs such as carry and borrow, and it has basic potential for considerably more complex functions than mere counting.

strobing or enabling, the strobe line can be used much like a system clock. For instance, the outputs can be disabled until all input transients have died away.

In a basic random-logic configuration, shown on page 126, the read-only memory performs combinational functions, such as code conversion, with the six data lines, while it can also perform control and sequential functions with the A and B inputs and the W and X outputs (or with some of the data lines as well). In normal operation, both the interrupt line A and the reset line B are at their 0 states. Thus, the W and X output lines are also at their 0 states. In this configuration, a 2,048-bit memory can store 256 words with 6 data bits and 2 control bits.

Now suppose an interrupt at the 1 level appears at the A input. This causes the W line to put out a 1, alerting the outside world that the read-only memory's output data is no longer valid. At the same time, the X line goes to its 1 state, if the reset is at 0, this drives the B input to its 1 state and causes the unit to latch. When the interrupt signal returns to 0, the outputs remain in their 1 states, due to the feedback loop, and the B line remains at 1. With the memory latched, a reset command is required before the other six outputs can represent the data or functions programed in that portion of the memory.

The gate driving the B input takes the place of an additional address or control line, and is the equivalent of a ninth input variable. With it, the 2,048-bit read-only memory has the same logic flexibility as one with 4,096 bits under the $\log_2$ rule. The single external gate makes the structure very easy to implement.

What the diagram shows is a normal combinational logic net acted upon by two sequential events—interrupt followed by reset—that stop it and then restart it respectively. The read-only memory's capacity can be used for combinational functions, sequential functions such as a modulus-16 counter, or in many other applications.

Many approaches have been championed as the most efficient implementation of LSI. One way to judge their economic merits is to compare the silicon chip areas they need to perform the average function. For example, a 2,048-bit read-only memory can be made on a 90-by-110-mil chip. According to our approximations, it is the equivalent of about 200 logic gates.

There are no LSI techniques today that can put a 200-gate random logic function on so small a chip. In fact,

no one would propose to put even 100 gates on such a chip. Thus chip economics favor the use of read-only memories even if our approximation were off by a factor of two. Forecasts of bipolar logic cells as small as 10 square mils have been made, but MOS FET storage elements have already gone beyond this level, to about 1 square mil per MOS FET. Of the 10,000 square mils on the chip in the photo about 65% is occupied by the wire-bonding pads, intraconnection wiring, and decode and sense circuits. Logic arrays require similar investments in area for input-output functions. Future improvements in process resolution and larger chip sizes will greatly increase read-only memory capacity because of the basic storage element's small size.

Moreover, semiconductor read-only memories require no custom engineering, wiring, packaging or testing on the part of the semiconductor manufacturer. Once the user submits his truth table to the manufacturer, no further negotiations are required. Only one mask, controlling the gate-oxide thickness, is altered to program a read-only memory. Logic arrays, by contrast, require the manufacturer to decipher logic equations and diagrams, to prepare a set of production masks based on these diagrams governing the type and chip location of logic cells and input-output devices, and to generate up to three metallization etching masks.

Differences in the gate oxide have virtually no effect on the production process; that is, read-only memories storing different data or implementing different logic designs are produced identically, so it is a standard production item. Its handling, flow, inspection, packaging, and testing are familiar to people on the production line, who thus don't have to learn the distinctions between different designs. Experience proves that this familiarity with a single design, or with a minimum number of designs, is not a minor point in the production of any IC. No special precautions or instructions are needed at any stage during the manufacturing process, from first diffusion to final test, and none need be paid for.

Perhaps the greatest benefit of read-only memory logic comes in testing. A device with 100 or 200 gates always poses severe testing problems: Every function that it should perform must be verified, and every incorrect function that it might perform must be weeded out. This complexity requires the logic-array manufacturer to develop either a special tester for each array that it builds, or a large general-purpose tester capable of testing virtually anything in digital circuitry. Either approach is expensive. But the read-only memory manufacturer can use a standard tester that rapidly checks out the memories in all applications—as memories or as logic.

Furthermore, the read-only memory need only be tested for its combinational functions, in addition to the usual electrical tests. Unlike an array of gates and latches, a read-only memory sequential-logic system can be checked out with the feedback loops open; then, if the combinational net functions properly, the sequential net will also work when the feedback loops are closed, because the loops simply change the output from one combinational function to another.●

References

1. Samuel H. Caldwell, "Switching Circuits and Logical Design," Wiley, April 1959.
2. John L. Nichols, "A Logical Next Step for Read-Only Memories," *Electronics*, June 12, 1967, p. 111.

A matter of bits

To the Editor:

In your article on read-only memories by Floyd Kvamme, it is claimed that a pair of cascaded ROMs allow two kilobits to define four independent functions of 12 variables each, a task that would normally require 16 kilobits. The four functions are far from being independent. The first eight variables (A through H) will define a given four bits to be input to the second ROM, but since there are only 16 possible combinations of these four bits, a number of other eight-bit addresses must produce the same output. The last four variables (I through L) will therefore produce the same variation of output functions (f_1 to f_4) for all common addresses.

Regrettably, I think that the only way to obtain four truly independent functions of 12 variables each is to use all 16,384 bits.

Christopher A. Brown
Research Department
British Post Office
London

■ Mr. Brown is correct in pointing out that in the most general case to define four independent functions of 12 variables each, 16 kilobits would be required. What the cascaded ROM technique does do, however, is create secondary functions which are common to the output functions. Thus, a cascaded technique provides an avenue for simplifying the total ROM problem solution depending on the particular problem. The two examples of cascading shown were, in fact, solutions to two specific problems. The user of ROMs for logic simulation is encouraged to attempt a ROM minimization by function factoring.

Making small ROM's do math quickly, cheaply and easily

Albert Hemel of Communication Products Corp. shows how combining lookup-table and equivalent-function techniques with ROM's averts the need for huge single-memory capacity

● A team of techniques, some old and some new, can become the winning combination for making inexpensive and widely-available read-only memories perform mathematical functions. The three members of this team are the familiar lookup-table approach that contains all possible combinations of a given mathematical function or arithmetic operation; the inexpensive read-only memories made possible by large-scale integration technology; and the equivalent-function approach wherein a large number is represented by the sum of several smaller numbers prior to implementation of the mathematical process.

The lookup table is basic to the new technique. However, instead of trying to store the complete table in a single memory, which in some cases would require a capacity exceeding 1 million bits, several smaller, off-the-shelf ROM's are used. The combination replaces the usual mass of gates and flip-flops ordinarily used to perform mathematical functions. Furthermore, the combination is fast—the lookup table-ROM approach involves only the delay through the memory and its associated gates. The method can be used for addition, subtraction, multiplication, and division as well as for computing exponential powers and square roots.

Multiplication is one of the simplest operations that can be carried out with a read-only memory. Basically, multiplication is repeated addition; that's exactly what

a desk calculator does. One of the numbers to be multiplied—the multiplicand—is added to itself as many times as the other number—the multiplier—specifies. Automatic desk calculators can take certain shortcuts; the simplest is multiplying by 10 merely by shifting the multiplicand to the right one digit position. To multiply by 27, for example, instead of adding the multiplicand 27 times, the machine adds it 7 times, shifts it right, and adds it twice more. To multiply by 207 the process would be the same except that the multiplicand would be shifted two places to the right; no addition would occur after the first shift because of the 0 in the multiplier.

Conventional logic arrays multiply in the same way, with one important difference: since they work with numbers in binary notation, the multiplicand is never added more than once following each shift. All the multiplier's digits are either 1 or 0; an addition occurs for a 1. But another shift is made immediately for a 0. This shifting-and-adding sequence is time consuming.

In any multiplication, whether decimal or binary, the number of digits in the product equals either the sum of the number of digits in multiplier and multiplicand, or that sum less one.

Therefore in a straightforward lookup table the number of bits per word must equal twice the above sum. Suppose the table contains all possible products of two four-bit numbers. Four input lines would be required for each

Multiplier. Four read-only memories and five monolithic four-bit adders can multiply two eight-bit numbers cheaper than can conventional sequential logic. Lighter and heavier shadings refer, respectively, to less and more significant bits in the result.

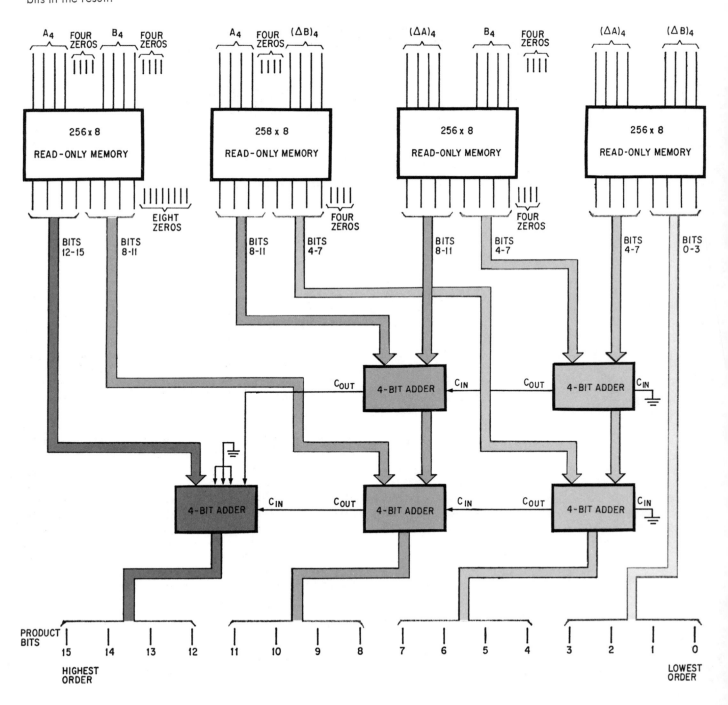

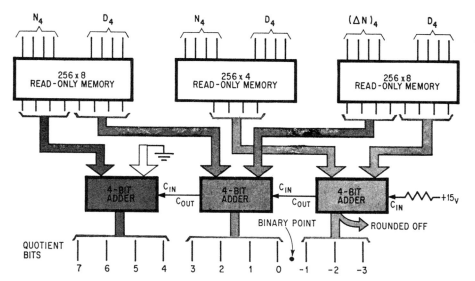

Divider. Three ROM's and three four-bit adders quickly and efficiently find the quotient of an eight-bit dividend and a four-bit divisor with accuracy out to 11 places.

number to be multiplied, or eight in all. These eight lines can carry $2^8 = 256$ different combinations of binary signals; each combination represents the address of one word in the memory. The memory's capacity would be 2,048 bits; since the product of two four-bit numbers can be as long as eight bits, the bit count in the memory would be $256 \times 8 = 2,048$.

This straightforward lookup table is as good as any method for performing a simple four-bit multiplication. But if the numbers are longer than four bits, the size of the memory grows very quickly. Thus, for two five-bit numbers, the word count is 1,024 and the output must be 10 bits long; total bit count is $1,024 \times 10 = 10,240$. For two six-bit numbers the total is $4,096 \times 12 = 49,152$. And for eight-bit numbers it is $65,536 \times 16$—more than a million bits.

No single memory with a million-bit capacity is available now, nor is one expected soon. If many small memories are interconnected to achieve this size, the cost becomes prohibitive.

But an equivalent lookup-table multiplier that works just as well as the big table can be built with much smaller memories. To design such a multiplier, represent each of the factors to be multiplied, A_8 and B_8, as the sum of two smaller numbers: one is simply the last four bits of the given number, the other is the first four bits followed by four 0's. Thus:

$$A_8 = A_4 + (\Delta A)_4$$
$$A_4 = XXXX0000$$
$$(\Delta A)_4 = \quad\quad\quad XXXX$$

Each X represents a binary 0 or 1. The other factor, B_8, is subdivided the same way.

With these numbers the original multiplication can be reconstructed as the sum of several four-bit multiplications:

$$A_8 B_8 = [A_4 + (\Delta A)_4][B_4 + (\Delta B)_4]$$
$$= [A_4 B_4] + [A_4(\Delta B)_4] + [(\Delta A)_4 B_4] + [(\Delta A)_4(\Delta B)_4]$$

These four products and their sum can be implemented in four 2,048-bit ROM's and five four-bit adders—all standard off-the-shelf items. They are manufactured by several companies, such as American Microsystems, Texas Instruments, Electronic Arrays Inc., Fairchild Semiconductor, and National Semiconductor. The multiplier shown opposite uses National's 256-by-8-bit MM 523, and also the Texas Instruments SN 7483 four-bit adders. Furthermore, the result appears at the outputs of the adders within one microsecond after the signals arrive at the memories' inputs.

These metal oxide semiconductor memories are used with adders built with transistor-transistor logic. This combination requires a 7.5 kilohm resistor to be connected between each memory output and a —12-volt supply. And, if TTL circuits are to drive the memories, each memory input should be connected through a pullup resistor to a +12-volt supply. In this case, every input is used twice, so the pullup resistors' value should be 3.75—half the normal value. Similar considerations to insure that the necessary current is available apply to the other designs described in this article—7.5 k ohms for inputs used only once, 3.75 k for inputs used twice, and 2.5 k for those used three times.

Each of the four memories has eight inputs and eight outputs, as in the simple example described earlier; but here the eight outputs are grouped into two sets of four. Each of these sets corresponds to one of four four-bit groupings in the 16-bit product. If the product bits are numbered 0 to 15, with bit 0 least significant and the furthest right, the groupings in the product

...multiplication and division are performed economically by breaking down the factors into the sums of two smaller numbers...

are bits 0-3, 4-7, 8-11, and 12-15.

The trailing 0's are not connected (for the inputs A_4 and B_4) as on page 134. However, they determine which of the four-bit groupings applies to a particular memory's output. The memory whose inputs are the $(\Delta A)_4$ and $(\Delta B)_4$ isn't concerned with any trailing 0's, so its outputs contribute to bit grouping 0-3 and 4-7 in the product. None of the other memories contributes to bits 0-3, so no adder is required for this output.

Four trailing 0's are associated with the inputs, and therefore with the outputs, of the two intermediate memories. These 0's are not connected to the memory, but they correspond to bits 0-3, so that the memories' actual outputs correspond to bits 4-7 and 8-11. The three memories that have at least one delta input produce a total of three contributions to bits 4-7; these three groups are combined in two four-bit adders to produce bits 4-7 of the product.

Finally, the last memory, which has no delta inputs, has eight trailing 0's appended to its outputs—four carried through from each of the two inputs. These correspond to bits 0-7, so that the memory's outputs are associated with bits 8-11 and 12-15. Therefore there are three memories whose outputs correspond to bits 8-11; these three groups are combined in two more four-bit adders to produce bits 8-11 of the product.

The four remaining outputs of the last memory alone would make up bits 12-15 of the product, except for the possibility of a carry bit from the lower-order adders. To incorporate this carry bit into the product, the fifth adder is required; like all the others, it has two four-bit inputs and one carry input. But it doesn't utilize all of its inputs. One of the four-bit inputs takes bits 12-15 from the last memory; the input carry takes the carry output from one of the lower adders. So far, the procedure is conventional. But there's another carry from another lower adder that has to be accounted for, and no other four-bit input. So the carry is connected to the least significant of the unused inputs, and the other three are grounded to hold them to 0. This is a rather profligate use of logic, and would never be economical except where integrated circuits are used. But it's less expensive to throw in another four-bit adder than to work up a special design from the individual IC gates.

A similar approach can be applied to division. When an eight-bit number, N_8, is to be divided by a four-bit divisor, D_4, the quotient could be thought of as four bits long—division is the inverse of multiplication, and the product of two four-bit numbers has eight bits. But with no restrictions on the divisor's magnitude, a full eight bits must be allowed for the quotient—in case the divisor is 0001, for example. Furthermore, there may be a remainder. To cover this contingency, the following example is set up for an 11-bit quotient, designated Q_{11}; the choice of 11 bits will be explained later. Of these 11 bits, three are to the right of the binary point, which corresponds to the decimal point in decimal notation; these three bits thus represent a binary fraction. Mathematically, the example $Q_{11} = N_8/D_4$ may be expressed as xxxxxxxxxxx = xxxxxxx/xxxx where the x's again represent either 1's or 0's in binary notation.

In a straightforward lookup table, the divisor and the dividend would require a total of 12 inputs, and the memory would contain $2^{12} = 4{,}096$ words of 11 bits each, or a total of 45,056 bits.

But if the 8-bit numerator is subdivided in the same way as the numbers in the multiplication example, the problem may be restated

$$Q_{11} = \frac{[N_4 + (\Delta N)_4]}{D_4} = \frac{N_4}{D_4} + \frac{(\Delta N)_4}{D_4}$$

where N_4 and $(\Delta N)_4$ are defined in the same way as

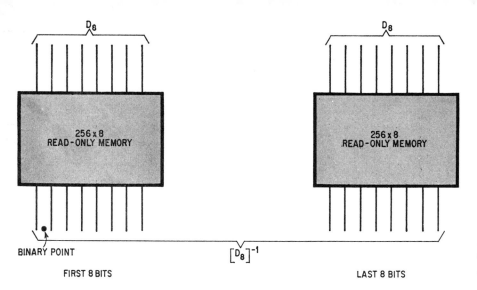

FIRST 8 BITS

LAST 8 BITS

$[D_8]^{-1}$

BINARY POINT

Inverter. With a large divisor, it may be easier to multiply the reciprocal than to divide directly. Reciprocals can be easily obtained directly from two ROM's.

the representations they correspond to in the multiplication example. Each of the two subsidiary quotients can be implemented with a 256-word ROM, but there's a catch that isn't found in multiplication.

In general, both quotients may have remainders that cannot be completely specified in a binary fraction 11 bits long—just as the fraction 3/32 cannot be completely specified in three decimal places. When the quotients are added together to make Q_{11}, since both of them may have been rounded off, they may create a cumulative error that makes the last bit position in the sum incorrect. To compensate, therefore, the two subsidiary quotients are implemented with an extra fractional bit—a fourth bit to the right of the binary point instead of three. Then, the lowest-order of these four bits is discarded at the output of the adder to provide the desired 11-bit accuracy.

Thus the N_4/D_4 portion of the final quotient can be implemented with a read-only memory of 256 words of 12 bits each. As shown on page 135, this is easily accomplished by using standard memories of eight-bit and four-bit word lengths connected in parallel. Typical ROM's such as National's MM523 can be used for the eight-bit word lengths, and the MM521 for the four-bit word. And just one additional eight-bit memory can be used for the N_4/D_4 portion. Since this N_4 dividend consists of only four bits, the necessary accuracy, four

places to the right of the binary point, is attained with only eight bits. The total is 5,120 bits with this technique, compared to 45,056 for the straightforward approach.

The 20 outputs from the three memories are combined in three four-bit adders in much the same way as was done in multiplication. One of the adders handles the four fractional bits and another the four low-order bits to the left of the binary point. A third adder is necessary for the four highest-order bits; it serves the same purpose as the fifth adder did in multiplication—to handle the effect of a carry from the other adders into these bits.

Ordinarily, when several small adders are used for summing large numbers, as in this example, the input carry to the least significant adder is held at zero with a ground connection; such a connection is shown in the diagram for multiplication, and also could be used in the division example. But in division, the lowest order bit is included only to prevent a cumulative rounding error, and is discarded in the final quotient. One convenient rule that can be applied to binary rounding is to add 1 to the lowest-order bit that is retained if the highest-order discarded bit is 1; this corresponds to the decimal rule to add 1 to the last digit if the highest-order discarded digit is five or more. This upward rounding can be insured by connecting the lowest input carry to a positive voltage, or leaving it disconnected, rather than grounding it. Either alternative holds the carry to a 1.

When the denominator is large, multiplying by the divisor's reciprocal may be easier than dividing directly. Finding the reciprocal of a binary number is not the same as complementing; it is the result of dividing the number into unity, and in general it will have a large remainder. Consequently, for accuracy, the reciprocal should have more bits than the original number. The diagram above illustrates in a general way how an eight-bit denominator is inverted using two 256-word-by-eight bit ROM's to produce a reciprocal value that's accurate to 16 binary places. When inverting larger numbers, whose leading bit is always 1, the reciprocal's leading bits are always 0. Then one of the two memories can be made smaller or eliminated altogether.

The four-bit adders used in the multiplication and division schemes, as well as subtractors, may themselves be implemented with read-only memories. The two operations are identical, except that in subtraction, one of

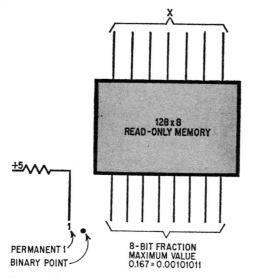

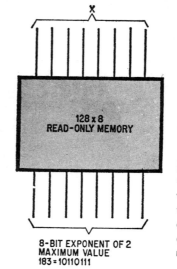

8-BIT FRACTION
MAXIMUM VALUE
0.167 = 0.00101011

8-BIT EXPONENT OF 2
MAXIMUM VALUE
183 = 10110111

PERMANENT 1
BINARY POINT

Exponential. Two ROM's can generate values of exponential functions over a wide range. One gives the fractional value, or mantissa—a characteristic of 1 always is used—and the other yields the exponent in a floating-point notation referred to the base 2.

the numbers involved is complemented before beginning the operation—its complement is used as part of the ROM address. However, there is little advantage in using ROM's, since integrated-circuit adders are readily available at low cost. But it's interesting to note some of the peculiarities that occur when addition is performed with this scheme.

It appears that an addition lookup table, containing the sums of pairs of four-bit numbers, would have the same number of entries—the same number of ROM words —as a table containing the products of such pairs. But this is not so. The adder table must allow for an input carry.

Thus a total number of nine input bits is needed for a four-bit adder—four for each 4-bit number and one for the carry. These nine bits address $2^9 = 512$ words, compared to 256 in the multiplication table. The greater number of words is partially offset by the fact that the sum contains no more than five bits, including an output carry. Thus the total number of bits in a ROM serving as a four-bit adder is $512 \times 5 = 2,560$, compared with the four-bit multiplier's 2,048 bits.

But just as in multiplication and division, the equivalent-function approach can simplify the adder design. For example, if a four-bit addition is considered as two two-bit additions, each with its own input carry, then the total number of input bits to each adder is five. This requires only $2^5 = 32$ words of three bits each, including an output carry, for each adder. The two adders then would require 64 words, and the output carry of one could be connected directly to the other's input carry. These 64 words thus could be packaged in a single unit containing only 192 bits, which is much less than the earlier 2,560 bits.

Raising values to an exponential power also works out quite conveniently with ROM's. Because the exponential function is one of the more rapidly increasing functions—exceeded among common functions only by the factorial—the outputs of a ROM containing values of the exponential should be expressed in floating-point notation—for example, ϵ^{10} expressed in floating-point notation is 2.2026×10^4, instead of 22,026.

However, floating-point notation need not be in the conventional power-of-10 format. In binary notation, powers of two are more convenient; the above example in binary is thus

$$\epsilon^{1010} = 101011000001010$$
$$= 1.01011000001010 \times 2^{14}$$
$$= 1.01011000 \times 2^{1110}$$

Here the exponent of ϵ is 10 in binary form; its value is expressed in binary form as a 15-bit number. This is finally expressed in base-2 floating-point notation as 1 followed by a 14-bit binary fraction, multiplied by 2^{14}. This fraction is shown above with the exponent in both a decimal and true binary floating-point format. In the latter, the fraction is rounded off to eight binary places.

Base-2 floating-point notation has two major advantages: it need not be reconverted into binary form for use in a system containing the function table, and its most significant bit is always 1. The latter permits this bit to be "free"—wired permanently outside the memory, rather than stored in it.

An exponential-function table containing values of ϵ^x, where x is accurate to seven bits, can be stored in two ROM's, each containing 128 words of eight bits each, as shown above. One of the memories, which could be National's MM 522 or equivalent, would produce the fractional part of the exponential value accurate to eight bits; the other would produce the exponent part of the function expressed in floating-point form. The input ranges from ϵ^0 to ϵ^{127} and the output from 1 to 1.167 $\times$

2^{183} or, in binary, to $1.00101011 \times 2^{10110111}$.

Such numbers aren't often encountered in practical applications. A more useful implementation might permit the 128 input values to range for example, from 0 to 63.5 in 0.5 steps; or to 31.75 in 0.25 steps; or to 7.9375 in 0.0625 steps, with successively higher resolution, depending on the position of the binary point. These correspond respectively to maximum output values of 1.528×2^{91}, 1.748×2^{45}, 1.870×2^{22}, and 1.368×2^{11}. In binary notation these are, respectively

$1.10000111 \times 2^{1011011}$

$1.10111111 \times 2^{101101}$

$1.11011110 \times 2^{10110}$

$1.01011110 \times 2^{1011}$

Any one of these versions would use the 128-word-by-eight-bit ROM for the binary fraction and a 128-word memory with a word length of four to seven bits for the exponent.

If an exponential function with both a wide range and high resolution is required, seven bits may not be sufficient for the input. This presents the same problem encountered in setting up a multiplication table for the product of two eight-bit numbers—it requires a much larger ROM than is practical.

But the solution to this problem is similar to that for multiplication—the exponent is divided into two parts

$$\epsilon^x = \epsilon^{(y + \Delta y)} = (\epsilon^y)(\epsilon^{\Delta y})$$

where, in the same manner as before, y contains all the higher-order bits of x followed by a string of 0's, and Δy contains the low-order bits of x. The two individual exponential functions are generated with two ROM's each. When the two exponential functions found in this way are combined, their bases, including the permanent high-order 1, are multiplied, and their exponents are added.

An exponential function of a constant other than ϵ can be obtained in the same way; it requires only that the read-only memories be programed with the proper values. But if the base of the exponential function is itself a variable, a very simple process is available for calculating its value. The process is based on the equivalence

$$A^x = 2^{x(\log_2 A)}$$

This equivalence holds true, of course, for any logarithmic base, including ϵ and 10; but 2 is used because it permits multiplication by a power of two by merely shifting the binary point, analogous to multiplication by a power of 10 in decimal notation.

The process requires that six ROM's be used—one to provide $\log_2 A$, four to multiply this log by x, and one to provide one of two subdivisions of $x(\log_2 A)$. These two subdivisions, in general, can be an integer part N and a fraction part F. With these subdivisions, the above equivalence equation becomes

$$A^x = 2^{x(\log_2 A)} = 2^{(N + F)} = (2^N)(2^F)$$

In this product, the number 2^F can be obtained from the sixth ROM, and the factor 2^N represents a shift of the binary point N places to the right.

For example, suppose A = 7 and x = 3. The value of $7^3 = 343$, but in terms of the equivalence, the steps are

$$7^3 = 2^{3(\log_2 7)} = 2^{3(2.807)} = 2^{8.421} = (2^8)(2^{0.421})$$

These are expressed in decimal notation for clarity; but in practice, of course, they would be in binary. The factor $2^{0.421} = 2^{0.0110110} = 1.01010111$; the factor 2^8 calls for the binary point to shift 8 places to the right, giving 101010111, which is equivalent to 343 in decimal notation.

For extracting square roots or higher roots, these combinational techniques won't work; there is no easy way to subdivide a large number into two parts, find the square root of each part, and then recombine the results. There are two complicated ways to go about it; one based on the binomial theorem; the other based on the Taylor series. But both are of limited value in practical applications.

However, the reverse process of finding the square or other fixed power of a number is quite easy with the ROM technique. The squares of all eight-bit numbers contain a maximum of 16 bits, which can be stored in a ROM of 256 words by 16 bits, yielding a total bit count of 4,096.

The ease of the method points the way to an iterative search technique for calculating square roots by trial and correction. The iterative search for the eight bit root, R_8, of a given 16-bit number, N_{16}, begins with using a trial root of $R_8 = 0$ as the address to the ROM storing all the squares. This trial root is then successively increased until the memory produces a number equal to or greater than the given number N_{16}; that trial root is the true root.

This process is fastest, on the average, if the most significant bit of the trial root is changed first from 0 to 1. If the output of the memory then exceeds the given number N_{16}, the most significant bit returns to 0; otherwise, it remains at 1. The same procedure then is used with the other bits of R_8. The circuits to control this sequence of trial roots and to compare the memory's successive outputs with the given number N_{16} can be made from standard IC flip-flops and comparators.

A rounding error often will occur if the ROM stores

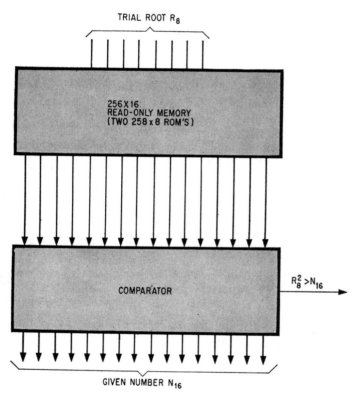

TRIAL ROOT R_8

256×16
READ-ONLY MEMORY
(TWO 258×8 ROM'S)

COMPARATOR

$R_8^2 > N_{16}$

GIVEN NUMBER N_{16}

Extractor. This scheme for obtaining square roots depends primarily on squaring a series of trial roots using a small ROM until a number is found that comes sufficiently close to the original number.

the squares of the trial roots R_8. Suppose, for example, the number whose root to be found is 280—in 16-position binary, this is 0000 0001 0001 1000. The successive eight-bit trial roots for this 16-bit number are 1000 0000; 0100 0000; 0010 0000; 0001 0000; 0001 1000; 0001 0100; 0001 0010; 0001 0001; in decimal they would be stated 128, 64, 32, 16, 24, 20, 18, 17. The squares of each of the first three trial roots are greater than 280; but the square of 16 is only 256. So the 1 is retained in the fourth position and 1's are tried in successively less significant positions until the last, corresponding to 17. This result is correct in this case, because the actual square root of 280 is 16.7332, correctly rounded off to 17. But if the number whose root was to calculated were 270, the same successive trial roots would be used. The result, however, would be incorrectly rounded off because the actual square root of 270 is 16.4317. This should be rounded off to 16.

To avoid this rounding error, the ROM can be programed to store $(R_8 - \frac{1}{2})^2$ instead of R_8^2. These two numbers differ by $(R_8 - \frac{1}{4})$ but the former differs from $(R_8 - 1)^2$ by $(R_8 - \frac{3}{4})$. Thus the memory's output will always be closer to the true square of R_8 than to the square of $(R_8 - 1)$. Using the same method of successive approximations, with an $(R_8 - \frac{1}{2})^2$ ROM, as was described above for an R_8^2 ROM, $(280)^{\frac{1}{2}}$ will be found to be 17 and $(270)^{\frac{1}{2}}$ will be 16.

An alternative procedure that would work just as well would be to begin with the largest possible trial root, 1111111, and change successive bits to 0 beginning at the most significant bit until the memory's output is less than the given number. With this alternative procedure, the memory should store $(R_8 + \frac{1}{2})^2$ to prevent the rounding error. ●

Bibliography

Radiation Inc., Application Note, Integrated Diode Matrixes, February, 1967.

John L. Nichols, "A logical next step for read-only memories," Electronics, June 12, 1967, p. 111.

Floyd Kvamme, "Standard read-only memories simplify complex logic design," this volume, p. 123.

National Semiconductor Corp., data sheets, MM521, MM522, MM523, and DM8200.

National Semiconductor Corp., Application Note #12, Digital Comparator.

Texas Instruments Inc., data sheets SN7401, SN7405, SN7474, and SN7483.

Chapter 6
Electromechanical and acoustic memories

Rotating disks and drums set peripheral memories spinning

Their fast access time gives them the edge over magnetic tapes,
but picking the best one for a specific application isn't easy
and requires detailed knowledge of their hardware and software

By Michael French
BCD Computing Corp., Deer Park, N.Y.

Growing in versatility, rotating disks and drums are more and more displacing magnetic tape as peripheral memories. But from the same versatility, confusion can arise simply as a result of the wide variety of technical choices that must be made before selecting a disk or drum for a particular job.

Should the memory be disk or drum? Should it be removable or non-removable, serial or parallel, self clocked or externally clocked? Ought the heads to be of the "flying" or in-contact type, movable or assigned one to a track? What kind of head switching arrangement should be selected? Should the records be of fixed or variable length?

The applications, of course, dictate the response to these questions—though engineers in the industry by no means always agree on the answers. For the technology's moved pretty fast in a comparatively short time and some of the basics—why heads "crash" onto drums, for example—aren't completely understood. In fact, it was only three years ago that IBM introduced its 2311 rotating removable disk memory that's since become the industry standard. Today, at least 20 firms make the disk packs and another 10 the compatible drives.

Rotating memories now have capacities ranging from 100 thousand to 4 billion bits, access times from 8.7 to 225 milliseconds, and cost from 0.5 cents to 0.02 cents per bit.

The ability to buy rotating memories from several different sources has acted as an important spur to growth. Another important factor has been the price drop accompanying higher recording densities and faster data transfer rates made possible by such advances as higher efficiency codes.

But perhaps the biggest boost has come from the increase in time sharing on large computers and real time data processing on miniature units. Both of these have created a need for peripheral memories with much faster access times than those offered by tape transports. Because such transports must read every record serially, access times are very long—on the average about a minute for a 1,200-foot reel of tape. In a disk or drum, on the other hand, where movable heads needn't read everything preceding a record, average access times are 87 milliseconds.

Thus, for real time applications like program swapping or airline reservation data banks, the rotating type memory is the only practical periph-

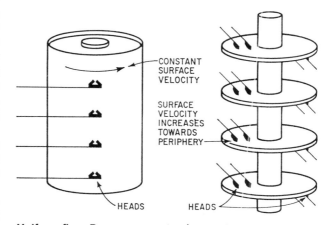

Uniform flow. Because every track on a drum memory is the same distance from the rotating center, surface velocity and, therefore, air currents under the flying heads are uniform. In disks, however, surface velocity and air flow rate increase toward periphery, making head design difficult.

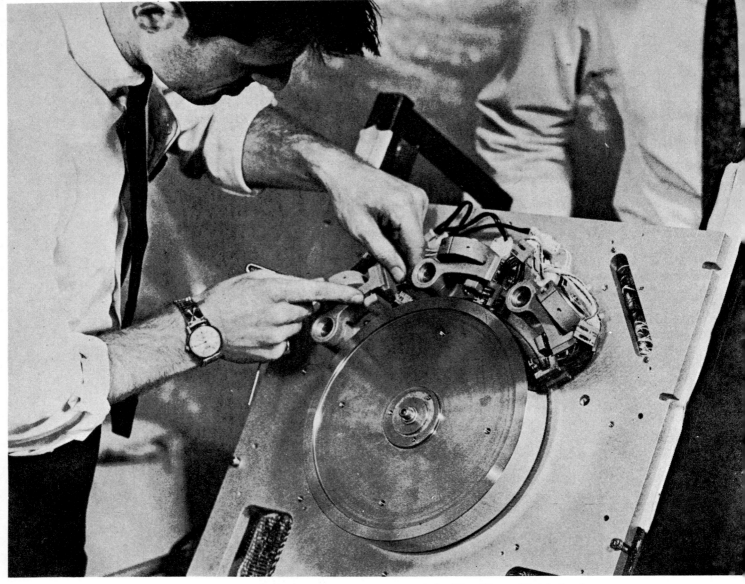

Low capacity. This low cost drum memory, made by Bryant, stores 1.2 million bits on 32 data tracks and has an average access time of 8.5 milliseconds.

eral storage medium. And for applications such as the sorting or merging of files, the need for considerably faster access time usually rules out tape.

One of the more controversial choices is that between head per track and movable head memories. Total access time of the first depends only on the times it takes to switch a head into the read or write mode—about 2 to 20 microseconds—and on the "latency time." The latter refers to the time it takes the desired portion of a particular track to rotate into position under a head. On the average, heads are half a rotational period away, and latency time averages between 8.7 and 16.5 milliseconds.

Movable head memories, however, include another delay because heads must travel from one track to another. On the average this takes between 50 and 225 milliseconds so that these memories are an order of magnitude slower than the head per track type. However, since the movable types use much fewer heads, they're also much less expensive. For instance, IBM's 2311, a 60 million bit mem-

ory, has only ten heads along a comblike arm and a one-in-ten selection matrix. All of the heads are positioned simultaneously, each one over a track on one of ten disk surfaces. (The total number of tracks available for reading or writing at one head position is called a cylinder.) This type memory costs about $26,000 and has a latency time of 12.5 milliseconds.

General Instruments' Magne-Head division offers a lower capacity and higher priced memory that stores 20 million bits. The higher price arises from the use of 512 separately mounted flying heads, one for each track, giving a total access time of 8.5 milliseconds.

Magne-Head's director of marketing Richard Martin, says, "In practice it's been proven that head per track memories can improve system data processing and throughput time by a factor as high as 10 to 1 over moving head memories. With central processing unit time being sold by the microsecond, computer efficiency versus application will be the major consideration, with basic hardware cost, within reasonable bounds, no consideration at all."

However, this opinion—typical of many in the industry—needs qualifying. Certainly, head per track memories are more economical for capacities under about 10 million bits because the cost of moving-head drives outweighs that of extra heads. But for most applications, where capacities over 50 million bits are required, it's too costly to include heads for each track and it calls for a very complex switching matrix.

However, in the 10 to 50 million bit range—where the bulk of the market is—the choice isn't at all clear. The economics vary with the application and the relative importance of speed and cost. Moving head memories that are compatible with the IBM 2311, for example, shift heads from one track to the next in 20 microseconds and travel an average distance (over 70 tracks) in 75 to 50 milliseconds. This includes time for removing mechanical brakes on heads and for damping out mechanical vibration. For applications, such as commercial time-sharing, the total access time of 87 milliseconds is sufficiently short and, since the computer isn't being used to perform other operations, doesn't raise costs.

Maneuvering for economy

Most of today's slow capacity units—offered by firms like Data Disk, Information Data Systems, and Alpha Data for as low as $5,000—are head per track memories. But for capacities between 5 and 50 million bits, some companies are selling compromise units that have movable drives with more than one head on each surface. Bryant Computer, the Computer Peripheral Corp., and National Cash Register make files that can read between a third and a sixth of their total storage capacity without moving their heads. And access time is less than with conventional moving head units because any single head doesn't have to move as far from one track to another. These memories cost about 30% less than comparable-capacity head per track units. And for some applications, access times can be reduced still further by writing records that are needed together on the same or adjacent cylinders.

A decision to use a movable head memory can, however, rule out drums, which are most often head per track units. For those who can use the IBM compatible disk memories, there are the advantages of lower cost and the choice of buying from a variety of suppliers.

Many disks have another advantage over drums—they can be removed from the memory and stored. This property is desirable for computer applications where alternate programs are used. For example, a computer might process payroll one day a week and perform engineering and production control tasks the remainder of the week.

However, for those applications that demand high reliability, very low error rate, and rugged construction, drums are the clear choice. Their long lifetimes—over 100,000 hours—and low error rates—

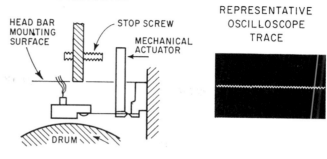

HEAD PAD RETRACTED

HEAD BAR MOUNTING SURFACE — STOP SCREW — MECHANICAL ACTUATOR — DRUM

REPRESENTATIVE OSCILLOSCOPE TRACE

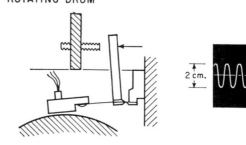

HEADS APPROACHING ROTATING DRUM

2 cm.

OPERATING POSITION

AIR FILM

4 cm.

HEAD GAP TANGENT MAXIMUM SIGNAL AMPLITUDE

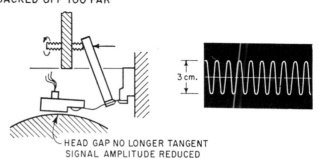

ADJUSTABLE STOP BACKED OFF TOO FAR

3 cm.

HEAD GAP NO LONGER TANGENT SIGNAL AMPLITUDE REDUCED

Flying low. In disks and drums, flying type heads ride a few millionths of an inch above rotating surface on film of air. When brake is removed, mechanical actuator moves forward until it is stopped by screw and, at the same time, head approaches surface, which starts to rotate. Amplitude of read or write signal is maximum when head gap is tangent to surface. If adjustable stop is backed off too far, signal amplitude decreases.

less than one transient error in every 10^{13} bits—derive from their relative immunity to head crashes. When heads smash onto the surface of a rotating disk or drum—instead of "flying" on a layer of air a few millionths of an inch above—magnetic material gets scraped off. Dust particles and mechanical instabilities are the chief causes of such crashes. Particles get between the head and surface where they act as abrasives that scour off magnetic material or they interfere with the head aerodynamics.

Drums minimize abrasion and head crashes because they're sealed and, therefore, keep out dust. (Removable disk memories, of course, can't be sealed.) While most non-removable disk memories aren't sealed, one line of disk memories—from the Digital Development Corporation—operates in a helium atmosphere and offers very high reliability. Equally important, drum heads are all the same distance from the rotating center, thereby guaranteeing a laminar airflow that's more than sufficient to keep the heads flying. By contrast, the flow of air under disk heads changes for each track and is small close to the disk center.

Drums have two other advantages: they rotate faster than disks (up to 24,000 rpm) and thus have faster access times and they can be packed with more information. Their potentially higher packing density results from their stronger head playback signal, which permits accurate readout of signals even though flux transitions are very close together.

Getting strong signals onto and out of today's narrow tracks and thin emulsions requires that heads either contact disk and drum surfaces or fly about 50 to 200 millionths of an inch above them. At these close distances it's just not feasible to position heads mechanically.

At first, air was blown through a hole in the head to maintain the surface to head spacing. But gradually these hydrostatic type heads have been replaced by hydrodynamic types. These fly above the surface on a film of air that's dragged along by the moving disk or drum. (The moving surface under the heads of an IBM 2311 disk memory, for example, generates a steady current of air since it travels at a rate of 64 to 93 miles an hour.)

Users of disk or drum memories don't have much choice in selecting types of flying heads, though they ought to be familiar with the problems that can come up. For instance, a power failure could cause the spring loaded heads to crash if the memory doesn't include a fail-safe retraction system. Fortunately, most drum and disk memories do. Also, if the head altitude isn't adjusted properly, playback signal level drops sharply. Another problem arises from mechanical vibration of the head. This modulates the amplitude of the playback signal, affecting both the memory's peak detectors and phase shifting networks. Good quality drum memories have modulation levels below 10%.

Almost every rotating memory sold today uses diode matrices to select signals from one head out of many. Noise is kept to a minimum by mounting amplifiers close to the read heads and connecting

Modular. In the Bryant AHO drum memory, heads are arranged 16 to a bar. This head per track unit offers access times as low as 8 1/3 milliseconds, and capacities up to 59 million bits. In another, more recent version, at right, heads are grouped nine to a pole piece to provide a more stable flying surface.

them with twisted pairs of shielded wires.

In the moving head types, the number of heads is small enough to allow one dimensional matrix selection. Lowering the head select line causes current to flow through the appropriate diodes. Current flowing from the write amplifier flows in alternate legs of a coil, saturating the track under it. In the read mode, small complementary impedance changes at the heads create differential voltage signals at the read amplifiers.

Head per track memories generally select heads in a two dimensional matrix. Heads, in an eight by 16 group, typically are mounted in a flying pad, which offers a larger and more stable aerodynamic surface than would individual heads. In the read mode, current flows from the source at the read amplifier through one of eight pairs of npn tran-

EXTERNALLY CLOCKED CODES

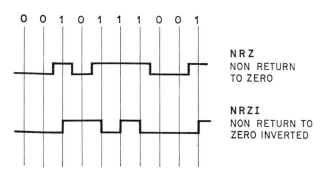

0 0 1 0 1 1 1 0 0 1

NRZ
NON RETURN
TO ZERO

NRZI
NON RETURN TO
ZERO INVERTED

SELF CLOCKED CODES

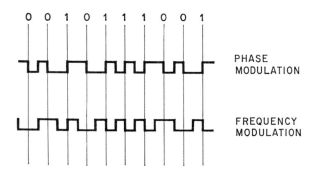

0 0 1 0 1 1 1 0 0 1

PHASE
MODULATION

FREQUENCY
MODULATION

HIGHER EFFICIENCY CODES

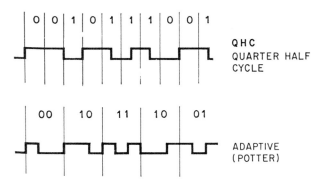

| 0 | 0 | 1 | 0 | 1 | 1 | 1 | 0 | 0 | 1 |

QHC
QUARTER HALF
CYCLE

| 00 | 10 | 11 | 10 | 01 |

ADAPTIVE
(POTTER)

Ins and outs. Several types of codes are used for writing and reading in rotating drums and disks. Simplest are the NRZ and NRZI externally clocked codes. In the first, 1's are recorded as magnetic flux saturations in one direction, 0's as saturations in the opposite direction. In NRZI, only 1's are recorded as flux transitions. Phase modulation notes direction of flux transition in cell middle, whereas frequency modulation notes presence or absence of transition. Higher efficiency codes offer higher bit packing densities but are economical only for high capacity memories. Quarter-half-cycle code 0's are written as transitions at end of bit cell, and 1's either as transitions in middle or as no transition. Potter code records two data bits for every three flux transitions.

sistors to the center tap of one of 16 read/write coils and then to ground through one turned-on y-address transistor. Typical track switching times for two dimensional arrays are 25 microseconds, head impedance levels are 500 to 1,000 ohms in series with 10 to 20 microhenries, and write currents are 70 to 120 milliamperes.

Telling time

Rotating memories offer the user a choice of four general types of clocking schemes and several different code patterns. In the simplest scheme—used on low-cost, low-capacity memories—a separate clock track provides both read and write synchronizing pulses that define the boundaries of the data bit cells. With the NRZ (non-return to zero) and NRZI (non-return to zero inverted) codes, this track provides synchronizing pulses directly in the write mode. Thus, the write clock frequency depends on the speed of the rotating disk or drum, thereby compensating for any variations. In the read mode, the pulse is delayed half a bit cell period to provide the sampling signal for both the output shift clock and the data.

With this external clocking scheme, at high packing densities it's possible for the read-sampling clock pulse and data to get out of phase, producing errors. Also, the NRZ and NRZI codes don't produce pulses in every bit cell and, thus, the read amplifiers have to handle frequencies covering several decades nearly down to d-c.

In the NRZ code, binary ones are recorded as magnetic flux saturations in one direction, binary zeros as saturations in the opposite direction. Thus, this code only requires a flux change when changing from one binary state to the other, and trains of binary ones and zeros produce no read back pulses. In the NRZI code only ones are recorded as flux transitions and a train of zeros doesn't produce pulses. However, there's no timing problem with either code when using seven or nine channel tape recorders because each character contains at least one transition to generate the clock.

Another method—the most common way of recording data in phase-modulation or double-frequency-modulation codes—provides external clocking for writing, and self clocking for reading. Used by most of the major independent memory manufacturers—Vermont Research, the Bryant Computer Corp., and Magne-Head, for example—this approach offers the highest recording densities and greatest reliability.

Both codes use up to two flux transitions for each bit cell. Phase modulation decodes data by noting the direction of the flux transition in the middle of the cell; double-frequency modulation, on the other hand, decodes by detecting the presence or absence of a transition in the middle of the cell. To read data, both codes reconstruct the clock from the encoded playback signal and then use the clock to decode the data bits. The codes are self clocking because at least one pulse appears in every data cell period during playback. For example, in double-frequency modulation, a binary one equals the clock frequency and a binary zero equals half this frequency. Both f-m and phase-modulation codes are fairly immune to noise and errors from transition shifting.

The IBM 2311 disk memory uses double-frequency modulation and a precision oscillator to provide both read and write timing. Data is transmitted to and from the memory in trains of 150 to 50 nanosecond-duration pulses. This system is reliable and doesn't require separately recorded read- and write-clock tracks on the disk. But it requires two flux transitions to record each data bit. And it's subject to errors caused by variations either in the mechanical tolerances of the disk drives or in the oscillator.

Bits and pieces

Two firms, the Computer Peripheral Corp. and Potter Instrument, are offering higher bit packing densities through codes that require less than two flux transitions per bit. However, due to the elaborate electronics required, these schemes are only economical for memories with capacities over 25 million bits.

Computer Peripheral's method uses a version of the Miller code to obtain one data bit per transition. (In the Miller code, zeros are written as flux transitions at the end of a bit cell; ones are written either as a transition in the middle of a cell if the preceding bit is a one or as no transition if the preceding bit is a zero.)

Potter's adaptive code only records two data bits for every three flux transition periods, but it still offers the highest bit packing densities because it allows flux transitions to be spaced closer together. By contrast, phase- and frequency-modulation codes offer 1,200 bits and 3,000 bits to an inch respectively for flying-head and head-in-contact memories.

Single transition per bit codes are harder to implement in memories for several other reasons besides needing additional encoding and decoding digital logic. Their reconstructed clock pulse doesn't appear in the same position in each data cell; the wide bandwidth of their detection amplifiers increases phase shifting, and the lack of symmetry in some data patterns increases error rate.

Yet, as the cost of integrated circuit amplifiers and decoding circuits drop, these codes should become more popular for large memories. At the same time, changing IC technology should favor self-clocked instead of NRZ and NRZI codes in smaller rotating memories.

Even though many rotating memories have separate clock and sector marking tracks—each with its own amplifiers—almost all have only one read amplifier and, thus, transfer data serially. The Vermont Research Corp., for example, sells a 4.2 million bit drum memory that has a bit transfer rate of 1.8 megahertz, or 225 bytes per second. If it had eight read/write amplifiers instead of only one, the bit transfer rate of this memory could be increased

to 14.4 Mhz, or 1.8 million bytes per second.

However, at least with high capacity memories parallel recording increases the possibility of skew (phase shifting) between tracks. In seven or nine channel tape transports, this problem is corrected by delayed sampling signals and, sometimes, by deskewing buffers.

Rotating memories use elaborate formatting schemes to indicate the bounds of fixed- or variable-length data blocks (records) and to synchronize free running external oscillators to detect readback signals.

It is a usual practice to write "preambles" of one to ten bytes before blocks of data to synchronize the read circuits. And some systems, like the Magne-Head drums and IBM disks, include guard bits at the end of each record. Between records there's usually a gap where there are no recorded signals. Envelope detectors in the read circuits identify these gaps as the extreme limits of blocks.

Files with fixed length records are the easiest to address and read since they don't require "count areas," or fields. In this type of formatting, sector blocks or markers are written onto the file by the seller and can't be changed by the user.

Since each record must be bounded by gaps, as the number of records on a track is increased the unusable space becomes greater and the data capacity decreases. Compromises are usually made between tracks containing many short records with many gaps, and tracks with one large record and maximum data capacity.

Signposts

Variable length formats waste even more data capacity. The IBM 2311 disk file uses this framing method. It contains synchronizing bits that indicate the number of bytes in variable data blocks and that note the status of each record. At the beginning of each record a "count area" contains status bits and field length bytes. Status indicators tell whether a track is usable or error prone, for example, if magnetic material has been rubbed off by a head crash. All commercial disk and drum memories have between 2 and 5% of their tracks set aside as spares. When a bad track is discovered, its records are rewritten on a spare.

Formats get quite complicated with very large disk files especially those used for high reliability, fast-access military applications that have redundant storage and storage-access mechanisms. These memories—generally movable head disk files with up to 90 heads per cylinder and parallel access channels—have one set of heads that read and write on one cylinder while another set performs a search for data.

If one data channel or head positioner requires maintenance, data is still accessible through the other channel. One popular disk file of this type, the IBM 2314, has nine independent disk files and packs that store a total of half a billion bits. Any eight of these packs are on-line at any one time. The ninth is a standby. ∎

Quite a big byte

To the Editor:

Michael French's article about rotating disks and drums makes a rather misleading statement about Vermont Research's 4.2-megabit drum memory. It has a bit transfer rate of 1.8 megahertz or 225 kilobytes per second—rather than the 225 bytes per second quoted in the article.

Also let me point out that our 8-megabyte drum is available in either bit serial or byte serial configurations with eight read-write amplifiers. The eight-bit parallel format at 2.0-megahertz clock rate gives us a 2 megabytes per second or 16 megabits per second data transfer rate, deskewed and self-clocked.

Please also note that the illustration of the flying head action on page 145 shows the single-reed mounting that is unique to Vermont Research products.

George Marchyshyn
R&D department
Vermont Research Corp.
North Springfield, Ver.

Boosting reliability of disk memories

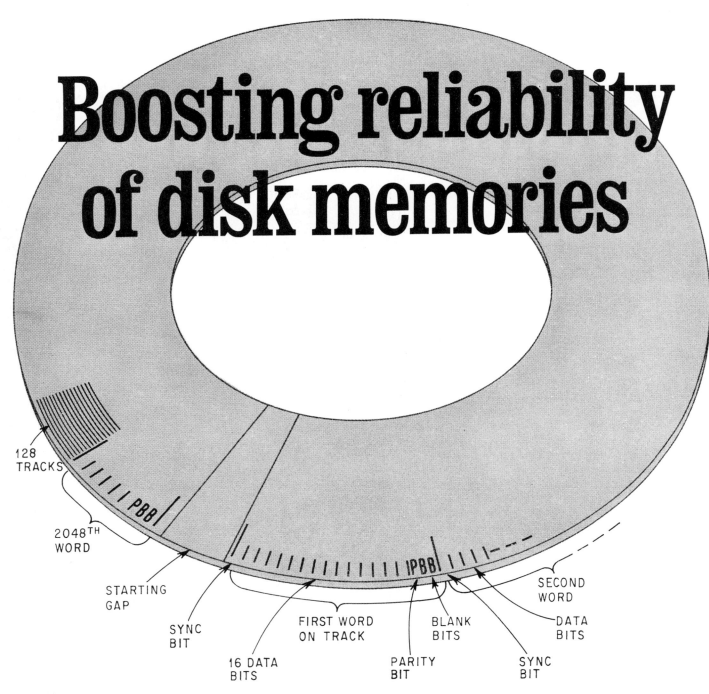

128 TRACKS

2048TH WORD

STARTING GAP

SYNC BIT

16 DATA BITS

FIRST WORD ON TRACK

PARITY BIT

BLANK BITS

SYNC BIT

DATA BITS

SECOND WORD

One in twenty. A synchronizing bit signals the beginning of every 16-bit word, of which 2,048 are recorded in each track; a parity bit and two blank bits follow the data. A gap 1/60th of a revolution in length separates the last word in a track from the first; but the 128 gaps don't actually line up in a pie-shaped sector as depicted in this diagram. Rather, because each track has its own read-write head, and because the heads are arranged in eight groups of 16 around the supporting casting, the gaps are also distributed around the disk.

Sound electronic design isn't enough by itself; good mechanical design can make the big difference, according to *Roland Boisvert* and *S. A. Lambert* of Digital Information Storage Corp.

● Mechanical design often has been ignored in electronic design, only to turn out to be the keystone without which otherwise technically sound and reliable equipment collapses. But if mechanical considerations in an electronic product are given very high priority, and are considered along with the design of the electronics, as in a new digital disk recorder with removable disks, the goal of high total reliability can be achieved:

▶ Timing reliability is high because read-write timing is controlled by synchronization bits interspersed among the data bits—and with only one sync bit in every 20 bit positions on the disk, against one in four or even one in two in some systems.

▶ Mechanical reliability is high because all major bearing surfaces run on air bearings rather than ball bearings, while the drive's mechanisms are controlled by fluidic logic instead of relays and solenoid valves.

▶ Data reliability is high because the disks are stored in sealed cartridges. From these they are loaded into the drive without being exposed to the dirt in room air.

Significantly, a major byproduct of the quest for mechanical reliability in the new recorder—Digital Information Storage Corp.'s DDR-1—is the first combination of effectively infinite storage capacity with fast access time. Removable disks provide the capacity, limited only by shelf space available for disk storage. Fast access results from having a read-write head for every track. These two features, a giant bonus when combined in one machine, are made possible by the air bearing's intrinsic self-centering property, which permits the disk to be accurately positioned relative to the heads, even as it spins at up to 3,600 revolutions per minute.

To permit a large quantity of data to be stored on each disk, some single-disk systems are arranged with storage surfaces on both sides of the disk. If the unit is removable, the two-sided arrangement requires read-write heads to be retracted during loading and unloading. But a head-retracting mechanism with one head per track would be so cumbersome as to be uneconomic, so these systems also require the heads to move from track to track preceding most reading and writing operations.

On the other hand, recording data on only one surface of the disk requires very small spacing between tracks. This can be close enough to cause crosstalk between tracks, and other problems, on disks using iron oxide coating; but when the magnetic recording medium is the nickel-chromium material that has become increasingly popular, these problems aren't serious. Nickel-chromium also permits tight packing of bits within a track. But close track-spacing means that the heads must be very accurately positioned over the tracks.

Accurate positioning, up to now, has precluded a removable disk. Enter the head-per-track approach—which has the added advantage of sharply reducing access

Simple. This view of the DDR-1's front panel also shows the slot through which disks are loaded into the machine from their storage cartridge, which is called a DISClosure. Here the machine appears on a table top, requiring the air compressors to be placed under the table or nearby. A stand is available that conceals the compressors in its base.

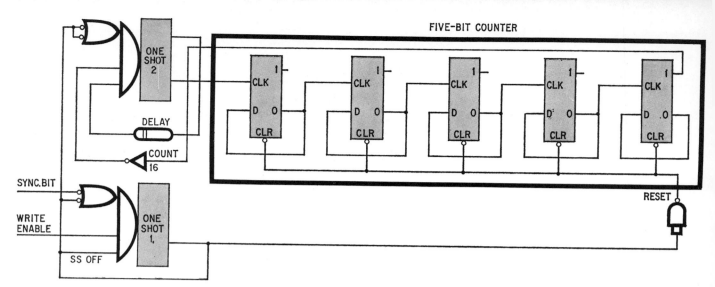

ONE SHOT 2

DELAY

COUNT 16

SYNC BIT

WRITE ENABLE

ONE SHOT 1

SS OFF

RESET

time. Thus a command from the computer to read or write data in a particular location on a particular track is delayed only by the time required for the location to come around under the head—at most one revolution of the disk—avoiding the additional delay for the track-seeking motion, which can be up to 10 times the rotational lag.

On many older fixed-disk storage units, synchronizing pulses are obtained from one of several timing tracks when writing or reading data in other tracks. But at high recording densities, the tolerances in these timing tracks become very critical. For example, the disk shows gyroscopic behavior under even slight external shock, causing a slight precession of the disk; or, under certain circumstances, it can set up a standing wave in the disk. Both the data and timing heads are mounted on flexible supports to ride out such disturbances, but they may ride in opposite directions and upset the phase relationship between the timing and data pulses.

These considerations—and a great many more—have forced designers of removable-disk systems to incorporate timing into the data tracks. These sync pulses necessarily somewhat dilute the density of the recorded data —sometimes to a very great extent, as when every other pulse is a sync pulse. But since in the DDR-1 only every 20th pulse is a sync pulse, dilution of the data density is almost negligible. It works because of a highly reliable method of clocking the data following every sync pulse,

and because of the machine's mechanical design details.

The reliability factor in the air bearing enters the picture here. For one thing, it tends to cushion external shocks, so that they are reduced in severity, if indeed they reach the disk at all. For another, because the air bearing is self-centering, it automatically compensates for any changes in the rotating mass comprising the disk, the supporting hub, the shaft, and the motor rotor as a result of external shocks or just ordinary wear and tear. Electronic engineers may not always realize the complexities involved when something spins in the presence of external forces. For example, the axis of rotation presumably passes through the center of mass—but not when the mass is unbalanced or when it is precessing gyroscopically.

Another detail is mounting of the read-write heads. In some systems, for example, they ride out transient disturbances in the disk because they sit on short horizontal arms that rotate a few degrees in a vertical plane around a support. The sideways component introduced by this rotation is only a tiny fraction of the vertical motion. But at high densities even that tiny fraction may be all or a large part of the distance between two bits, disrupting the timing of both read and write operations.

The DDR-1's heads are mounted on spring brackets secured against lateral motion at each end; the heads are free to move up and down as necessary, but can't move

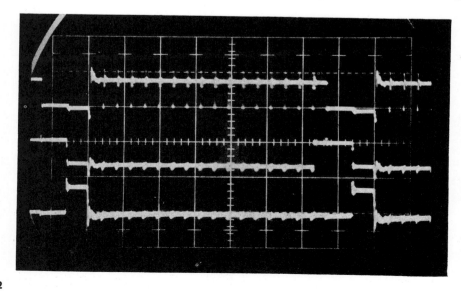

Word timing. These three signals generate all internal timing in the DDR-1. The top trace goes positive when the sync bit is read, and goes negative 17 times at 800-nsec intervals while reading or writing one word. The middle trace, rising 100 nsec after the 16th negative pulse, signals parity time; the bottom trace is the start signal for the next word.

Bits, words, tracks

Bits per word	16 plus parity and sync
Words per track	2,048
Data tracks	128
Words per disk	262,144 Expandable to 1,048,576 via three slave units
Average access time	16.67 msec (8.33 msec available)
Bit frequency	1.25 Mhz (2.5 Mhz available)

at all in a lateral direction.

When the DDR-1 receives a read or write command from the computer, it first selects the proper head for the desired track. Then it waits for the desired word to arrive under the head. A continuously running counter keeps track of the word that is coming up next, and when the counter matches the requested address, data transfer begins to or from the computer.

At this point, the DDR-1 sends an interrupt signal to the computer to request data for writing, or to indicate that the data is forthcoming on a read command. All disk storage units do this. But the DDR-1 also sends an early warning signal $16N + 5$ microseconds before the desired word is located; N is the number of words between the two interrupts. This number is wired into the machine; usually it's 4, but it depends on the user's requirements.

This early warning permits the computer program to finish an operation before attending to the disk; to start a routine to hold the computer's status while the disk operation is in progress; or perhaps to avoid starting a new task that it will have to discontinue shortly.

Each word stored on a DDR-1 disk begins with a sync bit, as shown on page 150, followed by 16 data bits, one parity bit, and two binary 0's that serve as a marker between words, for a total word length of 20 bits. There are 2,048 of these words in a single track, plus a gap of about 550 microseconds to indicate the starting point.

At the start of a read or write operation with an address less than the wired-in value of N, the early warning signal occurs at the beginning of this gap.

Coding is NRZI, a non-return-to-zero function, with change on ones; this is a common technique in which the disk coating always is magnetically saturated, and in which a 1 is represented on the disk by a flux reversal from saturation in one direction to saturation in the other. Successive 1's are thus depicted by flux reversals in opposite directions, whereas a 0 is represented by the absence of a reversal. As seen by the sense amplifier, therefore, the absence of a pulse shows a 0, and successive 1's, whether separated by 0's or not, are represented by pulses of opposite polarity generated by the alternating flux reversals. Parity is even—the parity bit insures that the number of bits in each word, including the sync bit, is even.

Timing depends on two single-shots and a five-stage binary counter, as shown at the top of page 152. One of the single-shots, when off, holds the counter in its reset state. At the end of the 550-μsec gap, the Enable line turns on, and the following sync pulse turns on the first single-shot, releasing the reset. It stays on for about 15 microseconds, long enough for the entire word to be written, then shuts off. But while on, it opens a gate to the second single-shot, which drives itself through a delay line and the same gate, and therefore oscillates at

. . . the whole disk-loading procedure is carried out by pneumatic and fluidic equipment; there isn't a single ball bearing anywhere in the business end of the machine.

Diode decoupling

A reasonably straightforward circuit, but one believed to be unique, shown below, decouples the sense amplifier from the write circuits, It begins with a write trigger (not shown in the diagram) which changes state whenever a 1 is to be written; the trigger's change turns on one of the two write transistors Q_1 and Q_2 and turns off the other, reversing the current through the winding in the head. This current originates at the +30-volt supply, and passes through switches in the selection matrix; it divides into two nearly equal parts to pass through matched resistors connected to the two ends of the head winding, whose resistance is much lower than that of the resistors. One of the currents passes through the head winding; they recombine and go to whichever of the two write transistors is conducting. When these transistors change state and reverse the current through the winding, the matched resistors damp the inevitable inductive kick, an improvement over a common design that has a center-tapped winding and no return path for inductive currents. Reversing the current in the winding reverses the saturation in the disk's surface according to the NRZI encoding.

Because the write transistors are connected to +15 volts, the diodes between their collectors and the sense amplifier are reverse-biased, so that the amplifier is decoupled from the write circuits.

When reading, both write transistors are turned off because the Write Enable line is off; the +30 volts in the matrix selection thus forward-biases the diodes and admits read signals in the millivolt range, riding on the large d-c bias, directly to the sense amplifier, which is floating at +25 volts. A capacitor at the amplifier's output blocks direct current, but passes data to the logic circuits.

This read-write circuit design carries with it a bonus: it can switch from write to read, or vice versa, in 350 nanoseconds. This permits the DDR-1 to read a word immediately before or after writing in the adjacent location on the same track. There is no waiting for a full disk revolution, as in most disk storage units.

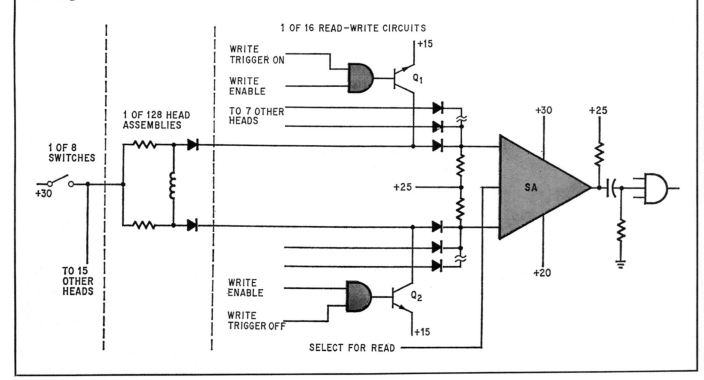

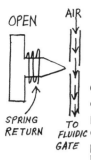

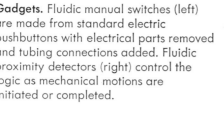

OPEN
AIR
SPRING RETURN
TO FLUIDIC GATE

CLOSED

Gadgets. Fluidic manual switches (left) are made from standard electric pushbuttons with electrical parts removed and tubing connections added. Fluidic proximity detectors (right) control the logic as mechanical motions are initiated or completed.

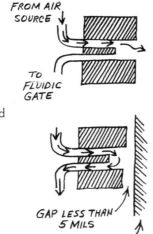

FROM AIR SOURCE

TO FLUIDIC GATE

GAP LESS THAN 5 MILS

DISK SURFACE OR OTHER RESTRICTION

1.25 megahertz. Its oscillations drive the binary counter, an array of five flip-flops—each a standard off-the-shelf product. The flip-flops actually are six three-input NAND gates on a chip, interconnected to act like a flip-flop; when the 0 output is connected to the data input, the circuit acts like a binary flip-flop, changing state with every positive shift of the clock input. This same 0 output is connected to the clock input of the following stage to produce the binary counting action.

The binary unit counts up to 16, then shuts off the oscillator. At that moment the second single-shot is on; when it turns off, it steps the counter again. The 17 pulses from the single-shot synchronize the writing of the 16 data pulses and the parity bit. Immediately after the 17th pulse, the first single-shot turns off, signaling the end of the word. The next sync pulse starts the process again, whether data is being transferred or not.

To interchange disks, the DDR-1 takes advantage of mechanical design ideas unique to disk storage units. First, disks not in use are kept in sealed cartridges. When a disk is to be loaded, the operator places one edge of the cartridge in a slot at the front of the machine. The mechanism opens the cartridge seal and a similar one on the machine, reaches into the cartridge, hooks onto the hole in the center of the disk, and pulls it into position underneath the motor shaft. At this point the operator must remove the cartridge, which recloses both

seals; then the motor shaft picks up the disk, accelerates it to the proper speed, and brings it up under the read-write heads. When the disk is unloaded, the sequence is reversed: the mechanism pushes the edge of the disk to get it into the cartridge, and reseals both the cartridge and the machine before the operator can remove the cartridge.

What's extraordinary is that the whole procedure is carried out by pneumatic and fluidic equipment; there isn't a single ball bearing anywhere in the business end of the machine.

Ball bearings have serious drawbacks in a disk storage unit. The disk must be capable of axial and rotational motion; ordinary ball bearings support only rotation, while specialized adaptations would require multiple bearings. Also, ball bearing wear subjects a rotating disk to undesirable motions, or even to development of a harmonically curved surface resulting from vibrations that are even multiples of its angular frequency of rotation as at left below. Lubrication doesn't always avert the problems, and the lubricant could pollute the magnetic recording surface.

These difficulties were averted with air bearings. Because air's fluid nature tends to equalize the pressure in any given mass of air, and because any off-center motion of the shaft tends to vary this pressure, the air bearing is intrinsically self-centering. And it's so friction-free that

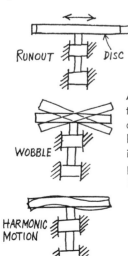

RUNOUT   DISC

WOBBLE

HARMONIC MOTION

Anti-wobble. The undesirable motions that can occur with ball bearings (left) are avoided in the DDR-1 with air bearings, shown at right. The shaft spins in a rotational bearing, and the hub and piston bear upward against thrust bearings, all films of air under pressure.

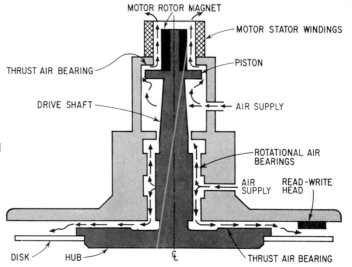

MOTOR ROTOR MAGNET

MOTOR STATOR WINDINGS

THRUST AIR BEARING

PISTON

DRIVE SHAFT

AIR SUPPLY

ROTATIONAL AIR BEARINGS

AIR SUPPLY

READ-WRITE HEAD

DISK   HUB   ℄   THRUST AIR BEARING

Fluidic logic

Air or any other compressible or incompressible fluid passing through pipes, jets and interaction chambers can be made to perform logic functions just as well as electronic circuits. In some way fluidic devices surpass their electronic counterparts—for example, in their resistance to nuclear radiation or their continued operation over wide temperature ranges. The principal limitation is speed; switching functions occur at speeds ordinarily measured in milliseconds, and at best in hundreds of microseconds. But in controlling relatively gross mechanical operations, as in the DDR-1, speed isn't critical and fluidics fill the bill.

Operation of fluidic logic devices is based on the tendency of a jet of fluid flowing parallel to the wall of a passage to adhere to that wall. A jet emerging from input duct A in the diagram, once it has attached itself to the wall of the left-hand outlet, as illustrated, stays there; nearly all the fluid volume exits through duct B. But a relatively small control jet at duct C can detach the main jet from its wall and force it against the opposite wall, where it remains after the control jet turns off. Now the major portion of the fluid exits through duct D. Another control jet appearing at E can switch the main jet back to its original position. This configuration behaves exactly the same as an electronic flip-flop; it has two stable states and remains in either state indefinitely unless it is switched to the other by a relatively small control signal.

A somewhat similar configuration implements the familiar NOR function in fluidics. Here the basic element, instead of being Y-shaped like the flip-flop, has one output leg in a straight line with the input and the other at a somewhat sharper angle than the flip-flop outputs. A laminar stream of fluid, flowing into the interaction chamber, continues straight through and attaches itself to the wall of the output leg in the absence of any control inputs at the side of the interaction chamber. Fluid emerging from this output represents the 1 state of the circuit. But a small control signal entering the interaction chamber through any one or more of the control input ducts can break this wall attachment and divert the jet to the other leg. Because of the relatively sharp turn from the input to the new output, the flow becomes turbulent and the jet doesn't attach to the wall—when the control signal turns off, the jet returns to the straight-through path. Thus the circuit is an implementation of the NOR logic function. Its operation as part of a larger logic array assumes that the 0 output, in which the flow is initially turbulent, is

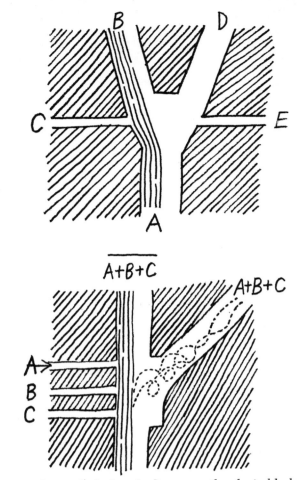

long and straight before feeding any other logic block, so that the flow again becomes laminar.

One of the benefits of fluidics is the ease with which fluidic large-scale integrated circuits can be put together. Almost all of the fluidic controls in the DDR-1 are built on a single lump of plastic about the size of an ordinary brick; "worm holes" in the brick are the passageways and chambers in which the fluidic logic functions are implemented. The fluidic brick isn't really as solid as it looks—it's made up of several layers of plastic, some with convoluted grooves and some with holes for connecting grooves in different layers.

Brick. In this assembly the two white layers contain arrays of fluidic NOR blocks; the other layers contain holes and channels that interconnect the blocks, when the "fan" shown here is closed and riveted together. This photo is of a dummy block; the assembly made for the DDR-1, by Pitney-Bowes Corp., contains four white layers.

Three layers. All electronic components are mounted on three 12-by-16-inch printed-circuit boards. Two boards carry the electronics common to all machines; the top board is tailor-made for a particular computer. Large center holes permit all three boards to fit over the housing for the floating piston and shaft.

it requires only a fraction of the torque a conventional bearing demands from the hysteresis-synchronous motor. And the air bearing, unlike the ball bearing, inherently permits axial motion.

Three air bearings are used: a rotational bearing surrounding the shaft that connects the drive motor to the hub supporting the disk; a thrust bearing above a floating piston that raises the shaft, hub, and disk into position for reading and writing, and another thrust bearing above the hub itself.

The floating piston, shaft, and hub [see p. 155] are cast as a unit; the motor rotor, which is a permanent magnet, is press-fitted onto the top of the shaft and becomes permanently a rigid part of the casting. After the disk has been mechanically latched onto the hub, air pressure on the piston raises it, together with the disk and the rotor. When the rotor enters the rotating magnetic field of the motor stator, the shaft begins to turn; by the time the shaft has reached its uppermost position, it is almost at its maximum speed.

At this point the piston is almost in contact with the bottom of the motor shell and the hub carrying the disk is almost in contact with the bottom of the shaft housing. In both places, a thrust air bearing is established—at the top by the air that pushes the piston up, at the bottom by air escaping from the shaft's air bearing. The differential pressure between each of these two thrust surfaces and the supply pressure controls the disk position with respect to the read-write heads with an accuracy of a few parts in 100 million, or a few hundredths of 1% of the nominal spacing between the disk surface and the read-write heads.

Since air already was available for the DDR-1's bearings, it was logical to use air in fluidic devices for controlling the recorder's mechanical motions.

In fluidics, as in electronics, a NOR gate is one of the simplest logic elements; from an array of NOR gates, logic functions of any desired complexity can be constructed [see "Fluidic logic," p.156]. These NOR gates, combined with a very simple proximity detector control, for example, removal of a disk from its cartridge provided the cartridge is in place and another disk isn't already in the machine.

Most of the air flows from the fluidic logic vents into the space around the electronic circuitry in the recorder, keeping the components cool. Then it recycles through a duct at the back of the cabinet to the blower at the bottom. A small part of the fluidic logic air, and all of the air from the bearings, pressurizes the interior of the compartment containing the disk loading mechanism and the read-write heads. As a result, when the seals on the compartment and on the disk cartridge open for loading or unloading, air flows out, keeping the interior of the compartment free of contamination. ●

Delay lines—key to low cost in keyboard machines

By Robert A. Tracy

Friden Inc., Palo Alto, Calif.

Although the delay line is one of the oldest forms of memory, it still remains a viable technology, appearing today in small serial computers and electronic calculators, as well as in communication networks, television, and radar systems. The original mercury lines were supplanted by devices of quartz or similar glassy material, and by magnetostrictive wires; now a newer type—the surface delay line—is making waves among engineers.

In essence, a delay line is a short-term information storage device that takes advantage of a mechanical vibration's very low propagation velocity relative to the velocity of electrical signals. It's used wherever volatility of stored data and relatively long access time aren't disadvantages.

There are three basic types of passive delay lines in use today. The oldest is the solid delay line, a prism of glass material in which signals are internally reflected at several faces while propagating from an input to an output transducer. Next is the wire line, in which a mechanical vibration is induced by a magnetostrictive transducer. The newest form is the surface delay line, in which the signals travel across the surface of the material rather than through its volume. And there are active delay lines of semiconductor material. In these devices a sound wave creates electrical effects that, in the presence of an electric field, react upon the sound wave to amplify it.

All passive delay lines are subject to certain fundamental limitations. One of these limitations is associated with the way sound attenuates as it is propagated through a material. For a given frequency f, the ratio of the amplitude at the end to that at the beginning of a time interval Δt is a double inverse exponential:[1]

$$\frac{\text{Amplitude at } (t + \Delta t)}{\text{Amplitude at } t} = (e^{-A_1 f \Delta t})\,(e^{-A_2 f^4 \Delta t})$$

A_1 and A_2 are constants. The term with the first power of frequency gives the effect of hysteresis in the material's stress-strain characteristics. This hysteresis arises from the energy lost when the material undergoes a strain—even a strain well below its elastic limit. The lost energy is dissipated in the form of heat, and, as the first-power term shows, is a function of frequency.

The fourth-power term gives the effect of scattering caused by the material's polycrystalline structure. In materials used for digital delay line memories, this term is usually negligible. It can be shown that when only the first-power term is considered, the maximum number of bits that a piece of material can store will be independent of the length of time the bits remain in the material.[2] That is, as Δt increases, f must decrease proportionally. (This isn't the same as saying the storage capacity is independent of the length of the material in inches.)

The material's storage capacity is inversely proportional to the constant A_1:

$$N_o = \frac{\pi \sqrt{3}}{A_1}$$

The number N_o may be used as a figure of merit for the material; some typical values are given in the table:

Memory materials

Material	A_1	N_o
Ni-Span C	.33	1.6×10^4
Beryllium copper	.14	3.9×10^4
Fused quartz	.015	36.3×10^4
Low-TC glass	.693	$.78 \times 10^4$

Even though the capacity is independent of the delay time, the latter is controllable. The most important variable is the temperature, which changes the physical length of the line and the modulus of elasticity of the material. The thermal coefficient of delay is the average of the thermal coefficients of expansion and of elasticity;[3] obviously if these are equal in magnitude and opposite in sign, the delay is constant with variations in temperature. This ideal condition is approached most closely in

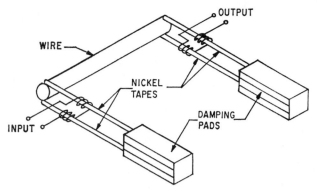

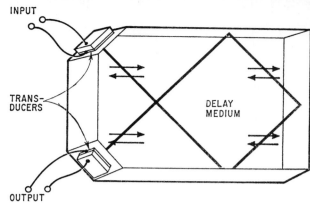

Twist. Current pulse in the input coil creates a tensile or compressive stress in the nickel tape, which twists the wire. This torsional stress travels down the wire, and transfers to the tapes at the other end. Output coil generates a signal as tape stresses pass through it.

Solid. Input transducer generates a wave in the block of glass that is internally reflected several times, producing a long delay time in a small piece of material, before arriving at the output transducer.

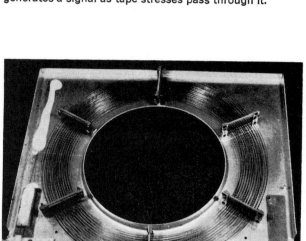

Pass through. This coil of beryllium copper wire circulates 20,000 bits at 1.5 megahertz with a signal-to-noise ratio of 20.

zero-TC glass made by Corning Glass Works and others, and in International Nickel Co.'s trademarked Ni-Span C, an alloy of nickel, chromium, titanium and a minute amount of carbon.

When the temperature can't be controlled, the maximum capacity of a delay line is

$$N_{max} = \frac{k}{\frac{d\tau}{\tau}\Delta T}$$

where k is the fraction of a period the bit is allowed to deviate from perfect timing, $d\tau/\tau$ is the thermal coefficient of delay, and ΔT is the temperature variation. Both Ni-Span C and Corning 8875 glass are often chosen for delay lines because they have very low coefficients of thermal delay.

Transducers also restrict delay line performance, but this is more a matter of fabrication difficulty than a fundamental limitation.

The typical wire delay line vibrates in the torsion mode, as at top left. The transducers are tapes made of a magnetostrictive material, such as nickel; coils are wound loosely around these tapes. A current pulse in the input coil generates a magnetic field, which causes a magnetostrictive change in the length of the tape inside the coil. If the tape shortens, this action generates a tensile stress; if it lengthens, the stress is also generated, but in this case it's compressive. Either way, the stress creates a strain pulse that is propagated away from the coil in both directions. At one end, this pulse is absorbed in the damping pad; at the other, it is converted into a torsion wave in the wire. Two tapes oppositely stressed by properly connected coils have a push-pull action. This torsion wave travels to the other end of the delay wire and is reconverted into an electrical signal by another pair of tapes and coils.

Sometimes only one magnetostrictive tape or a direct torsion-mode transducer is used. For example, the twenty-thousand bit wire delay line [photo at left] is constructed of beryllium copper with a single tape transducer at the transmitting end and a plated torsion mode transducer[4] at the receiving end. The line operates at 1.5 megahertz and has a signal-to-noise ratio of 20.

A current passing through the wire exerts control over the delay by heating the wire. The temperature can be increased or decreased to compensate for external variations; thus the delay can be kept constant or can be varied as desired.

The frequency limit of wire delay lines is about 4 or 5 Mhz. At higher frequencies solid delay lines are more practical, because the material is easier to control and the transducers easier to make.

In a glass, darkly

In a solid delay line shown above, the transducers are made of piezoelectric ceramic, such as lead-zirconate-titanate, that has been polarized in a strong electric field. The polarization direction

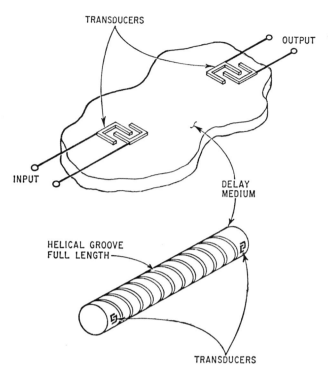

Surface effect. Sound waves that resemble water waves travel across the surface of this medium, either flat or helical, from one transducer to the other.

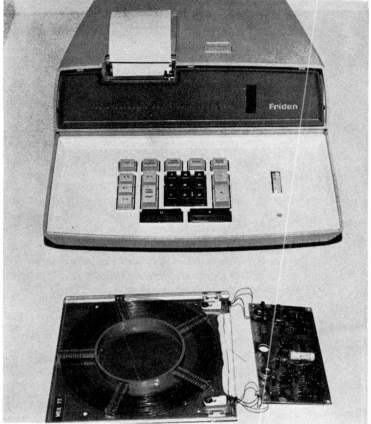

Line of action. The 1150 printing calculator's operation depends on the delay line in the foreground.

determines whether the vibration mode is shear, longitudinal in tension, or longitudinal in compression. The shear mode parallel to the reflective faces is usually preferred; it's less likely to generate new modes when it's reflected at the various surfaces.[5]

A typical solid delay line is Corning Glass Works' Type 9283. This uses the zero-temperature-coefficient glass and stores 2,048 bits at 8 Mhz. It operates reliably from 0° to 55°C without temperature compensation.

Fabrication problems limit the ceramic transducers used in these solid delay lines to thicknesses that operate only up to 20 Mhz. From 20 to 50 Mhz, quartz crystal transducers are employed. Recently, thin-film transducers of zinc oxide and cadmium sulfide have been developed that may be used from 50 Mhz to beyond 1 gigahertz.

On the surface

These transducers are also potentially applicable to a relatively new form of delay line of a solid material. Two kinds of surface-wave delay lines are shown above at left.

These ultrasonic surface waves, called Rayleigh waves, are very similar to water waves.[6] In a thin layer of material, the waves disperse or "break," much like ocean waves approaching a beach. But in material significantly thicker than the ultrasonic signal's wavelength, the losses are very low and the velocity of propagation is comparable to that of shear waves in the solid material. The losses are also very small on a convex surface, but become very high on concave surfaces.

Surface-wave delay lines are potentially very inexpensive and can store a large quantity of data. A single flat surface with vacuum-deposited transducers, as shown in the upper part of the sketch, could be fabricated for between $1 and $5. Its capacity obviously depends on its physical size, which is limited primarily by the difficulty of supporting the surface in such a way that no part of it can ever become even minutely concave. If that happened, the surface wave would be absorbed.

The helical configuration could store 10,000 words of 16 bits each in a one-inch diameter rod three inches long, at a cost of perhaps $20. The higher cost arises from cutting the groove to establish the helical configuration—for example, with an etching technique similar to that used in making integrated circuits.

In a delay-line memory, as the stored information appears at the output, it is immediately reloaded at the input. Thus it continuously recirculates with a time address rather than a physical location address. This time address—the moment at which a particular bit appears at the output—is in step with the data. Only when the data appears at the output of the delay line is it available for use; and only at that moment can new data be loaded in its place.

An example of a typical delay-line application is the Friden 1150 electronic printing calculator, shown above at right. The time addresses in the delay line are divided into six registers. The arith-

1	19	12	5	23	16	9	2	20	13	6	24	17	10	3	21	14	7	25	18	11	4	22	15	8

Interlacing. While calculator processes bit in position 1, six more bits go by. In the seventh position is bit 2, showing up just when the calculator is ready for it. While the calculator is working on bit 4, the delay line completes a full cycle, bit 1 is recirculated and bit 5 appears in the seventh slot after 4. This continues until bit 25 comes up; bit 1 reappears for new processing seven positions beyond 25.

metic unit shifts data within these registers, transfers it between registers, loads new data for storage, and unloads the stored data in the registers for output, as well as performing the standard arithmetic functions.

The cost of the delay line is minimized in the 1150 by permitting the time delay to vary with temperature and from machine to machine—thus bypassing critical design and fabrication problems. The home signal precedes the data propagated through the line; when it emerges, it opens a gate that starts the counter to provide timing and address information. When the last data has emerged from the line for either processing or recirculation, a signal from the address counter turns off the clock pulses that drive the counter. The dead time left over after the turnoff signal and before the home signal comes around again may be of any length without affecting machine operation.

Content-addressed memories have long been sought after for the more powerful computing machines, but most forms have been too expensive to be feasible. Delay lines provide a limited content addressing capability in a very simple way as shown below. In the search mode, the recirculating data passes through a search register in which it is compared with a tag that identifies the specific data. When a match is found, the immediately following data is directed into a buffer register.

The Friden 5610 Computyper uses this limited content-addressing technique in its program storage line. This gives the machine a programing capability with which it can execute sequential program steps, including both unconditional and conditional branching.

Interlacing, or gearing, is a third mode of memory operation with delay lines; it allows the use of high speed delay lines in a lower speed computer, greatly reducing access time. An interlaced delay line memory containing n bits produces several bits during each machine cycle, of which only the first bit is used. The number of bits per machine cycle and the total number of bits in the memory are selected so that a precession occurs as the delay line recycles, until access to all bits has been obtained, as shown above. Interlacing of registers is used in the Friden 1150.

Delay lines perform many other memory functions besides those in computers. For example, they appear as buffers in communications terminals, computer operated displays, and other peripheral equipment. And completely outside the computer field, new television and instrumentation applications are appearing at an increasing rate; radar systems, in which delay lines made their first appearance nearly 30 years ago, are continually finding new applications for them.

Keeping pace with expanding utilization of delay lines are advances in design,[7] materials, and transducers. And significant strides are being made in understanding the behavior of phonons—the fundamental science of delay lines. Even delay lines that provide internal amplification have been built.[8] One of these has single crystals of cadmium sulfide interspersed between conventional delay lines; the crystals transduce the signal from one line to the next and amplify it at the same time. They act like amplifiers inserted in a transmission line. ■

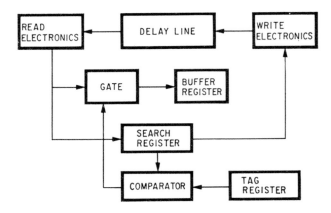

Associative. A delay line has a limited content-addressable capability because it is constantly recirculating all its data, even when it's not doing anything with it.

References

1. W.P. Mason, "Physical Acoustics," Academic Press, 1964, Vol. 1, Part A, p. 445.

2. R. Dickinson, "Wire Delay Line Materials," Friden, Inc., internal report, 1968.

3. G.G. Scarrott and R. Naylor, "Wire-Type Acoustic Delay Lines for Digital Storage," Proceedings, Institution of Electrical Engineers, Part B, Supplement 3, 1956, p. 497.

4. Z. Kitamura, H. Terada, and S. Hidaka, "The Magnetostrictive Film Transducer for Ultrasonic Delay Lines," IEEE Transactions on Magnetics, Sept. 1966, p. 206.

5. D.L. Arenberg, "Ultrasonic Solid Delay Lines," Journal of the Acoustical Society of America, Jan. 1948, p. 1.

6. Igor A. Viktorov, "Rayleigh and Lamb Waves: Physical Theory and Applications," Plenum Press, 1967.

7. G.L. Heiter and E.H. Young, Jr., "A 100-Mhz, 1,024-Bit Recirculating Ultrasonic Delay-Line Store," Digest, International Solid State Circuits Conference, 1968, p. 108.

8. A.R. Hutson, J.H. McFee, and D.L. White, "Ultrasonic Amplification in CdS," Physical Review Letters, 1960, p. 359.

A choice for serial memories

By David C. Uimari

Corning Glass Works, Raleigh, N.C.

When designing serial memories with capacities of from 100 to 20,000 bits and bit rates of from 1 to 2 megabits per second, an engineer may choose to use either glass memory modules or metal oxide semiconductor shift-register circuits. Whatever his decision may be, he will find that both glass memory modules and MOS shift registers are useful as digital delay lines of 20 microseconds to a few milliseconds, as buffers in computer systems, and as temporary storage to refresh the volatile image in a cathode-ray tube display; they are also used in digital integrators, digital differential analyzers, and serial adders. One of their more sophisticated applications is for buffering different input and output rates, using interlacing techniques in which adjacent bits in the memory arrive or depart at nonadjacent times. Either kind of serial memory can produce the desired result in any of these applications; but they differ in cost, frequency response, and other parameters.

In both approaches a data bit inserted at one end of a device appears at the other end some time later—for the case of 100 bits at 1 megabit per second, 100 microseconds later. For longer term storage, the source is disconnected from the device after the maximum number of bits has been loaded; then the output, after shaping and amplifying if necessary, is connected to the input so that all the data circulates continuously.

While glass delay lines don't work well at frequencies below 2 megahertz, their range of operation extends up to 50 Mhz. Memory modules made from these delay lines can operate at as low a bit rate as desired, with appropriate interleaving or encoding techniques. Also, the power-supply requirements of glass memory modules are simpler; they need fewer different voltages than do the MOS circuits. Furthermore, glass memories need no external bit-for-bit synchronizing and can accept signals from, and deliver them to, most standard integrated circuits without special level-shifting circuits at the interfaces. In addition, their power dissipation doesn't depend on operating frequency.

On the other hand, MOS doesn't work too well at data rates above 2 megabits per second, and over 5 megabits the circuits must be multiplexed—several slower circuits must operate in parallel, with successive bits routed to different circuits in rotation. Below 1 megabit, MOS is usually better than glass; indeed, at these lower frequencies, the tradeoff is actually between MOS and magnetostrictive delay lines rather than between MOS and glass delay lines.

Nevertheless, the MOS approach has an advantage over the glass memory approach in terms of size and weight. While the power supplies, clocks, and level shifters required by MOS diminish this edge, adequate planning will minimize this problem. In MOS about 4,000 bits in eight flatpacks, together with associated external circuits, will fit on a 4½-by-6-inch printed circuit board weighing 8 ounces; a glass memory module of the same capacity, while occupying the same amount of space, would weigh 14 ounces. Furthermore, an MOS shift register of half the capacity would be about half the size, whereas the 2,000 bits in glass would take up the same volume as 4,000 bits.

Random access isn't possible with either technique, except on a time-dependent basis. To obtain any particular bit, one must wait, on the average, half the time required for a single bit to propagate through the memory, because the data in a serial memory is accessible only at the input or at the output. This limitation usually isn't a serious obstacle when the data is serial to begin with—as when it arrives from a telephone line or other communication channel.

These memories are also dynamic—the data is lost if it doesn't move continuously through the memory. In a glass memory, the data propagates alone through the memory once it has been launched; power and clocking are necessary only to resynchronize it when it appears at the output. But an MOS memory needs clock pulses to push the data along. While MOS static shift registers can be built, in which the clock can be stopped indefinitely

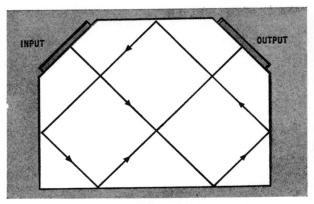

Five cushion. The shape of the delay line in a glass memory insures several reflections for the propagating sound wave, thus prolonging the delay within the glass.

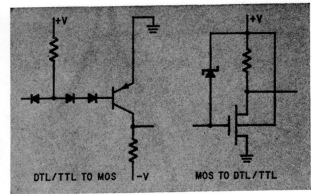

Level shift. Circuits like these are sometimes required to translate between high MOS voltage levels and the lower levels used in bipolar circuits.

without losing data, they still require continuous power—and they are intrinsically larger and more costly than dynamic MOS memories.

Serial memories are most economical—whether MOS or glass—in capacities of 100 to 20,000 bits. For fewer than 100 bits, arrays of flip-flops are feasible; integrated bipolar circuits are generally used, but MOS has made some inroads in this area. For more than 20,000 bits, ferrite cores and electro-mechanical media, such as rotating disks and drums, cost less per bit.

While the frequency tradeoffs between MOS and glass are generally found between 1 and 5 megabits per second, other considerations may be involved. The memory function can't be divorced from the rest of the system, and these frequency and capacity limits shouldn't be construed to say that it can. For example, if physical size is important, MOS may be the best choice in an application where otherwise a magnetostrictive delay line would be less expensive. Or if power dissipation is a problem, a glass memory may pay off even at an unusually low frequency. Also one can't ignore assembly cost, testing cost, or ultimate reliability.

Happy circumstance

Glass delay lines themselves have been used for many years but they are now enjoying an increase in the number and variety of applications. This is a result of the heavy emphasis on speed, and the need for frequencies that approach the resonant frequency of the glass-transducer combination. Widespread use and demand along with increased production volume have cut the cost per unit to the point where glass is now competitive in many areas where it was not before.

Quite simply, a glass delay line transmits mechanical energy from an input transducer to an output transducer. The delay arises from the relatively slow velocity of propagation, and can be as great as 350 microseconds because the path inside the glass is usually much longer than the dimensions of the glass, as shown above. A glass memory module includes the delay line with its transducers, and driving, sensing, and regenerating circuits.

The bulk glass from which a glass memory is made must have properties that permit it to be formed to the proper shape economically; it must also have a minimum temperature coefficient of velocity and a minimum frequency coefficient of attenuation.

Glass that meets the temperature coefficient requirement has a coefficient of linear expansion that is equal and opposite to the coefficient of its elastic modulus. This glass is relatively soft, as glass goes, and is easily formed into the proper shape—pentagonal, for example—usually by grinding or by pressing it in a mold when it's hot.

Close tolerance

This forming operation is quite critical. In this kind of glass the velocity of sound is about 10,000 feet per second, or a tenth of an inch per microsecond. But the tolerance on the time delay is typically ±15 nanoseconds, which restricts the tolerance on the path length, including several reflections, to ±0.0015 inch.

Two kinds of piezoelectric transducers are in common use—quartz crystals above 10 Mhz and lead zirconate-titanate (PZT) below that point. Sometimes both are used, although PZT is fragile at high frequencies. However, with a judicious use of both available transducer materials, a single memory can operate at any frequency in the range of 2.5 to 50 Mhz. At lower frequencies the energy beam spreads inside the glass far enough to reflect from the top and bottom of the slab as well as from the edges. These extra reflections increase the attenuation sharply, to an unacceptable level.

Either type of transducer is metallized on both sides and attached to the glass with cement or solder. Connecting wires are attached to the transducers by soldering.

Unlike the MOS memory, the cost of a glass memory is relatively insensitive to the number of bits per package, up to 5,000 bits. A larger piece of glass can store more bits; and since the fabrication cost are much greater than the material costs, the size of the glass has little effect on the price of the complete unit. In other words, a 5,000-bit mem-

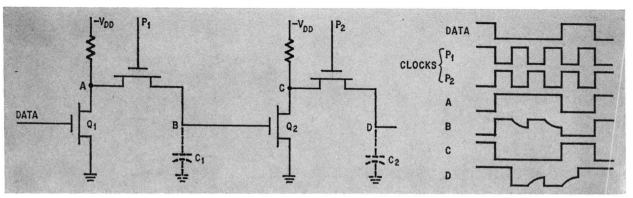

Dynamic. Gate capacitance of transistor Q_2, shown here as C_1, picks up the inverted data at A when P_1 is negative, retains it long enough for P_2 to transfer it to the gate capacitance of the next stage. Charging and discharging rates determine minimum and maximum frequencies of the circuit.

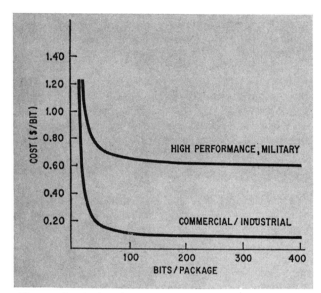

Cheaper by the hundred. MOS memories cost less per bit when large numbers of bits are squeezed into a single package. But a wide temperature range boosts costs.

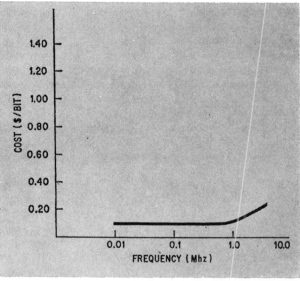

Corner plot. At higher frequencies the cost of an MOS memory suddenly rises, almost like the attenuation of an amplifier.

ory would cost only slightly more than a 50-bit memory operating at the same data rate.

As with the MOS devices, the cost per bit of a glass memory increases when the operating temperature ranges increases—typically, by 10% to 20%. But costs are almost constant as frequency increases.

The case for MOS

An MOS memory can be fabricated as a large-scale integrated circuit with several hundred bits on a single silicon chip. These capacities are possible because of the extremely small size of most MOS transistors.

The most common type of transistor used today in MOS shift registers is the p-channel field-effect transistor. This device comprises two p-type re-

gions—the source and drain—diffused into a wafer of n-type silicon, with an insulating layer of silicon oxide and a metallic layer—the gate—deposited between them. That portion of the n-type silicon directly under the gate is the channel. When the gate acquires a negative charge from an external circuit, it drives the n-type carriers from the channel, which thereby becomes p-type and establishes a low resistance between the source and drain. Thus the transistor turns on.

Most MOS shift registers use negative logic—with the binary 0 state at ground and the binary 1 at a negative voltage, somewhere between −7 and −24 volts. These levels are difficult to obtain from standard bipolar IC's; they require level-shifting circuits such as shown at the right on page 164 to translate to and from the bipolar signals, which generally range from 1 to to 5 volts.

Recently an improved manufacturing process has been developed for producing shift registers that operate directly with standard bipolar logic levels. This process eliminates the need for level shifters.

Charging the capacitance

The gate, together with the channel and the insulating oxide, forms a capacitor that charges and discharges as the transistor turns on and off. Since this charging action passes current through an external resistance, it takes time; and the time constant is the principal limiting factor on the speed of MOS circuits. This capacitance is also large enough to serve as the storage medium in a dynamic shift register; it retains charge for a long enough time to define the state of the next stage in the register.

A typical dynamic shift register stage is shown at the top of page 165.

Because the MOS transistor can be so small, many shift-register stages can be made on a single chip of silicon; and with multi-chip packaging, several chips can be packaged together. Thus a single small package could contain quite a large memory. Up to 256 bits in a single package are readily available off the shelf, and chips and packaging techniques are improving every day, indicating the availability of still larger memories in the near future.

Prices now range from 5¢ to 50¢ per bit, in quantities of 1,000 chips; the price per bit of larger chips, as well as larger quantities of chips, tends to be lower, as shown in the graph on the left on page 165. But the price tends to increase slightly for higher frequency MOS circuits, as shown in the right hand graph, or for wider operating temperature ranges.

Future developments

It's safe to predict that MOS costs will drop radically. Modules now priced at 5¢ per bit show every promise of dropping further before long. And their performance will improve—operating data rates will be somewhat higher, and ways will be found to use more moderate data rates with less complex clock requirements. Circuits that need lower-voltage power supplies will certainly be developed.

Glass memory modules are available now at prices as low as 2½¢ per bit. While the percentage drop in cost of these modules will probably be less than that of MOS shift registers, both devices are expected to continue to be cost competitive in the future—especially in the higher bit capacities. And the advantages of glass at high data rates, and its simple operation, will also help preserve its niche in the market. In addition, even higher data rates and longer delay times appear probable, with the development of better materials and better circuits. Longer delay times, of course, correspond to a lower cost per bit. ∎

Chapter 7

Advanced technology

Optical techniques light the way to mass-storage media

By M.D. Blue and D. Chen

Honeywell Research Center, Hopkins, Minn.

Optical techniques, though still in an early stage of development, offer a number of advantages in mass-storage applications. In fact, beam-alterable, beam-addressable mass memories are a definite possibility within the foreseeable future.

Optical methods permit information-packing densities greater than those possible with magnetic recording, which provides a different approach to problems of power consumption, weight, and mechanical complexity. In the meantime, of course, computer systems and applications are evolving to the point where ever greater storage capacities are required.

Given the present rate of growth in data processing, 10-billion-bit memories are conceivable. With optical techniques, such a memory could be contained in less than a square foot of surface. Magnetic techniques on the other hand would require at least 100 times as much area.

Researchers in their approaches to optical memories take advantage of all the latest tricks of the trade—such as holography, high-resolution photographic emulsions, and photochromism. They use lasers to vaporize material or to heat it above some critical temperature, where it can be affected by external magnetic or electric fields.

An optical beam, for example, can be focused to a diffraction-limited spot size whose diameter is approximately equal to the light wavelength. Thus when the wavelength is 1 micron (near infrared) the potential density of resolvable focused spots is more than 100 million per square inch. Visible light wavelengths are about half a micron, which makes the potential density of stored information even greater.

By contrast, magnetic recording—on drums, disks, cards, and tapes—currently offers densities of about 100,000 bits per square inch. Improved materials and techniques might conceivably increase density to a million or so, but it's limited by signal amplitude and noise, in turn determined by tradeoffs in track width, track spacing, and surface-to-head distance.

Given these available densities, therefore, a memory of ten billion bits requires 10,000 square inches of magnetic recording surface, or an area eight feet square. This is obviously too large to be addressed directly in a single module; if divided into smaller areas, problems of mechanical motion in access arise.

The performance of various types of computer memories plotted on a storage capacity-access time plane [see page 170], illustrates the general tradeoff between capacity and access time. Viewed in this way, the projected performance of optical mass memories can include a larger capacity, a shorter access time, or both.

A typical optical memory, diagramed on page 171, uses a laser as a light source. It is thus distinguished from an optoelectronic memory, whose light is internal to the element [see following article]. Almost all proposed optical memories use lasers to get light of high power density (very bright), spatial coherence (waves in phase), or both. The light-beam modulator is a high-speed switch. The beam-deflection system directs the modulated beam to the recorded information, either mechanically—with a scanning prism arrangement, for example—or electrically, using electro-optic or acoustic techniques. The light beam emerges from the deflection system and passes through the storage plane, whose information content alters the beam's character—that is, its intensity, its phase, or its polarization. It then is focused onto a detector, whose signal fluctuations can be interpreted as binary 1's and 0's.

This mode of operation in an optical mass memory system imposes several general requirements on the storage medium:

- It must be readable by the beam, and changeable except in special applications requiring a very

How optical memories compare with other mass-storage units

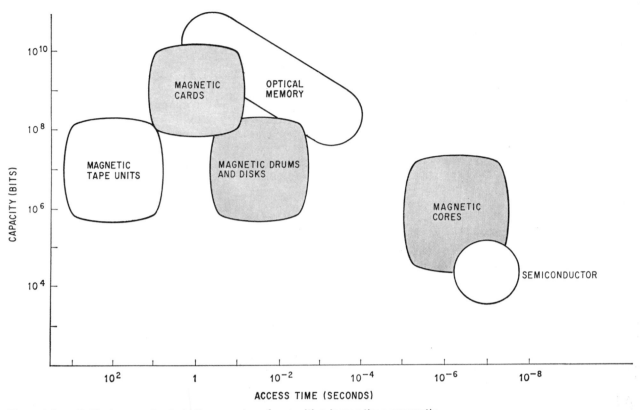

Big and fast. Optical memories hold the promise of capacities larger than presently available units, yet significantly faster than today's big ones.

large permanent memory.
- It must require a reasonable beam intensity.
- It should operate at a reasonable temperature—preferably room temperature.
- Its intensity threshold must permit repeated reading and tolerate scattered beam intensities without affecting the stored information.
- It must be stable over extended periods of time.
- It must be effectively grainless to permit recording information at high densities.

Permanent storage

A novel approach to optical read-only memories, studied at Bell Telephone Laboratories, stores information in a rectangular array of holograms, each of which contains a page of information.[1,2] The holograms are recorded on a high-resolution photographic plate; thus the information cannot be altered. Each page, or individual hologram, is read by illuminating it with a laser beam, which reconstructs the image—an array of light and dark spots corresponding to 1's and 0's. These are detected by an array of photodiodes. Each hologram can produce a reconstruction at the same location at the readout plane, and as a result, the same array of photodetectors can monitor the entire surface of

the hologram array.

The Bell Labs group, using the holographic technique, demonstrated a system with a capacity of about 4 million bits, and now suggests extending this technology into a system with 100 times the capacity and an access time of less than 10 microseconds.

To erase old and store new information in this system, an alterable material that can record holograms is needed. A photochromic material may turn the trick; such materials are described later in this article.

Photographic emulsions are generally more sensitive than photochromic and other direct recording approaches. The chemical processing of photographic emulsions after exposure effectively amplifies the latent image. However, the advantage of amplification is offset by the delay that the chemical processing requires. Because of the time lag, the information isn't available for reading immediately after writing.

High-resolution photographic emulsions are also permanent. However, they fill the bill for applications that require high information storage density in a fixed form using optical techniques. Recording densities greater than 10^9 bits per square inch have been achieved,[3] and various coating methods are possible. Writing schemes that use diffraction techniques reduce sensitivity to dust and dirt; these schemes are somewhat analogous to the holographic approach.

Standing waves within the thickness of the photographic emulsion offer another approach toward increasing information storage density. This standing wave occurs when a light beam exposing the film to store a 1 reflects off the substrate below the emulsion and interferes with itself. In doing so the beam sets up a periodic layer structure in the developed silver image, and has a spacing related to the light's wavelength, or color. Light is masked out of areas where 0's are stored, so that these spots remain unexposed. When a beam of light reflects from the developed emulsion, it reproduces the information stored by the light that originally exposed the emulsion. In principle, by using a number of light sources of different colors, many bits could be stored and retrieved at each location in the memory.[4]

Laser on tape

Several proposed laser writing schemes are based on material removal or vaporization by laser beam bombardment. For example, the Precision Instrument Co. has an experimental digital-tape recording system called the Unicon [Electronics, Feb. 3, 1969, p. 52]. It uses a one-watt argon laser, controlled by an electro-optic modulator, which vaporizes 1.5-micron holes in an opaque coating on a clear polyester tape. The tape itself is not damaged. This system records data at several megabits per second, with information densities above 10 million bits per square inch. A lower-power laser, too weak to alter the opaque coating, reads the information from the tape. The stored information is permanent.

Scientists at the National Cash Register Co. report laser beam recordings on evaporated metallic films[5] 500 to 1,000 angstroms thick, and on organic coatings several microns thick. In this technique a helium-neon gas laser with a maximum power of 38 milliwatts, focused to a spot 1.8 micron in diameter, records more than a million spots per second. A two-dimensional scanner permits direct facsimile recordings of capital letters approximately 30 microns high.

Itek has studied an optical memory system which uses a laser to write on 10-inch-diameter storage disks coated with photographic emulsion. Data is recorded on five-micron-wide tracks within a 1-inch band at the outer edge of the disks. A store of 650 disks, each holding 200 million bits of data, gives on-line random access to approximately one trillion bits of data.

Beam-alterable memory

A photochromic-holographic optical memory overcomes some of the disadvantages of photographic emulsions, and has some advantages of its own. Photochromism[6]—a characteristic of many organic dyes and other organic or inorganic compounds—is a reversible change in a compound's absorption spectrum when it's irradiated with a specific wavelength of light. In general, short wavelengths cause the spectrum to shift toward the red; longer wavelengths shift it back toward the blue. Thus, a photochromic material that is transparent to visible light can be darkened by ultraviolet irradiation and bleached by visible or infrared light. Alkali halides, such as potassium iodide and potassium bromide, are examples of these crystals. Other materials are transparent only to infrared light; they can be "darkened" by visible light and "bleached" by infrared. The darkened crystal absorbs radiation of a specific wavelength, and continues to transmit other radiation. For example, a material might appear to the eye to change color from yellow-orange to blue-gray, because the red component of white

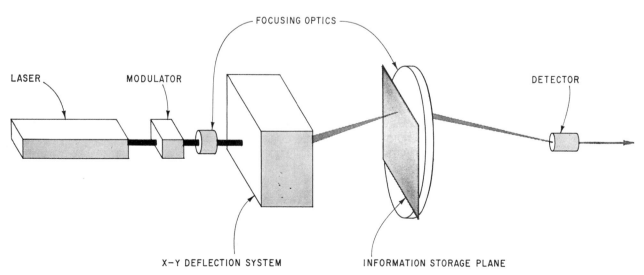

Components. All optical memories require these basic parts, most of which can be implemented in various ways. Common to most of them is the laser, which is both bright and coherent.

light would be absorbed.

Carson Laboratories Inc. took the photochromic approach, and built a system in which the same laser beam bleaches and subsequently reads the alkali halide crystal. The crystal must be heated to approximately 80°C during recording and cooled to 0°C during readout. Its operation requires a high energy level, in terms of much power or a long time; it takes 100 seconds of bleaching to produce a 5% density change when the helium-neon laser's flux density is 50 megawatts per square centimeter and its wavelength is 6,328 angstroms.

Other companies studying photochromic techniques for computer memory applications include RCA, the Univac division of the Sperry Rand Corp., the International Business Machines Corp., NCR, the Control Data Corp., and Itek.

These memories have some unique advantages. Since information can be stored three-dimensionally, the volume instead of the area of the medium is available for storage. Using holography in combination with photochromism, information about each bit is distributed over the entire area of the hologram, so that the memory isn't sensitive to dust particles or mechanical damage. The light deflector's specifications are simpler and the illumination need not be uniform over the hologram area. Photochromic media employ molecular or atomic phenomena and are therefore virtually grainless. Other properties of holograms permit a memory system to be organized in a variety of ways.

But present photochromic media are subject to fatigue after repeated operation, long-time instability, lack of a well-defined threshold of intensity—that is, the media are too nearly linear—and sensitivity to scattered light. Research is under way to solve many of these problems.

Lights and magnets

Magnetic materials when combined with optical systems lead to several novel approaches for reversible storage media. Now that high-power lasers and materials that have improved magneto-optical properties have been developed, the laser can induce usable changes in the magnetic storage medium. Typically, a focusing system concentrates the laser energy on a small region of the material. Information is written in the material with a thermomagnetic effect.

Honeywell Inc. is currently studying how to store information in thin magnetic film of a manganese-bismuth alloy.[7] This material, in thin-film form, can be magnetized perpendicularly to the film plane, with two stable magnetic states; in both of these it exhibits the magneto-optic Faraday effect. In one stable state, the magnetic field is directed upward through the film. In the other state, the field is directed downward. Regions in the film magnetized up or down correspond to binary 1's and 0's.

The films are first saturated magnetically so that all regions are in the same state. To write information, a laser beam is focused onto a small region, whose temperature rises rapidly. At a temperature

of 360°C—the alloy's Curie · temperature—this region loses its magnetization. As the region cools, the magnetic flux from an external field or from the surrounding region aligns the magnetization in the desired direction. This localized region now stores a bit of information. This is called a Curie-point writing technique.

Stored information is retrieved using the magneto-optic Faraday effect. A beam of plane-polarized light from a beam deflector passes through the desired region of the film. Because the film is magnetized, it rotates the plane of polarization of the transmitted beam, one way for a stored 1, the other for a 0. If an analyzer has been set to extinguish light from a 0 bit, then a region magnetized the other way will rotate the beam in the opposite direction, so that it is partially transmitted by the analyzer. A photodetector reads the stored information.

New twist

This readout technique requires a medium, such as MnBi, that has a high Faraday rotation. This rotation is about half a million degrees per centimeter of the material's thickness; but since the thickness in this case is measured in angstroms, the actual rotation is only a few degrees.

The Curie-point writing technique would seem to be inherently slow, depending as it does upon heating a localized region. However, typical laser pulses as short as 0.1 microsecond have been used successfully. After all, spot sizes are only one or two microns in diameter; as a result the amount of material to be heated is very small.

These tiny spots, spaced from 5 to 10 microns apart, can have a density of from six to 24 million bits per square inch.

This writing technique is also applicable to other ferromagnetic materials, notably europium selenide and europium oxide. IBM has been actively engaged in using these materials to demonstrate a technique for an optical memory.[8] These media have a very large Faraday rotations, but their Curie temperatures are very low—4.2°K for EuSe and 60°K for EuO—so that they must be operated in a cryogenic environment.

Multilayer films whose components have different Curie-temperatures, can also store data using the Curie-point writing technique.[9] Heating a spot in the multilayer film to a temperature above the Curie point of one of the component films reduces the coercive force of all the layers as a whole to a lower level. An external field slightly above this level then writes data in that spot without affecting the rest of the film.

Garnet adds up

Single crystal garnet materials for magneto-optic memories have been investigated at Bell Labs and at Univac. Gadolinium iron garnet (GdIG), for example, has some very interesting magnetic properties.[10,11] This material's total magnetization is attributed to two opposing sublattice magnetiza-

Optical mass memory performance

Material	Writing technique	Writing speed, bits/sec	Readout technique	Readout speed, bits/sec	Erasure	Packing density, bits/cm²	Stability
Manganese bismuth	Thermomagnetic Curie-point writing using 10-mw laser beam; magnetization determined by field near Curie point (350° C)	10^6	Magneto-optic effect	10^8	Applied magnetic field and coincidence laser heating	4×10^6	Good below 340° C
Alkali halide	Photochromic process; illumination by ultraviolet or blue beam causes absorption spectrum of bits to shift toward red	10^6	Absorption of light	10^6	Near infrared laser or heat	10^6	Poor
Europium oxide	Thermomagnetic Curie-point writing using low-power laser beam; magnetization determined by field near Curie temperature ($-190°$ C)	10^7	Magneto-optic effect	10^8	Applied magnetic field and coincidence laser heating	10^6	Must be below $-190°$ C
Garnet	Thermomagnetic compensation-point writing using low-power laser beam; magnetization determined by field near compensation temperature ($15°$ C $\pm 3°$ C)	10^4	Magneto-optic effect	10^8	Applied magnetic field and coincidence laser heating	10^5	Must be at compensation temp.
Ferroelectric	Combination of photoconductivity and ferroelectric effect. Light beam reduces resistance of photoconductive layer, allowing the applied field to affect ferroelectric polarization.	10^4	Discharge current sensing	10^8	Destructive read only	10^4	Good

tions. At a certain temperature, called the compensation temperature, the two magnetizations cancel in a way that results in a very large increase in the coercive force over its normal value. This compensation temperature can be near room temperature—usually slightly below.

Wafers of this material have only two stable magnetic states, similar to those of manganese-bismuth films. With the crystal magnetically saturated in one state, switching localized regions into the other state stores information in those regions. They can be switched by locally raising the temperature from the compensation level with a focused laser beam, and simultaneously applying an external magnetic field exceeding the coercive force. A small temperature rise—approximately 3°C in GdIG—sharply reduces the coercive force which is the magnetic field required to reverse the local magnetization. Therefore the applied field can switch the heated region, but will not affect the unheated region, which remains at the compensation temperature.

The smallest regions that can be switched on a smooth wafer of GdIG are approximately 100 microns in diameter, corresponding to about 64,000 bits per square inch. Smaller regions have been obtained by scribing the material into squares. Using this approach, information packing densities approaching a million bits per square inch have been achieved.

Scientists at IBM have recently succeeded in preparing thin films of GdIG chemically. This thin film medium can support a packing density of 10 million bits per square inch, but it requires a higher magnetic field to write, and a larger temperature rise.[12]

Ceramic sandwich

Ferroelectric material, like ferromagnetic material, can have two stable polarization states. Applying an electric field switches the material from one state to the other, just as magnetic fields cause a switch of magnetization in ferromagnetic materials. These basic properties make ferroelectric materials such as barium titanate and triglycine sulfate appear suitable for an alterable medium.

The "ferrotron" scheme suggested by the Marquardt Corp. is an interesting application of ferroelectrics to optical memory.[11] This device consists of a photoconductive and a ferroelectric layer sandwiched between two electrodes; the electrode next to the photoconductive layer is transparent. When the photoconductive layer is dark, it prevents the electric field applied at the electrodes from reaching the ferroelectric layer. But a light beam focused on a particular spot of this device reduces the photoconductive layer's resistivity at that spot. Consequently, the external field reaches the ferroelectric layer at a localized region and orients its polarization accordingly.

The written information is read out by discharging the ferroelectric medium when the beam addresses it. The direction of the discharge current indicates the direction of the polarization, and thus indicates that a 1 or 0 had been stored.

The readout is destructive because it removes the stored electric charge. A nondestructive readout in the ferroelectric would be possible using the electro-optic effect, which would alter the character of a polarized light beam as mentioned previously. But the development of a ferroelectric optical memory lags other techniques. The main difficulties are in the material preparation and in the lack of well-defined switching thresholds in many practical ferroelectric materials. Recent studies in polycrystalline electric ceramics suggest these difficulties eventually will be resolved.

The major approaches to optical memories are summarized in the table on page 173. The performance figures are estimates, based on material limitations on in some instances or preliminary experimental results. ∎

References

1. F.H. Smits and L.E. Gallaher, "Design considerations for a semipermanent optical memory," Bell System Technical Journal, July-August, 1967, p. 1,267.

2. L.K. Anderson, "Holographic optical memory for bulk data storage," Bell Laboratories Record, Nov. 1968, p. 319.

3. J.A. Altman and H.J. Zweig, "Effect of spread function on the storage of information on photographic emulsions," Photographic Science & Engineering, May-June, 1963, p. 173.

4. H. Fleisher, P. Pengelly, J. Reynolds, R. Schools, and G. Sincerbox, "An optically accessed memory using the Lippmann process for information storage," Optical and Electro-Optical Information Processing, MIT Press, Cambridge, Mass., 1965, p. 1.

5. C.O. Carlson, E. Stone, R.L. Burstein, W.K. Tomita, and W.C. Myers, "Helium-neon laser: thermal high-resolution recording," Science, Dec. 23, 1966, p. 1,550.

6. A. Reich and G.H. Dorion, "Photochromic high-speed large-capacity semi-random access memory," Optical and Electro-Optical Information Processing, MIT Press, Cambridge, 1965., p. 567.

7. D. Chen, J.F. Ready, R.L. Aagard, and E. Bernal G., "Laser-addressable manganese-bismuth film: key element in a high-density optical memory," Laser Focus, March, 1968, p. 18.

8. G.Y. Fan and J.H. Greiner, "Low-temperature beam-addressable memory," Journal of Applied Physics, Feb. 1, 1968, p. 1,216.

9. D. deBouard, "Feasibility study of a large-capacity magnetic-film optical memory," IEEE Journal of Quantum Electronics, May, 1968, p. 378.

10. J.T. Chang, J.F. Dillon, Jr., and U.F. Gianola, "Magneto-optical variable memory based on the properties of a transparent ferrimagnetic garnet at its compensation temperature," Journal of Applied Physics, March, 1965, p. 1,111.

11. Norman Goldberg, "A high-density magneto-optic memory," IEEE Transactions of Magnetics, Dec. 1967, p. 605.

12. R.E. MacDonald and J.W. Beck, "Magneto-optical recording," 14th Annual Conference on Magnetics and Magnetic Materials, Nov. 18-21, 1968.

13. S.C. Requa and J.M.N. Hanlet, "Externally sensitive solid-state image storer," Space/Aeronautics, August, 1964, p. 87.

Optoelectronic memories: light to read out by

By Richard D. Stewart

General Electric Co., Syracuse, N.Y.

Optoelectronic memories have two unique features: First, their electrically bistable, light-emitting storage elements are completely independent of their detectors, which read out the stored information. Second, partly as a result of this isolation, much intermediate processing can be done during readout—in fact, almost as a part of it.

Optoelectronic memory technology, however, has a long way to go. The big problem is system design; even though some remarkable devices have been invented, such as the light-emitting switch and the electroluminescent-photoconductor cell, few advances have been incorporated into practical systems.

The isolation means that there's no limit to the number of detectors that can be operated simultaneously, in any kind of sequence or pattern. Readout can be serial, parallel, or by block. If the application warrants it, even reading and writing can be simultaneous—although not in the same element, of course. And the light emitters and detectors can operate with different ground references without interference.

By contrast, most other forms of storage elements are built into a linear array that permits reading or writing in only one element at a time, so they are intrinsically serial. Some configurations permit reading or writing in an entire row or column at a time, but this is the closest approach to true parallel operation of nonoptoelectronic arrays, short of operating several small arrays at once, and it's very expensive. Designers must take care to eliminate ground loops and other paths for spurious signals.

While the data is being read out, intermediate processing can be done with an opaque mask, a filter, or a Kerr cell. Thus, with optoelectronics, an associative memory, for example, could be built; or a correlation function could be applied to the data as it is being read out. For example, if an optoelectronic memory contained the digital equivalent of a pictorial image, correlation would permit the image to be separated from a noisy background, or would establish the existence of certain characteristics in the image. This technique has already been used successfully in a fingerprint identification experiment.

The General Electric electronics laboratory is currently developing new ways to fabricate high-density arrays of optoelectronic elements, not only for memories as such but also for memories with optical readout—that is, for displays. In another current program, the British Ministry of Technology is evaluating optical mass memory storage techniques. International Computers Ltd. is building an optical read-only memory, based on a cathode-ray tube scanner, photographic data store, and a photomultiplier readout. The system is designed to store 65,536 words of 69 bits each. This program's results will indicate the capability of an optoelectronic system based on well-established optical components.

The difference between optoelectronic and electro-optical memories should be kept carefully in mind. Optoelectronic memories contain an array of electrically bistable light-emitting elements, any of which can be turned on or off, so binary data can be stored. Because each bit requires a separate electrically switchable element accessible from the array's exterior, optoelectronics is most suitable for small, fast memories, such as scratchpads.

Electro-optical memories, on the other hand, store data in some kind of mask that transmits or obstructs a beam of light [see preceding article].

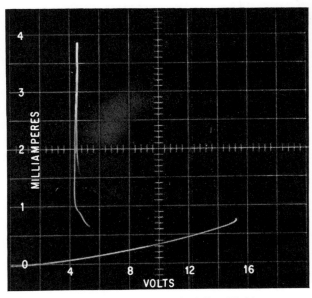

Threshold. Voltage-current characteristic of light-emitting switch shows threshold, where gradually increasing current suddenly begins to climb steeply as voltage drops back. Curve is also discontinuous with decreasing current.

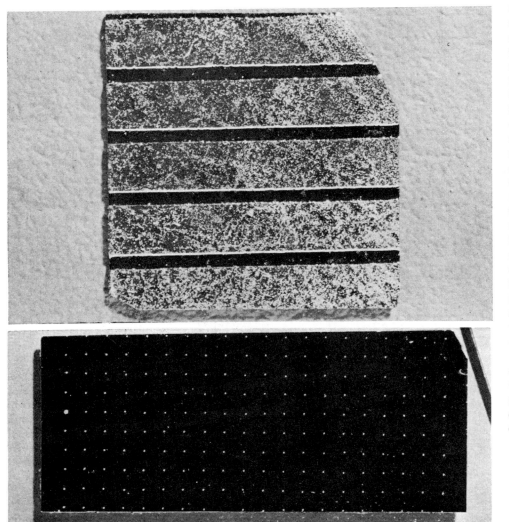

Etching. Black stripes are semi-insulating substrate, showing through where p-type material (gray) has been etched away to isolate the columns in a memory array about ¼-inch square. Continuous gray material connects the anodes of a column of diodes. The bottom photograph shows the reverse side of a ½-by-1 inch wafer that, except for size, is similar to the one above. Each white dot is a spot of n-type material. A memory array would be made from this wafer by evaporating a thin-film resistor beside each dot, then connecting the resistors in rows perpendicular to the columns, as shown on page 178.

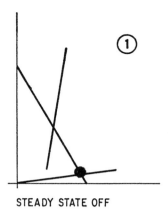

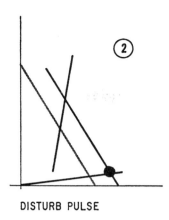

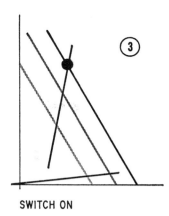

STEADY STATE OFF

DISTURB PULSE

SWITCH ON

(LIGHT EMISSION)

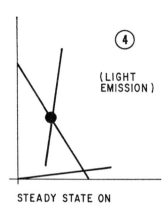

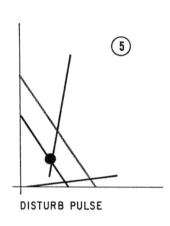

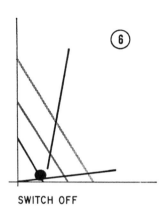

STEADY STATE ON

DISTURB PULSE

SWITCH OFF

Disturbance. In the matrix on the next page, a single disturb pulse at either end of a diode has no effect on it, but pulsing both ends of the same diode can change its state. These six diagrams trace the sequence of events.

Since the mask can be large and the data densely packed, the electro-optical memory is suitable for bulk storage. Also, because often the data in the mask cannot be changed easily or at all, most electro-optical units are either read-only or updatable memories, that is, data can be added but not removed.

Optical feedback

Several kinds of devices or combinations of devices meet the requirements of an optoelectronic memory. One simple combination is the photoconductor and neon bulb; a similar unit is the electroluminescent-photoconductor (EL-PC) cell. These devices are connected as a series circuit, with optical feedback to establish bistability. Once the bulb or EL device begins to emit, its light reduces the photoconductor's resistance, ensuring that the emission continues. In addition, the emitted light indicates the storage cell's state. It's turned on by applying a momentary overvoltage to the series circuit, or by shining an external light source on the PC element; it's turned off by removing the power

momentarily.

The combination, however, is larger than monolithic circuitry. A much smaller cell is a combination of a silicon integrated flip-flop and a light-emitting diode. The silicon IC provides the threshold and storage action. In this configuration the light emission is solely for external detection; it doesn't enter into the circuit function.

A light-emitting switch developed by GE embodies the concept of an optoelectronic memory element in a single device.* It's essentially the only unit now being developed. Unlike a light-emitting p-n diode, the LES contains a layer of semi-insulating material between the p and n regions. This material's resistivity—generally between 10^5 and 10^6 ohm-centimeters—is considerably higher than that of the usual doped semiconductor, which is about 0.01 to 1 ohm-cm, yet isn't quite as high as that of an ideally pure, or intrinsic, semiconductor-- about 10^8. (The classic insulating materials, such

* The LES device was investigated for memory and display applications under military contracts AF30(602)-3615 and DA28(043)-01486(E), respectively.

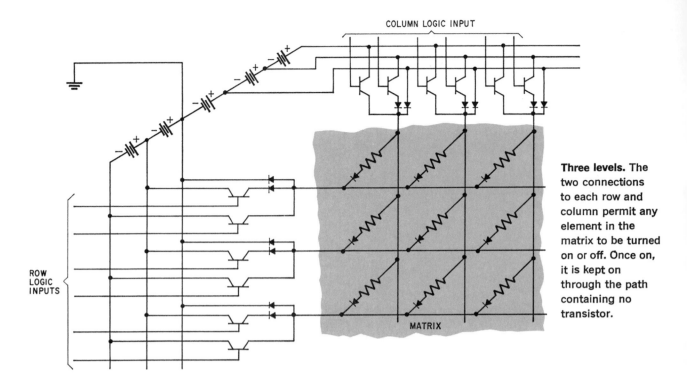

COLUMN LOGIC INPUT

ROW LOGIC INPUTS

MATRIX

Three levels. The two connections to each row and column permit any element in the matrix to be turned on or off. Once on, it is kept on through the path containing no transistor.

as rubber or porcelain, have resistivities of about 10^{15}; copper is about 2×10^{-6}.) This material also distinguishes the LES from the superficially similar p-i-n diode, whose interposed layer's resistivity closely approximates that of intrinsic material.

The LES, when properly biased, will maintain a steady state with either high or low impedance. Its voltage-current characteristic curve, shown on page 176, and the diagrams on page 177, show how it does this. In the low-impedance, or "on" state, the LES emits radiation characteristic of its bandgap. For a gallium arsenide structure this radiation occurs near 8,800 angstroms, similar to the GaAs p-n emitter. Since the LES emits no radiation in the high-impedance mode, its state can be interrogated by sensing its optical output.

To use any optoelectronic device in a practical memory, many units must be integrated into a high-density array. The LES structure is well suited to this array fabrication, because the individual device element consists of a p region and an n region formed on opposite faces of a high-resistivity wafer. The isolation between adjacent devices depends on the starting wafer's bulk resistivity; since this is on the order of 10^6 ohm-cm, several tens of megohms are easily achieved.

To apply an optoelectronic storage element as a memory, appropriate signals must be presented to each element in the array so that it can be switched independently from the high-impedance or "off" state to the low-impedance or "on" state, or vice versa. These can be obtained from three-level drivers connected to the rows and columns of the array, as shown above. Writing a 1 into a particular element in the matrix requires each of the two drivers that control the element's row and column to apply half the selection voltage. This increases the voltage applied to the element above its threshold level, switching it to the low-impedance state. Writing a 0 is similar; the applied voltage is reduced below its lower stable level.

Because data retrieval is optical, it's independent of the switching electronics. The read part of the memory consists of an image sensor system that can sample each of the storage locations. This can be done serially, in parallel, or in a combination of both. The most basic detector system is an array of photodetector elements—one for each of the emitters. Several kinds of solid state arrays of photoconductors, photodiodes, or phototransistors are available for this function.

Another type of detector can be made from a vidicon sensitive to near-infrared light. One difficulty in this approach is aligning the electron beam to a particular location on the photo-cathode corresponding to a specific storage element. A potential solution entails a discrete diode array for the vidicon cathode, so that a unique correspondence exists between each emitter and detector. Similar photodiode vidicons have been successfully operated at Bell Telephone Laboratories at densities of about a million per square inch. ∎

Bibliography

E.I. Gordon, "Beam-scanned vidicon," Bell Laboratories Record, June 1967, p. 175.
G.C. Gerhard and H.A. Jensen, "Visible light-emitting switch," Applied Physics Letters, June 15, 1967, p. 333.
A.M. Barnett and H.A. Jensen, "Observation of current filaments in semi-insulating GaAs," Applied Physics Letters, May 15, 1968, p. 341.
"Electro-optical mass memory," Data Processing Magazine, July 1968, p. 23.

Sonic film unit is a sound bet

A strain wave moves along a substrate under an isotropic magnetic film
in experimental memory that reads and writes, is nonvolatile,
and isn't saddled with mechanical contrivances

By Rabah Shahbender
RCA Laboratories, Princeton, N.J.

Strain waves interacting with magnetic film elements form an unusual memory—the sonic film. In the technique, which RCA Laboratories has been investigating for several years, strain waves travel at the speed of sound along a substrate under an anisotropic magnetic film, taking advantage of the latter's magnetostrictive properties to record data in it. The aim is to produce a block-oriented random-access memory (Boram), in which blocks of data are accessible randomly at electronic speed but from which data can be retrieved only a whole block at a time, not in individual words.

It's still an experimental technique; current work is primarily in improving ways to launch the strain wave and in measuring its characteristics. This research will probably continue for at least another year, after which a program must be undertaken to develop methods to deposit the film, make the transducer, package the unit mechanically, and so on—probably one or two years' more work.

[Ed. note—Since this article was originally published, RCA Laboratories discontinued the sonic film project. See note p. 188.]

Like those of the planar thin-film memory, the sonic film memory elements are a series of thin-film spots or strips deposited on a substrate of glass or similar material. But the sonic film memory is capable of nondestructive readout; whereas planar thin-film memories, in general, have destructive readout—that is, all information taken from them must be regenerated if it is to be available for later reuse. [Cylindrical thin films, or plated wires, are also capable of nondestructive readout; see the article on page 29 of this volume.]

Like the sonic delay line, the sonic film depends on a piezoelectric element from which high-fre-quency mechanical pulses propagate through a substrate. But the sonic film memory is nonvolatile, whereas the data stored in a sonic delay line vanishes when power is shut off.

Like the electromechanical disk or drum unit, the sonic film memory can transfer data from individual blocks or tracks at very high rates. But the sonic film memory isn't saddled with mechanical supports, linkages, drive motors, and the like, and it doesn't have to wait an average of several milliseconds, as does the mechanical unit, before it can start reading from a particular block. Furthermore, it's capable of much better volume utilization. That is, bits can fill up every cubic inch of memory instead of being scattered about on the surface.

The simplest configuration for a memory block is a series of continuous strips of anisotropic magnetic film deposited on one surface of a glassy substrate, similar to a biologist's microscope slide, as shown on page 180, top. The best results are obtained with a substrate of fused silica. The film's anisotropy creates a much larger remanent flux in a particular direction, called the easy axis, than at right angles to that direction—the hard axis. An ultrasonic transducer of lead zirconate-titanate or similar material is attached to one end of the substrate, and an ultrasonic absorbing medium is attached to the other, to prevent echoes from generating spurious outputs. Two conductors on opposite sides of a plastic sheet are put over the magnetic film strips. One conductor is the bit line, parallel to the film's hard axis; the other is a sense line, parallel to the easy axis. One of these has a zigzag pattern; which one depends on the orientation of the film relative to the direction of strain wave propagation and on whether a longitudinal or shear wave is

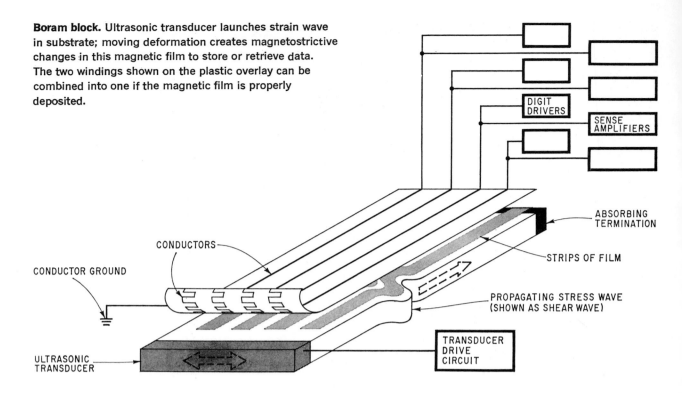

Boram block. Ultrasonic transducer launches strain wave in substrate; moving deformation creates magnetostrictive changes in this magnetic film to store or retrieve data. The two windings shown on the plastic overlay can be combined into one if the magnetic film is properly deposited.

DIGIT DRIVERS

SENSE AMPLIFIERS

ABSORBING TERMINATION

STRIPS OF FILM

PROPAGATING STRESS WAVE (SHOWN AS SHEAR WAVE)

CONDUCTORS

CONDUCTOR GROUND

TRANSDUCER DRIVE CIRCUIT

ULTRASONIC TRANSDUCER

used. For the longitudinal wave, the direction of propagation is parallel to the direction of strain; for a shear wave, the two are perpendicular, with the strain parallel to the plane of the film. Any of these configurations works, but a shear wave gives the best results.

To enter data into the block, the ultrasonic transducer launches a strain wave that propagates along the glass at the speed of sound—3,760 meters per second in fused silica. For a strip 30 centimeters long, this strain wave would arrive at the absorbing medium 80 microseconds after it was launched. As it passes each bit position on its way along the substrate, the strain wave reduces the switching threshold of the film at that position, because of the film's magnetostrictive properties. Pulses of current in the bit line can reverse the magnetization of the strained regions of the film without affecting that of the unstrained regions; properly timed pulses can therefore write data in the film as the strain wave moves along the substrate.

Likewise, as a strain wave passes a given region of the film in the absence of a writing pulse, the film's magnetization rotates slightly but doesn't reverse; this rotation generates a voltage in the sense winding. The polarity of the induced voltage depends on the remanent state of magnetization corresponding to the stored data.

This description is somewhat oversimplified. Actually, either rotation of the easy axis or reduction of the anisotropy field, or a combination of both, can be used for either writing or reading. But in any case, a single sequence of bits can be serially stored in the film, and serially read out again. Data can be processed several bits at a time—in characters or full computer words, for example—by using

the necessary number of film strips on the substrate, each with its own digit and sense line and its own drive and sense circuits.

The diagrams and oscilloscope traces on page 181 show the results of tests on a sonic film memory device. These particular tests were performed on a substrate lacking an absorbing termination at the end opposite the ultrasonic transducer, so that echo signals are present. Also, the substrate had discrete film spots, measuring 20 by 50 mils, as shown below, instead of a continuous strip of film, and it had a large round patch of film in the center for testing the film's B-H loop. Other tests have shown that a continuous film strip is feasible for this memory. If

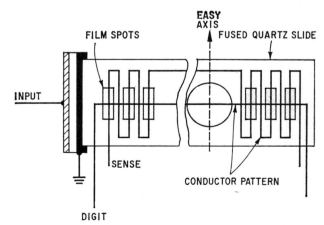

FILM SPOTS

EASY AXIS

FUSED QUARTZ SLIDE

INPUT

SENSE

DIGIT

CONDUCTOR PATTERN

Test blocks. Initial tests were performed on this unit using individual patches of film and two separate conductors. The round spot is for testing the film's B-H loop. Later tests showed that continuous film and one conductor are feasible.

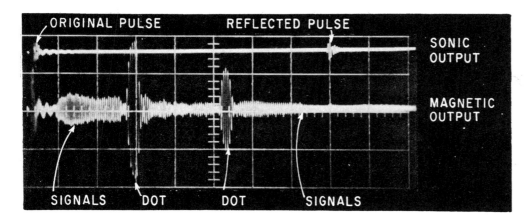

Composite signals. Upper trace shows original and reflected pulses in transducer; lower trace is signals read from film spots as sonic pulse propagates through substrate. Scales are 1 mv and 5 μsec per division.

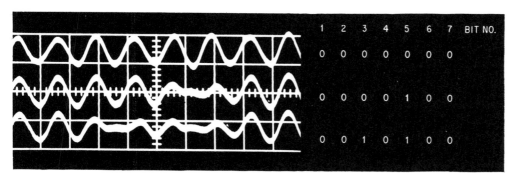

	1	2	3	4	5	6	7	BIT NO.
	0	0	0	0	0	0	0	
	0	0	0	0	1	0	0	
	0	0	1	0	1	0	0	

Data pulses. In one test, pulses generated by passing sonic wave represent binary 0's; where a 1 no pulse. Scales are 0.5 mv and 0.2 μsec per division.

the film's easy axis is at an angle to the strain wave's direction of propagation, the sense and digit functions can be combined in a single winding.

The oscilloscope trace of the composite sense signal, in the top photo, also shows in its upper trace the original driving pulse and the pulse generated by the sound wave reflected from the far end of the substrate. On the lower trace are the outputs from the individual magnetic spots and a large blip generated by the round center patch. Both of these are duplicated in reverse, with reduced amplitude, as the echo pulse returns.

The sense signals from seven adjacent bit positions, expanded in the bottom photo, include 0's in all seven positions, a single 1 in position 5, and 1's in positions 3 and 5 in the three traces. A distinct change in the sense signal character is visible for the stored 1's. The encoding used in this example generated a pulse for a 0 and essentially no pulse for a 1. The reverse coding, of course, could be used instead. Timing for a series of missing pulses in succession is established by strobe signals in the amplifier.

The length of a bit in inches or centimeters is determined by the length of the strain pulse from leading to trailing edge, which is the product of the velocity of sound in the substrate and the time duration of the strain pulse. To enter data in the memory, a strained magnetic region must switch completely in less than the time required for the strain wave to pass that region.

If bits are packed onto the film at 20 per centimeter—much less than the tightest feasible packing in this technology—the strain pulse must be no more than 0.5 millimeter long. If the wave travels at 3,760 meters per second, its duration is about 125 nanoseconds, and it therefore passes a particular point in 125 nsec. Then the magnetic film must switch in less than 125 nsec—considerably less, because higher densities are more practical and there must be a margin for error. This implies a switching time of about 10 nanoseconds.

Furthermore, the current pulse that causes this switching cannot have much overdrive, or it will switch unstrained bit positions as well as the one that is strained. The switching threshold is reduced to about half its unstrained value as the strain wave passes; the current pulse should be just strong enough to clear the strained threshold reliably without affecting any unstrained part of the film.

Densities, in general, are determined by transducer characteristics. If the density is too high for a particular kind of transducer, pulse crowding will occur between adjacent bits as they interfere with one another. To a certain extent, this interference can be overcome by appropriate encoding techniques, such as phase modulation. These techniques, which guarantee at least one phase change in every bit position regardless of whether it is a 1 or a 0, are similar to those that permitted bit packing densities on magnetic tape to increase from the 556 bits per inch that was standard only a few years ago to the 3,500 or so commonly found today.

Of the various parameters of a magnetic film, the most important ones entering into the sonic film's operation as a memory are the anisotropy field, H_k, the coercive field along the easy axis, H_c, and the direction of the easy axis relative to the direction of the strain, ϕ.

The anisotropy field expresses numerically the tendency for the magnetization to lie along one of the two axes in the film. It's shown graphically in the hysteresis loops measured in the two directions, drawn below. An ideal material for the sonic film memory, when unstrained, would have a perfectly square loop in the easy direction and no loop at all in the hard direction, and these directions would interchange when the material was sufficiently strained. The best films for this purpose approach the ideal quite well. They are made from about 60% nickel, 25% iron, and 15% cobalt.

The coercive field, of course, is simply half the width of the hysteresis loop along the easy axis. It's the field necessary to reduce the remanent magnetization to zero.

Both the anisotropy field and the direction of the easy axis are affected by strain. The easy axis tends to line up with the direction of the strain—discontinuously so, if the strain is great enough and applied at right angles to the original easy axis. And the anisotropy field can increase or decrease with strain, depending on the strain's magnitude and whether it is tensile or compressive. Both the anisotropy direction and the anisotropy field as functions of strain have been derived analytically; the graphs on page 183 are plots of these derivations.

In the first graph at left, the rotation of the magnetization θ_r is plotted against the normalized strain, with the angle ϕ between the unstrained easy axis and the direction of strain as a parameter. The easy axis can be established in any direction when the film is deposited in a suitably oriented magnetic field. The normalized strain is the ratio of the actual strain to the strain that produces the discontinuous rotation at $\phi = 90°$; for highly magnetostrictive nickel-iron films the latter is 10^{-4}.

This graph shows that if the strain is applied parallel to the easy axis ($\phi = 0°$), the easy axis doesn't rotate at all. On the other hand, if the strain is applied at right angles to the easy axis, the axis jumps suddenly through 90° to align itself with the strain when the latter reaches the critical value $K = 1$, or 10^{-4}. (Of course, this is only a theoretical result, based on the analytical derivation. Truly discontinuous rotation in the mathematical sense is physically impossible. In practice, because of microscopic variations in the substrate material, the strain isn't at exactly right angles to the easy axis at every point in a sample, even a small one, nor is it exactly the same value everywhere in the sample. As a result, the easy axis rotates quickly—not discontinuously—through *about* 90° when the normalized strain is *about* 1.)

In the second graph, at right on page 183, the normalized anisotropy field, H_k, is plotted against normalized strain, again with ϕ as a parameter. Normalized anisotropy field is the ratio of the actual field to the field existing in the absence of strain. Positive strain is tensile, and negative strain is compressive; either one can increase or reduce the anisotropy field, depending on its direction relative to the unstrained easy axis. The graph shows that for positive values of K greater than 1, and with $\phi = 90°$, the anisotropy field appears to become negative. This is a result of the discontinuous rotation of the easy axis under these conditions.

These theoretical predictions apply also to cylindrical thin films, although the details are different, of course. The predictions have been checked out experimentally.

PZT transducers

There are many piezoelectric materials, but not many that are suitable for a sonic film memory. One of the few both suitable and commercially available is lead zirconate-titanate, known as PZT from the chemical symbols for its components, Pb, Zr, and Ti. PZT transducers with a resonance frequency of 4 megahertz are readily available and are easily bonded to the ends of fused-quartz substrates; they generate ultrasonic pulses that propagate almost ideally. Unfortunately, the bit density for which this frequency is suitable is only about 25 bits per inch.

For a density of 100 bits per inch the resonant frequency is 16 Mhz. PZT transducers at this frequency are also available, but they're harder to handle, and the pulses they generate tend to travel through the substrate with velocities that are a function of frequency. Since a square pulse contains many frequencies, its shape deteriorates as it travels under these conditions, to the detriment of the output signal. The pulses are also likely to convert to other modes, analogous to the various electric and magnetic modes in a waveguide; these modes propagate at widely differing velocities, and thus produce spurious signals.

For still higher densities, up to 200 bits per inch, transducers of cadmium sulfide are being developed. These transducers are evaporated onto the substrate in somewhat the same way that the thin films are evaporated. Their resonance frequencies are in the range of 20 to 50 Mhz. These transducers, and the characteristics of the strain pulses that they generate, are the principal subjects of present in-

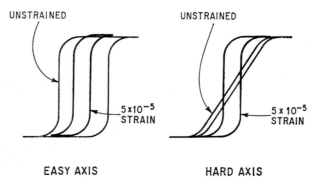

EASY AXIS · HARD AXIS

Toward isotropy. Sonic film's operation depends on the difference between the magnetic hysteresis loops in the easy and hard directions and the effect that strains has on them—narrowing one and widening the other.

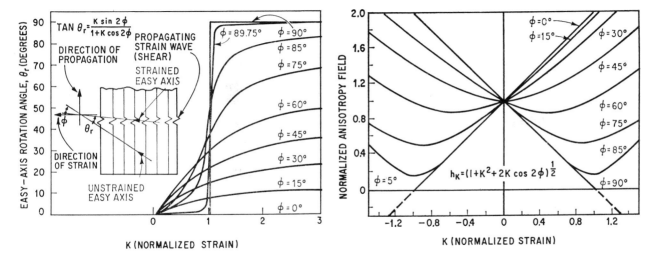

Twist, push, and pull. Amount of easy-axis rotation caused by strain wave depends on strain's magnitude and angle relative to original easy axis, plotted at left. Inset defines the angles. Diagram at right shows how strain diminishes difference in magnetic properties between the film's easy and hard axes.

vestigations in the sonic film technology.

A sonic film memory system would comprise a large number of substrates, each carrying several film strips storing information. Each strip is equivalent to a data track, containing a number of bits depending on the bit density and the track length. These parameters in turn are limited by the resonant frequency of the driving transducers, as described above, and the attenuation of the ultrasonic pulse as it propagates in the substrate. This attenuation is not excessive in a substrate 10 inches long; if the density is 200 bits per inch, each track could hold 2,000 bits. As many as 50 tracks could be deposited on a single substrate and driven by a single transducer, resulting in a capacity of 100,000 bits per substrate. Each track would require its own digit-sense conductor with associated circuitry. Because readout is nondestructive, a small number of sense-digit circuits could be shared by a large number of tracks; data read from unselected tracks need not be sensed for regeneration.

Only 10 such substrates would provide storage for a million bits. Capacities of many megabits would thus be available in a relatively small number of substrates. In such a system the access time is determined by the speed of the circuits that select the transducers—presumably about a microsecond. After a transducer was selected and a strain wave launched along a substrate, the bit transfer rate would depend on the bit density and on the velocity of sound in the substrate—typically 32 megabits per second at 200 bits per inch density.

As mentioned previously, the sonic film memory's performance is similar to that of an electromechanical magnetic disk or drum system; its bit transfer rate is similar, but the sonic film's access time is much faster—a microsecond, compared to the drum's 30 to 40 milliseconds. In the electromechanical system the bit transfer rate depends on the bit density and on the relative velocity between the storage medium and the recording head. The velocity is limited by mechanical considerations to a few hundred feet per second, so that megabit transfer rates are obtained by packing the data at high density. In the sonic film memory, the velocity is that of sound, many thousands of feet per second, permitting high bit rates at modest densities.

From a device point of view, the sonic film memory resembles a fast thin-film memory. But the latter's word-selection circuits are replaced by the ultrasonic transducers, each of which provides access to many more bits than the usual circuits.

Writing and reading in a sonic film memory cannot be interleaved; once a track has been selected all of it is loaded with new data, or all the old data is retrieved. This bypasses the digit transient recovery problem of other high-speed memories.

Without these transients, the sense amplifiers need not discriminate against much noise. In fact, the only noise present is the thermal noise in the amplifier itself. Because of this, even though the sonic film is block-oriented, its performance is almost as good as the performance of a wholly random-access memory. ∎

Bibliography

J.A. Rajchman, RCA Technical Note No. 346, 1959.

E.N. Mitchell, G.I. Lykken, and G.D. Babcock, "Compositional and angular dependence of the magnetostriction of thin iron-nickel films," Journal of Applied Physics, April 1963, p. 715.

H.L. Pinch and A.A. Pinto, "Stress effects in evaporated permalloy films," Journal of Applied Physics, March 1964, part 2, p. 828.

H. Weinstein, "Static and dynamic stress effects on cylindrical ferromagnetic films," Journal of Applied Physics, March 1966, p. 1,003.

H. Weinstein, L. Onyshkevych, K. Karstad, and Rabah Shahbender, "Sonic film memory," American Federation of Information Processing Societies, Conference Proc. Vol. 29 (Fall Joint Computer Conference), 1966, p. 333.

L. Onyshkevych, "Strain-sensitive thin magnetic films," Journal of Applied Physics, February 1968, p. 1,211.

Cryoelectric memories: best hope for large and fast storage units

The devices will be both speedier and cheaper than present types;
a single driver can handle a great number of storage elements
and a single amplifier can sense many memory positions

By Robert A. Gange

RCA Laboratories, Princeton, N.J.

Faster and cheaper memories than any available now—that's the promise held out by research on cryoelectric memories.

In a cryoelectric unit, one driver can actuate up to 10,000 times as many storage elements as in conventional magnetic or semiconductor memories, and a single amplifier can sense as many more memory positions. What's more, these elements can work very fast, with minimum noise, because they have very low power densities and an extremely nonlinear transition between the superconducting and normal states.

The basis for these assertions is a "technology performance index" that compares various memory forms from the point of view of a physicist rather than that of an engineer. This index shows that further development of cryoelectric technology is very worthwhile, even with room-temperature magnetic and semiconductor technologies' rapid evolution. Even the sophisticated refrigerators to attain the extremely low operating temperatures that cryoelectric memories require are only a minor problem.

One large-scale cryoelectric memory design has been successfully worked out. It relies upon a new memory element and a new organization to maximize speed and minimize cost. And it indicates that the predictions based on the technology performance index are fully realizable.

Cryoelectric memories are based on an exotic physical phenomenon called superconductivity—the disappearance of electrical resistance from certain materials at temperatures near absolute zero, in the absence of a magnetic field [see "Removing resistance," p. 187]. These memories can be built of a large number of ring-shaped storage elements, each of which can retain a small electric current that circulates indefinitely in the absence of resistance, just as a ferrite core retains a magnetic flux indefinitely.

To compare the inherent performance capabilities of different systems based on different technologies but serving a common purpose, a common denominator must be found that transcends design innovation and is more basic than such parameters as speed. Such a denominator can be derived from physical constants such as the speed of light and the characteristic impedance of transmission lines.

In all memory systems, an input signal selects a particular bit or word in preparation for storing data or interrogating previously stored data. It propagates along a line of B bits spaced X meters apart, during a time interval determined by the length of the input line, BX, and the velocity of propagation $1/(LC)^{\frac{1}{2}}$, or

$$T = BX(LC)^{\frac{1}{2}}$$

where L and C are the distributed inductance and capacitance per meter of the input line. But the characteristic impedance of the input line is

$$Z_o = (L/C)^{\frac{1}{2}}$$

assuming that the line is lossless. In terms of characteristic impedance, therefore, the propagation time along the line is either

$$T = BXCZ_o \quad \text{or} \quad T = BXL/Z_o$$

substituting for L or for C respectively.

Therefore, if the maximum number of bits per second transferred to or from the system is β,

$$\beta = B/T = Z_o/LX = 1/CXZ_o$$

The second equality applies to cryoelectric and other magnetic memories, and the third to metal oxide semiconductor memories, in terms of the ruling reactance in the respective cases.

This represents an absolute upper limit on the rate at which information can be stored or retrieved.

An output constraint, α, corresponding to the input constraint, β, depends on the technology being considered.

In a magnetic memory, each storage element couples a useful maximum flux linkage, ϕ, to the output. This is less than the total input flux for that bit, because of losses in the memory. The input flux per bit equals the product of the input current, V_{in}/Z_o, and the inductance per bit, $L_{in}X$. The output parameter, α, is, by definition, the ratio of the minimum input voltage to the maximum output flux or

$$\alpha = V/\phi_{out}$$

Substituting the greater value of the input flux in the denominator of this fraction

$$\alpha > \frac{V}{(L_{in} X) \, V/Z_o} = \frac{Z_o}{L_{in} \, X}$$

An analogous situation exists in semiconductor memories built with MOS storage elements, except that the coupling constraint relates to electric charge instead of flux linkage. The MOS element couples a maximum charge, Q, to the output. This is less than the input charge; the latter, in turn, equals the product of the input voltage, IZ, and the capacitance per bit, CX. In this case, the definition of the output parameter, again denoted by α, is the ratio of the minimum input current to the maximum output charge, or

$$\alpha = I/Q$$

Substituting as before,

$$\alpha > 1/CXZ$$

The cryoelectric system is actually a form of magnetic memory, but the former's losses are quite small, and an additional factor must be included in the output parameter inequality:

$$\alpha > Z/LX \ \gamma$$

This factor, γ, is necessary because the memory's output, some seven orders of magnitude smaller than that of other magnetic memories, requires a high-gain amplifier, which is at the temperature of liquid nitrogen or at room temperature. (Even the former—about $-200°C$—is warm compared with the elements' operating temperature.) This temperature difference is important because it permits the amplifier gain to be increased with no attendant increase in thermal noise.

Although the cryoelectric memory is free of common-mode and other forms of coherent noise, the transition from cryogenic to room temperature generates thermal noise. This remains relatively small if the memory output signal is boosted by a transformer on the cryogenic side of the interface, so that the thermal noise is only a small fraction of the signal presented to the amplifier.

The factor γ depends on the transformer turns ratio, the inductances in the storage element that determine current paths when data is being stored, and the ratio of the currents used when data is being stored. The maximum value of γ is about 360; currently attained values are closer to 5 or 10.

Because the input parameter, β, is the maximum number of bits per second transferred into the system, it's also a measure of system bandwidth. The output parameter, α, is the ratio of an input quantity to an output quantity, and as such is a measure of system cost.

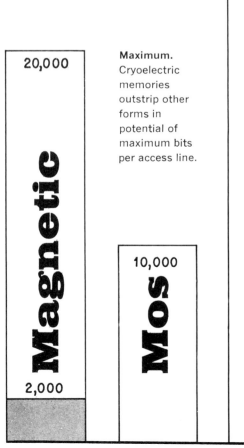

Maximum. Cryoelectric memories outstrip other forms in potential of maximum bits per access line.

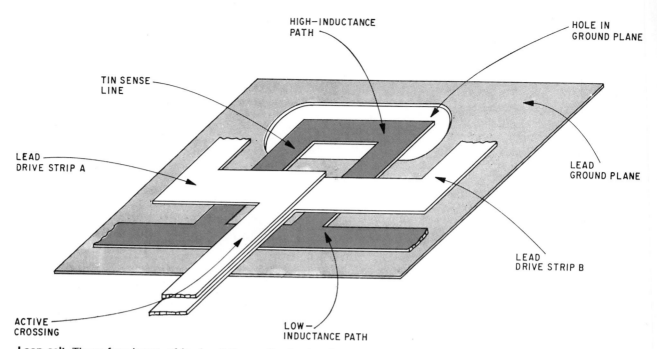

HIGH—INDUCTANCE PATH

HOLE IN GROUND PLANE

TIN SENSE LINE

LEAD DRIVE STRIP A

LEAD GROUND PLANE

LEAD DRIVE STRIP B

ACTIVE CROSSING

LOW—INDUCTANCE PATH

Loop cell. These four layers of lead and tin are the basis of a large cryoelectric memory. A circulating current in the tin loop corresponds to a stored binary 1. The increased inductance created by the hole in the ground plane tends to maintain this circulating current; current in the drive line sets up resistance in the loop, which tends to oppose the circulating current.

For example, of two systems, the one that requires the higher input voltage costs more because more energy passes through a given volume of it in a given time, and therefore it has higher dielectric losses. This translates into a larger number of drivers to activate a given number of bits, or fewer bits activated by a given number of drivers.

The higher input voltage also implies a higher input impedance and, for a comparable bit capacity, a higher inductance per unit length of line. This in turn means a longer propagation delay, or, again, fewer bits activated per driver.

The same higher input impedance also implies a longer time constant. This means it takes longer to decode an address, or that fewer lines can be addressed in a given time by a single decoder.

Higher input voltage also implies more noise coupled to the sense lines, with consequently fewer bits per amplifier, increasing costs still more.

Similar considerations are higher driver voltages, higher bit voltages, higher power supply requirements, and higher voltage stress. The last increases costs by reducing reliability.

And of two systems, the one with the lower output flux or charge requires better amplifiers and has a poorer signal-to-noise ratio.

Clearly, then, the ratio of β/α should be as large as possible. But equally clearly, the ratio has natural upper bounds that cannot be circumvented through design innovation. These upper bounds are 1 for other magnetic and semiconductor memories and γ for cryoelectric memories.

Expressing the ratio β/α in terms of the individual expressions is rather awkward. But these can be re-evaluated as follows: For cryoelectric and other magnetic memories, in which α is the ratio of input voltage to output flux:

$$\frac{\beta}{\alpha} = \frac{Z_{in}}{XL_{in}} \cdot \frac{\phi_{out}}{V_{in}}$$
$$= \frac{1}{I_{in}} \cdot \frac{I_{out} \, L_{out}'}{XL_{in}} \cdot \frac{B}{B}$$
$$= \frac{I_{out}}{I_{in}} \cdot \frac{L_{out}'}{L_{in}'} \cdot B$$

The input flux was expressed as flux per bit, but the output flux is the total. It equals the output current times the total output inductance; the prime in the formula distinguishes total inductance from the corresponding inductance per meter. Multiplying the entire expression by B/B introduces the number of bits into the denominator, converting that term to the total input flux. (L_{in} is in henrys per meter and XL_{in} in henrys per bit, so BXL_{in} is measured in henrys.)

For semiconductor memories, the ratio α is that of input current to output charge:

$$\frac{\beta}{\alpha} = \frac{1}{CXZ_{in}} \cdot \frac{Q_{out}}{I_{in}}$$
$$= \frac{C_{out}' \, V_{out}}{C_{in}XV_{in}} \cdot \frac{B}{B}$$
$$= \frac{C_{out}'}{C_{in}'} \cdot \frac{V_{out}}{V_{in}} \cdot B$$

In these expressions the ratios of output to input inductance and capacitance are clearly visible and can be designated r_x. Likewise, the ratios of output to input current and voltage can be renamed r_y. Then the ratio β/α, which is equivalent to bandwidth per dollar, can be expressed:

$$\frac{\beta}{\alpha} = r_x\, r_y\, B < 1$$

for other magnetic and semiconductor memories, and

$$\frac{\beta}{\alpha} = r_x\, r_y\, B < \gamma$$

for cryoelectric memories.

Orders of magnitude

In the former, the input and output propagation velocities can be assumed to be equal, which means that $r_x = 1$. The inductance ratio r_y in a magnetic memory can range from about 5×10^{-5} to 5×10^{-4}; the capacitance ratio in the semiconductor memory is just about in the middle of this range, or 10^{-4}. These lead to the maximum module sizes for these two forms of memory: 2,000 to 20,000 bits per access line in a magnetic memory, and about 10,000 in MOS.

In a cryoelectric memory, however, r_y is about 7×10^{-6} and r_x only about 0.4; these quantities show that the maximum number of bits per access line can be as high as 2×10^7, or 20 million.

Thus a much larger number of bits in a cryoelectric memory is accessible with one driver or detectable with a single amplifier. Experimental results corroborate this prediction.

Only one large-scale cryoelectric memory has been successfully designed and built. The work was done at RCA Laboratories, and the second-generation results were announced upon completion [Electronics, April 17, 1967, p. 111]. Further work has substantially increased the packing density without sacrificing either output signal amplitude or the operating tolerances on drive currents. These are typically 200 microvolts and ±10%. The highest density arrays built to date have a quarter-million bits in 24 square inches. This is the largest cryogenic array ever built that works consistently over the entire area, as verified by numerous statistical measurements.

The lack of success of other attempts is attributed to the narrow dimensional tolerances required, the insufficient attention paid to system considerations in designing the elements, and the dependence on cryoelectric address decoders instead of room-temperature decoders.

Generation gaps

The second-generation storage element consists of four metallic layers electrically insulated from one another, as shown opposite: a lead ground plane with holes etched in it, a tin digit strip containing a series of loops (one for each storage cell), and two lead drive lines. This is similar to the first-generation element, but the rearranged holes

Removing resistance

Fifty-eight years ago the Dutch physicist H. Kamerlingh Onnes—who three years previously had been the first person to liquefy helium—discovered that mercury's electrical resistance suddenly disappeared if it were cooled to within about 4° above absolute zero. Other metals he was familiar with because less and less resistive as they were cooled, but their resistance eventually leveled off at a value and at a temperature that depended on how pure they were.

Onnes named the new phenomenon superconductivity, and called materials that exhibited it superconductors.

Shortly after Onnes' discovery, other investigators found that if a superconducting metal were placed in a sufficiently strong external magnetic field, it regained its resistance. The threshold implied by the word "sufficiently" is called the critical field.

Second property. Superconductors were thought to be simply ideal conductors until 1933, when they were found also to be perfectly diamagnetic—that is, in the presence of a subcritical magnetic field the field was wholly excluded from the interior of the material except for a thin layer a few thousandths of a mil under the surface.

By itself, this diamagnetic property might be explained by postulating that applying a field to a superconductor sets up eddy currents in its surface. These eddy currents would have associated magnetic fields equal and opposite to the applied field, and in the superconductor the eddy currents would persist indefinitely, in the absence of resistance.

But it isn't quite that simple. If a magnetic field is applied to a superconductor at room temperature, the eddy currents exist while the field is applied and then die away, so that the field passes through the material. Then if the superconductor is cooled below its critical temperature while the field is maintained, it actually expels the field when it becomes superconductive.

and digit strips permit a significantly higher density. Current in the drive lines produces a magnetic field that switches the tin in the digit strip immediately beneath into the normal state. The drive lines themselves remain superconducting. Ordinarily the digit current passes under the drive lines, but when that part of the loop becomes resistive, the current is diverted to the other side of the loop, where the inductance is higher because of the hole in the ground plane. When the drive currents turn off, the entire loop returns to the superconductive state; the inductance establishes a circulating current in the loop that corresponds to a stored binary 1; absence of current indicates a 0.

A third-generation anisotropic structured element attains even higher density by putting the drive lines over the high-inductance part of the loop without increasing the lines' inductance. Details of the technique are proprietary.

In the cryoelectric hybrid system built from these

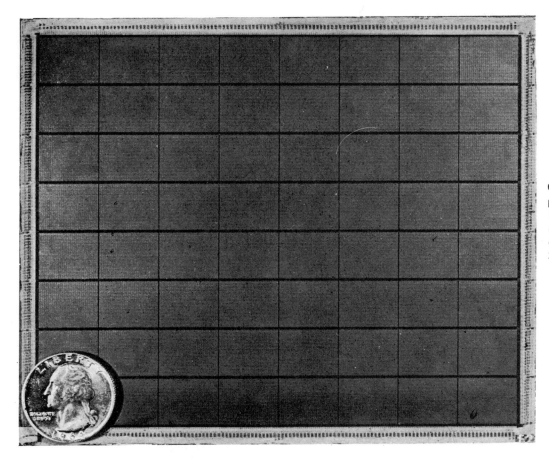

Cold array. This plane contains 262,144 cryo-electric storage elements in 24 square inches.

elements, the drive-line inductance is negligible even when the bit capacity is very large, because the superconducting metal is diamagnetic—it excludes all magnetism from its interior. (This property, incidentally, justifies the name "cryoelectric" for this form of memory. Cryogenic is too broad—it covers all low-temperature phenomena—and cryomagnetic implies ferromagnetism, not diamagnetism.)

The diamagnetic property also effectively eliminates all interaction and noise coupled through the substrate. Only one pair of decoders and drivers, therefore, is required for the entire system, and they can be made very small and simple. Furthermore, they may be kept at room temperature, so that they can be checked out independently of the memory array. Low interaction and noise also permit the sense signals to be unambiguously detected even when they are very small, so that the storage elements themselves can also be very small and closely packed.

Cooling the cryogenic portion of the memory isn't difficult, with currently available refrigeration equipment. Although the cost of this equipment is perhaps half that of the entire system, the ultimate size that the technology performance index predicts would require a refrigerator whose cost was small relative to that of the entire system.

If such a system suffered even a minor failure, it would be out of operation for quite awhile, because cooling it to cryogenic temperatures after making the repair would take several hours. But the chances of its ever breaking down are very small, because at 3.5°K nothing deteriorates.

Other work

Much of the cryogenic memory work outside RCA Laboratories seems to be principally of academic interest. Some researchers are studying the Josephson junction—a sandwich of a thin normal layer between two superconductors that behaves somewhat like a tunnel diode—but this device is still far from any practical applications. Several projects were under way at one time to develop a cryogenic associative memory, but most of these have been discontinued or cut back; the projected costs remained very high relative to the rapidly decreasing costs of other technologies.

Ed. note—In a private conversation during the preparation of this volume, Dr. Gange disclosed that RCA had discontinued work on cryoelectric memories. The company decided that the economic advantages of the technology were insufficient to justify further investment. Presumably economic considerations were also responsible for the demise of the sonic film memory [p. 185] at RCA and of a similar project at Sylvania Electric Products, Inc.

Ferroelectric memories for special applications

By Alvin B. Kaufman

Litton Systems Inc., Woodland Hills, Calif.

For certain applications, polycrystalline ferroelectric materials promise a high-performance memory at a very low cost. These applications include frequency control and the identification of persons seeking access to secured areas. Such memories are amenable to batch processing, capable of high storage density, and resistant to nuclear radiation. Moreover, they produce signals many orders of magnitude larger than those generated with solid state magnetic memory devices.

Ferroelectric memories are well suited for immediate use in certain industrial jobs where only a single word—without addressing logic—is required for a control process. For example, they can be employed in remote meter-reading schemes or in multichannel radio receivers, where linear-select memories can act as a binary code to control a precise frequency and thus to select the individual channels.

To write data in a ferroelectric memory requires the application of a 75-to-150-volt signal for as much as a millisecond—somewhat less for higher voltages. The pulse establishes oriented domains within the ferroelectric material in somewhat the same way that a current pulse polarizes (magnetizes) a ferromagnetic material. Several differently polarized regions can exist in the same device, storing several independent bits.

Two different approaches have been taken to data retrieval. In one of these, application of an interrogating voltage pulse generates another pulse of the same or opposite polarity depending on the polarity of the ferroelectric material; the output voltage pulse can be used directly with MOS or converted to a current pulse to drive bipolar semiconductor circuits.

In the other approach, a ferroelectric wafer's opacity, which depends on its domain orientation, permits data to be read out with a beam of light impinging on an array of photodetectors behind the wafer.

With either retrieval method, the ceramic's piezoelectric and optical characteristics depend on the properties of the orientable domains. And since this orientation is essentially permanent and needn't be disturbed by reading, the ferroelectric memory has a nondestructive readout capability at speeds greater than a megahertz. Once established by a writing signal, the orientation stays put regardless of environmental change or power failures.

These memories aren't in wide use at present, however, and for several reasons. First, many potential users consider ferroelectric devices to be unproven. Second, since the ferroelectric device is voltage-sensitive, it cannot easily take the place of a current-sensitive magnetic memory. It's also quite slow to write. Further, the logic that decodes addresses for a ferroelectric array is expensive because it requires diode or transistor isolation to decouple the elements from one another. And finally, the basic memory element looks like a three-port device; its implementation in an array thus appears easier than it really is.

Taking the wrong path

Another factor to be considered: ferroelectric memory elements are capacitive both with respect to each other in an array and with respect to the printed-circuit wiring associated with the array. This capacitance sets up paths through which unaddressed bits may appear at the output, creating errors or uncertainty in the addressed data. And the isolation needed to block these second-order paths is likely to be expensive.

In a ferroelectric memory from which data is retrieved optically, similar second-order paths are likely to exist in the write circuits, so that data can sometimes be loaded in the wrong place. Also the read circuits, which use a light source and an array of photocells, are likely to be complex.

These considerations make the future of ferroelectric memories in computers rather bleak. Large-scale integrated decoding circuits might overcome some of the problems, but the use of LSI in this sphere seems unlikely in the immediate future. Electrically alterable read-only memories remain an attractive application, but magnetic memories have a big head start here.

The most useful form of ferroelectric memory is the piezoelectric bender, shown below. This device consists of two pieces of ferroelectric material bonded to the opposite sides of a thin metal plate and containing a pattern of electrodes on their outer surfaces. Because the material is piezoelectric, a voltage applied to one of the electrodes causes the entire device to deform physically; this deformation, in turn, generates output voltages at the other electrodes, again as a result of the piezoelectric property.

The polarity of the output voltage depends on how the material under each electrode was polarized during a previous writing operation. This memory can produce several volts in its output signal and can drive bipolar, metal oxide semiconductor, and silicon controlled rectifier circuits directly.

In one recent application developed at Diginetics Corp., a small ferroelectric memory was embedded in a printed-circuit board, as shown on page 191, to make a kind of electronic key. When the fully-assembled key, encapsulated in an opaque dyed epoxy, is inserted in a readout device, it generates a combination of voltage signals that are compared with a preset combination in the reader. If the combinations match, the reader produces a signal that could be used for credit identification or to provide access to restricted areas. The combination stored in any particular key can be easily changed by an encoder device, but is, according to Diginetics, extremely difficult or even impossible to duplicate.

The photograph shows a 13-bit memory capable of 8,192 different combinations. However, a 20-bit memory, of the same physical size, could provide more than a million different combinations.

These keys have a number of advantages over the magnetically encoded cards now used in similar applications, the most important being the fact that it's hard to alter data stored in the ferroelectric device. The magnetic code, on the other hand, can be easily changed, deliberately or accidentally. Furthermore, the ferroelectric data isn't as readily ascertained as the magnetic, even if there's no intent to alter it.

Today's most commonly used ferroelectric material is a lead-zirconate-titanate composition, sometimes doped with bismuth or niobate. This material's principal disadvantage is its high writing voltage; if a material could be developed with a

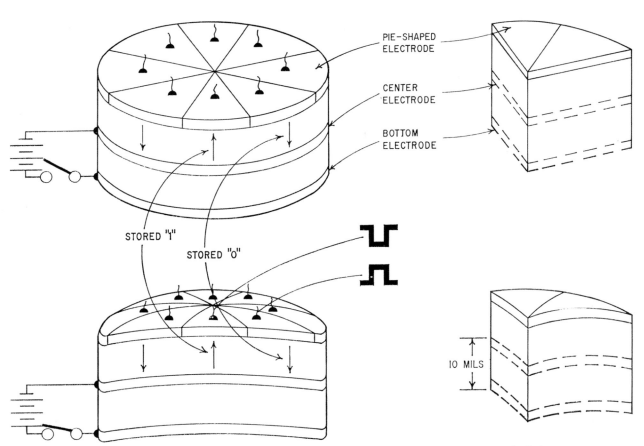

PIE-SHAPED ELECTRODE

CENTER ELECTRODE

BOTTOM ELECTRODE

STORED "1"

STORED "0"

10 MILS

Bender. A voltage applied to the bottom layer of this $1 piezoelectric wafer bends it; because both layers are bonded to the center electrode, the top layer also bends, producing output voltage signals.

Two keys. The ferroelectric wafer, when embedded in opaque epoxy, makes a key that's much harder to duplicate than the old-fashioned variety.

voltage in line with a computer's normal d-c power supplies, computer applications might suddenly seem more attractive.

Also such transparent ferroelectric materials as bismuth oxide and niobate glass-ceramic are being considered for use in certain types of displays. ■

Bibliography

"See-Through" Ceramics Create Optical Memory, Electronic Design, Nov. 8, 1967, p. 26.

A.B. Kaufman, "Memories shot from guns," Electronics, Feb. 5, 1968, p. 98.

"Unlocking memories," Electronics, Sept. 16, 1968, p. 57.

A.B. Kaufman, "Ferroelectric Memories for Security and Identification Applications," Proc. Conference on Applications of Ferroelectrics, Washington, D.C., Oct. 10-11, 1968.

C.E. Land, "Ferroelectric Ceramic Electro-Optic Material and Devices," ibid.

Charles F. Pulvari, "An improved field-controlled polarization transfer device and its application in an associative memory having a 48-bit word length," ibid.

Nonvolatile and reprogramable, the read-mostly memory is here

Integrated arrays combine amorphous and crystalline technologies; new memories could help realize promise of microprograming

By R. G. Neale and D. L. Nelson, *Energy Conversion Devices Inc., Troy, Mich.*
Gordon E. Moore, Intel Corp., *Mountain View, Calif.*

☐ Both the read-only and random access varieties of semiconductor memories leave something to be desired in many applications. RAMs' volatility allows data stored to disappear if power fails. On the other hand, ROMs' inflexibility commits them to data that cannot be changed.

A new kind of integrated circuit, the "read-mostly memory," avoids these problems. An integrated array of amorphous and crystalline semiconductor devices available in sample quantities, the RMM can be programed, read, and reprogramed repeatedly. And once programed, the RMM retains data unless it's intentionally altered. The RMM, therefore, doesn't need the data storage on card, tape, or disk required to back up a RAM if power fails. And the same RMM can be used even if the program must be changed; there's no need for the time-consuming and expensive process of making new masks and fabricating a new IC, nor is it necessary to substitute an electrically programable but fixed type circuit.

Microprograming—a computer technique in which a programer can at will change an operational code or sequence—probably will emerge as the most important application for these devices. The great promise of the microprograming concept has yet to be fully realized—even though the idea originated almost 20 years ago—because of the difficulty and cost of changing the contents of microprogram stores with available memory devices.

Several fertile areas exist where the read-mostly memory's special property of electrically alterable, nonvolatile data storage could be usefully applied:
▶ Airborne computers, which often require a different set of data for a particular mission or operational situation.
▶ Industrial control systems, in which "canned cycles" —stored instructions—must occasionally be altered for new tooling, instrumentation, or test procedures.
▶ General purpose computers in which, even though storage of fixed data is required, it is still desirable to make changes in the data during the design phase.

Physically, the new 256-bit RMM's organization is a 16-by-16 matrix of amorphous semiconductor cells, which must be isolated from each other by integrated silicon p-n junction diodes, as shown on opposite page, to prevent spurious paths in the array. The 122-by-131-mil chip size gives a packing density comparable to that of bipolar or MOS techniques, and should improve with fabricating experience. The chip is enclosed in a 40-lead ceramic dual in-line package.

Each cell in the memory consists of an Ovonic amorphous semiconductor device and an isolating diode in series on a silicon substrate, as shown opposite. The Ovonic structure itself consists of a film of amorphous semiconductor material between two molybdenum electrodes. Many such cells—series combinations of Ovonic devices and silicon diodes—are arrayed over the silicon chip, with each cell addressable by an x-y grid, as shown on opposite page, below. The cell behaves like a nonvolatile bistable resistor with an on-to-off resistance ratio of about 10^3.

Without the series diodes, a few adjacent Ovonic devices in the on (low resistance) state might make the Ovonic device being interrogated appear to be on when it's really off. The resistance of the adjacent on cells would shunt the off resistance. With the diodes, however, the back resistance of the diodes added to the on resistance of the adjacent cells prevents this ambiguity.

Despite some superficial resemblances, the amorphous semiconductor memory is quite a different animal from the electrically alterable, fusable type of memory recently introduced by such companies as Radiation Inc., Motorola Semiconductor, and the Solid State Scientific Corp. Although both types can be programed in the same way, the fusable type's program can't be changed, whereas the amorphous semiconductor RMM can be reprogramed repeatedly.

Changing the memory cell from a high-resistance (disordered) to a low-resistance (ordered) state and vice versa—that is, programing—is done by applying a pulse of a certain voltage, current, and duration. The cell can then be interrogated, or read, without changing its state by applying a constant current and measuring the voltage to determine whether the Ovonic device is in its high or low resistance state.

What defines a set or a reset pulse is not so much its energy as its energy-time profile. Thus, the SET, RESET, and READ operations for the 256-bit memory array require significantly different drive conditions, with voltages varying from a few volts to 25 V, currents from a few milliamperes to over 100 mA, and pulse widths from nanoseconds to milliseconds.

Typical configurations for SET, RESET, and READ driving are shown on the next page. Preparatory to a SET operation, the critical voltage of the Ovonic memory must first be exceeded and a current of several milliamperes must flow for several milliseconds to ensure stable conversion to the low resistance state. This action is accomplished by bringing a selected y line (connected to the cathode of the memory cell to be set) to ground through a saturated transistor. Simultaneously holding all other y lines at 25 V (the inhibit voltage) reverse biases the other diodes and thus isolates the memory cells. At the same time, a selected x line (connected to the anode of the memory cell to be programed) is driven by a 5 mA constant current source at 25 V to insure that the amorphous semiconductor is in the ordered state. The drive voltage, however, must not be allowed to increase above 25 V, since a breakdown of the isolation diodes might result.

In the RESET operation, the procedure is similar except that the current source is increased to 200 mA and the pulse width is reduced to 5 μs. As with the SET operation, the voltage is limited to 25 V.

To read a cell it's merely necessary to apply a fixed current to the cell and measure the voltage drop. A low voltage indicates an on (or SET) cell, and a high voltage indicates an off (RESET) cell.

The circuitry for the READ operation must identify the SET and RESET states of a cell quickly. A typical READ condition is a 2.5 mA constant current applied to the selected x line and a grounded y line. The READ output voltage will then be less than 3 V for a SET memory cell, 5 V for a RESET cell.

The memory cell array's line capacitance and the storage time of the isolation diode determine reading speed. For fast reading, the large capacitance of the y line should be driven by a low-impedance source. The small capacitance of the x line should be driven by a constant current source to forestall excess current through the amorphous memory switch. Such conditions could produce an array access time of about 65 ns. However, the access time for the system would be somewhat longer because of the propagation time of the decoder and driver circuitry.

Of course, the drive circuitry will vary with the particular system. Some applications may not require SET or RESET circuits in the system itself; programing would then be done by external equipment. Also, dropping the 25 V requirement for setting makes the READ circuit relatively easy to implement.

The simplicity and cost of the READ circuit depends

Array. The isolating diodes and Ovonic switches are connected in series across an x- and y-address line. The RMM consists of 256 such combinations.

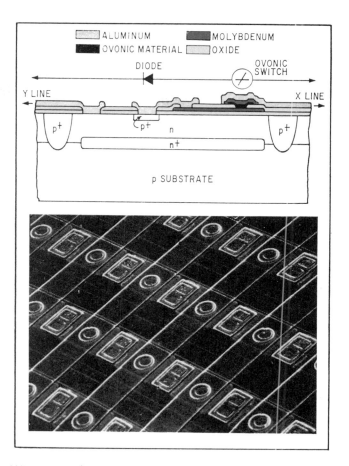

Winning combination. Each read-mostly memory cell contains a thin-film of amorphous semiconductor material deposited on a single-crystal silicon substrate in series with a silicon diode. The metal stripes—the x-address lines—connect the doughnut-shaped Ovonic switches. Running perpendicular to the stripes the y-address lines buried in the silicon connect the figure-eight-shaped silicon diodes. The diagram at top details the cross section of a complete memory cell.

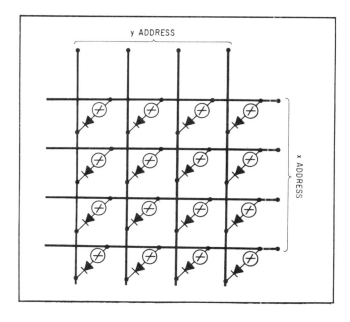

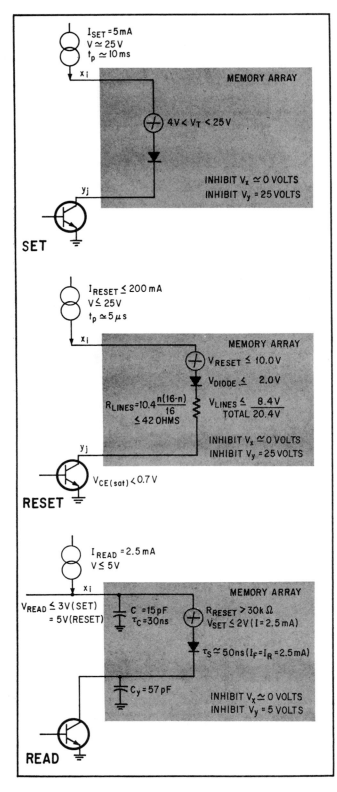

How to read. The operations of SET, RESET, and READ require significantly different values of voltage, current, and pulse duration. Typical conditions are shown in this diagram. The inhibit voltages are for the x and y lines, respectively; n is the number of diodes; V_T is the critical voltage of the amorphous semiconductor; t_p is the pulse duration, and $τ_C$ and $τ_S$ are the time constants affecting READ speed.

on speed requirements: at lower speeds, simple pull-up resistors will suffice, but higher speeds necessitate active pull-up drivers.

One of the knottiest aspects in the RMM development was how to integrate the amorphous-semiconductor memory cells and the silicon substrate containing the isolation diodes. The processing conditions and sequence had to be adjusted to insure compatibility with both types of device.

The problem centered on the aluminum that connects the isolation diodes to the Ovonic devices. This aluminum must be alloyed to the silicon substrate to assure a good contact. However, alloying requires a temperature of about 550°C, which would be too high, since it would also destroy the amorphous semiconductor materials.

This impasse was resolved by depositing and etching the molybdenum film that serves as the lower electrode for the amorphous semiconductor and then alloying or sintering the aluminum to both the silicon diode and the molybdenum. A clear molybdenum surface contact is thus left for the amorphous semiconductor. The aluminum applied over the amorphous semiconductor cell in a subsequent step need not be alloyed, since it doesn't contact the silicon.

As in other p-n junction isolated silicon ICs, the breakdown voltage is an important consideration. The diodes consist of p-type regions of material in n-type channels, as shown on the preceding page. Each of the 16 n-type channels contains 16 diodes. The maximum voltage that appears across the n-type channels must not exceed the breakdown voltage between the n-type channel and p-type isolation channel.

The resistivity of the n-type channel is about 20 Ω per square for the process used (the same process used to make transistor-transistor logic ICs). For a square memory cell (Ovonic device and isolating diode combined), the line resistance for 16 diodes would be 320 Ω. A RESET current of 100 mA passing through the channel develops a voltage drop of 32 V. In the TTL process, however, breakdown voltages usually range from 25 to 30 V, and the channel isolation would fail.

Diffusing a shallow n+ region along the channel reduces the channel's resistivity from 20 Ω per square to 3 Ω per square and, hence, the voltage drop across it. Moreover, no extra process step is required as the n+ diffusion is needed anyway to establish an ohmic contact between the aluminum and the n-type channel.

In addition, the diode channels have both ends shorted by an aluminum conducting strip around the outside of the array, reducing the effective interconnection resistance to the cells. This places the channel in parallel with the addressing line, reducing their effective resistance. Thus, the channel resistance for a channel of n cells is nR/4 when both ends of the channel are shorted, whereas it would be nR without the short.

Repeatability of SET and RESET cycles was the prime concern at the outset of the RMM development. Large quantities of devices were therefore tested to

Benign disorder

The useful bistable characteristic of amorphous semiconductor material depends on a reversible phase transition between two states of greater and less disorder—high resistance and low resistance. To understand the effect, consider the diagram of a thin film of amorphous semiconductor in a memory system, shown below. (The physics of amorphous-semiconductor switching are explained in detail in *Electronics*, Sept. 28, 1970, p. 61.)

To switch a cell to the low resistance state, a voltage exceeding a certain threshold value V_t is applied across the amorphous film. This is an electronic process, not a thermal one, which switches the film and establishes an initial conducting condition that enables electrical energy to be deposited in a confined film channel. A 50-microjoule pulse applied in about 10 milliseconds heats the amorphous material sufficiently to change phase from a disordered or glassy state to a more ordered structure.

The crystallization, or ordering process, is related to the participation of carriers from the valence band—those that form the bonds in the material—in the conduction process. The removal of these carriers from the bonds allows atomic restructuring to take place more easily. Accompanying this change is a drop in resistance of some 3 or 4 orders of magnitude. The sequence of events is called SET process.

The duration of the SET pulse is important. For example, a pulse of only 0.1 ms won't create a permanent change in the amorphous film even though the pulse's amplitude is greater than the critical value V_t. The memory cell will switch to the low resistance state, but when the pulse terminates, the cell reverts to the high resistance state. But with a 10-ms pulse, the cell will remain in its low resistance (or on) state after the pulse is removed. The cell then can be continuously interrogated nondestructively. This is called the READ operation.

To return the cell to its high resistance (RESET) state, the material must be changed back to the disordered state. This is achieved by applying a high current for a short period (approximately 5 microseconds). With about 5 μJ of energy deposited in the cell, the heat generated returns it to the amorphous state, as shown below. The cell cools rapidly, and the disordered, high-resistance state is maintained at room temperature. A typical cell with critical voltage of 15 v is about 1.5 micrometers thick and 5 μm in diameter; such a cell cools to room temperature in about 1 μs.

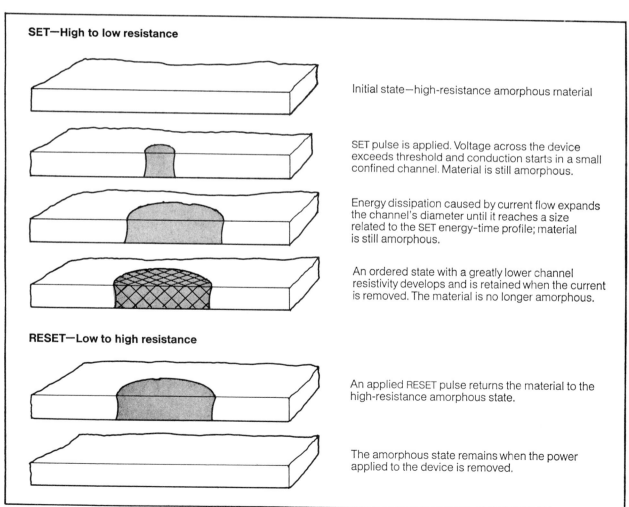

SET—High to low resistance

Initial state—high-resistance amorphous material

SET pulse is applied. Voltage across the device exceeds threshold and conduction starts in a small confined channel. Material is still amorphous.

Energy dissipation caused by current flow expands the channel's diameter until it reaches a size related to the SET energy-time profile; material is still amorphous.

An ordered state with a greatly lower channel resistivity develops and is retained when the current is removed. The material is no longer amorphous.

RESET—Low to high resistance

An applied RESET pulse returns the material to the high-resistance amorphous state.

The amorphous state remains when the power applied to the device is removed.

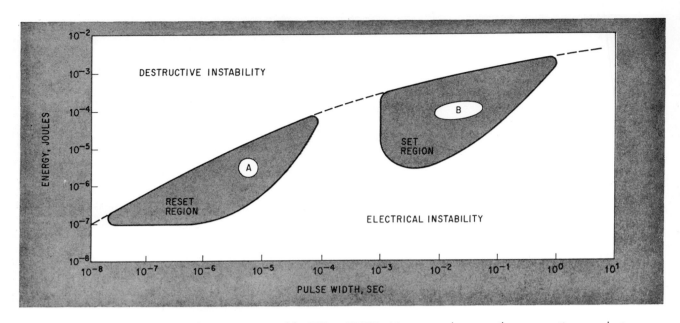

Time and energy. To ensure that the memory is stably SET or RESET without any damage, the energy-time product should fall within the shaded regions. Also an effective change of state requires sufficient RESET energy to reconvert the entire volume of material that has been SET. Thus, a cell that has been SET in region B must be RESET in region A

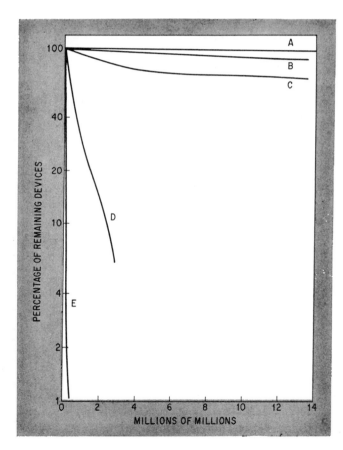

Life cycles. Relatively small changes in the composition of material will affect the operating lifetime of amorphous memory cells. Replacing two atomic % of one constituent in a three-element glass with another shifts the lifetime from the short-lived curve marked E to the long-lived curve marked A.

evaluate the effects of repeated cycling on various switching materials and geometries, and under differing processing and operating conditions. Thousands of test cycles were made.

It was found that the composition of an amorphous semiconductor can dramatically affect the lifetime of the device. The curves shown at left illustrate the effect: the nearly vertical short-lifetime curve (marked E) represents a three-element glass amorphous semiconductor.

The addition of only 2 atomic percent of an additional element shifts the cycle lifetime behavior to the nearly horizontal long-lifetime curve (marked A). The three upper curves represent material compositions that Energy Conversion Devices is studying and optimizing for use in the RMM.

The energy-time combination used for SET and RESET also profoundly affects life expectancy. Certain regions on an energy versus time plot result in effective setting and resetting, as shown above. An energy-time combination that falls below the regions defined by the roughly triangular regions will not produce a stable change in the state of the memory cell, not even after repeated cycling.

Another consideration is the energy-time balance; a cell set with a certain energy within the SET safe area must be reset at a compatible energy in the RESET safe area. Thus, if a cell is set within the ellipse marked B on the energy diagram, then the proper RESET condition should lie within the circle marked A.

The reason for this correspondence requirement is that the area of the converted region in the amorphous semiconductor film depends on the SET energy-time. Thus, as more material is converted to the ordered state, a larger energy is required to achieve a stable reconversion. □

Chapter 8

Memory testing

Memory testing is a task that comes in layers

By Leonard Kedson and Alan M. Stoughton

Computer Test Corp., Cherry Hill, N.J.

Like memories themselves, memory testing technology forms a hierarchy. Yet, despite an ascending scale of complexity, each level in the hierarchy shares some attributes common to the levels above and below. These common factors superimposed on the hierarchy lend a degree of complexity to memory testing that isn't always readily apparent to engineers not directly involved in the technology.

At the first level is the testing of individual storage elements—be they ferrite cores, lengths of plated wire, or some other type. Elements that pass the individual tests are assembled into arrays, which then undergo a higher level of testing. Finally the arrays are combined with drive and sense electronics and other circuitry and are tested again, this time at a system level.

Obviously, the nature of the tests performed on the elements depends on the type of element. And, to a certain extent, this specificity carries through to array testing. But at the system level the memory is a black box in which data can be stored and from which it should be retrieved without change; system testing is therefore largely independent of the kind of element itself.

Test methods for the different types of memories are similar in concept if not in detail. But because ferrite-core memories are the most widely used and most understood, they are used here merely to explain the underlying principles of the testing techniques.

From the bottom up

If element, array, and systems tests are considered as successively higher horizontal layers of tests, then tests that are common to all layers correspond to vertical cuts through them. These vertical cuts represent characterization tests, production tests, and quality-control tests.

Characterization tests are usually made on new core types or new array designs to establish product specifications. Their results may be plotted as curves similar to those on p. 200, which show how a core's performance differs as a function of drive current variations. Similar curves may be plotted to show the effect of temperature and other operating parameters.

Production tests are usually run on a 100% basis to detect and isolate deficiencies in components or in workmanship. They are generally the same in all manufacturing plants, but often differ in detail. Their result is very simple: acceptance or rejection of the unit being tested.

Quality-control tests are performed on random samples selected after the production tests to assure full compliance with product specifications. Rather than simply accept or reject, these tests measure and record actual core parameters; the results are often processed statistically.

At the array level, not only must each individual element be tested again for proper operation, but the way it is affected by its neighbors in the array must also be evaluated. Interactions may occur among neighboring storage elements because of half-select noise or because of parasitic effects among address and sense wires that thread the elements. Array tests usually require several passes through the array, using different storage patterns and drive currents to measure these effects fully.

Characterization tests for memory arrays define operating margins within which error-free operation can be expected. These margins, presented graphically, are called shmoo plots. Theoretically, they should be polygons in two dimensions or prisms in three dimensions, depending on the number of independent variables. But because inherent electrical noise tends to round off the corners, the plots become irregular closed curves, whose shapes explain their name—the shmoo was originally a curvy little comic-strip character. Shmoo plots are

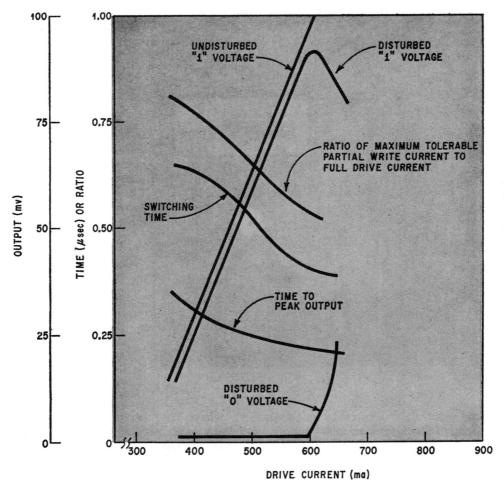

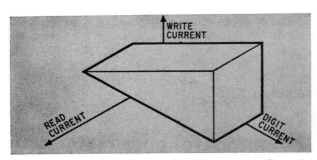

Theoretical. Satisfactory operation of a memory element depends on all currents going through it having optimum values. Above is the relationship between the theoretical maximum variations for these currents.

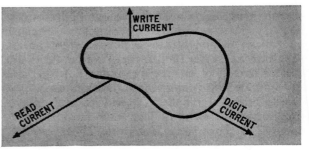

Actual. Noise and other parasitics round off the sharp corners so that the region of satisfactory operation is pear-shaped rather than prismatic. The curve is called a shmoo plot.

one method of defining the acceptance limits for subsequently manufactured arrays. They are also used for defining the operating range over which system electronics must operate.

Production tests of arrays assure compliance with design specifications and also detect such manufacturing defects as broken or chipped cores, missing cores, or wiring errors. These tests, like production tests of cores, usually call for acceptance or rejection of the array without recording specific core response values. Although a single fault in an array is sufficient cause for rejection, the entire array must be tested and all defective locations identified. In most cases rejected arrays can be repaired and do not need to be thrown away.

Quality-control tests run by manufacturers on arrays are primarily to assure good workmanship and uniform performance. They are often duplicated by users as part of an incoming inspection.

Both element and array test systems use sub-

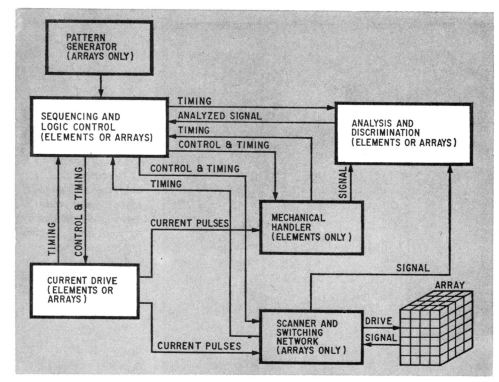

Dual role. Functions in color are used in both element and array testing equipment. Other functions are particular to one or the other level of testing.

systems for sequencing and control, for current pulse driving, and for analysis and discrimination.

The sequencing and control subsystem includes pulse generators that may operate at frequencies up to 25 megahertz, and logic that controls the pulse train distribution and timing. These pulse trains are usually low-power voltage signals that trigger precision current or voltage amplifiers and measurement discriminators; the amplifiers drive the array elements, and the discriminators measure the voltage response. The applied current pulses must have a fast rise time, a sharp corner at the top without overshoot or ringing, and a flat top; and they must retain these characteristics linearly over a wide range of amplitudes, widths, and delays. Amplitudes, for example, can vary from 10 milliamperes to more than 1 ampere. These requirements impose severe constraints on the design of the current-drive subsystem.

In a typical analysis and discrimination subsystem, a 100-megahertz differential amplifier and several types of discriminator circuits may be used to measure the single transient output signal. Different types of discriminator circuits determine whether the signal amplitude exceeds a threshold at its peak or at some prescribed time; compare the peak amplitudes of two simultaneous signals with one another; determine the elapsed time from the beginning of the drive signal's rise to the output signal's peak; and temporarily store the results of these measurements. These discriminators must be capable of resolving voltage and time measurements with millivolt and nanosecond accuracy.

In addition to these basic subsystems, element testers require mechanical handlers to position

each element. These may be manual, semiautomatic, or fully automatic. And array testers require an addressing subsystem to select individual elements or subarrays in the array. The functions of the addressing subsystem are to generate patterns of data for evaluating worst-case noise conditions and signal-to-noise ratios, to cycle through the entire array, to stop temporarily or recycle at an address when an error is detected, and to provide controls for testing selected areas of the array. ∎

Computers for core tests

By William R. Blatchley

Computer Test Corp., Cherry Hill, N.J.

Computer-controlled testers for ferrite cores and core arrays are poised to replace traditional semiautomatic test systems. In many applications, computer control not only does the job faster and cheaper, but is more accurate as well.

Time and dollar savings on the production line arise directly from the computer-controlled tester's ability to establish or change test parameters rapidly and concisely. In addition, the flexibility of computer programing provides the user a hedge against obsolescence of his test equipment.

Computer control. Computer Test Corp.'s Delta 400 is an example of a computer-controlled array tester. It saves hours of the operator's time because the stored program sets up the test parameters. The computer, a Scientific Data Systems Sigma 2, is to the right of the teletypewriter.

Although manual testing is still in wide use and probably will remain so for quite some time, it is subject to some rather pronounced disadvantages that render it quite unsatisfactory.

For example, the operator must set a large number of controls both to define various operational characteristics of the memory being tested and to establish precise values of the test equipment's outputs to the memory. Some of the characteristics are the ranges of the parameters used in the test, the drive pulse sequences, and the data patterns that generate the worst noise levels. Then, when the test is under way, the operator must adjust these controls to obtain the proper waveforms, as he observes them on an oscilloscope, over wide ranges to close tolerances.

Time and money

Not only is this procedure tedious and repetitious but it also causes equipment to remain unused because it's easier to duplicate pieces of test equipment for different memory products than it is to readjust the setting on a single test rig when the product run changes.

Furthermore, no two operators will get the same results on identical products, because of subjective differences. And finally, because setting the controls consumes too much time, marginal testing such as plotting shmoo curves is held to a minimum, or omitted entirely—particularly since such tests are to be run on the completed system.

Special-purpose automatic test equipment that isn't computer-controlled doesn't necessarily solve the problem. Such equipment is very expensive and can be used for only the lifetime of a particular array design. Few manufacturers of core arrays can afford to underwrite the cost of a different custom-designed tester for each of his products; no manufacturer of test equipment can afford to underwrite these costs for the industry.

Control, not monitor

Computer-controlled testers offer a way out. They are much easier to set up than the manual systems and are far more versatile—yet they are as simple to operate as a special-purpose tester.

Every computer-controlled test system—as distinguished from a manual tester with a computer monitoring its outputs—has three important characteristics:

- Its current drivers, discriminators, and other key circuits are programable to work with different amplitudes, rise times, and other parameters.
- It has a display and recording arrangement to show exactly what inputs it provides to the memory being tested.
- It can automatically enter new information at predetermined points in the test sequence, such as new current rise times, new pulse widths, or new thresholds.

In a typical test system that has these characteristics, shown above, the controls can be set in less than five minutes, because all the pertinent information is available on paper tape. Out of these five minutes, 33 seconds is spent on the current drivers, which require from 15 minutes to two hours on manual systems. A few more seconds go for printing instructions that tell the operator how to set the console switches for specific results. Following the basic test, the system can always read new instructions from paper tape that direct it to execute variations on the test without operator intervention.

These testers have many applications today and hold out the promise of almost unlimited applications in the future. For example, they are already effective for multiplexed testing, mixed-lot testing, marginal testing, shmoo plots, and, in general, all testing that goes beyond accept/reject.

In multiplexed testing, the system and the operator can work independently on one or more arrays simultaneously. This requires the system to have two or more sets of current drivers and switches, but the production volume can be doubled, or perhaps more than doubled.

For example, during the five minutes an array is being tested, the operator can be connecting another array to the second set of drivers. Then, while the second test is going on, he removes the first array and connects a third.

In mixed-lot testing, the quick setting of the controls in a computer-controlled test system permits much more thorough testing of the arrays in a given time than would be feasible, or even possible, with manual testing.

Seven times as fast

For example, suppose seven arrays of seven different designs are to be tested in a given eight-hour shift. If the controls on a manual tester can be set for any of the types in an hour, most of the day's work would consist of resetting them, and a total of only one hour's testing would be accumulated—an average of only about 8½ minutes per array. That's barely enough time to verify that the assembly works the way it should—let alone enough time for a thorough test of the array.

But setting the controls on the computer-controlled tester—five minutes for each array—adds up to only 35 minutes for all the arrays, leaving 445 minutes for testing, or more than an hour for each array, which leaves more than enough time for a thorough workout.

Marginal testing on a single product provides assurance that the array works equally well at both ends of the published current specifications. This requires different control settings for the two ends of the range for each array tested. In a manual test, a typical approach would be to set the controls only once for each end of the range and connect each plane twice, because connecting planes is quicker than setting controls.

But with the computer control, setting involves only running a paper tape through a reader; this can be done twice for each array, so that the array

need be connected only once. Depending on the exact time required for setting up and connecting, this can more than double the production in a given period of time.

Shmoo made easy

Shmoo plots usually aren't made on planes when manual methods are used; they are put off until the memory system is assembled because on planes they take too much time. In their simplest form, they require every word in the memory to be cycled and checked for an error for every combination of two drive currents. These currents are varied in small increments over a range wider than the range the memory will encounter in normal use.

Obviously, making all those small changes in the x and y drives can take a lot of time. For this reason, even simple shmoo plots made manually can take days to complete—whereas a computer-controlled tester can do the job in an hour. Furthermore, once the job is started, it runs by itself—an attendant is no longer needed.

Although simple computer-controlled testers use discriminators capable of making an accept/reject decision, it's easy to add complex circuitry that can measure the American Society for Testing Materials' standard test parameters—the time taken for an output signal to reach a peak, the amplitude of that peak, and the time for the core or other memory element to switch completely. These complex circuits also permit histograms, or distribution curves, to be made; and they need not be removed for a return to the simple accept/reject level, as in production testing.

What's to come

Computer-controlled testers are capable of almost unlimited applications. As memory technology advances, new test methods will be necessary. These methods, which will be easy to implement with computer-controlled testers, will make special-purpose testers obsolete.

For example, 2½-D memories only recently became very popular, but many suppliers and users of test equipment found themselves with rooms full of special-purpose equipment that became obsolete almost overnight.

Read-only memories of various kinds are becoming more common every day, and large-scale integrated-circuit memories appear to be just around the corner. Only the developers of these memories know now what kind of test equipment is likely to be needed, and they're not talking about their thus-far proprietary designs.

When these designs hit the market, users with computer-controlled testers will be able to adapt rather quickly, laying out cash only for new programs and maybe a little for new connectors, jigs, and other accessories.

But the howl that went up when 2½-D came out will be heard again from those who are sticking to manual and special-purpose equipment. ∎

Exercising memory systems with worst-case bit patterns

By Charles R. Elles

Computer Test Corp., Cherry Hill, N.J.

and Elwood A. Dance*

Scientific Measurement Systems, Inc.,
Moorestown, N.J.

It's not enough to test only memory elements and assembled arrays. After these tests, connecting the array to its drive, sense and control circuitry completes the memory system; and only after this complete system passes its own level of testing can there be any reasonable assurance of high reliability, for the unit as a whole.

In a system test, the drive and sense electronics and memory address, data, and timing logic have been installed; the memory is operated during the test under normal conditions, at normal environment, as specified for its ultimate environment.

Generally the best test of a memory system—as opposed to memory elements or arrays—is a functional test: Can information be stored and retrieved without error at full memory speed? In other words, can complex patterns of digital data stored at each address location be completely retrieved without error?

Worst-case patterns, which depend on the wiring configuration of the memory, determine to what degree inherent noise affects the memory's stored data. This noise is either generated in the half-selected cores or capacitively coupled from drive to sense lines. When the noise is too great, the discriminator may detect it and erroneously indicate the presence of a 1 in place of a 0, or a 0 in place of a 1.

Besides the obvious all 1's and all 0's, a variety of other data patterns are useful. Among the simpler patterns are checkerboards, double checkerboards, checkerboards shifted by one bit, interlaced rows of 1's and 0's, and their complements. Large memories may require more complex patterns to generate the worst-case noise conditions that they may encounter in use.

Memory exercisers

A memory exerciser contains address, data and timing logic that generates these patterns, stores them in the memory being tested, and recovers them at memory speeds. It is made up of an address counter—which coordinates all memory op-

* Formerly with Computer Test Corp.

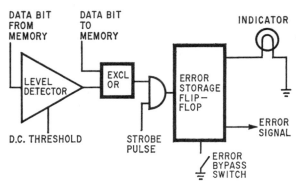

Detector. Any pulse from the memory, identified as a 1 or a 0 by the level detector, is compared in the exclusive-OR gate with the binary value that it should have. When the values are different at the time of the strobe pulse, the flip-flop records an error, and the indicator warns the test operator. One circuit exists for each word bit.

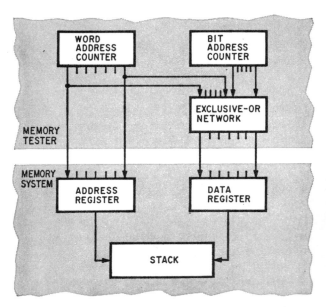

Pattern generator. Exclusive-OR network combines bits in exerciser's two address counters and transmits them to memory's data register, to load pattern into array.

erations—a pattern generator, mode controls, and timing circuitry.

The address counter is usually organized in straight binary form. If the memory being tested contains 2^n words of k bits each, the address counter is n bits long. This counter specifies the memory location being tested at any instant; at this location all k bits are checked in parallel. To generate any of the checkerboard or other specialized patterns, a second address counter of k bits specifies the individual bits, as shown directly above. For example, a memory containing $2^{12} = 4,096$ words of $2^4 = 16$ bits each would require an address counter of 12 bits to specify every word, and 4 more bits to specify individual bits in each word for the data patterns.

In this example, individual bits in the data pat-

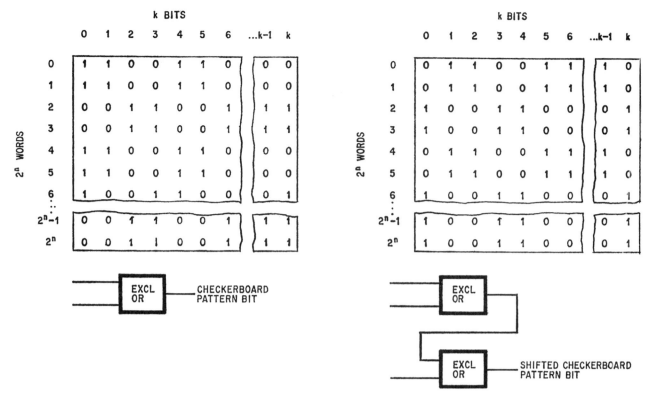

Checkerboards. The second least significant bit of the n-bit address counter is combined with the second least significant bit of the k-bit address counter to generate a worst-case checkerboard pattern, left. A slight variation in the circuit produces the same pattern shifted one bit to the right. Both circuits use exclusive-OR gates.

tern are defined as a function of the address. Other data patterns can be entered from punched paper tape, programed with patchboards, controlled manually from the front panel, or permanently wired into the exerciser.

During normal operation, the counter starts at zero and counts one for each memory cycle that is performed until the maximum address is reached. All memory locations are thus sequentially tested. This process can be repeated—that is, the test may be recycled as many times as desired in a search for transient errors.

Using manual control switches on the panel, the operator selects upper and lower address limits or selects only one location. Lamps indicate the memory location under test.

A bank of exclusive-OR circuits compares each output data word, bit for bit, with the pattern originally stored. When there's an error, a comparator output lights an indicator on the front panel that pinpoints the data bit in error. This may also cause the machine to enter a preprogramed error mode that helps to isolate the error.

Different courses of action

Once an error is detected, different options are open to the operator. Much depends on the test being performed. In acceptance testing, the best course is to count the error and continue the test; the number of accumulated errors is then displayed after the test has been run to completion.

In troubleshooting, however, the defective address and the error bit must be ascertained. Stop-on-error and error-recycle modes are important aids in this task. To locate the source of error, the exerciser can stop and display the contents of the address counter and data error flip-flops. If the error is transient, the machine can continuously recycle the memory at a single address, while the operator investigates the cause of the error.

One-shot timing

Mode control and exerciser timing are derived from internal read and write timing pulses, or from an external source. In one system, one-shot multivibrators provide this external timing—two are used for each read-write pulse. One multivibrator defines the pulse position, and the other, triggered from the trailing edge of the first, controls pulse width. These multivibrators must be stable to within 0.5% and must have a duty-cycle capability that approaches 100%.

Logic levels in general-purpose exerciser systems rarely match those of the memories under test. Interface circuits therefore are placed between the exerciser logic and the memory. With these circuits, which are designed to drive terminated transmission lines, the operator can select and set the logic levels required to match the memory system being tested. ∎

Boosting plated-wire yield: which knob to adjust?

By Gary Chernow

Computer Test Corp., Cherry Hill, N.J.

Fast switching, low power dissipation, and nondestructive readout make plated wire an attractive memory element. But these features may be accompanied by a serious production disadvantage—the medium's unpredictable yield, sometimes as low as 30%, which severely restricts the length of usable pieces of wire. Several solutions to this problem are being investigated.

A closed-loop process could be solution to the yield problem. In this process, test results obtained on-line would be fed back automatically to the manufacturing process, varying critical parameters and allowing plating, testing, and cutting of the wire at speeds of up to 100 inches per minute.

Wire is now plated and tested continuously at speeds ranging from 10 to 30 inches per minute. But there is no feedback from the testing to the plating operation, except when an operator decides that the rejection rate is too high and makes a manual adjustment. For example, he may adjust the temperature of the electrolyte, vary the concentration of the plating solution, or change the plating current density; but between the times when he makes these decisions and adjustments, many flaws may be detected in the wire produced.

For these tests, a closed-loop system is perhaps easier to envision than to implement, because of the adjustments that test results dictate. They include such factors as film thickness, alloy composition, surface roughness of the substrate, the anisotropy field, the film's magnetic history, and so on. All these parameters affect the stability of the film's domain and wall structure, which in turn affect the output signal's behavior. But there's no clear correlation between the results of a test and the parameter to be adjusted; such correlation is a prerequisite of automatic closed-loop control.

Data is recorded in plated wire by magnetizing the thin film of plating material in either direction around the wire; the magnetizing force is the resultant of currents in a perpendicular word strap and in the wire itself. To read out the stored data, a word current acting alone tilts the magnetization vector of the wire away from its circumferential direction; the resulting flux change induces an emf between the ends of the wire. When the word current is removed, the vector is returned to its rest position by its anisotropic energy, thus permitting nondestructive readout.

The testing operations measure four quantities: the intrinsic amplitude of a readout pulse from the wire, the effect of disturb currents in both the word and bit directions, and the effect on a particular bit cell of repeated reading and writing operations in adjacent cells. These measurements are usually made immediately after the last step in the plating process. In one instrument for making the measurements, the wire passes through a frictionless electrical contact such as a cup of mercury, then through three word straps—each of which generally makes one turn around the wire—and finally through another mercury cup. The word straps carry the word current, just as in the complete plated-wire array. During the test, the bit cell being tested is under the middle word strap, while the other two straps are used for reading and writing in adjacent cells. The mercury cups establish contacts for bit current through the wire itself. Because there is current in the wire during the plating process as well as during testing, the upstream mercury cup is grounded and a current source is connected to the downstream cup. This prevents the bit current and the plating current from interfering with one another.

Step-by-step procedure

One common test uses a sequence of four steps: First, 0's are written 1,000 times into each of the three cells under the three word straps, one cell at a time, after which a 1 is written once into the middle cell. This 1 is then read out and the amplitude of its readout pulse recorded. This first step thus requires about 3,000 separate operations.

In the second step, the same 1,000 0's in three cells and the single 1 in the middle cell are written as before, but then a word current passes through the middle cell's word strap 1,000 times in the absence of a bit current in the wire. This is tantamount to 1,000 read operations, but the peak is stored only at the 1,000th time. Because of the disturbing effect of repeated reading in one position, the peak will be slightly lower than previously.

The following step is essentially the same as the second, except that 1,000 bit-disturb current pulses pass through the plated wire, while no current passes through any word strap. This further reduces the peak of the middle cell's output, which is stored again.

Finally, the 1,000 0's and the single 1 are written again, followed by an additional 1,000 0's in each of the two adjacent cells. Again the middle cell's 1 is read out and stored.

After all four steps have been completed, the ratio is taken of the peak output pulse in the second, third and fourth phases to that in the first. These ratios should be uniform along the full length of a segment of plated wire, and are more important than the absolute amplitude of the pulses; for if disturbances from adjacent cells cause too great a

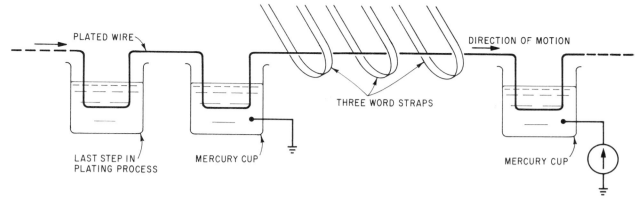

Nimble. Plated wire coming out of the manufacturing process is tested as it passes through the middle one of the three word straps. The other two help to simulate an actual memory environment. Mercury cups are electrical contacts for bit current in the wire during testing. 32,000 cycles are executed while the wire moves only a few mils.

shrinkage of the output pulse, the data cannot be interpreted. On the other hand, because a single sense amplifier serves the whole wire, it can be adjusted to work with the absolute amplitude of that wire's output over a wider range than the allowable shrinkage caused by the disturbances that arise from adjacent cells.

These four sequences add up to about 16,000 operations. The entire procedure is then repeated with complementary data—1's replacing the 0's, and the 0's substituting for the 1's, for a total of 32,000 operations. Repeating the process with complementary data establishes the skew factor of the plated wire, or the degree to which the film's easy axis differs from a perfectly circumferential direction. Although 0's and 1's produce output pulses that are nominally equal in amplitude and opposite in polarity, skew tends to make one pulse lower than the other.

Handle with care

In making these tests, the 32,000 read and write cycles are performed while the wire moves no more than 4 mils, or 1/10 of a bit cell length; if the wire moves at 30 inches per minute, these 32,000 operations must be completed in 8 milliseconds, allowing about 250 nanoseconds per cycle. Repeating the test every 4 mils insures that the wire's characteristics are uniform along its length.

Not all tests are now performed on-line. One important off-line test is for zero magnetostriction. Plated wire's magnetic characteristics must not be changed when the wire is physically stressed. To this end, the characteristics of the plating material are carefully controlled and great pains are taken to mount each segment of wire in an array so as to protect it from stress. Nevertheless, selected wire segments that pass the on-line test are subjected to pulling or twisting while their B-H characteristics are being measured. If the magnetostriction isn't zero, the physical stress will change the shape of the B-H loop; if the change is excessive, the plating process must be adjusted. This test is difficult, but

Tester. This device contains the apparatus diagramed.

not impossible, to implement on-line.

Another off-line test is a plot of sense output versus write current and bit current, called a window test. This test is the plated-wire analog of the shmoo tests carried out on ferrite core arrays, except that there is only one independent variable for each plot instead of two. These tests require a considerable length of time to make, even with automatic equipment, so it's impractical to carry them out on a moving wire. This being the case, the window test probably won't be on-line at any time in the foreseeable future. Instead, the plots are made at intervals of 10 or 15 minutes on samples taken from the on-line test; a comparison of successive tests is one indication of the plated film's uniformity. ∎

Bibliography

Tentative Methods of Test for Nonmetallic Magnetic Cores . . . , American Society for Testing Materials, Standard C-526-63T.
Sampling Procedures and Tables for Inspection by Attributes, MIL-STD-/105D, April 1963.
C.P. Womack, "Schmoo Plot Analysis of Coincident Current Memory Systems," IEEE Transactions on Electronic Computers, February 1965.
Frank S. Greene Jr., "An Automatic Ferrite-Core Tester," Computer Design, April 1966.
J. Hubbs, "What's Wrong With Pulse Instrumentation," IEEE, Nov. 11, 1967.
C.J. Walter, A.B. Walter, M.J. Bohl, "Setting Characteristics for Fourth Generation Computer Systems," Computer Design, August 1968.
Alan M. Stoughton, "Computer-Controlled Memory Testing," Modern Data Systems, August 1968.
George A. Fedde, "Plated wire: a long shot that's paying off," Electronics, Nov. 11, 1968, p. 124.

Chapter 9
Special memories

Military masses its cores for battlefield conditions

By Bryan W. Rickard

Electronic Memories Inc., Hawthorne, Calif.

Up in the air or down to earth, a military environment for electronic equipment usually implies a wide temperature range and high humidity in which the equipment must operate reliably, while withstanding severe vibration and shock. These conditions are particularly severe for computer memories, since they must handle all the programs and data for a variety of tasks—often in the midst of battle.

To achieve reliability under these conditions, the cores in military memories are usually made of lithium ferrite, and the core mats are mounted on rigid frames, instead of being suspended in midair by their selection wires. Furthermore, all exposed conducting materials are coated with a moisture-resistant material to avoid shorting by contamination, and all cabling is securely tied down.

In general, the military core memory is designed and built in accordance with the appropriate military specifications for use in aircraft, missiles, ships, or ground-based equipment. These specifications insure that the materials, parts, and processes used are consistent with the military's basic requirements for human engineering, utility, value, and quality control.

Lithium ferrite's wide temperature range is a result of its crystalline structure, in which monovalent lithium replaces divalent and trivalent ions in a complex bonding structure [see p. 19 in this volume]. But lithium ferrite cores can't solve all the temperature problems of military memories. Drive currents through even the best lithium cores must be temperature compensated. Since the coercive force of the material decreases as the temperature goes up, the drive currents must also decrease, at approximately the same rate. These currents are usually controlled by temperature-sensitive resistors or diodes mounted in the stack. As the temperature increases, these devices control the drive circuits to admit less current through the drive lines.

But using these devices creates a subsidiary problem—namely, making sure that all cores controlled by a given drive line are at the same temperature as the monitoring device, or nearly so. A great many factors can affect the temperature gradient within a memory, some of which are discussed below:

■ Operating duty cycle is one of the more obvious factors. The more often a memory is cycled, the more often its cores switch; each switching action requires energy input, most of which is dissipated in the form of heat. If the rate of energy input is greater than the rate of heat dissipation, the memory's temperature rises.

■ Within a given cycle of the memory, the ampli-

Battle ready. This memory stack, designed to withstand the stresses and strains of military applications, can store 4,096 words of eight bits each. Current-steering diodes are visible on the top layer.

tude and duration of the drive current pulse also affect the rate of energy input. The minimum pulse needed to switch the cores establishes lower bounds on amplitude and duration.

▪ For a drive current pulse of given amplitude and duration, the size of the wires that thread the cores determines the energy input to the memory, and therefore the rate of heat dissipation.

▪ Operating data patterns affect the heat input to the memory in two ways. Firstly, a preponderance of 0's in the data pattern increases the heat input, because cores into which a 0 is written are kept from switching by current in an inhibit winding. The inhibit current is about the same magnitude as either of the two selection currents, but it passes through a much longer wire. This wire cannot be made very large in diameter because it has to pass through very small cores along with several other wires. Its small size and its length therefore make its resistance rather high, and current through this resistance will therefore generate a good deal of heat.

Secondly, since reading and writing 1's in a data pattern switch the cores, and hysteresis converts some switching energy into heat, a preponderance of 1's increases the amount of this converted energy. However, this is a relatively minor factor as far as temperature gradient is concerned,

except when a fast memory repeatedly cycles at a single address, creating hot spots wherever 1's are stored in the word at that address.

▪ Air pressure and air flow affect the temperature gradient in some memories, but generally are less important considerations for military memories, since many of these depend on conductive cooling. Heat developed within a conductively cooled stack is conducted through the metallic structure to a heat sink, from which it reradiates to the environment. By using conductive cooling, structural limitations that might inhibit the access of air to the memory can be ignored; its use also eliminates the danger of dust and other contaminants brought in by air currents, which eventually would block the air flow; and in some circumstances such as spaceborne and high-altitude applications, there is no air.

▪ Rapid ambient temperature change may cause a temporary failure by creating large thermal gradients within a stack—even though it may operate satisfactorily under equilibrium conditions. For example, when an aircraft scrambles from an arctic base, its equipment bay's temperature increases rapidly as it absorbs heat from the engine; the sudden heat from the firing of weapons is another factor. This kind of problem can be a particularly difficult one to diagnose, because of its transient nature. To avoid it, the cores must have the widest possible temperature coefficient—generally less than 1 milliampere per degree Centigrade, and their thermal conductance must be high.

- Internal thermal conductance—core to core, and core to temperature sensor—should be as high as possible, both to keep the internal temperature even and to avoid difficulties with rapid ambient changes. Establishing a high conductance in these areas more or less assures high conductance from cores to heat sink, which limits the cores' upper temperature extreme but has little relevance to internal gradient. High thermal conductance is obtained by bonding the cores on metal frames, and by joining the frames with accurately fitted spacers or side plates that contact the frames over a large area. The drive wires also conduct heat as well as electricity. Heat conduction paths are also necessary on or past the end boards, which carry selection diodes and interconnecting printed circuits; these boards are usually made of epoxy glass, which is a material that has a very low thermal conductivity.

A well-designed military-memory stack can withstand shocks of over 1,000 times the force of gravity applied in a few milliseconds, and sustained vibration of over 30 g's—in spite of the fact that the crushing strength of a ferrite core is only about 50 grams—about the same as that of a glass bead of the same size. The mechanical structure is very rigid and has no resonant frequency within the range of excitation frequencies encountered in most turbine- and rocket-powered craft.

Each core is bonded to the planes in such a way that a pull of several grams—many thousands of times the weight of a single core—is required to detach it.

Weak link

The magnet wire on which the cores are strung is a potential source of mechanical failure. It is subject to fatigue; it is weakened by chemical changes that occur when it is soldered; and it may be kinked and scratched during stringing. When the memory vibrates, the wire may rub against the cores, causing wear. Careful design and construction are necessary to guard against these vulnerable points.

The military core memory is also protected against atmospheric hazards. Humidity and contamination could be responsible for both open-circuit and short-circuit failures in a memory. Open circuits can result from metal corrosion that breaks a conducting path; short circuits can occur when moisture and contaminants build up on adjacent conductors until they come in contact.

Coating all uninsulated circuits with a material impervious to moisture prevents the electrolytic build-up, but does not necessarily prevent corrosion. Even though the coating ordinarily withstands the kinking and twisting that often occurs when the fine copper wire is threaded through

several hundred cores of rather abrasive material, it nevertheless may develop crazing and pinholes through which moisture can attack the metal when a high d-c voltage is present.

To prevent these failures, arrays are manufactured in extremely clean surroundings. Production-line personnel handle the fine wire with extreme care to avoid damaging the insulation. And the completed memory is thoroughly tested at temperature extremes, to insure that they meet the appropriate military specifications.

The general-purpose memory contains many diodes—either individual glass-encapsulated diodes, which are very rugged and reliable, or integrated assemblies of several diodes in a single multilead package, which promise to make even higher reliability.

When the diodes are installed in the stack, care is taken to avoid stress on the interface between the diode leads and glass body, and to keep the soldering heat at a minimum.

Outlook

Adequate environmental performance has already been achieved in militarized memory stacks, to the extent that no dramatic improvements in the necessary characteristics are likely to occur. On the contrary, recent trends indicate that exposure requirements will become less rather than more severe over the next few years, permitting a relaxation in the specifications.

In the past, military memory system organization has lagged behind commercial development by several years, possibly because military agencies prefer to use time-proven techniques. Therefore today's trends in commercial core memories, such as 2½-D organization and the use of smaller, faster cores, haven't yet appeared widely in the military market, but they will probably be accepted in due time. The reputation of the military for pushing advanced developments doesn't extend to the field of core memory technology.

In addition to the general-purpose 3-D core stack, the military also requires many different specialized memories for various purposes. These include magnetically pure systems, which must be completely devoid of external magnetic fields to avoid interfering with other nearby magnetic equipment—for example, those instruments in a spacecraft which are designed to measure the magnetic field of the moon or another planet. Other examples of specialized memories are those with nondestructive readout, those that operate at ultra-high speeds, and those that dissipate ultra-low power. Many of the design and production considerations apply to these as well as to general-purpose memories; and the engineering and production know-how obtained from meeting the more sophisticated requirements often can increase performance at the general-purpose level. Conversely, specialized memory production wouldn't be possible without the foundation supplied by experience with standard general-purpose memories. ∎

Core-memory driver runs cooler

Dual-mode device reduces heat dissipation by automatically switching
to a low-power constant current source after generating fast-rise pulse

By Charles J. Ulrick

Collins Radio Company, Cedar Rapids, Iowa

Core-memory current drivers initially must supply a great deal of power to generate fast pulse rise times. But once this is accomplished, all that power is no longer required, and the excess amount is dissipated in unwanted heat. Less than half the power generated in conventional core drivers actually gets delivered to the load. And the wasted power heats up transistors in the current source, adversely affecting the circuit's reliability.

To generate pulses with fast rise times in core windings, drivers require voltage sources four and five times larger than those used to power ordinary integrated circuits. But once the pulse's rise time has been effected, the energy requirement to maintain a constant current through the winding drops sharply. A current-monitoring circuit operating as a voltage generator and as a current generator dissipates much less power than ordinary drivers, has a cooler ambient temperature, and can be packaged in integrated circuit form.

When the circuit is triggered, a large voltage is delivered to the selected core, generating a fast-rising pulse across its inductive load. Current through the core winding increases and is sensed by a comparator which, at a selected current amplitude, switches off the large voltage supply and automatically substitutes a constant current source with a low supply voltage.

The circuit consists of a differential amplifier, Q_3-Q_4, that activates either of two voltage supplies, +5 volts and +12 volts. A resistor bridge, R_1, R_2, R_3, R_4, and R_s, feeds the input terminals of the differential amplifier.

A push-pull circuit, Q_1 and Q_2, supplies a reference voltage, V_{REF}, of —5 volts or +12 volts to the differential amplifier's input depending on the input logic swing.

The core driver is inactive when the reference voltage is at —5v and triggers when the push-pull circuit applies +12v to the amplifier's input.

As soon as +12 volts appears at V_{REF}, the resistor bridge becomes unbalanced. The differential amplifier, acting as a comparator, senses the voltage difference across R_s. The output current through R_s rises to a steady state value, I_o, of approximately $R_2 V_{REF}/R_1 R_s$.

After V_{REF} switches to +12 volts, Q_3 of the differential amplifier conducts very heavily, turning on transistors Q_5 and Q_7. These transistors, in a Darlington configuration, connect the +12-volt power supply to the inductive load through resistor R_s. The pulse's leading edge continues as long as the +12-volt supply is applied.

While the +12-volt supply generates the pulse's leading edge, the +5-volt source remains cut off because Q_6's base-emitter junction is reverse-biased.

As the current through the inductor approaches the steady state value I_o, Q_3 of the differential amplifier conducts less and less. Current through the Darlington pair decreases and the voltage delivered to the load begins to drop. Q_5 and Q_7 cut off when the load voltage of +5 volts is reached.

But the voltage never drops below 5 volts, because at this level transistors Q_6 and Q_8 are conducting, applying the current source to the load. Little or no current flows through the Darlington pair as long as R_5, R_6, and R_7 are selected properly.

Quick switch. This core driver operates in two modes to reduce power losses. When activated by the input control logic, the 12-volt supply kicks in to deliver the power necessary to generate a 50-nanosecond rise time. Once the desired current level is reached, the 5-volt supply takes over and delivers a constant current with much lower power dissipation. The reduced power requirement makes this circuit suitable to be packaged as a thin-film IC.

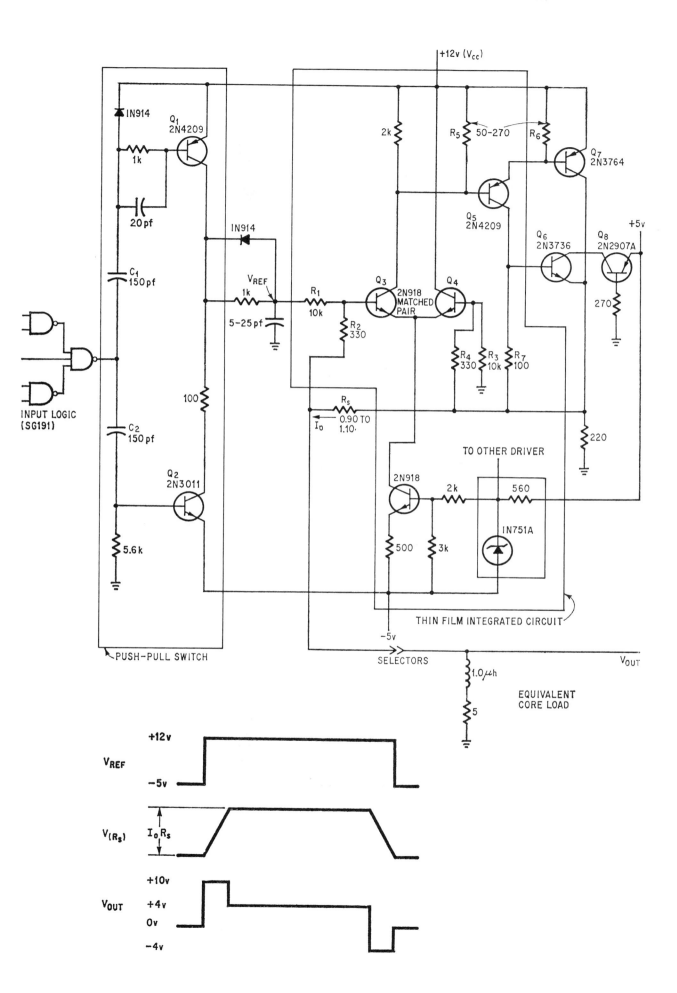

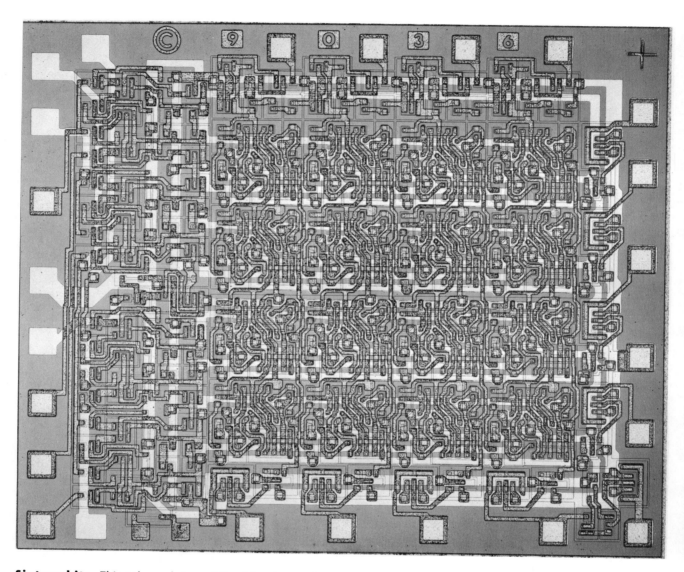

Sixteen bits. This enlarged view of the chip, shown also at the bottom of page 219, shows details of Fairchild's 4102 associative memory, one of the earliest successful designs that got an adequate number of bits on a chip with an access time short enough to be useful.

Associative memory chips: fast, versatile –and here.

At last bipolar ICs are both large
enough and fast enough to
make practicable 16-bit
off-the-shelf associative processors

By James Bartlett, John Mudge, and John Springer,
Fairchild Semiconductor, Mountainview, Calif.

● Thanks to the evolution of integrated circuit technology, associative memories at last are a commercial reality. And along with their availability as off-the-shelf chips comes their promise of speeding many types of digital operations. For by taking over some simple processing operations, the associative memories eliminate a computer's need to spend time pulling data out of storage and putting it back in just to let its central processor take a quick look.

Structurally, an associative memory resembles an ordinary read/write memory with the addition of a comparator for each bit. A set of inputs, called a descriptor, goes to all the comparators, which match the inputs against the stored words. If a particular word is identical to a descriptor, its comparators produce a "match" signal and the word is made available by the memory at its output.

In a contents-addressable memory, the simpler way to use an associative memory, descriptors and stored words contain an equal number of bits, so that a descriptor matches at most one stored word. But when the memory is used as an associative processor, descriptors contain fewer bits than the stored words, and each descriptor may match a whole group of words—any and every word that includes those bits. Thus, instead of handling just one match signal at a time, the associative processor must be able to handle several simultaneously. It also must be capable of analyzing only parts of stored words and ignoring the rest of the bits in that word.

These requirements are important constraints in designing an associative memory because they increase the number of pins a chip needs per bit. For one thing, the possibility of multiple matches means that a memory needs a match-signal pin for each word. Otherwise there's no way of telling from which word a match signal is coming. In memories that don't have to deal with multiple matches, the signals can be encoded according to their origin and sent to a single pin, which is connected to a decoder.

For another thing, selective matching—or masking— of a portion of a stored word adds one pin for every block of bits to be masked. (In a truly versatile memory it would be possible to mask any bit randomly.) Each masking pin carries an "enable" signal to a comparator or block of comparators. Any comparator receiving this signal then puts out a match signal without receiving a descriptor.

Masking also is used in the write operation to prevent new data from being written into the masked fields. New data enters the memory via the descriptor pins with the help of a write-enable circuit.

There are several ways of building an associative memory. Even general purpose computers can be used but, not being optimized for the job, they're impractically slow.

A faster processor can be built in a serial scheme, like the one shown on the next page. A shift register for each word bit is required, and the length of each register in bits equals the number of words. While circulating through the registers, the stored information is compared with the descriptors. When a match is obtained, the contents of the address counter are read out to indicate where the matched word is stored. One complete circulation at most is required to complete the search.

But with a parallel arrangement of memory cells it's possible to have even faster associative memories. They can also be very large, since the cells may be connected to form words of any length and any number of words.

For maximum speed, it's desirable to combine the logic of the comparator circuitry and the storage elements of the memory on the same structure. Metal oxide semiconductor designs have been tried because of the large number of bits which can be placed on an MOS chip, and because of the low-power features of this technology. However, MOS circuits that are economical to produce are not fast enough for a good associative memory—they take as long as 300 to 500 nanoseconds to produce a match signal. Bipolar associative memories can do the job 10 times faster, but have been limited to relatively few bits per chip because bipolar logic requires more space and power.

This bits-per-chip limitation has long been the principal obstacle in the way of associative processing. But improvements in bipolar IC technology have made it possible to produce associative-memory building blocks of adequate size. One such block is Fairchild's 4102—a 16-bit array organized as four bits by four words on a chip 80 mils by 95 mils. (A 32-bit array would have required a 140-mil-by-95-mil chip, but the yields of chips larger than 110 mil by 110 mil are

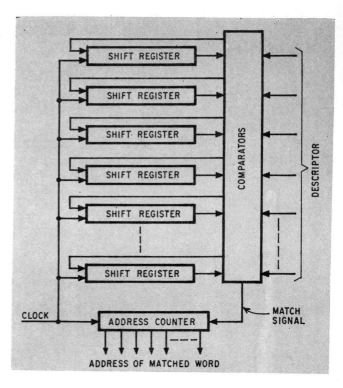

One approach. With its single set of comparators, a serial associative memory can process only one word at a time. Therefore, if the registers hold N words and the clock's period is T seconds, a complete search takes NT sec. In a parallel memory the time is T sec.

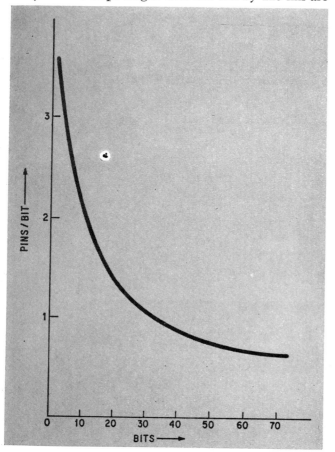

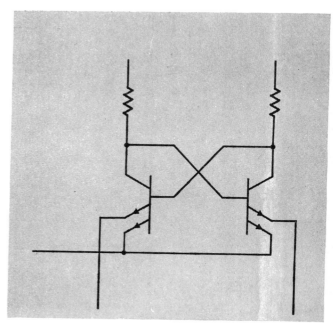

Sensitive. This latch is often proposed as the basic cell structure for associative memories. The problem: the circuit is hard to control over the full TTL temperature range.

More bits, but . . . As the number of bits on an associative-memory chip goes up, the pins-per-bit figure goes down. Unfortunately, very large chips with a lot of bits can't be made economically.

An associative memory from paper to chip

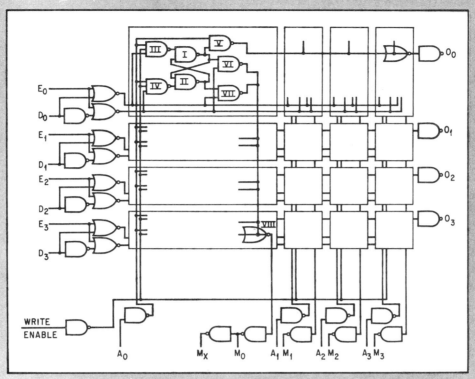

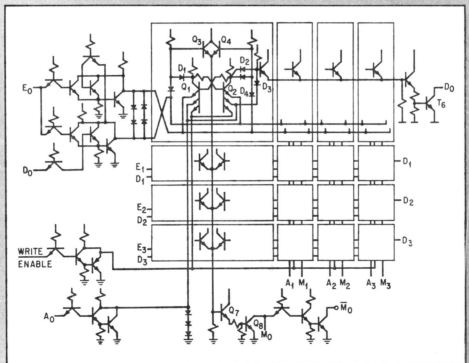

A = ADDRESS INPUT

D = DESCRIPTOR INPUT

E = ENABLE INPUT

M = MATCH OUTPUT

O = STORED-DATA OUTPUT

M_X = INVERTED MATCH OUTPUT

very sensitive to the quality of processing.)

As the photograph shows, most of the area of the 4102 is taken up by the 16 cells, each with its own storage element and comparator. The rest of the chip contains circuits for address selecting, match detecting, and input processing.

Considerable reduction in chip area per bit was achieved by using two layers of metal instead of one. This eliminated cross-unders, with their associated voltage drops and parasitic capacitances, which tend to increase circuit delays. But despite the compactness of the cell design, the storage cell current is only 2.5 milliamperes, representing a dissipation of 12.5 milliwatts per bit, or 30 mw/bit including the dissipation of the peripheral electronics.

The number of pins required by the 4102, however, did limit its bit capacity. The curve on page 218 is a plot of pins-per-bit versus number of bits for an associative memory chip. The 4102 has 24 pins—four address, four descriptor, four enable, four match and four output pins for the memory's four words, plus one pin for an inverted match signal, a write-enable pin, and two power pins.

At the 16-bit level there can be two approaches to the design of an associative memory. The first is to use a simple latch like the one shown at the bottom of page 218, as the basic storage element. However, as a rule, this latch must be accompanied by sense and drive circuits with operating parameters that are difficult to maintain over wide temperature ranges. Since it's desirable for the memory to function over a range compatible with the TTL ($-55°C$ to $+125°C$) the simple latch approach was rejected.

The cell structure actually adopted was derived from the logic diagram shown on p. 219. NAND gates I and II form the bistable storage element; gates III and IV are for addressing and writing data into the memory; V allows the stored data to be read out; and VI, VII, and VIII form the exclusive NOR function for detecting the mismatch between data in the storage element and the descriptor information.

These functions can be readily implemented by the circuit shown below the logic diagram. Transistors Q_1 and Q_2 form I and II's bistable latch, with the multiple emitters doing III and IV's job of entering data and addressing. Diodes D_2 and D_3 are the read-out gate, V. And D_1, D_4, Q_3, and Q_4 perform the match/mismatch function of VI, VII, and VIII.

An associative memory, such as this one, is ideally suited for systems where information is stored and retrieved with a key word. For example, in an airline reservation system it's necessary to store an identification number for each flight along with information about that flight, such as destination and number of unreserved seats. If the flight number is used as the address at which the other data are stored in the memory, then retrieval of the other data is only possible when the flight number is known. A more flexible approach would be to store the information n a contents-addressable memory.

The figure below shows what such a memory system might look like, with four 16-bit words formed by tying together the address inputs and the match outputs for corresponding words in four 4102's. The match outputs are connected to a word selector, whose outputs address the stored words. The memory initially is loaded with the flight number in the first six bits (field X), the reservation status in the next six bits (field Y), and the destination code in the last four bits (field Z). The enable inputs for the first six bits are tied together to form E_1, those for the next six bits form E_2, and those for the last four form E_3.

With this system it's possible to request data on all flights to a particular airport. When the proper destination code is applied to field Z and E_1 and E_2 are activated, matches are produced in all words containing that code. The word selector then addresses in succession each word that produced a match, so that the words may be read out in sequence. Alternatively, if information regarding a specific flight is desired, the flight number is placed on the field X data inputs; the word containing information about that flight matches the data in field X; the selector addresses that word; and it appears at the memory's output terminals.

Another advantage is worth noting. There are

Plane control. Working in this airline reservation system, the associative memories deliver data on the basis of flight information, destination code, or reservation status. Enable signals mask those fields that are not to be compared, while descriptors go to the remaining bits.

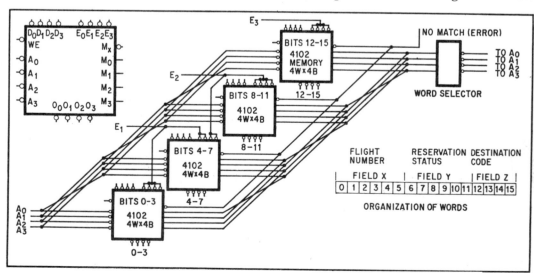

no restrictions on the storage locations of identification codes, other than that they be unique.

One of the most attractive uses of associative memories is as a liaison between a conventional semiconductor memory and a core memory. Such an arrangement gives a computer an access time approaching that of the semiconductor memory, even though most of its storage is in core.

The general technique is to divide the computer's core memory into blocks. The assumption is that once an address in a particular core block has been requested, it's probable that many more addresses in the same block will be requested. So, whenever the central processor requests data from an address in a particular block, the entire block is transferred to the semiconductor memory. The associative memory holds a code representing the blocks of core which have been transferred to the semiconductor memory, and, when an address from one of these blocks is requested, it recognizes the code and retrieves the data by going straight to the semiconductor memory.

Another place where an associative memory can play a part is in a bubble-up memory, so called because vacant locations always come to its top. A bubble-up memory is a stack of stored words. When a word is read from anywhere in the stack; the word is removed; all words above it "drop down" filling the vacant slot; and the word read out is placed at the top. When a new word is to go into the memory, the bottom word is dropped, and the new word is written in at the top.

The advantages are that the most recently used information is always near the top of the stack, and that the stack itself always contains the most frequently used information.

The easiest way to design a bubble-up memory is to make the data storage locations themselves shiftable because this is the simplest way to keep track of the stored words. But addressing data from the stack then is difficult because the data are constantly moving around. If the bubble-up memory has an associative memory, however, the latter can instantly recall any word, regardless of its physical location in the stack. ●

One by one

An associative processor needs some way of handling, one at a time, the multiple match signals that a set of descriptors may produce. Typically a word selector, like the one shown below, does the job. When descriptors are applied to the memory, this selector's latches store the match signals. The priority encoder selects one signal and sends it to the decoder which addresses the word in the memory that produced the match. Then the latch resets, and the encoder selects another match signal. The decoder output can also be used to address a stage register to the selected word.

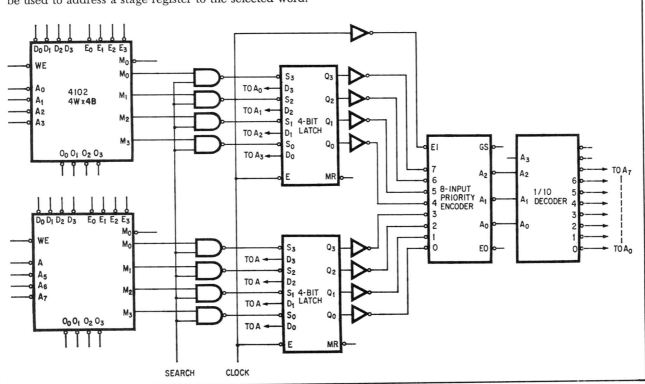

With associative memory, speed limit is no barrier

Advances in plated wire and semiconductor arrays gave the impetus
that moved associative memories out of the lab and toward production,
and thus offering designers the advantages of simultaneous processing of data

By Jack A. Rudolph, Louis C. Fulmer, and Willard C. Meilander
Goodyear Aerospace Corp., Akron, Ohio

● Spurred by new developments in plated wire and semiconductor arrays, associative memories for computers have left the conceptual stage and moved into operational hardware. Associative memories—which store and address data by content rather than specific address location—must be made of elements that can process data as well as store it. With the advent of plated wire and semiconductor arrays, these functions can now be implemented in a relatively simple and economical manner.

Associative memories have another valuable characteristic: they will process several operations simultaneously, thus alleviating the strain of designing high-speed systems that are already pushing the limits of transmission line propagation time.

Addressing by content also reduces the amount of computer time and memory capacity required to keep track of constantly changing locations. These nonproductive housekeeping and bookkeeping chores have taken up an increasing proportion of time and capacity as hardware technology has advanced. The advantages of associative memories are sufficiently important that they have kept an increasing number of researchers busy over the last 14 years.[1]

Furthermore, the development of plated-wire and semiconductor arrays permits the extension of the associative memory concept to associative processors, which handle matrixed data in much the same way as large parallel processors, such as the Illiac 4 at the University of Illinois.

An associative memory in its simplest form contains:
▶ An array of storage elements, with nondestructive readout (NDRO) capability.
▶ A comparand register that specifies the content by which desired data is recognized.
▶ Logic circuits that perform the exclusive-OR comparison.
▶ A match/mismatch register, which is an array of flip-flops connected to the storage elements through sensing amplifiers.

A computer doesn't need an address code to keep track of words stored in an associative memory. Instead, the computer specifies the content of the words it needs —and out come the words, wherever they were stored.

Usually the matching data itself is of little value, because it's already available in the comparand. But a match on all the bits of a comparand may indicate that other desired data is available in another memory for which the associative memory serves as a control or index; or a match may indicate that some event has occurred that requires responsive action. Or a search may be made for words a few of whose bits match a corresponding few in the comparand. In a pure associative memory, the few bits used in a search can be any of the bits in the word, at the programer's option; the unused bits are masked. A variation is a content-addressed memory, containing words with both associative and nonassociative bits; following a search through the associative portion, a readout of the matching words yields both associative and nonassociative parts.

For example, an associative or content-addressed memory could contain the entire payroll record for a company. One memory word per employee would contain name, job title, wage rate, deductions, personal data, and so on. From such a memory, in a single cycle, a computer could call for the payroll records of all employees who make $17.82 a week; all the records would be found at once, regardless of how many of them there were.

To accomplish this, the identifying information— $17.82 in this case—is placed in the comparand register. Logic circuits compare each bit of the comparand with the corresponding bit in all the words of the memory. One strobe pulse per comparand bit produces output signals for all matching bits; flip-flops in the match/ mismatch register store these signals.

Therefore, the contents of the match/mismatch register at the end of a series of strobe pulses in successive bit positions indicate which words in memory matched (or mismatched) the word in the comparand register. Hence, all words in the memory are simultaneously compared, on a bit by bit basis, with the comparand word, and the words that respond, if any, are indicated by the state of the word flip-flops.

Suppose, for example, a small associative memory containing four words of four bits each is to be searched

223

for a match, as shown below. Initially, all four flip-flops in the match/mismatch register are turned on. The first strobe pulse compares the first bit position of all four words with the first bit in the comparand. In three of the words shown, there is a match in the first position; this match blocks the strobe's passage through the exclusive-OR logic. But since there's a mismatch in the first word, the strobe pulse gets through the exclusive-OR and resets the first flip-flop. This takes only a few nanoseconds—equal to the strobe pulse's duration plus the propagation time through the array.

Immediately after the first comparison a second strobe pulse tests the second bit positions in all four words. This pulse also finds a mismatch in the first word, and the logic would have turned off the first flip-flop had it not already been off. Furthermore, there is another mismatch in the fourth word, so that its flip-flop is now turned off.

At the third strobe pulse, a match is found in the first and fourth words, but since mismatches were previously found in these words, their flip-flops remain off. Meanwhile another mismatch is found in the second word, so its flip-flop turns off too. This leaves only the third-word flip-flop on. And since the fourth strobe pulse doesn't find another mismatch in the third word, the third flip-flop stays on. Thus, the contents of the match/mismatch register show that the third word matches the four-bit

word originally placed in the comparand register.

The time required to search the entire memory for a match or mismatch with the comparand word depends on the number of bits in the comparand and the rate at which the bit-by-bit strobe takes place—typically the rate is 100 to 300 nanoseconds per bit. Search time, ignoring cable propagation delays, is independent of the number of words stored in the memory. And it's this factor that permits the orders-of-magnitude smaller execution time of, for example, file search routines.

However, large memories usually have longer cables whose lengths vary to a greater degree than those in small memories; these factors affect search times. To minimize this problem, a memory is divided into modules and the cables routed to achieve identical lengths.

Before information can be written into an associative memory, some indicator is needed to show which locations in the memory are either empty or contain unwanted data. One indicator is a bit position in each word to represent the status of that word. For example, a 1 could show that the data is still required and a 0 that the location is available for new data. The write operation is then preceded by a single-bit search to find an empty location for the word to be written.

Thus, the programer need not know exactly where or how big the empty spaces are. His data simply disappears into the memory; when he needs it, he calls for an associative search. Likewise, he can store the data in any order, because the associative search takes place on all words simultaneously. Thus, the associative memory eliminates the time that conventional machines must spend sorting data for storage and restructuring dynamically changing data files.

Every associative memory discussed up to this point—including the content-addressable memory—has been essentially only a single-function memory: that is, it searches only for those words that exactly match the comparand.

However, adding a few more features produces an even more useful associative memory design. In the diagram on the next page, the response store contains the sense amplifiers and match/mismatch register for all words in the memory. Additional circuitry, in the response resolver, scans the states of the flip-flops in the match/mismatch register at the end of a search operation to produce the desired results. These might

Match. In this simplified associative memory, four successive strobe pulses compare the four bits in the comparand register one at a time with bits in the memory array. At the start, all positions in the match/mismatch register contain 1; every mismatch found in the array (light shading) resets the register position corresponding to that word to 0. After four strobe pulses, only the third position of the match/mismatch register still has a 1, showing that only the third word in the array (dark shading) matches the comparand.

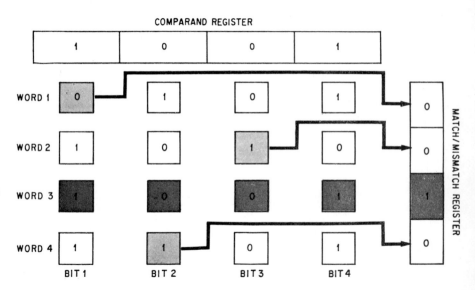

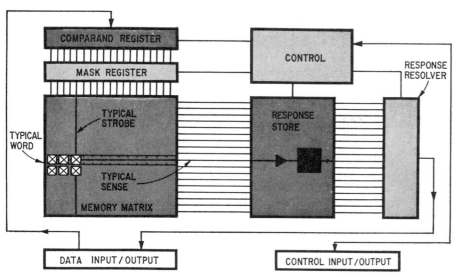

System. Basic associative memory contains an array of storage elements, a comparand register, and a response store (dark shading). Additional functions can be performed if a mask register and additional logic and controls (light shading) are added

include a count of the number of matches or mismatches instead of a mere indication of them. Thus, a program may not need information about individuals who make $17.82 a week, but rather how many employees there are at that rate to determine the cost of increasing their salary to $22.04 a week. Or, having identified a word that is to be processed, the response resolver can control the reading out of the word, either serially through the response store, or in parallel. Serial readout is much slower, of course, but, depending on the system that the associative memory is linked to, it may be suitable for a particular application.

Additional features permit still more flexibility. For example, the mask register permits a search to be performed only on selected bits in the comparand, not the whole comparand, as mentioned previously. With the mask register the programer defines which fields or portions of the comparand he wishes used in the search. Or a search could locate all words whose numeric value is greater than the comparand, or less than it. Furthermore, both types of searches could be combined in a between-limits search if a second comparand register were used; this would locate all words that are numerically between two values.

In terms of the previous example, a search for an exact match of selected bits would be necessary to locate those employees with a given salary. Likewise, a search for numeric values greater than the comparand could locate employees who were taller than 6 feet; a less-than-comparand search could locate those who had been working for the company less than 18 months; and a between-limits search could learn who among the work force had more than one year of college but less than four.

Modifying the response store permits the execution of more complex instructions: for example, "Find all employees with red hair who make between $20 and $25 a week and have been working here more than 35 years."

Several associative memories have been built and tested. A few of these were part of classified projects, so that a complete list of all associative memories built to date is not available. But the table on page 227 contains a representative listing.

The largest of these, shown on p. 226, is the 2,048-word unit developed in 1968 by the Goodyear Aerospace Corp. for the U.S. Air Force's Rome Air Development Center. This ferrite-core unit executes 15 kinds of searches on its 50-bit words, and it can perform 31 operations related to the memory's interface with RADC's Control Data Corp. 1604B computer. The entire instruction set has been incorporated into the 1604B software.

In associative memories, as in most other memories, the speed, cost, and maximum word length are affected by the kind of memory element used. But in associative memories, the cost is greatly increased by the electronic circuits connected to each word. This is perhaps the main reason why these memories aren't mass produced.

Some experimenters have attempted to build associative memory elements made of cryotrons and planar metallic films. However, magnetic ferrite elements—either simple toroids or multiaperture devices—have proven most successful in associative memories large enough to function in a computer system. However, these elements are limited in speed and dissipate considerable power.

At Goodyear Aerospace, however, both high speed and low power dissipation have been recently achieved with a special type of plated-wire array. In conventional types, current in a "strap" that passes once or twice around a group of parallel wires generates data-read pulses from all the wires at once—one bit from each wire. But in the Goodyear approach, because search operations are performed one bit at a time on corresponding bits in the memory, the strap carried the strobe signal instead of a word-readout signal. Thus, the associative plated-wire array organization is orthogonal to the conventional array, as shown on page 227. In this arrangement, successive bits in a single word are stored along a single wire rather than in corresponding positions in adjacent wires.

This rearranged organization creates a serious write-disturb problem—the effect on a particular bit position when a write operation is repeatedly performed on an adjacent bit position. Conventional arrays suffer less from this problem. To write a word in a conventional array, current is switched into a single strap and into all the wires—in one direction to write a 1, and in the opposite direction to write a 0. Stray magnetic fields from the strap tend to affect bit positions under adjacent straps, particularly when the write operation is repeated. In conventional arrays the design of the straps, and of keepers—a layer of magnetic material on top of the straps to regulate the magnetic field's dispersion—effectively eliminate write disturb.

In Goodyear's associative memory, on the other hand,

Special functions in practice

Several companies have tinkered with associative memories to perform control functions in conventional computers. Recently, for example, a small associative memory of 64 words by 16 bits was incorporated experimentally into an IBM 360 model 40 computer to regulate the memory space made available to time sharing users. Another experimental project at IBM used a 124-by-64 associative memory for fast code-pattern identification in a performance monitor and data reduction processor. But closer to practicality is the 64-word associative memory in the Burroughs computer that serves as a control unit for the Illiac 4 parallel processor. This memory performs an instruction look-ahead function.

In commercially available machines, the "cache" memory in IBM's 360 models 85 and 195 has certain associative properties. The Control Data Corp. also is reportedly using a small associative memory for internal bookkeeping in one commercial machine; so was the General Electric Co., at least up until its merger with Honeywell, Inc.

a write operation involves current in many straps and in only one wire. All the straps together present much stronger stray fields that affect many bits in many wires; and again, the effect is accentuated when a similar pattern is rewritten many times using the same straps. As in conventional arrays, attention to strap and keeper design has overcome the problem; Goodyear also uses special wide-tolerance plated wire.

Even though the plated-wire array offers advantages, this technology for associative memories will eventually yield to large-scale integrated circuits, even for large memories. Relatively small semiconductor associative memories—up to 64 bits—are available today, but they haven't yet been incorporated into memory systems of substantial size. They'll become practical for large associative systems about the same time as they become practical for large address-oriented memories.

The cost per bit for associative memories is greater than that for conventional memories. A prototype ferrite-core associative memory containing about 100,000 bits can be fabricated for $3 to $5 per bit; in production, the cost might drop to $1.50 to $2 per bit. Plated-wire associative memories, on the other hand, range from less than $1 per bit in prototypes containing 1 to 10 million bits to 15¢ or less per bit in production by 1972. But this is still much higher than the price for conventional ferrite-core and plated-wire memories, which now cost only 5¢ to 10¢ per bit.

The main reason for higher cost is that the associative memories require logic circuits at each word, whereas conventional memories need only drivers and amplifiers for each bit of one word. For example, the big associative memory built by Goodyear for RADC contains 2,048 words of 50 bits each; the memory requires 2,048 essentially identical logic circuits in its response store. But a conventional memory of equal size would require only 50 sets of drivers and amplifiers. Also, an associative memory's response store and resolver make the memory a kind of small computer that can execute a variety of complex instructions. This capability is intrinsically more expensive than mere storage.

However, this price differential isn't so great if the total operating system cost is considered. Associative systems require simpler software and save time when searching through a file for data of a particular type.

These higher costs, in the past, have limited the appli-

Big fellow. Largest practical associative memory built to date is this unit at RADC, containing 2,048 words of 50 bits each.

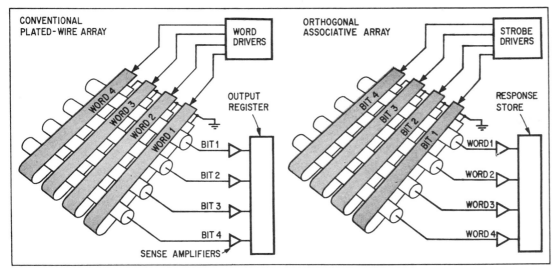

Orthogonal. Associative capability is obtained from conventional plated-wire array by reversing the roles of drive strap and wire. Conventional array (left) has one word per strap; each wire carries corresponding bits in different words. Associative array (right) has one word per wire; straps sample corresponding bits in different words.

cations of associative memories. But today, plated-wire technology has already brought the cost down substantially, and semiconductor technology promises to bring it down even further—generating new interest in associative memories and development of new applications. These generally fall into four classes:

▶ As a peripheral device, which is connected like tape drives, magnetic disk units, and so on.

▶ As a special-function memory, apart from the main memory—rather like a special scratchpad or accumulator.

▶ As the main memory of a computer.

▶ As an associative processor.

Except for a few special cases, an associative memory connected as a peripheral device would not be cost effective. Several studies[2] indicate that input/output subroutines take up more time transferring data between the computer and the memory than do the operations within the memory itself. The subroutine can't keep the associative memory busy. Goodyear's big 102,400-bit memory at RADC is connected as a peripheral, but RADC provided a direct access channel between the two memories to keep the associative memory from getting bogged down in the main memory's subroutine.

As a special-function memory, the associative memory would be introduced into the design of the computer as a hard-wired portion of the control system to perform a single function with great efficiency. For example,

the memory could be part of a processor's executive system; or if a program demands more than the available main-memory space, the associative memory can handle the swapping of program "pages" between the main memory and a drum or other bulk-storage unit. [See also "Special functions in practice," p. 226.]

As a computer's main memory, the associative memory would have to be exceptionally large by today's standards. It would also probably be most feasible in content-addressable form rather than as a pure associative memory. But, as yet, it's never been tried—partly because it would be very expensive, and partly, perhaps, because of the large present investment in address-oriented system software, little of which could be easily transferred for use in such a system.

Perhaps the most significant use of an associative memory would be as an associative processor. This application requires the match/mismatch logic to be modified to include arithmetic capability at every memory word. Such a processor would be considerably more versatile than a conventional computer that executes one instruction at a time on a single pair of data items. And for some tasks, it could approach the capability of a large-scale parallel processor.

The basic associative memory, in such a processor, performs not only logic search operations, but arithmetic operations as well. Each word in the modified associa-

Delivered Associative Memories (partial listing)

Year	Customer	Contractor	Associative storage device	Memory size	Associative searches	Interface
1963	Dept. of Defense	Scope Inc.	Multiaperture ferrite device (transfluxor)	1,024 words × 24 bits	Exact match	I/O channel
1963	U.S. Air Force, Rome Air Development Center	Stanford Research Inst.	Linear split-C cores	1,100 words × 281 bits	Exact match	Special device
1964	U.S. Navy Bureau of Ships	Goodyear Aerospace	Multiaperture ferrite device (MALE)	256 words × 30 bits	Exact match; Greater than; Less than; Between limits	I/O channel
1965	U. S. Air Force, Avionics Laboratory, Wright-Patterson Air Force Base	Philco-Ford	Multiaperture ferrite device (Biax)	1,024 words × 48 bits	Exact match	I/O channel
1968	U.S. Air Force, Rome Air Development Center	Goodyear Aerospace	Biased logic Ferrite core (Biloc)	2,048 words × 50 bits	Exact match; Greater than; Less than; Maximum; Minimum; Next higher; Next lower; Between limits	Direct memory access to computer
1970	Air Force Avionics Lab	Texas Instruments	MSI-MOS	128 words × 50 bits	Exact match	Special device (classified)

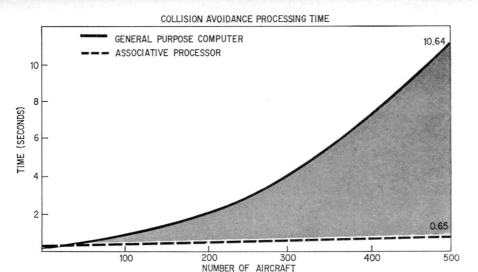

Margin. Because an associative processor can check out the current status of many radar tracks at once, it can predict the likelihood of collisions in an area containing hundreds of aircraft soon enough to permit action to avoid collision. A conventional computer, on the other hand, is hard pressed simply to predict collisions before they actually occur.

tive memory together with the word's related electronic circuits—which are somewhat more complex than those required for the basic associative memory—can be programed for specific tasks. The circuits could, for example, add the contents of two fields of a word and store their sum in a third field of the same word. The addition is executed serially by bit, and would, therefore, be much slower than in a conventional computer, which adds bits in parallel. But the same "add" instruction is executed in the modified associative memory simultaneously on all words in the memory, or on any selected set of words; therefore, the average add time is inversely proportional to the number of words in the set.

Since the operation of an associative processor involves more writing than a basic associative memory would the Goodyear plated-wire design with its high speed, low power, and resistance to disturbs is particularly useful in an associative processor.

In one associative processor, built by Goodyear for the U.S. Air Force Material Laboratory, at Wright-Patterson Air Force Base, the time required to add two 12-bit fields is 20 microseconds. This is very slow compared to today's high-speed conventional computers; however, this design would be capable of executing the same command on up to 3,000 words simultaneously. This yields an effective add time for the set of as little as 7 nanoseconds per word. Since each word in an associative processor is both its own data store and arithmetic unit, it's economical to have rather long word lengths; in Goodyear's design the words are 256 bits long.

Perhaps the associative processor's first task would be in a command-and-control data processing system. Such systems characteristically execute the same computer program identically on every member of a large set of data; and new data entering at extremely fast rates continuously replaces the old data. Furthermore, all the data must be processed in real time. Thus, such a system inherently takes advantage of the associative processor's parallel processing capability and extremely high execution speed.

A typical example of such a system would be in multiple target tracking in radar systems; another would be conflict prediction in aircraft traffic control systems. Both systems involve large quantities of data in the form of radar target tracks, which are continuously changing. In an associative processor, all the data concerning

a single target track can be stored in one memory word. The processor handles every track simultaneously by the same algorithm; thus, in the collision avoidance problem, it enjoys a speed advantage of 16:1, as shown above, over the conventional approach, which processes each track separately and sequentially. In simple target tracking the advantage over conventional machines may be as high as 2,000:1. ●

References

1. A.E. Slade and H.O. McMahon, "A Cryotron Catalog Memory System," Proceedings, Fall Joint Computer Conference, 1956, p. 115.
2. A.G. Hanlon, "Content-addressable and Associative Memory Systems—a Survey," IEEE Transactions on Electronic Computers, Aug. 1966, p. 509.

Bibliography

E.C. Joseph and A. Kaplan, "Target-track Correlation with a Search Memory," Proceedings, 6th National Convention on Military Electronics, June 1962, p. 255.

A. Apicella and J. Franks, "A High-speed NDRO One-core-per-bit Associative Element," Proceedings, International Conference on Magnetics, April, 1965, p. 14.5-1.

E.E. Eddey, "The Use of Associative Processors in Radar Tracking and Correlation," Proceedings, National Aerospace Electronics Conference, 1967.

K.E. Batcher, "Sorting Networks and Their Applications," AFIPS, Conference Proceedings, Spring Joint Computer Conference, Vol. 32, 1968, p. 307.

W.C. Meilander, "The Associative Processor in Aircraft Collision Prediction," Proceedings, NAECON, 1968.

Design house finds 'one for all' can apply to custom memories, too

One plan offers a memory maker lower costs if other manufacturers can use its design; a price and performance guarantee comes with it

By Lawrence Curran
Electronics' staff

Memory design houses traditionally stand jealous guard over customers' proprietary rights. But the alert management of Technology Marketing Inc. discovered that many companies don't object if their custom-designed memories are manufactured and used by others. In the process, TMI found a way to reduce costs for some customers and also turn a profit for itself.

The young Santa Ana, Calif., firm offers customers two options: the usual exclusive design contract and a lower-priced version. Under the latter arrangement, other companies can manufacture essentially the same memory developed for someone else. These licensees don't pay development costs, but instead give TMI a license transfer fee.

Started little more than a year ago by Robert Lowry and George Wells, TMI probably is unique in the industry because of its guarantee, which it feels rivals Sears Roebuck's. TMI promises "satisfaction with the job" and assures customers that they can manufacture the specified memory in their own facilities at the quantity prices agreed upon. The company says it will foot the bill for excess development and manufacturing costs.

Lowry and Wells, either of whom acts as company president on any given day depending on the nature of the negotiation, only found out in the last few weeks that their customers don't always care whether or not they have ex-

clusive ownership of the memory systems TMI designed for them. Lowry believes that TMI's policy of licensing the same design to

more than one company will account for the major portion of future business.

He feels most customers, usually

Young oldtimers

Even though he's only 36, George Wells, the technical half of the Lowry-Wells team that heads Technology Marketing Inc., goes back to the early days of core memories. He was a circuit designer in RCA's computer group from 1958 to late 1961. In that year, he visited and worked with engineers at Telemeter Magnetics Inc., in Culver City, Calif., on designing a formidable memory project for which the firm was subcontractor to RCA. This was a 1.5-microsecond unit, and the 30-mil-diameter cores—and all the associated tooling and stringing techniques—had to be developed for it. At the time, 50-mil cores were the smallest in general use.

One of the now-prominent "names" then affiliated with Telemeter Magnetics was Trude Taylor, who left in the summer of 1961 to create Electronic Memories Inc., now Electronic Memories and Magnetics Corp.

Because Telemeter Magnetics was one of the first commercial core-memory companies in the United States, and because Wells recognized its potential, he was receptive when officials of the Southern California firm asked him to come to work for them. He started there in January 1962, just after the company was sold to Ampex Corp., and became its Computer Products division. Wells kept in touch with Taylor, however, later joining Electronic Memories to handle core memory systems.

He resigned from the post in 1968, and Lowry, then associated with System Design Associates, lured Wells to his company, which later spawned Microdata Corp. and its minicomputer-manufacturing subsidiary, MicroSystems Inc. SDA was a consulting company, and Wells developed the group's memory system design business, including the memory for MicroSystems' Micro 800 minicomputer.

Lowry says the computer's memory was ready before the rest of the machine, and SDA officials felt the memory could be sold. But this would have conflicted with SDA's charter as a consulting house. The memory consulting activity was set off separately, and Wells and Lowry eventually parted amicably with SDA-Microdata to form TMI. They got a running start in the memory design business with a $250,000 backlog from SDA.

Lowry's path shows fewer turns than Wells's. Now 42, he was the first salesman on Decision Control Inc.'s payroll back in June 1963. The firm was sold to Varian Associates, becoming Varian Data Machines in June 1967. Lowry was director of International Marketing when he left to join SDA in January 1968. He and Wells started TMI in March 1969.

computer manufacturers, will agree to let their designs be used elsewhere because they don't want to sell memories. Since they save money by manufacturing their own memories in house, they don't object to TMI selling the same design two, three, or four times over. In such cases, all TMI has to do is to design different custom interface hardware.

Under the licensing arrangement, TMI covers development costs, then charges each customer a manufacturing license-transfer fee to partially offset the considerable documentation that accompanies TMI-designed memory prototypes. The license-transfer fee will range from $10,000 to $20,000, Lowry says. Then each customer pays TMI a royalty on every system it builds. This will be set up on a sliding scale—possibly $200 for each of the first 100 memories built, $175 for each of the next 100, and so on until a fixed limit is reached.

The recent switch to the license-royalty arrangement could kick TMI's sales upward. But it won't affect the number of totally new designs TMI will undertake, about 12 to 20 a year. Four months is the average cycle time for a custom design, and TMI can handle about five at a time, with three in final checkout simultaneously.

No production. TMI has no intention of manufacturing any memories itself. "What puzzles many customers," Lowry says, "is that we turn them off quickly when they ask us to manufacture their memories." The price quotes on a job are so thorough that customers often assume TMI is seeking the production contract as well as the design contract.

Lowry feels there's good reason not to be a manufacturer, particularly of standard memory systems. First, computer memories have graduated from the days of small quantity orders to the point where orders for thousands aren't unusual and TMI doesn't ever want to do more than $1 million a year in memory design sales; it wants to be selective enough to maintain quality design, its stock in trade. Lowry says. "The black art is gone from memory design," he asserts. "It takes experienced people, but it's now a science."

Exclusive customer ownership

arrangements will account for the bulk of TMI's projected 1971 sales of $1 million since the licensing royalty arrangement is so new.

No extras. If TMI exceeds its estimated development costs in its price quote, there's no extra charge to the customer, and if it costs the customer more than TMI has estimated to manufacture the memory in quantity, TMI will make up the difference. To date, most jobs have come in 6% to 8% below TMI's estimate. "This is because 94% of the manufacturing costs derive from materials whose prices are known" Lowry reports.

"We felt the industry was ready for a company that would assume full responsibility for what it does," Lowry asserts. "We guarantee client satisfaction. There are no qualifications, and we have to make it right if he's not satisfied. This philosophy dictates selectivity."

Since most customers anticipate volume production, TMI's designs must use readily available parts to insure simplicity of manufacturing and good reliability. The firm insists that there must be at least two sources for components in its designs, and it takes an active role in negotiations for such major items as core stacks to prevent cost overruns. TMI advises customers not to string the cores themselves but to let the core supplier do it, and provide the circuit boards and decode diodes. Thus, Lowry says, TMI customers can get custom stacks as completely tested assemblies that can be bought from multiple sources. TMI also favors completely pluggable core stacks without the backplane wiring that makes for additional labor charges and possible error.

The package TMI offers includes not only the design specifications and prototype models but all the documentation needed for the customer to turn the job over immediately to his manufacturing facility. TMI will use the customer's symbology, drafting standards and numbering release system on the customer's own title block vellums, if desired. TMI also will document the core stacks using, say, the Ampex, Electronic Memories and Magnetics, or Ferroxcube symbology and numbering release system, including their suppliers' testing procedures. Then TMI's customer

can turn the prints over to any of a number of stack makers for immediate production. There's no production-delay wait for drawings to be converted to another format.

ECL, too. While most of TMI's designs have been core memories, Wells has designed a system for Standard Computer Corp. in Santa Ana, Calif., that employs emitter-coupled logic. This is a 2½-dimension, 10-million-bit memory used in Standard's own IC-7000 computer and sold separately by the firm for use with IBM's System 360, models 65, 67, and 75. Using 20-mil cores, the unit has a full cycle time of 700 nanoseconds; with 18-mil cores, the cycle time is cut to 500 nsec.

"We were looking for TMI to put us into the memory business and they did it," says Standard's David Keefer, vice president for research and development.

Wells cites these TMI goals: in a three-wire, 3-d system with volume production, "we're looking at an 800-nsec cycle time"; in a 2½-d system, Wells says, 500-nsec speeds are easy to attain with cores or semiconductors, and future cores will increase that speed.

"In a three-wire, 3-d system," Wells says, "the cost of the memory is the same whether the cycle time is 900 nsec or 2 microseconds, but the power supply cost is greater for the faster memory. Also, speeds of 900 nsec dictate moving air for cooling, a cost and noise item. Most manufacturers will trade speed for lower cost."

TMI has designed memories for several minicomputers, including the 1-μsec, 400-word-by-18-bit system for Raytheon Computer's model 704; a 1.6-μsec, 1,000-or 4,000-word by eight-bit system for Monitor Data Systems' new model 708 machine; and a 4,000-word by 16-bit memory for the Ruggednova, the military version of the Nova, made by a Data General Corp. licensee. TMI also designed a 2-μsec, 2,000-word by 18-bit memory for a large industrial data base system made by Data Pathing Inc., Sunnyvale, Calif., and is designing the memory for Omnicomp Computer Corp.'s new Omnus-1 minicomputer. Omnicomp also is in Santa Ana, Calif., and expects to introduce the machine later this year.

Chapter 10

Memory systems

For sophisticated calculators, core arrays are worth the price

By Thomas E. Osborne

Hewlett-Packard Co., Palo Alto, Calif.

A random-access memory costs more than a serial memory, but the design freedoms and simplifications it allows in electronic calculators and other small machines more than make up the difference.

Serial memories were characteristic of those first-generation electronic calculators that began to appear on the market about 1963. These memories —usually magnetostrictive delay lines, though a few rotating magnetic disks were used—were substantially faster than their mechanical forebears.

The designers at that time considered using core memories, the only form of random-access memory then available, but they invariably decided in favor of delay lines on a cost-comparison basis. The cost differential was partly in the storage medium and partly in the peripheral circuitry—but partly also in the designer's imagination.

First, the designers saw cores as hundreds of tiny components that had to be strung with two, three or even four wires. They compared these with a delay line—a single piece of wire coiled up, with transducers capable of imparting a high-frequency acoustic signal at one end and of sensing it, after a propagation delay, at the other.

A second factor counting against core memories was the large number of relatively expensive high-current transistors required by their drivers. The delay line needs only a single driver—and it's not a high-current device. Also, the core array employs many sense amplifiers, while the delay line requires only one. And for all the drastic price reductions transistors and core arrays have undergone in the past few years, a delay line is still cheaper.

Furthermore, most manufacturers of core memories were apparently slow to supply samples and reluctant to build the small arrays required in electronic calculators. On the other hand, the delay-line manufacturers were quick to quote very low prices and to back them up with samples.

However, the designer of an electronic calculator doesn't design a memory; he designs a system containing a memory. He must therefore choose a form of memory that permits him to meet his specifications at a reasonable cost. Since the design philosophies of the core calculator and delay-line calculator are quite different, it's hard to say which type of memory results in the lowest system cost in a given application. But generalizations and estimates that take into account the limits of the two technologies can be made.

In general, then, it can be said that a calculator requiring less than 500 bits of storage favors the delay-line memory, while the calculator with more than 1,000 bits of storage favors the core memory. The 500-to-1,000-bit territory, between these two categories is the area of contention.

One factor affecting the crossover: the cost per bit of a core array decreases more rapidly as the memory size increases than that of a delay-line memory. But what establishes the core's economy is the fact that sophisticated calculators capable of automatically executing highly complex operations require more than 1,000 bits of storage; and in devising such stores, the freedom offered by a core memory results in a more efficient design.

It would take a great deal of space to elaborate fully upon all the efficiencies the use of a core memory affords a design. For one thing, the core memory is free from the delay line's unyielding timing requirements. Information transported throughout a delay-line system must be rigidly scheduled, and this rigidity significantly influences the functions and design philosophy of the calculator. A design with a core memory is free from all but minor timing restrictions.

Calculator designers have indeed capitalized upon these freedoms to produce more sophisticated devices. Their products can do floating-point arithmetic, carry out complex arithmetic functions, and be easily programed to execute a sequence of operations. Since a core memory in nonvolatile, it can retain information when power is removed from the system; this is not true of a delay-line memory. Another important advantage of the core memory over the delay line is its inherently higher speed—especially in machines with a large storage capacity.

From a practical viewpoint, little is gained by going to higher speeds in nonprogramable calculators. Almost all electronic calculators can perform any single operation in 2 seconds or less; some can do it in milliseconds.

But with programable calculators capable of executing hundreds of arithmetic operations in sequence automatically, speed becomes important.

The Hewlett-Packard 9100A calculator, a machine with a core memory, can solve a common problem 50 times faster than can a delay-line calculator. For example, where a typical delay-line machine needs about 7 minutes to solve a typical problem involving a set of transcendental equations—whose coefficients involve logarithms, trigonometric functions, and the like—by making a series of successive approximations, the HP 9100A can do the job in 7 seconds.

If the memory in the HP 9100A were programed to simulate the operation of a serial delay line, its bit rate would be 4 megahertz—four times faster than most magnetostrictive delay lines.

Of course, calculators with serial memories will continue to handle calculations under the step-by-step control of human operators. In fact, these machines will continue to take the largest share of the market for electronic desk calculators. And for now, their serial memories will be delay lines.

But for stored-program machines capable of carrying out complex calculations automatically, random-access memories—currently ferrite-core arrays—will get the nod.

But both delay lines and core memories will eventually be supplanted by integrated-circuit arrays—shift registers in place of delay lines as serial memories, and flip-flop registers in place of cores as random-access memories. ■

'Cache' turns up a treasure

By Donald H. Gibson

Systems Development Division, International Business Machines Corp., Poughkeepsie, N.Y.

and W. Lee Shevel

Component Division, International Business Machines Corp., East Fishkill, N.Y.

Caught between the devil and the deep blue sea is the designer who wants to build a computer that incorporates both high speed and large main-memory capacity—say 10 million bits or more. His quandary: such a memory is large physically, and the rate at which data can move is limited by the speed of light.

In practice, the data may take more than 100 nanoseconds to traverse the distance between a storage location in the memory and a register or other location in the processor, while the processor's cycle is likely to be less than 100 nsec. Speeding up the memory wouldn't minimize this mismatch, and it might even boost the memory's cost to an unacceptable level.

The trick is to use two memories. Such a hierarchy, properly organized, can resolve the clash between design objectives and the laws of the physical universe.

One is a buffer, small and fast to match the speed of the processor, and close in for quick accessibility; the other is large and relatively slow, but able to transfer large batches of data into the small memory in a single cycle.[1] Thus the two memories have approximately equal bandwidths, but their cycle times differ by a factor of, say, 10 to 16.

For example, the IBM System 360 model 95 had a multiunit processor whose basic machine cycle was 60 nsec and had a main memory of of approximately 10 million bits. When the main memory, standing alone, was exercised under the control of its own circuits, a pulse could travel from the main panel into the memory array itself in 60 nsec, to begin the actual reading out of data. Yet the functionally identical signal, originating at the adder in the processor when the memory operated as part of the system, took 180 nsec—three times as long—to travel into the array and initiate the same process. A larger memory would have required an even greater time spread.

But in the 360/85, the buffer memory, or "cache," is used for the first time in a production-line computer. The cache is a monolithic semiconductor memory packaged inside the processor and it is 12 times as fast as the main memory, or "backing store." The latter is in a separate frame several feet away along a direct line and further away along the connecting cables. The cache contains instructions and data immediately required for processing, and exchanges these directly with the processor, as shown at left, which thus needs only occasional reference to the backing store.

Big one

The backing store in the 360/85 is available in several capacities; the largest contains ap-

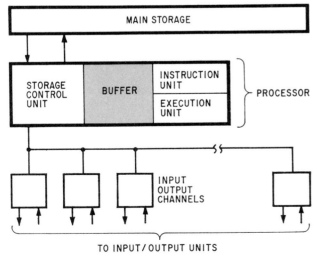

Cache. Like a squirrel's store for the winter, the processor keeps a supply of instructions and data readily available in the high-speed buffer.

Mouthful. This frame stores one million bytes of data or instructions; any group of 16 bytes is accessible in 960 nanoseconds. It's part of the main memory for the IBM 360/85.

proximately 4 million eight-bit bytes. This biggest configuration comprises two 2-million-byte frames, each with its own controls and error-correction circuits; within each frame are two 1-million-byte modules, one of which is shown above, each made of eight subunits containing 16,384 words of 72 bits per word. These eight subunits are electrically organized as four 16K-by-144-bit memories, reading out two 72-bit words in parallel in each cycle. The 72 bits include eight 8-bit bytes and eight redundant bits that work with error detection and correction circuits. The backing store is made with conventional toroidal ferrite cores 21 mils in diameter,

which switch in less than 200 nsec. They are wired into a stack of 36 planes, each plane a square array 128 cores on a side.

The cycle time of the modules in the larger-capacity backing store is 960 nsec. Access time of each 16K-by-144-bit element is 415 nsec. When placed in the physical configuration of the 360/85, the memory's access time as seen from the processor is 960 nanoseconds—the same as the module's cycle time. The difference between 415 nsec at the memory frame and 960 at the processor is accounted for by transmission delays in the cable and propagation lags in the priority and error-correction circuits.

In the 4-megabyte backing store, the four 1-megabyte modules are interleaved four ways, permitting new cycles to be initiated in each module at 80-nsec intervals. Thus, with interleaving, the main memory's time slot temporarily matches that of the buffer—a request for data from the main memory produces two 72-bit words or 16 eight-bit bytes from the first module, 960 nsec after the request is issued; but it also automatically triggers interleaved requests for data in the other modules, and this other data arrives in 16-byte groups at 80-nsec intervals. But no single module can be accessed a second time before the end of its 960-nsec cycle.

Little one

The second key element of the hierarchy is the buffer memory. This unit, or cache, on the IBM 360/85 is available in sizes of 16K, 24K, and 32K bytes (K = 1,024). The 16K-byte unit contains 16 cards, identical in function and in components, each with a 1K byte capacity.

The storage cells on each card are contained in an 8-by-9 array of modules in the center section of the card; these are surrounded by circuits for addressing, writing, and sensing. The modules are based on IBM's half-inch-square solid logic technology (SLT) substrates. Each holds two silicon chips, and each chip contains an 8-by-8 matrix of storage cells. Thus each module holds 128 binary storage cells.

Other memories could be structured using the same set—for example the cache in the 360/195. In fact, this system utilizes the buffer even more efficiently than the 85.[2] The 85 also has smaller memory registers of 64 to 256 bytes that are composed of these same modules mounted on smaller cards. The smaller registers have a faster access and cycle time of 25 to 30 nsec.

Ultimate—almost

This system of a cache memory operating with a backing store attains 64% to 96% of the system performance that could be theoretically achieved with a single memory of cache speed and of backing-store capacity, housed within the processor. If the actual cache always contained the data required by the processor, the performance would be 100%; and even when the program was care-

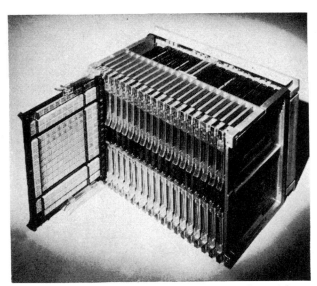

Buffer. These 16 cards can hold 16,000 bytes for quick access by the 360/85 processor. The data arrives in groups of 64 bytes from the memory.

Small but fast. This silicon chip, shown on the nib of a pen, contains 64 memory cells that deliver data in as little as 54 nsec, in the 360/195.

fully constructed to have the required data in the cache as seldom as possible, performance was 64% of the theoretical maximum. To date, no actual customer's program has been worse than the most severe worst-case programs. If these percentages hold for a 16K cache, they would be somewhat higher for larger caches, because, obviously, the proportion of data found in the larger cache is higher.

These results were obtained by a simulation process, and verified in an exhaustive study that employed cycle-by-cycle timing modules for a number of cache system designs, and actual programs of IBM 360/65 and IBM 360/75 users.[3] From the results of simulation runs on these designs and programs, detailed timing charts were prepared of program performance on a machine with a cache.

Questions and answers

These charts provided answers for the major questions that arise in evaluating the cache concept: How large should the cache be? What optimum block size should be transferred between backing store and cache? How does performance vary with backing-store access time?

The study produced highly favorable results. It disclosed that cache capacity of 16K to 32K bytes is sufficient for holding, on the average, 95% of all storage requests made by the central processing unit. When extended to the model 195, the study showed that the proportion of storage requests satisfied in the cache averages 99%. A block of 64 bytes represents the proper amount of information to bring into the cache when a backing store access is required. System performance varied no more than 10%-15% as backing store access time ranged from zero to two microseconds,

corresponding to a wide range of cycle times for the main memory, and of cable lengths between it and the processor.

These results correspond reasonably well to the findings for an IBM 7000 series machine.[4]

The cache concept has proven feasible largely because the set of programs to be run on a cache system have addressing patterns readily adaptable to the concepts. This is true because programs usually comprise lists of instructions in successive locations to be executed in sequence, and because blocks of data also are usually in successive locations. They don't have to be, but it would be more effort for programers to scatter them around and it wouldn't have any advantage.

The cache concept, as implemented in the System 360/85, has proven to be as good as expected. But one interesting point has been established by the hardware that was not established by the simulation, because the hardware includes a switch on the console to disable the cache. With this switch set in the disable mode, all programs require three to four times as long to complete as when the cache is working. It's one of several controls that disable certain parts of the machine; they keep the system running at reduced speed in the presence of a component failure that otherwise would stop the machine completely. ∎

References

1. M.V. Wilkes, "Slave Memories and Dynamic Storage Allocation," IEEE Trans. on Electronic Computers, April, 1965, p. 270.
2. C.J. Conti, "Concepts for Buffer Storage," IEEE Computer Group News, March 1969, p. 9.
3. J.S. Liptay, "Structural Aspects of the System 360/Model 85: the Cache," IBM Systems Journal, Vol. 7, No. 1, 1968, p. 15.
4. D.H. Gibson, "Consideration in Block-Oriented Systems Design," AFIPS Conference Proceedings, Vol. 30 (Spring Joint Computer Conference), 1967, p. 75.

Outcome. Further work along the lines of the project described in the following article produced over 100 models of memory systems, all faster than the originals; this system, Ferroxcube's FI-3, is an example of the newer series. Capacities range from 1,000 to 8,000 words of six to 18 bits each, all with full-cycle times of 3 microseconds.

Backward step opens up route to new products and new markets

Product planning has some definite lessons to offer the industry, says Ferroxcube's *Jack Buckwalter;* by modifying core size to slow a memory and reduce cost, task force achieved mass production and wide sales appeal

● In their race for speed and miniaturization, manufacturers of computers and associated equipment often overlook a potentially vast market of commercial and industrial users. Caught in the backwash of the onrushing state-of-the-art technology, these would-be users neither require nor can they afford highly sophisticated hardware. What they need are products planned specifically for their needs—both in performance and in price.

Such an approach was taken by the Ferroxcube Corp., a manufacturer of memories. In essence, Ferroxcube started by backing away from the leading edge of technology in developing a core memory. By sacrificing one feature—speed in this case—designers were able to develop new low-cost systems that are opening new markets. This approach permitted further cost reductions in manufacturing and synergistically came up with techniques for mass producing and marketing advanced technology products.

Ferroxcube's one step backward, two steps forward approach called for a multidiscipline redesign team to systematically question market, development, application, and manufacturing assumptions about memories. After three successive redesign efforts, the team came up with a magnetic-core memory that could be mass produced for only one-third the cost of the original computer-oriented memory.

A similar backward step can be profitable in a wide range of products—especially those sophisticated electronic products that currently are not widely accepted in industrial markets. A few obvious ones are tape transports that could be redesigned for applications requiring only low data rate and small physical volume; line printers for applications that overtax a strip printer, but don't need full page-printout capacity or speed; and alphanumeric displays.

The evolution of Ferroxcube's product line to fit fresh marketing objectives reflects the value of close cooperation among market research, product development, and manufacturing engineers. This cooperation spawned several valuable lessons:

▶ Product development must be a team effort, without rank, and the team must represent the views of customer, factory, and internal and external technology.

▶ Cost effectiveness is best achieved by a multiple-pass design, in which the team successively tests the fundamental premises, the fundamental techniques, and the evolved refinements. In memory redesign, these correspond respectively to the premise that slower speed will cost less, interboard wiring can be reduced, and the subassemblies of the finished product can be reorganized for lower cost.

The chief aim of the redesign was to bring down the cost per bit of storage in the memory devices that

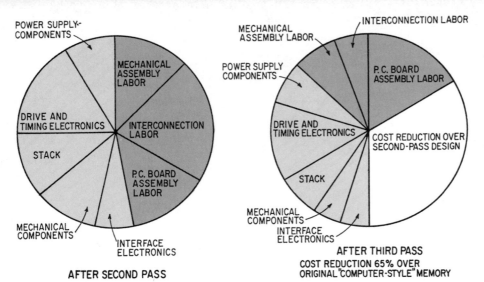

POWER SUPPLY-
COMPONENTS

MECHANICAL
ASSEMBLY
LABOR

DRIVE AND
TIMING ELECTRONICS

INTERCONNECTION
LABOR

STACK

P.C. BOARD
ASSEMBLY
LABOR

MECHANICAL
COMPONENTS

INTERFACE
ELECTRONICS

AFTER SECOND PASS

MECHANICAL
ASSEMBLY LABOR

INTERCONNECTION LABOR

POWER SUPPLY
COMPONENTS

P.C. BOARD
ASSEMBLY LABOR

DRIVE AND
TIMING ELECTRONICS

COST REDUCTION OVER
SECOND-PASS DESIGN

STACK

MECHANICAL
COMPONENTS

INTERFACE
ELECTRONICS

AFTER THIRD PASS
COST REDUCTION 65% OVER
ORIGINAL "COMPUTER-STYLE" MEMORY

Third pass. Following the design and manufacturing cost reductions, new modules, which could be combined into memories of almost any size, were defined within this framework. They cut the two-pass cost by another third and the original cost of a fast memory by about two-thirds.

were offered to the noncomputer market at the time. The initial purchase price is the most persuasive factor to a designer when he selects components for industrial process controls, instrumentation, small business machines, and automated machinery. Sales to these designers never developed into the kind of market that memory manufacturers had hoped for. Designers continued to find enough reliability for their purposes in relays, crossbars, and other electromechanical memories.

Not even the electronic memories' vaunted qualities such as data volatility, nondissipative storage, data-handling versatility, and nondestructive readout could overcome a reluctance to pay more per bit and more per function. Designers also refused to be swayed by the fact that maintenance costs per bit over 5,000 hours for an electronic memory are negligible. Over the same period, the maintenance cost for an electro-mechanical memory, though considerable, still didn't bring its cost up to the level of electronic memories.

While these facts were generally known, their implications were not clear when the Ferroxcube team began its study in 1966. The study produced a fundamental set of observations:

▶ Computer-grade memory systems are always much faster than industrial and commercial users require.
▶ Faster memories cost more to build.
▶ Faster memories cost more to use, because, for

example, the system to which they are connected must have faster rise times and better noise immunity.

▶ Industrial and commercial users are generally not interested in memories with cycle times faster than about 2 to 10 microseconds. But, within that speed range, they would be interested in memories that were as easy to buy as conventional relays, crossbars or tape and card devices—provided the memories cost much less than the conventional devices.

In examining these initial observations, the task force, which comprised a marketing expert, an applications engineer, a digital circuit designer, and a manufacturing specialist, drew on its combined expertise. The group raised the question: Would the costs for slower memories—much slower, maybe 10 times slower than the standard 1 to 2 μsec designs that were then offered—actually be low enough to bring them into line with those of other storage devices?

To answer the question, the researchers first tested basic design assumptions. They selected a conventional 2-μsec computer memory, and tried redesigns that would cut cost without affecting reliability or function, with the exception of cycle times, which were allowed to be anything up to 20 μsec. Changing one parameter, such as increasing core size, gave a pyramid of economies, ranging from less expense for stringing the cores to fewer profit-robbing rejects. So, after the first

FIRST PASS COST REDUCTION

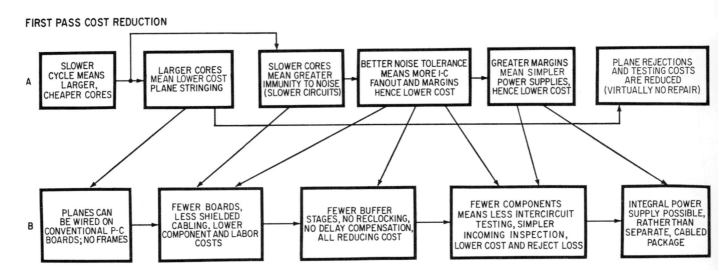

A

SLOWER CYCLE MEANS LARGER, CHEAPER CORES

LARGER CORES MEAN LOWER COST PLANE STRINGING

SLOWER CORES MEAN GREATER IMMUNITY TO NOISE (SLOWER CIRCUITS)

BETTER NOISE TOLERANCE MEANS MORE I-C FANOUT AND MARGINS HENCE LOWER COST

GREATER MARGINS MEAN SIMPLER POWER SUPPLIES, HENCE LOWER COST

PLANE REJECTIONS AND TESTING COSTS ARE REDUCED (VIRTUALLY NO REPAIR)

B

PLANES CAN BE WIRED ON CONVENTIONAL P-C BOARDS; NO FRAMES

FEWER BOARDS, LESS SHIELDED CABLING, LOWER COMPONENT AND LABOR COSTS

FEWER BUFFER STAGES, NO RECLOCKING, NO DELAY COMPENSATION, ALL REDUCING COST

FEWER COMPONENTS MEANS LESS INTERCIRCUIT TESTING, SIMPLER INCOMING INSPECTION, LOWER COST AND REJECT LOSS

INTEGRAL POWER SUPPLY POSSIBLE, RATHER THAN SEPARATE, CABLED PACKAGE

A look over the shoulder

When the coincident-current magnetic-core memory was first produced commercially, about 15 years ago, the computer market was the only market for it.

About 10 years ago, independent core-memory manufacturers—that is, those who did not also build computers—were saying that the cost of core memories could be reduced only by developing mass markets other than the computer market. Everyone spoke bravely of the widespread potential use of core memories in industrial process systems, in small business machines, in numerical-controlled machines, in instrumentation and data-acquisition systems, in telemetry, and so on; but, no one manufacturer was able to develop and sustain a demand large enough to justify mass production.

About five years ago, a number of independent memory-system manufacturers introduced large catalogs of moderately priced memory systems, in which the sizes, performance characteristics and prices of hundreds or even thousands of models were given. But none of the units in their catalogs were available off the shelf; indeed, most manufacturers had never built more than one out of 100 of the many basic sizes and types specified in their catalogs. Prices were still high, because they were geared to short runs.

This is where the Ferroxcube team came in.

And of course, where anyone is successful in a venture, competitors are sure to follow; Ferroxcube's success with low-cost memory systems has been no exception. In the two or three years that these systems have been on the market, swarms of other manufacturers have followed suit—notably the Standard Memories Corp., Datacraft, Sanders, and Fabri-tek. In fact, Fabri-tek is reported to have begun a second round in the cost-cutting effort. Varian Data Machines has aimed at the same market, but with the Cadillac among memories—a good but expensive design.

Nevertheless, Ferroxcube is still shipping something like a thousand systems a month, and expects to see a seller's market that will grow for some time—with no lack of competition.

Two passes. In cutting the cost of a ferrite core memory, the first task was to simplify design, in the steps at top. This simple design then permitted cost reductions in manufacturing (bottom).

design pass, the team had an 8-μsec memory, with costs gratifyingly reduced.

In the second design pass, the manufacturing engineer introduced techniques and configurations that further reduced the cost of the system, as shown on the bottom of the diagram on page 240. These changes required somewhat different circuits, and allowed some component reduction. They brought the cost down even more, but the group saw ways to reduce costs even further.

In the third and final pass, the team members analyzed the final package. They found that a large proportion of the cost was for cable installation and mechanical assembly—labor that cannot readily be automated. On the basis of this finding, they recommended a change from functional modularity to aggregate modularity. Subassemblies containing many single-function circuits, such as drivers and decoders, would be dropped in favor of subassemblies containing an almost complete memory system. They should be made in such a way as to allow the number of bits per word, the number of words, or both, to be extended almost indefinitely, by stacking the subassemblies together.

This approach not only cut costs quite sharply, as shown on page 240, but also increased reliability greatly because it drastically reduced the number of interconnections. It was, of course, ideal for mass production because these "memory slices" could be manufactured almost continuously. The particular bit-word combinations in which they would ultimately be packaged and sold could be left for later. Certain other modules, that needn't be produced in the same quantities as the memory "slices," were designed as separate entities. These include timing generators; only one is needed for many "slices" of memory.

Marketing experts found the cost per bit of this new design to be acceptably low, and applications engineers found that its compatibility with existing industrial systems was pronounced. For example, many users were able to use the memory without any experience with core memories or dynamic logic.

The catalog that was first issued for these new memory systems listed over 300 standard designs, all based on only nine modules, combined in various bit-word formats.

The market acceptance of this new class of memories —by all groups, from nonelectronic machine-tool designers to logic specialists who plan small data processors—was everything the company could have hoped for. Less than a year after their introduction, production of all modules was continuous, at rates exceeding the minimums needed for economical production.

Having achieved the major objective—a degree of market acceptance that would sustain large-scale production—the same marketing/engineering/production task force sought to extend the benefits of this volume to faster memories. The resulting new generation attains full-cycle speeds of 2 to 3 μsec, and split-cycle speeds of 1 to 2 μsec, and can be modified to operate even faster. The principal changes in design are integrated logic circuits for most of the control and decoding electronics, improved sense amplifiers, and faster cores. These faster memories are now produced at about the same low prices as were the original 8-μsec first-generation designs—thus opening still wider markets for the small memory system. ●

Chapter 11

Of historical interest

Weaving wires for aerospace jobs

By Richard A. Flores

Librascope Group, Singer-General Precision Inc., Glendale, Calif.

Woven plated-wire memories have demonstrated their mechanical and electrical integrity when operated in a simulated aerospace environment. They dissipate very little power and potentially can be manufactured very economically.

The Librascope group of Singer-General Precision Inc. has since 1964 devoted a research and development program to devising woven-wire memories capable of nondestructive readout and producible at low cost. This effort has produced a line of NDRO memory products for use in severe aerospace and military environments. They're made from wide-tolerance plated wire by a weaving process that reduces the number of connections required by other manufacturing techniques.

Librascope's work is carried out under terms of a license from Toko Inc. The Japanese firm has continued developing the process for commercial applications, and recently announced arrangements for the use of the woven memories in a Japanese version of Univac's 9000 series computers [Electronics, Sept. 16, 1968, p. 236].

Warp and woof

In the first step of the manufacturing operation, the wire is plated, tested, and cut to length. [This much of the process is basically similar to Univac's, described on page 29.] The wires are then inserted in tunnels in a mat woven on an automatic loom. These mats, typically 4 inches square, consist of straight wires 5 to 8 mils in diameter—what textile weavers call the woof—with smaller wires—the warp—woven across them in an over-and-under pattern. When the larger wires are

pulled out of the mat, they leave tunnels into which the plated wires can be inserted. The mat can be woven directly on the plated wires, but at some risk of putting kinks in them that would affect their magnetic properties.

Wherever the smaller wire crosses the plated wire, it defines a bit cell on the plated wire. These smaller wires are spaced typically 40 to the inch along the plated wire, although their exact spacing depends on the intended application.

A particular advantage of the weaving technique is that it can produce rather complex multiturn coils that require lower word currents and less expensive electronics than single-turn coils, and dissipate less power.

For example, in the word-line pattern shown on page 246, an individual line weaves across the array of plated wires in an over-and-under fashion and returns in an under-and-over pattern. The result is that every plated wire has a current loop around it with exactly one turn, and the turns around adjacent wires are in opposite directions. That line can be the word line by itself if the application requires it, or it can be connected in series with other word lines to produce coils of as many turns as desired; the diagram shows a two-turn coil. Alterations in the weaving process produce different numbers of turns and different directional patterns in a practically infinite variety.

Two other important features of the weaving technique appear in the diagram. First, some of the warp wires are left unconnected to provide spacing within and between the word coils. Because of this, the field can be shaped for optimal operation in a

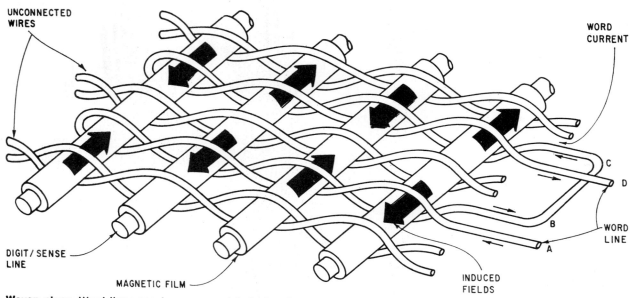

Woven plane. Word lines passing among plated wires in an over-and-under pattern make coils that can be interconnected to produce any of a wide variety of field patterns (heavy dark arrows) in the plated wire.

specific application and for reduced interaction between coils.

Second, adjacent coils can have opposite magnetic polarity so that the magnetic fields are closed through them rather than between them. Thus, current entering a terminal A and passing over the first plated wire, returns under it to point B. But this is connected to C, from whence the current passes under the wire and returns over it to terminal D. The polarity reversal reduces the line's self-inductance, so that low-voltage constant-current drive circuits can be used. These circuits further cut electronic costs and power dissipation.

Besides the spacer wires and coils, the mat contains a magnetic keeper wire plated with permalloy in somewhat the same way as is the main plated wire. It increases the homogeneity of the drive field and reduces creep between bits—a characteristic of films that under certain conditions can destroy the data in a particular bit cell when the adjacent cell is repeatedly cycled. The keeper wire is essentially a low-reluctance path between word coils on a single word line, as at top right.

When adjacent word coils are opposite in polarity, these low-reluctance paths between them permit each coil to produce a larger field without disturbing the bits under adjacent coils. And the coils produce a sufficient field with word currents

Over the hurdles

The computer industry was long rife with rumors about Librascope's difficulties with the woven-wire memory. The company did indeed have problems, but it stayed with the technology for some time.

One of the biggest problems cropped up in 1967 when Librascope built an 8,000-bit breadboard model for an aerospace customer. The breadboard worked well and Librascope was asked to build a larger version, but the customer's funds were curtailed. So, under a cooperative compromise, Librascope built two more stacks and the customer built the associated electronic circuitry. Unfortunately, these memories didn't turn out too well; the weaving technique still had some bugs in it, and the customer's electronics didn't mate properly to the stacks. But the customer had to accept the memories because both his money and time were running out.

Along with these woes, some of Librascope's key people chose that moment to seek greener pastures.

Nevertheless, development continued, while the company set up a pilot production line and landed three contracts that it hoped would lead to substantial production rates later on. Based on the 64,000-bit module it announced in the summer of 1968, Librascope maintained a production capacity of perhaps 100 stacks a year. Until its potential market seemed to dry up, the company considered that module its basic building block.

Librascope's disk memories, made by the same division that handled woven wires, were so very successful that they were rewarded with more R&D money than woven wire. When the Singer Co. acquired Librascope's parent, General Precision, Inc., in the spring of 1968, it took a hard look at the woven-wire operation and kept it going for almost a year. But it finally discontinued the effort in April, 1969.

—Lawrence Curran, Wallace B. Riley

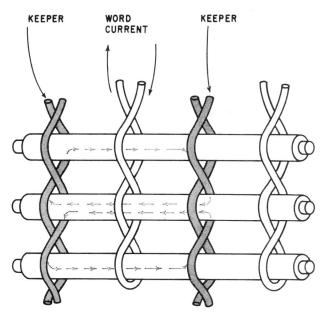

Keepers. Plated wires woven into the mat along with the word lines improve memory operation.

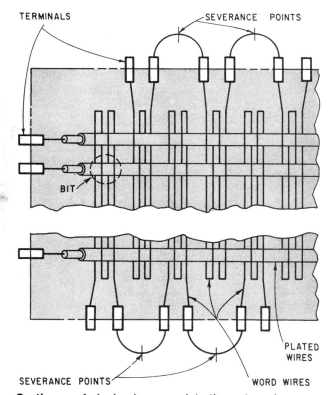

Continuous. A single wire woven into the mat can be cut afterward, simplifying interconnections.

that are reduced 25% by the use of a keeper. Likewise, output voltages are increased by a similar percentage because the field is homogeneous.

The effect of the keeper is localized—it does not load all the word coils, as a continuous ferrite keeper would. The latter is a sheet of magnetic material laid down over the mat or array of wires, also to provide a low-reluctance path; some experimenters have tried it.

The weaving operation takes place on a converted textile loom, which can weave any number of configurations and has two significant features:

 • It can weave word line coils as one continuous strand with terminals at the ends of each coil. This minimizes the number of interconnections, thus reducing fabrication costs and increasing the reliability of the woven mats. In the most common pattern for a random-access plane, the wires are cut after weaving at points between word coils, as shown at bottom left.

 • It has a Jacquard head, allowing individual control of each wire, and of the weave pattern, by either punched paper tape or punched cards. With this control, woven-wire mats can be fabricated with the data permanently and unalterably woven into the matrix, a capability unique to woven-wire technology. The loom controls the way a word coil intersects a digit line, thus producing special patterns automatically. The polarity of each bit location within a word coil is established when the weave goes over or under that particular location.

Weaving for read-only

For example, an adjacent pair of plated digit wires can be connected in series and segmented in 0's and 1's, depending on whether the word-coil pattern is over-and-under or under-and-over at a particular bit cell. If the word pulse current travels under the first digit wire and over the second, the bit stored will be a 1. If the converse is true, it will be a 0.

These permanently woven read-only memories provide nondestructive readout storage that cannot be altered and is unsurpassed for holding repetitive data such as tables, fixed programs, or reference information.

Using this basic technology, Librascope has demonstrated fully operational stacks at the shock, acceleration, and vibration levels called for by the appropriate military specifications.

A full memory system has been breadboarded and tested over a temperature range from —20° to +85° C. This system, weighing less than 4¼ pounds and displacing less than 40 cubic inches, stores 4,096 words of 20 bits each and dissipates 250 milliwatts of power when cycling at 100 kilohertz. Its standby dissipation is only 5 mw.

The cost advantage of woven-wire batch fabrication has yet to be demonstrated. However, fully automating the processes of wire fabrication and testing will reduce the basic costs of a woven plated-wire memory. The weaving process is inexpensive. Soldering mat connections to the printed-circuit board that supports it could be done quite rapidly, and inserting the plated wire into the woven mat and connecting the wire to the circuit board could be greatly speeded by inexpensive tooling. It therefore appears quite feasible to build a low-cost aerospace memory on a production-line basis.

Batched. In this enlarged photograph, the individual permalloy toroids are visible, threaded by copper conductors that act as drive and sense wires. The permalloy and copper were etched from continuous layers deposited on an epoxy board (dark background).

Potential for batch fabrication exists with etched permalloy memories, says
Donald F. O'Brien of Laboratory for Electronics; permalloy toroids and
copper conductors turned out by the thousands make up the memory plane

Etching memories in batches

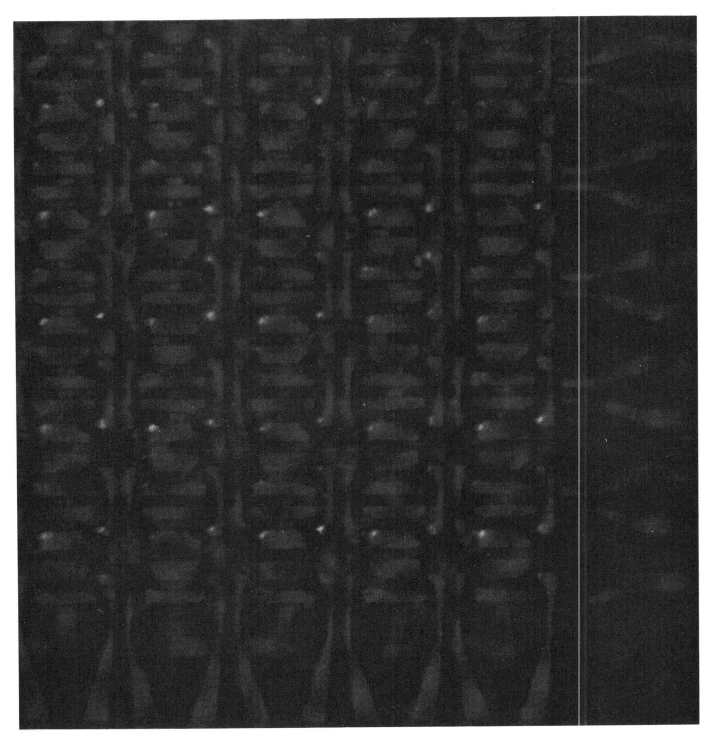

● What batch fabrication does for semiconductors, it can do for memories—improve yield, simplify handling and testing, and lead to extensive miniaturization. Specifically, in the case of etched permalloy memories, the fabrication step, when executed at the level of complete planes rather than at the level of individual elements, produces several thousand bits of memory at a clip.

In addition to this prime advantage, etched-permalloy technology carries with it certain particular good points that arise from the materials used, the memory's physical structure, and the way it's put together. Permalloy's magnetic properties are well known, and closed flux structures can be formed, thereby avoiding air gaps and insuring high output levels. Also, the memory lends itself to the formation of proven organizations, such as the 3-D layout for ferrite-core stacks. The permalloy structure is a monolithic structure and needs no external support. Furthermore, it is made in much the same way as multilayer printed-circuit boards.

In operation, the memory is economical and it is mechanically rugged. It holds up over the full military temperature range in the presence of radiation. Other features include very little power dissipation, and densely packed and nonvolatile data. In addition, employing the memory elements as nonlinear mixers of two frequencies delivers a nondestructive readout capability;

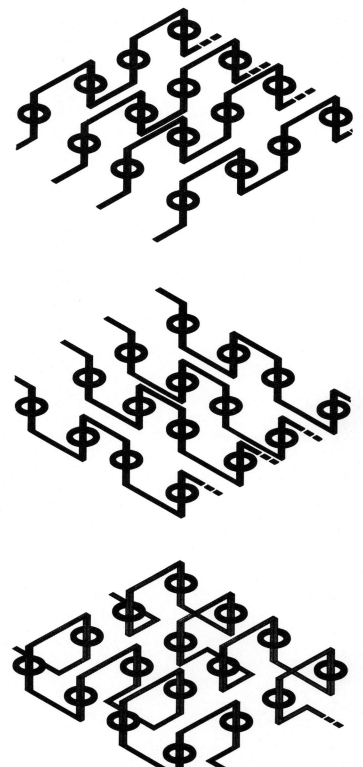

Zigzag. These drawings show the convolutions of the individual copper conductors in an etched permalloy plane.

the phase of the output corresponds to the stored data.

Building the memory basically involves the successive depositions of copper and permalloy on a polymeric supporting medium, with intermediate steps that etch toroidal storage elements from the permalloy, and drive and sense conductors from the copper. The finished planes can then be assembled into stacks, using another batch-fabrication process developed by the former Electronics division of Laboratory for Electronics Inc. The technique was applied in the production of a random-access mass memory and a low-power avionics memory. Both have proven to be feasible.

However, the memory's principal limitations are slow speed and small output signals. Twice as long as those of ferrite cores, the memory's cycles can be shortened only by going to a considerably more expensive form of permalloy and more complex and expensive drive circuits. But, at the same time, because of its lower speed, the memory dissipates only about a tenth of the power of a ferrite-core array and requires much smaller drive currents. As for its small outputs, special sense-amplifier circuits can detect them, or, in the case of 2-D organization, an increased drive current can produce a larger output.

At the outset, five different patterns are drawn at 125 times actual size; they must register perfectly. Representing only a small portion of the plane, the artwork is reproduced photographically by a step-and-repeat process while being reduced to its finished size. The stringent accuracy—±0.0002 inch accuracy across a 12-inch square, horizontally and vertically—maintained during reduction forced LFE to construct a special camera that at the time was well ahead of the state of the art. Today, comparable cameras are in common use by integrated-circuit mask makers.

After an inspection verifies accuracy and registration, the pattern of the first conductor level is etched on an ordinary copper-clad epoxy board. In the photo on page 249, the dark background is the underlying epoxy; the next-darkest pattern is the conductors made in this first etch.

Additional applications of epoxy cover the copper pattern. A layer of photoresist is added, exposed, and etched to make a large number of holes in groups of three. Each group lies directly over the ends of the etched conductors.

Now, a thin sheet of permalloy containing 1% molybdenum, added to boost its magnetic properties, is laid on the epoxy layer, which insulates the permalloy from the etched copper. Etching the permalloy leaves a pattern of toroids, 23 mils outside diameter and 17 mils inside diameter, just visible as dark gray circles in the photo. Each toroid surrounds a group of three holes.

Next, the toroid layer is filled in with epoxy; this surface then receives a coating of photoresist. The holes are etched for the second time through several layers of epoxy and photoresist to the copper. These holes are then filled to the top with copper by successive steps of electroless deposition and electroplating. Thus, the path for electrical contact runs through copper "mesas" to a final solid layer of copper. This top layer is bonded, with plenty of heat and pressure, to insure contact with all mesas—nearly 250,000 on the largest planes. Etching this layer of copper produces the top layer of conductors—the lightest shade in the photo.

The copper conductors of the completed plane are checked for continuity and short circuits. The usual magnetic tests performed on any magnetic memory verify the plane's ability to accept data written into it, to resist disturbances by noise and half-select current pulses, and to read out the data accurately upon request. Only a few significant tests are carried out during fabrication: registration is checked visually, and the permalloy is checked for magnetic properties before deposition.

Actually, the process involves over 40 steps whose end product is an array of permalloy toroids "threaded" with three sets of conductors—all visible in the photo and separately diagramed on page 250. One set passes up through the first toroid in a north-south column. A second set passes down through the first toroid in an east-west row. These two correspond respectively to the x and y selection lines. The third set, a combined sense and inhibit line for 3-D operation, serves two rows at once as it passes from left to right across the array, as shown in the photo.

Two typical examples of completed planes are shown at the top of page 252. The smaller of these contains 2,048 toroids wired in a linear-select organization for a low-power avionics application. Diodes, in the solder pads visible in the photo, prevent sneak currents from generating false outputs from unselected words.

The larger plane in the photo contains about 83,000

Large and small. Two typical etched-permalloy planes contain 2,048 toroids (left) and nearly 83,000 (right) for linear-select organizations. Larger plane includes a substantial number of redundant toroids.

Stacked. Batch-fabrication also applies to stacks of etched permalloy planes. Specially drawn wire fits notches precut in the sides of the stack, thus interconnecting corresponding etched conductors.

toroids in a square array, 288 on a side. The photo on page 249 is an enlargement of a portion of this plane. Several redundant lines in each direction can be pressed into service, should any toroids or any connections between mesas and etched conductors turn out to be bad.

Interconnecting these planes into stacks also takes advantage of a batch-fabrication process. First, all the planes are placed in contact with one another in the same registration as they will be in the completed stack. Then a diamond wheel cuts notches, 12 mils deep, in the ends of the conductors. Fifteen-mil spacers are inserted between the planes, and specially drawn wire, cut to lengths equal to the height of the stack, is inserted in the notches. The wire's cross-section fits the notches exactly. Finally, the four edges of the entire stack are solder-dipped. This completes the assembly of stacked permalloy planes, except for the attachment of connectors to the soldered wires for cables that fed the drive and sense circuits.

Two feasibility models of etched permalloy memories have been built. One of these is a low-power avionics version for Wright-Patterson Air Force Base, under contract AF 33(615)-2838. The other is a mass memory for the Rome Air Development Center built under contract AF 30(602)-3826.

In the low-power avionics version, 1,024 words of 32 bits each are stored; the cycle time is 2 microseconds.

Its organization is linear select, or 2-D, in a folded arrangement shown on p. 254. In this mockup, a single horizontal word strap between the front and rear edges contains a single four-bit word, isolated with the aid of diodes not shown here. The toroids switch like ferrite cores. Data stored in the toroid is read out through the paired dark and light sense lines—one pair of lines per bit—and detected with differential amplifiers. Two sense lines for each bit pass in opposite directions through the toroid to reinforce the signal detected by the amplifier, while canceling the noise.

The output signal of etched permalloy, especially in the 2-D organization, is only a millivolt or so, compared to 10 to 15 mv for plated wires and as much as 80 mv for ferrite cores. This problem can be overcome by employing a read overdrive in the 2-D organization, at the expense of part of the technology's low-power advantage; or by using more sophisticated sense amplifier designs that can reliably detect such small signals, in either 2-D or 3-D organization. There's still a third possibility for 3-D that was tried out in the mass memory version, which contains 1.3 million bits and can read out any word nondestructively in 20 usec.

For nondestructive readout this memory uses each core as a nonlinear mixer; a-c currents of 1 megahertz and 600 kilohertz are sent into the selected x and y lines respectively, and the sum frequency, 1.6 Mhz, is detected on the sense line. The phase of the sum frequency, determined over 10 or more cycles of the a-c signal, denotes the state of the core. This reading technique makes small output signals easier to detect, permits speeds closer to those attainable with ferrite cores, and allows nondestructive readout as well. This idea was first proposed in 1954 by Bernard Widrow, then at the Lincoln Laboratory of MIT. However, in conventional memories the phase of the a-c readout can't be reliably determined because the coupling capacitance between drive lines varies too much. The technique works in the etched permalloy stack because the etching technique controls the coupling capacitance much more closely.

Problems still remaining in this technology include simplifying the organization, refining the design and fabrication for large-scale production, developing reliable miniaturized connectors, and refining the drive and sense circuits.

In the mass memory built for the Air Force, each x and y line had a switch at each end; two switches had to close before a line could be selected. Ordinarily every unselected switch has a small amount of leakage, and a substantial amount of coupling occurs between drives lines when the two-frequency a-c drive is used. Using two switches reduced the leakage to a point where spurious signals didn't appear on the sense line. Experiments indicated that a conventional one-switch selection scheme could be developed, with the line ends opposite the switches connected to a common bus.

The density and smallness of etched permalloy memories aggravate even further the always difficult task of designing connectors with contacts that are sufficiently close together and have sufficiently low resistance and high reliability. And of course, as in any technology, small design changes are often necessary when a product goes into production, and there's always room for peripheral circuit improvement. ●

Folded. This linear-select mockup
illustrates the interconnections in an
etched-permalloy stack, arranged for
maximum signal output and
minimum noise.

Changing of the guard

While this manuscript was in preparation, Laboratory
for Electronics Inc., sold its proprietary interest in
the etched permalloy technology to Cambridge Memories Inc., Newtonville, Mass. The latter organization is
developing the technology further.

Lower costs for longer words

By Albert M. Bates

Burroughs Corp., Paoli, Pa.

As main computer stores, planar thin-film memories offer more speed and shorter access times—and thus greater throughput—than any other technology available today. Along with these advantages, the thin-film memories dissipate less power than two-dimensional and 2½-D ferrite-core arrays of comparable speed, and an order of magnitude less power than the most recently reported bipolar semiconductor types. And, taking speed and word length into account, their cost per bit is low.

For these reasons, thin films stand a good chance of displacing ferrite cores as the mainstay of memories over the next few years, but the rising tide of semiconductor technology may make their reign a short one.

The Burroughs Corp. has been working on thin-film storage for more than 10 years. The first product of this work, a 300-nanosecond scratchpad memory containing 128 words of 16 bits each, went into the company's D825 computer in 1961. More recent examples include a 500-nsec main memory of 16,384 words of 52 bits each for the B8500 computer, Burroughs' largest third-generation machine, and a 200-nsec memory module of 2,048 words of 64 bits each for the Illiac 4, a giant parallel processor being built by Burroughs for the University of Illinois.

The B8500 main memory, which contains more than 850,000 bit cells, dissipates less than 845 watts, or less than 1 milliwatt per bit; that figure includes dissipation from the associated electronic timing and control circuits. A fast 2½-D core memory of comparable speed, on the other hand, dissipates about 1,200 watts, or 1.4 milliwatts per bit.

Comparison with metal oxide semiconductor arrays is impractical in this context because MOS stores haven't yet been built in size and speed ranges even remotely similar to those of thin-film memories.

A film-memory system costs less than other types in relation to speed and word length. The chart on page 256, which compares films with 2½-D and 3-D core memories, shows how the relative cost per bit—along the vertical axis—varies with word length—along the horizontal. The capacities of the memories are indicated by the curves. In every case, larger memories cost less than smaller memories; and longer words, up to a point, are cheaper than shorter words.

The most expensive item in small memories is the electronic circuitry that decodes addresses. But for a given address complexity, extending the word lines to include more bits per word costs only a negligible amount and thus drops the cost per bit sharply. However, there's a catch. Every additional bit in a word requires additional sense-digit circuitry, and that expense eventually overtakes the cost of address decoding.

In the chart, the curves for 3-D memories are almost flat, indicating that the cost of these memories is almost independent of word length. The cost curves do begin to rise for exceptionally long words, however.

The point of minimum cost for 2½-D memories is off the chart to the left, indicating an exceptionally short word—perhaps only a couple of bits. The cost per bit for these memories rises quite sharply with increasing word length.

But with a thin-film memory, long words are the cheapest; and the larger the memory's total capacity, the longer the lowest-cost word becomes. The lowest-cost word length for a memory of 2^{20} bits—about a million—would be about 200 bits. For this very reason, the main memory in the B8500

255

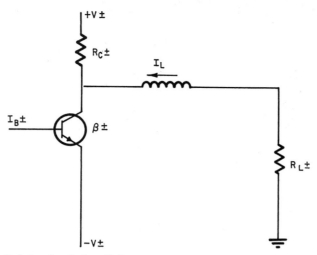

Points of variation. Tolerance in each of the components indicated contributes to a driver circuit's overall tolerance.

Cost vs. word length. The minimum cost for this film is shown here to be reached for longer word length and larger capacities than for either 2½-D or 3-D core memories. For 2½-D minimum cost is for very short words; for 3-D cost is almost independent of word length. Cost rises when sense-digit cost overtakes address decoder cost.

computer holds just about a million bits in 4,096 words of 240 bits each. Of these bits, 208 are used in actual system operation while the other 32 are spares.

Rock bottom

Though the chart is drawn in terms of relative cost per bit, the 2.5 level shown for thin films actually corresponds to about 2½ cents per bit, a cost considered a feasible ultimate low for memories of this type. Present costs are somewhat higher, because some design refinements haven't yet reached the production line.

Film memories are less expensive than core arrays because their memory planes are batch fabricated while cores must be manually strung or soldered, and because the driving circuitry is less complex, thanks to the negligible reactance on the drive lines and the aforementioned use of saturating transistors.

Greater tolerance

The thin films' power-dissipation characteristics are due in part to the small amount of material involved when the film switches, and in part to the wide tolerances on drive currents and the consequent simplicity of the drive circuits.

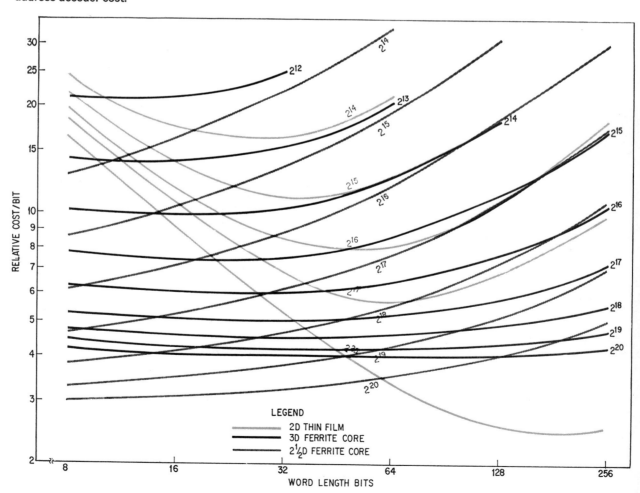

Although the drive currents in the thin-film memories operating in the destructive readout mode are about the same magnitude as those of core arrays, their tolerances are 10% to 15%, compared to 2% or 3% for cores. (Thin-film memories have also been designed to operate in the nondestructive readout mode, which doesn't need as large a drive current. However, these memories also generate a small sense signal and thus require separate circuits for read and write drivers; in general, their electronics are more expensive in this mode. All Burroughs thin-film main memory designs are DRO, and NDRO won't be considered further in this article.)

The wider tolerances on drive currents are permissible because the nickel-iron films used are less sensitive to temperature than are ferrite cores, and involve different switching mechanisms.

Most thin films in memories are of a nickel-iron alloy that is magnetically anisotropic, that is, it is more easily magnetized in a particular direction than at right angles to that direction. Furthermore, in the easy direction, these films have nearly square hysteresis loops similar to those of ferrite. In the hard direction they are almost linear.

Saturating circuits

The thin-film memory operating in the DRO mode requires only enough current to switch it; the upper current limit established by ferrite's temperature sensitivity isn't present. This makes for greater design freedom as well as for wider current tolerances. For example, saturating transistor drivers can be used where the current can be permitted to vary as much as 15%. Because its collector-to-emitter voltage is smaller than that of a nonsaturated transistor, the saturated transistor dissipates less power and contributes less to the system's over-all temperature rise. Also, circuits that saturate are easier to design and build than those that don't.

To store a bit in a thin-film memory, a word current rotates the bit cell's magnetic vector and a bit current establishes the direction in which the vector "flops back" when the word current turns off. Neither current can seriously affect another cell. The phenomenon called "creep"—the tendency of data to disappear when it's under an idle line located between two repeatedly addressed lines—is eliminated for all practical purposes by the spacing of the storage elements and by line impedances.

In most ferrite-core designs, the switching current is the sum of two closely controlled currents in different wires. Too large a current will affect cores on the wire that shouldn't be switched, and the exact amount of current that can cause switching depends on the core's temperature. The degree of precise control necessary under these conditions precludes the use of saturating transistors as drivers.

The fact that thin-film memories can use saturating transistors improves their power-dissipation properties even more. Because each of these tran-

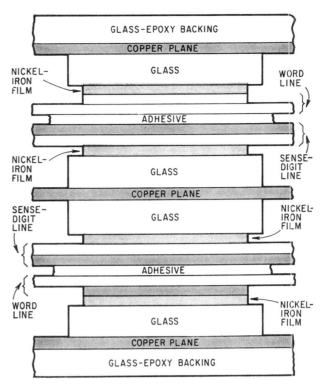

Glass stack. Thin-film array on glass substrate is assembled into a glorified club sandwich.

sistors can provide more current than nonsaturating types can, fewer of them are needed. This not only further reduces dissipation, but lowers the temperature at the junction within each transistor and the voltage stress on the transistor. It thus increases the mean time between failures.

As an added bonus, the modest dissipations and voltages indicate that integrated drive circuits will eventually be batch-fabricated on a single substrate, of silicon, with all the inherent advantages of that approach.

Power-supply voltages for thin-film arrays are also much lower than those of core arrays; a drive line for a film can be designed as a triplate strip line—one flat conductor between two ground planes—a configuration that reduces the parasitics between adjacent lines. The film cells also present a negligible inductive load to the drivers compared to the substantial back voltage and consequent spikes on the power-supply bus that exist in a ferrite-core array.

Talk is cheap

Two-dimensional organization of multiple word lengths give a system with a thin-film main memory access to several words in only a few hundred nanoseconds, and permit it to write as many words in one memory cycle. In the B8500, four words are accessible at once in 200 nsec.

Films are capable of switching in 5 nsec or less, whereas present-day standard cores 20 mils in diameter take anywhere from 100 nsec on up. Smaller cores, if and when they go into production,

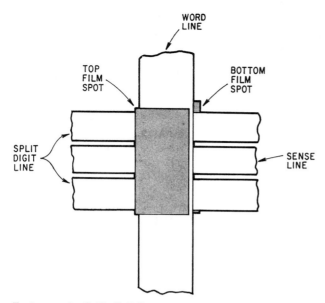

WORD LINE

TOP FILM SPOT

BOTTOM FILM SPOT

SPLIT DIGIT LINE

SENSE LINE

Facing spots. Split digit lines, straddling the sense line, and word line pass between two film spots facing one another on glass substrates.

can switch faster, but they're still far slower than the films. One false impression should be corrected here. It's often assumed that to maintain their high speeds, film memories have to run hot—to practically cook. Actually, their operation is low-voltage and relatively cool.

In the B8500, an array of rectangular spots of 1,500-angstrom-thick nickel-iron alloy on glass substrates is backed by a solid copper sheet on a glass-epoxy board, as shown on p. 257. The easy axis of magnetization is parallel to the long side of the rectangles, whose shape contributes more to the anisotropy than would squares or round spots. Two of these arrays are placed face-to-face, with the film spots registered over one another and with intervening lattice of word, sense, and digit lines of copper-laminated Kapton tape—a polyimide film manufactured by Du Pont.

The two face-to-face spots in each bit cell establish a flux path similar to the one in a toroidal ferrite core; the path lies entirely in magnetic material except at the ends of the cell, where the flux jumps a small air gap to pass from one spot to the other. This configuration is much more reliable than a single spot, which would require the flux to return from one end of the cell to the other through the air. The single spot would yield only half the output for a given cell area, and would be more easily disturbed by stray magnetic fields and neighboring drive fields.

Word lines are about the same width as the film spots' narrow side, and generate a magnetic field parallel to the "hard" axis of magnetization when current passes through them. Each digit line is split in two, with the sense line between the halves; the three together are about as wide as the long side of the film spot, as shown above. When

a current in the word line forces the spot's magnetization to turn from the easy to the hard axis, the rotation generates a pulse in the sense line. Then, while the word current is still present, identical currents in the two digit lines set up a resultant magnetic vector that determines the direction of magnetization in the spot—one way or the other along the easy axis—after the current turns off.

The sense and digit lines must necessarily be parallel to one another. If the digit line was not split and was laid alongside the sense line, it would have a stronger effect on one end of the rectangular spot than on the other; the sense line would pick up a weak signal or none, reducing the memory's reliability.

If a single digit line was laid atop or underneath the sense line, the two would be coupled differently to the spot and tightly coupled to each other, generating much noise.

In the B8500, two of these face-to-face pairs are assembled back to back. Their common ground plane is the solid copper sheet backing each (the glass epoxy coating is eliminated at the center of this sandwich but protects the outside copper layers). All the word lines are connected to this common plane at the end opposite the driver circuits as shown below. The outside ground planes are also connected to the center plane at this point, producing the triplate strip line configuration for the word lines.

One memory plane basically comprises three copper sheets, four sets of film-on-glass arrays, two sets of lattice laminations, and associated electronic and mechanical hardware. (This is oversimplified; each copper sheet, for example, is in two pieces to ease the assembly procedure.) A memory plane of 1,024 words of 208 bits is assembled in a mass soldering operation lasting less than an hour. The necessary electronic circuits are added to this assembly, and four of the resulting frames are put together to make a single memory module. Each B8500 system contains from 12 to 16 modules, depending on the customer's application, and thus his memory requirements.

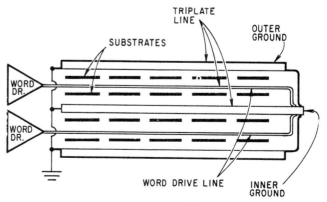

TRIPLATE LINE

OUTER GROUND

SUBSTRATES

WORD DR.

WORD DR.

WORD DRIVE LINE

INNER GROUND

Common ground. Word lines and all ground planes, connected at one point, establish triplate strip line.

Bibliography

E.E. Bittmann, "Thin-Film Memories: Some Problems, Limitations, and Profits," Proc., International Conference on Magnetics, April 1963, p. T-149.

H.P. Louis and W.L. Shevel Jr., "Storage Systems—Present Status and Anticipated Development," IEEE Trans. on Magnetics, September 1965, p. 206.

R.H. Jones and E.E. Bittmann, "The B8500 Half-Microsecond Thin-Film Memory," American Federation of Information Processing Societies, Conf. Proc., vol. 31 (Fall Joint Computer Conference), 1967, p. 347.

IEEE Journal of Solid-State Circuits, special issue on large-scale integration, December 1967.

J. Reese Brown, "High-Speed Magnetic Memories," Modern Data Systems, February 1968, p. 62.

A.V. Pohn and R.J. Zingg, "Magnetic Film Memory Systems," IEEE Trans. on Magnetics. June 1968, p. 146.

Patriarch. The Illiac 1, long ago dismantled, was one of the first 15 or so digital computers. Completed in 1952, it contained a Williams-tube memory—an array of 40 cathode-ray tubes each with 1,024 spots on its screen. The spots were either large or small, corresponding to 1's and 0's; capacitive sensors outside the tubes detected the size of the electron "splash" as the CRT beam passed over each spot. Unlike some of the technologies described in the following article, the Williams tube is not likely to be revived.

Exotic storage applications often revive old memories

By Robert W. Reichard

Computer Control Division, Honeywell, Inc., Framingham, Mass.

As hazardous as predicting the future of the computer industry is deprecating its past—because supposedly "dead" technologies, that perhaps originally were ahead of their time, sometimes come to life again. Even so, computer memories have generally evolved in an orderly manner, for economic reasons; the few mavericks that have had an impact have done so primarily because of special applications, of one sort or another.

The pace of technology and the requirements of applications have caused a proliferation of memory technologies. This proliferation has been so broad that no memory form can be pigeonholed in a particular type of application; there have always been, and will always be, wide areas of overlap. This overlapping has been largely responsible for the success of some technologies and the demise of others; in addition, the more widely a technology can be used, the more likely it is to pay off.

One prime example of an old technology's new life is the rebirth of the 2½-D core memory after a decade of disuse. This memory form is an elementary coincident-current memory which contains, on one drive-current axis, as many drive circuits as there are bits in the word; these circuits are logically enabled or disabled to write a 1 or a 0 respectively. This technology was considered state-of-the-art 13 years ago,[1] although some of its characteristics—such as a mean time between failures of well under 100 hours—appear ludicrous today.

With the wisdom of hindsight, the 3-D memory can be considered an improvement on the 2½-D, which required more drive circuits. A 2½-D memory containing n-bit words requires $(n + 1)$ sets of selection and drive circuits, whereas a 3-D memory requires only two sets of circuits regardless of the number of bits per word.

But the renaissance of the 2½-D came about for several reasons. Among these reasons is the much smaller size of standard cores now than 10 to 15 years ago; through these tiny cores the 2½-D needs only three wires to be threaded, instead of the four that the usual 3-D design needs. There is another reason: circuits, on the whole, are cheaper and much more reliable than they used to be, permitting a degree of prodigality in their

use that would have been unthinkable in the middle 1950's.[2]

Nor are 2½-D memories alone in enjoying such a resurrection. Not long ago engineers at Bell Telephone Laboratories built a memory out of quartz delay lines.[3] For their application—a signal-processing system for the U.S. Navy—only this rather antiquated technology provided the high access rate that the application required. Although the unit's maximum latency was 750 microseconds, the data was retrieved in blocks, with a new 48-bit word made available every 25 nanoseconds; the system thus resembled a magnetic drum with an enormously high bandwidth.

Evolution, not revolution

The development of memories that are faster, cheaper, larger in capacity, smaller in physical size, and more reliable is compelled to obey the force of economy. Trying to improve all these parameters simultaneously, while staying within the bounds of economy, results in evolutionary, rather than revolutionary, change.

Yet, as the exception proves the rule, occasionally a product has appeared that offered an extraordinary improvement in one characteristic at the expense of two or three others; some of these memories have been profitable to their developers, but none lasted very long or were built in large numbers. For example, the Ampex Corp. built some memories several years ago that were very large, very complex, and very costly. The company sold them to only a few non-government customers besides the military agency that funded their development; they were the only memories then available that had microsecond cycle times, and the users needed that speed at almost any price.

Such innovations, while lacking a wide market, often contribute to the industry's viable base, from which more useful products later evolve. Furthermore, sometimes their unique advantages can be developed for a particular value.

Magnetic logic, for example, was quite a fad at one time, but declined in interest for various reasons—manufacturing problems, among others. But those who persisted in studying it found its requirements for little or no standby power and its insensitivity to radiation made it ideal for applications whose unusual requirements insulated them from the pressures of the marketplace.

Most of these applications, of course, are in the aerospace industry. Even so, during the interval between fad and fruition, multiaperture devices for magnetic logic proliferated; however, few of these saw even isolated uses, and one company actually went out of business as a result of its overcommitment in this area.

Tradeoffs

Military applications, also on occasion, require memories whose attributes would be unacceptable elsewhere. Thus a system that is intrinsically slow is nevertheless often suitable because it dissipates less power or is more reliable than more conventional systems. For example, a militarized core memory typically has an access time about one-quarter the full cycle time, instead of about one-half, as is the case in commercial versions; this is so because, to keep its semiconductor circuits as reliable as possible, it works with low voltages whose waveforms have long risetimes, thus slowing them considerably. [The ferroelectric memory described in the article on page 189 is another such intrinsically slow device.] In other memories small size and light weight may be required, even at high cost.

A divergence of technology has also occurred in the telephone industry, which enjoys a built-in market. The telephone companies don't need expert salesmen to tout their wares; on the contrary, the telephone markets are highly predictable and can be precisely characterized. It's therefore possible to manufacture memories for telephone exchanges that wouldn't be commercially marketable; the application requires extraordinarily high reliability and minimal maintenance, but performance and physical size are only minor considerations. Examples of such developments include the twistor, made of a flat metallic ribbon wound around a cylindrical wire; and the ferrite-plate memory, essentially a large collection of cores in a monolithic unit. Because the telephone companies could predict the need for these memories far in advance, they had plenty of time to finance them, to develop them and to recover the investment—situations that are rarely present in the commercial arena.

End use of a product also creates divergence in technology. On the one hand, where a product is to be sold on the open market, it must be modular and capable of being used with various combinations of optional accessories; on the other hand, where a product is to be used as a subassembly in a large number of identical units, its attributes can be optimized for that particular application.

Imaginative designers will always continue to produce revolutionary ideas. Some of these ideas have never been seriously tried out. Others have been tried and failed. Their originators have often been influenced by trends in other technologies.

Memory categories

Address-related

Random access
Sequential access
Interlaced access
Pushdown storage
Content-addressable

Data-related

Serial format
Parallel format
Electrically alterable
  read-only
Mechanically alterable
  read-only
Fixed read-only
Content-addressable

Data rate-related

Fast read, fast write
Fast read, slow write
Slow read, fast write

Environment-related

Temperature tolerant
Humidity tolerant
Electromagnetic
  radiation resistant
Shock and vibration
  resistant
Corrosion resistant
Pressure tolerant

Support-equipment related

Limited power
  dissipation
Non-volatile
  (no standby power)
Limited size
Limited weight
Reliability
Cost
Modularity

Semiconductor developments, for example, led to the idea of the tunnel-diode memory, which has never breached the cost barrier; low-temperature physics generated interest in cryogenic stores.

Likewise, pure intuition has produced concepts with biological analogs. For example, a neuristor structure has been proposed that, like nerve fibers in animals, propagates signals without attenuation, and that conceivably could be interconnected in large networks like the human nervous system. Another similar structure is the cryosistor, which operates at very low temperatures and depends on unusual ionization phenomena in semiconductors at those temperatures.

It's always wise to keep an eye on the reasons for the failure of those ideas that didn't quite make it; advances in technology may obviate them, and at the same time make a previously impractical idea quite valuable. Also, evaluation may show how to avoid committing the same mistakes again.

Historical analysis should never be used to discredit a new idea; the latter's time may not yet have come. For example, storage at a molecular level—such as storing images in crystals using Bragg-angle holography—has been an idea of basic researchers for a long time. One of these days somebody may perfect this technique or invent some other molecular device, permitting a system engineer to design a memory surpassing any previous units in capacity and compactness.

Similarly, researchers should continue working with neuron-like devices. These are basically serial storage elements, and in that respect are elementary; the unsolved problems are in clocking, input-output, and multiple branching, and these problems are by no means necessarily unsolvable.

Great temptation

The proliferation of memory technologies creates a great temptation to try to categorize the wide variety of application requirements into mutually exclusive groups. This is difficult, even though the table shown above seems to indicate it's easy. It's equally difficult to establish a relationship between the various memory technologies, past and present, and each of the groups. It's nevertheless helpful to try this pigeonholing procedure, as background.

Plated-wire memories illustrate the problem. These are usable in each of several categories: as scratchpads (high-speed, small-capacity read-write memories); as main storage units (medium-speed, large-capacity read-write memories); and as microprogram units (high-speed, medium-capacity electrically alterable read-only memories). Thus they can't be made to fit in any one category.

Each grouping of technologies in the table is supposedly independent of all the others. Within each group, the various categories indicate the different approaches that have been required or could conceivably be required.

Under the heading "Address-related," for example, the random-access category is the basic mode required in most computers. The push-down store is also sometimes known as the last-in first-out memory. It is related to the content-addressable store, from which data is retrieved in terms of content rather than location. Both approaches have been proposed for use in the same memory in one recent application.[4] The sequential mode, or first-in first-out mode, is most useful in simple data accumulations. In these sequential memories data can be stored or retrieved from any given block only in the order in which it was stored. The interlaced mode is one where data is read out at a different rate or in a different format than that in which it is written. An example of this is Raytheon's Cortic radar signal processor.[5]

In the data-related categories, the serial and parallel formats are self-evident. The mechanically alterable read-only form would be most useful as a catalog that could be expediently changed when necessary, but only by mechanical process. Electrically alterable read-only memories are similar, except that their alterations, when necessary, must be quicker than the mechanical form permits; obviously the electrically alterable form must also incorporate safeguards against accidental alteration by the wrong person at the wrong time. An example of a fixed read-only store would be a mathematic table or a dictionary.

The fast-read, fast-write data rate is probably the best known and most often used, and therefore can be considered a norm. But it's not always the best for specific applications. A fast-read, slow-write memory would be more suitable in a data gathering application, as in an automatic tester. A memory of this description has been built that reads conventionally in about 250 nanoseconds but takes 100 times as long to write, using a degaussing process, because in its application—telephone switching—writing new data occurs only rarely and when it does occur it's a radical event.

A slow-read, fast-write memory would be re-quired in an application where the output rate is limited by other factors. Such an application is storing digitized television pictures quickly in an unmanned spacecraft and transmitting them slowly back to earth. Such variations from the norm permit independent design of read and write circuits.

The environment-related constraints may affect the memory directly, or may only require it to be isolated from them to some extent. For example, military equipment is subject to wide temperature variation, which can be compensated for directly with special magnetic cores or indirectly with heated core stacks or temperature-compensated power supplies.

Some memories are subject to unexpected exposure to electromagnetic radiation. For example, magnetic thin-film memory design, which isn't seriously affected by temperature fluctuations, must take the earth's magnetic field into account. And more than once the cause of an intermittent system failure has been traced to a high-powered airport radar that periodically swept across the computer.

Ambient pressure can be as low as zero in outer space or as high as several thousand pounds per square inch in ocean deeps. Obviously, the same piece of memory equipment won't have to withstand both extremes, but one or the other may have to be accounted for in a design.

Support equipment directly affects the memory design, and strongly depends on the memory's application. For example, a memory in a spacecraft has very limited power available to it, and both it and its power supply are subject to stringent size and weight constraints. Furthermore, their reliability must be predictable and very high. As a result, spacecraft memories bear very little resemblance to commercial equipment.

Since these design parameters usually differ subtly from one system to the next, development costs can't be spread out over a lengthy production run. As a result, costs of such systems are often an order of magnitude higher than those of commercial equipment of similar performance. ∎

References

1. M.A. Alexander, M. Rosenberg, and R. Stuart-Williams, "Ferrite core memory is fast and reliable," Electronics, Feb. 1956, p. 158.

2. R.W. Reichard and W.F. Jordan Jr., "A Compact Economical Core Memory with All-Monolithic Electronics," Conference Proceedings, American Federation of Information Processing Societies, Vol. 32 (Spring Joint Computer Conference), 1968, p. 253.

3. P.S. Fuss, "1.36-million-bit High-speed Delay Line Memory," Electronic Communicator, May, 1968.

4. R.B. Derickson, "A Proposed Associative Push-down Memory Concept," Computer Design, March, 1968.

5. John D. Collins, "Putting the squeeze on radar signals," Electronics, Jan. 22, 1968, p. 86.

Index

Index

268

Thin film (*Cont.*):
    planar, 39, 42, 45, 49, 52, 255
        and strain waves, 179
Tracy, Robert A., 159
Transistor array as read-only memory, 119
Transmission line:
    bifilar, 16
    reflections in, 12
Triglycine sulfate, 173
Triplate stripline, 257
Tunzi, Burton R., 67
Turnbull, John L., 19
Twistor, 262
Two-phase logic circuit, 68

Uimari, David C., 163
Ulrick, Charles J., 214
Unicon, 171
Univac Division, Sperry Rand Corporation, 29, 45

Vieth, Robert F., 52

Waffle-iron memory, 57
    variations of, 58
Whalen, Robert M., 23
Whiskers (*see* Rod memory)
Womack, Charles P., 52
Woven-wire memory, 245